NAGC Pre-K–Grade 12 Gifted Education Programming Standards

The Pre-K–Grade 12 Gifted Education Programming Standards should be part of every school district's repertoire of standards to ensure that the learning needs of advanced students are being met.

The new edition of this popular book helps schools understand the updates to the standards, which have a renewed emphasis on equity and inclusion. The six standards focus on student outcomes in learning and development, assessment, curriculum planning and instruction, learning environments, programming, and professional learning (updated from professional development used in the 2010 version). This book details these standards and provides suggestions for implementing each one. It also includes sample assessments of student products and performances, which will assist schools in developing program and service evaluation benchmarks.

This book is a must-have for school leaders and gifted education professionals who want to offer the most effective services for gifted and advanced students. It is a service publication of the National Association for Gifted Children (Washington, DC). This designation indicates that this book has been jointly developed with NAGC and that this book passes the highest standards of scholarship, research, and practice.

Susan K. Johnsen, PhD, is Professor Emerita of Educational Psychology at Baylor University. She has written three tests for identifying gifted students and more than 300 articles, monographs, technical reports, chapters, and books related to gifted education.

Debbie Dailey, EdD, is Associate Professor of Education and Chair of the Department of Teaching and Learning at the University of Central. She serves as treasurer for Arkansans for Gifted and Talented Education, Chair of the STEM network at National Association for Gifted Children, and President-Elect for Council for Exceptional Children-The Association for the Gifted.

Alicia Cotabish, EdD, is Associate Professor of Teaching and Learning at the University of Central Arkansas. Alicia is the former past-president of the Arkansas Association of Educational Administrators and currently serves as Co-Chair of the National Association for Gifted Children Standards Committee.

NAGC Pre-K–Grade 12 Gifted Education Programming Standards

A Guide to Planning and
Implementing Quality Services
for Gifted Students

2nd Edition

Edited by Susan K. Johnsen, Debbie Dailey,
and Alicia Cotabish

Routledge
Taylor & Francis Group

NEW YORK AND LONDON

Second edition published 2022
by Routledge
605 Third Avenue, New York, NY 10158

and by Routledge
2 Park Square, Milton Park, Abingdon, Oxon, OX14 4RN

Routledge is an imprint of the Taylor & Francis Group, an informa business

First edition published by Prufrock 2011

Library of Congress Cataloging-in-Publication Data
A catalog record for this book has been requested

ISBN: 9781032144979 (hbk)
ISBN: 9781646322299 (pbk)
ISBN: 9781003236863 (ebk)

DOI: 10.4324/9781003236863

Typeset in Palatino
by Apex CoVantage, LLC

Contents

Contributor Biographies   vii

Preface   xiv

1   **Introduction to the 2019 NAGC Pre-K–Grade 12 Gifted Programming Standards**   1
Susan K. Johnsen, Alicia Cotabish, and Debbie Dailey

2   **Designing Supportive School Environments for Social and Emotional Development**   35
Thomas P. Hébert

3   **Addressing Gifts and Talents, Racial Identity, and Social-Emotional Learning Regarding Students of Color: Challenges and Recommendations for Culturally Responsive Practice**   58
Donna Y. Ford, Kristina Henry Collins, and Tarek C. Grantham

4   **The Assessment Standard in Gifted Education: Identifying Gifted Students**   94
Susan K. Johnsen

5   **The Curriculum Planning and Instruction Standard in Gifted Education: From Idea to Reality**   128
Joyce VanTassel-Baska

6   **Differentiation: Standards Inform Best Practice**   152
Julia Link Roberts

7   **Programming Models and Program Design**   176
Cheryll Adams

8   **Professional Learning Standards**   214
Sandra N. Kaplan, Jessica Manzone, and Julia Nyberg

9   Using the NAGC Standards for Program Development
    and Improvement   230
    Keri M. Guilbault and Alicia Cotabish

10 State Models for Implementing the Standards   253
    Wendy Behrens and Mary L. Slade

11 Aligning Gifted Programming Standards with ISTE Standards
    for Enhanced Student Outcomes   277
    Debbie Dailey, Jason Trumble, and Michelle Buchanan

12 Advocating for Implementation   303
    Susan Corwith and Chin-Wen Lee

Appendix A 2019 *Pre-K–Grade 12 Gifted Programming Standards*   322

Appendix B Assessments for Measuring Student Outcomes   344
    Tracey N. Sulak and Susan K. Johnsen

Contributor Biographies

Editors

Susan K. Johnsen, Ph.D., is Professor Emerita of Educational Psychology at Baylor University. She is editor-in-chief of *Gifted Child Today* and co-author of *Identifying Gifted Students: A Practical Guide, Using the NAGC Pre-K–Grade 12 Gifted Programming Standards, Classroom Management for Gifted and Twice-Exceptional Students Using Functional Behavior Assessment, Independent Study Program*, and more than 300 articles, monographs, technical reports, chapters, and other books related to gifted education. She has written three tests used in identifying gifted students: *Test of Mathematical Abilities for Gifted Students* (TOMAGS-2), *Test of Nonverbal Intelligence* (TONI-4) and *Screening Assessment Gifted Students* (SAGES-3). She is past president of The Association for the Gifted (TAG), Council for Exceptional Children, and past president of the Texas Association for Gifted and Talented (TAGT). She has received awards for her work in the field of education, including NAGC's Ann Isaac's Award, NAGC's President's Award, and CEC's Leadership Award.

Debbie Dailey, Ed.D., is an associate professor of Education and Chair in the Department of Teaching and Learning at the University of Central. Prior to moving to higher education, Debbie was a high school science teacher and gifted education teacher for twenty years. Debbie currently serves as treasurer for her state gifted association (Arkansans for Gifted and Talented Education), Chair of the STEM network at NAGC, and President for CEC-TAG. Debbie has authored and co-authored multiple journal articles, books, book chapters, and products focused on K-12 STEM and gifted education. She has delivered numerous professional development workshops and presentations at local, state, national, and international venues.

Alicia Cotabish, Ed.D., is an associate professor at the University of Central Arkansas. She is the Past-President of the *Arkansas Association of Gifted Education Administrators* (AAGEA), and currently serves as the Member-at-Large representative for the *American Education Research Association – Research on Giftedness, Creativity, and Talent* (AERA-RoGCT). She was the recipient of the 2015 National Association for Gifted Children *Early Scholar Award* and 2012 the country in areas such as differentiation, instructional coaching, and curriculum design. Jessica is a former classroom teacher from Baltimore, Maryland.

Julia Nyberg, Ed.D., is a professor at Purdue University Global in the Department of Education and Communication. Dr. Nyberg was a K-6 classroom teacher and professional development expert before entering higher education. Dr. Nyberg's research focuses on curriculum and instructional design for diverse gifted and advanced students. Dr. Nyberg speaks at state and national conferences and provides demonstration lessons for school districts related to her expertise in curriculum design and differentiated instruction. Dr. Nyberg serves on numerous professional organizations, including as the executive director for the California Association for the Gifted.

Julia Link Roberts, Ed.D., is Mahurin Endowed Professor of Gifted Studies at Western Kentucky University. She is the executive director of The Center for Gifted Studies and The Carol Martin Gatton Academy of Mathematics and Science in Kentucky. Dr. Roberts is the President of the World Council for Gifted and Talented Children, Chair of Accreditation and Standards for The Association for the Gifted, Chair of the Kentucky Advisory Council for Gifted and Talented Children, and Legislative Chair of the Kentucky Association for Gifted Education. Dr. Roberts has been honored with the NAGC Ann F. Isaacs Founder's Memorial Award, the Acorn Award for Faculty Excellence, the Palmarium Award, and the NAGC Distinguished Service Award. She writes about and presents on curriculum/differentiation/assessment, advocacy, policy, STEM leadership, as well as gifted education and talent development. Dr. Roberts directs Saturday and summer programming.

Mary L. Slade, Ph.D., is a professor in the Department of Early Childhood Education in the College of Education at Towson University. Mary's teaching includes early childhood education as well as gifted, talented, and creative education. Mary is one of the inaugural FACET teaching fellows for the university with a focus in online learning. Dr. Slade has worked on state and national levels in the field of gifted education by serving on boards of directors, co-hosting state conferences, and serving on various committees. Mary served two terms as a member of the Board of Directors for the National Association for Gifted Children (NAGC) and was awarded the early leader award. In addition to other NAGC initiatives, Dr. Slade was the editor of the initial publication of NAGC Pre-K-12 Programming Standards.

Tracey N. Sulak, Ph.D., joined the faculty of Baylor University in 2013, where she serves as graduate faculty in the Department of Educational Psychology and coordinates the Master of Arts in Teaching in exceptionalities. She has taught a wide variety of courses from statistics to multicultural education to assessment of students with exceptionalities, but most of her teaching has been in the area of academic development of students with exceptionalities. Her research interests include broadening participation in STEM education with an emphasis on students with twice exceptionalities, teacher development, and student motivation. She has served in multiple roles in organizations like the American Montessori Society and the American Educational Research Association.

Jason Trumble, Ph.D., is Associate Professor of Education at the University of Central Arkansas where he teaches preservice and inservice teachers to effectively integrate technology, content, and pedagogy. He is the program coordinator for the UCA education specialist degree in digital age teaching and learning. Dr. Trumble's research focuses on the intersection of teaching and technology as well as STEM learning, assessment practices, and emerging technologies.

Joyce VanTassel-Baska, Ed.D., is the Jody and Layton Smith Professor Emerita of Education and founding director of the Center for Gifted Education at The College of William and Mary in Virginia where she developed a graduate program and a research and development center in gifted education. She also founded the Midwest Talent Search and the Center for Talent Development at Northwestern University. Dr. VanTassel-Baska has published widely including 32 books and over 650 refereed journal articles, book chapters, and scholarly reports. Her most recent books are: *Talent Development: Theory, Research, and Practice* (Ed.) (in press) and *Curriculum Planning and Instructional Design for Gifted Learners* (3rd edition) (2020) (with Ariel Baska). She has received numerous awards for her work, including several from the National Association for Gifted Children, Mensa, the American Educational Research Association, and the World Council on Gifted and Talented Education. She was selected as a Fulbright Scholar to New Zealand in 2000 and a Visiting Scholar to Cambridge University in England in 1993.

Preface

Overview of the NAGC Pre-K–Grade 12 Gifted Programming Standards

Susan K. Johnsen, Debbie Dailey, and Alicia Cotabish

Growing out of the need for more rigorous and measurable standards and higher expectations for academic performance, standards have been developed for teacher preparation, programming, and specific content or discipline areas. These standards have been used for the design of assessment-based accountability systems and the accreditation of both teacher preparation and K–12 programs. Based on new or updated knowledge about how students learn, research-supported pedagogical strategies, and changes in society and culture influencing student learning needs, it is important to continuously revisit and revise standards.

Gifted education has been and continues to be an integral part of the standards movement. The initial Pre-K–Grade 12 Gifted Programming Standards were developed in 1998 and revised in 2010. In 2017, the National Association for Gifted Children (NAGC) Professional Standards Committee was tasked with reviewing and updating the 2010 standards. The 2019 standards reflect the effort of that group and other stakeholders including members of NAGC, members of Council for Exceptional Children-The Association for the Gifted, State Gifted Education Directors, NAGC Network leaders, and the NAGC Board of Directors. The 2019 standards were revised based on the latest research and practices in gifted education and reflect the evolving conceptions of giftedness with a renewed emphasis on equity and inclusion (see the Programming Standards in Appendix A).

The six standards focus on student outcomes in learning and development, assessment, curriculum planning and instruction, learning environments, programming and professional learning (updated from professional development used in 2010). All of the standards are aligned to evidence-based practices, which are known to be effective in working with gifted and talented students, and are sensitive to the dual goals of equity and excellence. These programming standards are the focus of this book, *Using the NAGC Pre-K–Grade 12 Gifted Programming Standards*. The authors of these chapters were guided by the following questions:

1. What standards relate to the focus area (e.g., social/emotional development, curriculum, identification, and so on)?
2. How are these standards supported by research and effective practices?
3. How might teachers, schools, and school districts use these standards?
4. How might teachers, schools, and school districts assess student outcomes?

Along with addressing these questions, each author has provided specific examples of ways that the standards might be implemented.

In Chapter 1, "Introduction to the NAGC Pre-K–Grade 12 Gifted Programming Standards," Susan K. Johnsen, Alicia Cotabish, and Debbie Dailey examine how the 2019 Pre-K–Grade 12 Gifted Programming Standards (Programming Standards) fit within the national context, identify the needs for Programming Standards, explain the process used for developing the Programming Standards, outline the general principles underlying the Programming Standards, contrast the 2010 Programming Standards with the 2019 Programming Standards, describe each of the Programming Standards and their related research, and make recommendations for their use. Uses include self-assessment, professional development, program evaluation, and advocacy.

In Chapter 2, "Designing Supportive School Environments for Social and Emotional Development," Thomas P. Hébert identifies four themes emerging in the standards related to social and emotional development: self-understanding; awareness of learning and affective needs in gifted students; personal, social, and cultural competence; and appreciation of talents within gifted young people and their recognition of ways to support the development of their gifts and talents. For each of these themes he provides research that supports specific practices. He concludes his chapter by describing ways that a teacher might create a classroom environment that is designed to support the social and emotional development of students.

In Chapter 3, "Addressing Gifts and Talents, Racial Identity, and Social-Emotional Learning Regarding Students of Color: Challenges and Recommendations for Culturally Responsive Practice," Donna Y. Ford, Kristina Henry Collins, and Tarek C. Grantham examine the six standards using a multicultural lens and a gifted lens. They provide a cultural framework for interpreting, conceptualizing and building upon the newly revised standards. In particular, they align the programming strands to the Culturally Responsive Equity-based Bill of Rights for Gifted Students of Color (Ford et al., 2018; 2020) and provide a greater emphasis on social-emotional learning among students of color. The chapter is divided into four sections guided by the following questions:

1. What are some of the cultural differences and needs of GATE students of color?
2. How are the 2019 NAGC standards responsive to the needs of GATE students of color?
3. Why is attention to racial identity a responsive, equitable, and efficacious social-emotional learning approach for designing strategies and assessing student outcomes?
4. What are implications for GATE coordinators and other educational professionals?

They conclude their chapter with a call for educators to understand that gifted students of color have different cultural needs from their White classmates and to align their work with standards that are equity focused and culturally responsive and promote racial identity development.

In Chapter 4, "The Assessment Standard in Gifted Education: Identifying Gifted Students," Susan K. Johnsen identifies the foundational principles that inform the standards on identification and then describes ways of establishing equal access (Student Outcome 1) and using and interpreting a variety of assessments to identify students' interests, strengths, and needs (Student Outcome 2) so that gifted students from diverse backgrounds are identified (Student Outcome 3). She includes criteria and an example form to use in organizing data for placement and guidelines from the Office of Civil Rights for examining bias in the overall identification procedure.

In Chapter 5, "The Curriculum Planning and Instruction Standard in Gifted Education: From Idea to Reality," Joyce VanTassel-Baska provides an overview of curriculum planning, a definition of differentiation, necessary curriculum planning documents (e.g., curriculum framework and scope and sequence), and curricular emphases within the standard. She then reviews research that supports the curriculum standards and provides two curriculum models that respond to the demands of the programming standards. Next, she adds methods for assessing student outcomes and ways that the curriculum planning and instruction standards might be used. She concludes the chapter by providing recommendations for implementing a standards-based curriculum.

In Chapter 6, "Differentiation: Standards Inform Best Practice," Julia L. Roberts focuses on instructional strategies for differentiation in classrooms. These instructional strategies include planning for differentiation, preassessing to ensure that each student is learning, and implementing learning experiences that match each student's interest, learning preferences, and readiness. She emphasizes the importance of educators working together to implement the standards with the instructional goal of continuous progress. She concludes the chapter by providing specific differentiation strategies, programming options, and needed policies and procedures for implementing the standards.

In Chapter 7, "Programming Models and Program Design," Cheryll M. Adams provides information that allows school personnel to make appropriate choices for programming for gifted students. She initially describes effective programming and services that have clearly articulated elements (e.g., philosophy, goals, definition, identification plan, curriculum, teacher selection, professional learning, and program administration). She then provides evidence-based programming options for acceleration, enrichment, and grouping. She concludes by describing state level initiatives and two programming examples.

In Chapter 8, "Professional Learning Standards," Sandra N. Kaplan, Jessica Manzone, and Julia Nyberg begin by aligning the purposes of professional learning (i.e., relevance, support, continuity, and visibility) with the NAGC standards and describe the features of effective professional learning. They describe the five barriers that need to be addressed in order for professional learning to be effective and provide a continuum for matching the professional learning activity to implementation options. They end the chapter with a discussion on how technology has changed the face of professional learning, allowing greater access to learning experiences through online delivery formats.

In Chapter 9, "Using the NAGC Programming Standards for Program Development and Improvement," Keri M. Guilbault and Alicia Cotabish focus on program evaluation to identify and document gaps in programming and services. They begin the chapter discussing how the standards can be used by state department personnel, gifted education program coordinators, and classroom teachers. They provide evidence for the necessity of using self-study when planning, developing, implementing programs and improving programming and practices. They describe a revised tool that can be used to identify and document programming and service gaps. Using the self-study tool, they provide model examples of ways to use a gap analysis and action plan charts in implementing the standards. They conclude the chapter by describing two scenarios of ways that a program coordinator and a classroom teacher used the standards.

In Chapter 10, "State Models for Implementing the Standards," Wendy Behrens and Mary L. Slade describe how state departments of education use national standards for evaluating and improving state standards, approving gifted plans and programs, and monitoring compliance with state regulations. In their survey with state directors of gifted education, they examined the frequency of standards use at state and local levels. They conclude the chapter with a case study and vignettes depicting illustrative exemplars of the implementation of the standards.

In Chapter 11, "Aligning Gifted Programming Standards with ISTE Standards for Enhanced Student Outcomes," Debbie Dailey, Jason Trumble, and Michelle Buchanan align the International Society for Technology in Education standards for students and educators with the gifted programming standards (student outcomes and evidence-based practices). They include a discussion of each gifted programming standard, aligning the student outcome to the appropriate ISTE student standard and evidence-based practices to the appropriate ISTE educator standard. After the discussion of each standard, they provided a practical classroom or program application that can be used to improve student outcomes and promote achievement in technology-rich environments.

In Chapter 12, "Advocating for Implementation," Susan Corwith and Chin-Wen Lee discuss how to insert gifted programming standards into school improvement conversations and advocate for gifted learners. They connect elements of the frameworks with literature on effective advocacy found in the field of gifted education. They provide key questions and examples to engage readers in authentic applications in the field. Next they describe how leaders in gifted education can advocate for their use. They suggest three advocacy strategies when presenting the standards and provide a sample scenario for each.

The appendices offer rich resources for practitioners. The programming standards appear in Appendix A. Each standard is preceded by a description and followed by student outcomes and evidence-based practices. Appendix B provides freely available assessments and resources for measuring student outcomes and evaluating programs in these areas: creativity, critical thinking, curriculum, interests, learning and motivation, multicultural, products and performances, program planning and evaluation, and social, emotional and psychosocial skills.

As part of the workgroup, we would like to thank the Pre-K–Grade 12 working group members for their development of the programming standards, Chin-Wen Lee and Keri Guilbault, with special thanks to the chair, Susan Corwith. We will continue to work on developing resources and making presentations related to these standards. We would also like to acknowledge Katy McDowall, Prufrock Press, for her editorial assistance. We hope that you find this book helpful in implementing the NAGC Pre-K–Grade 12 Gifted Programming Standards.

Introduction to the 2019 NAGC Pre-K– Grade 12 Gifted Programming Standards

Susan K. Johnsen, Alicia Cotabish, and Debbie Dailey

The standards movement has grown exponentially since 1983 when *A Nation at Risk* was published (National Commission on Excellence in Education, 1983). The Commission recommended that schools, colleges, and universities adopt more rigorous and measurable standards and set higher expectations for academic performance. Since that time, all states have adopted some form of standards-based education system and professional associations have developed standards for teacher preparation and program services. While the Every Students Succeeds Act (ESSA, 2015) grants states more authority over their school accountability than the No Child Left Behind Act of 2001, it still holds schools accountable for student achievement. States must submit plans to the U.S. Department of Education showing accountability indicators of academic progress and school quality or student success of *all* students. School districts may select evidence-based strategies that are tailored to local needs. Since gifted and talented students deserve to be included, gifted educators must have standards to become actively involved in the development of state plans and in local conversations about effective practices.

Currently, gifted educators have two sets of standards—those that address teacher preparation and those that address Pre–K-12 programs. This

DOI: 10.4324/9781003236863-1

characteristics of effective programming and services in gifted education and ensuring a degree of consistency across schools and school districts (Johnsen & Clarenbach, 2017; Johnsen & VanTassel-Baska, 2016; Johnsen et al., 2008). Educators in gifted education can point to evidence-based practices that are important to implement. Without standards, services to gifted and talented students are left to the discretion of decision-makers who may or may not have a background or even an interest in gifted education.

In a recent survey conducted by the National Association for Gifted Children's Professional Standards Committee as part of the standards review process, the top three uses of the current Programming Standards were reported as planning and implementing research-based gifted education programs, program evaluation, professional development and teacher preparation (Corwith & Johnsen, 2021).

In planning and implementing programs and services, the Programming Standards can provide a structure for defining critical benchmarks; developing policies, rules, and procedures; identifying practices that are the most effective for students with gifts and talents; and providing points for discussion and collaboration among educators, families and other community stakeholders (Corwith & Johnsen, 2021). In this way, policymakers can focus on what is important in gifted education, and schools are able to evaluate all aspects of their programs and set benchmarks for improvement.

Since professionals in gifted education are more aware of evidence-based classroom practices essential to improving outcomes for gifted and talented students, they can be used as a guide for professional development of individual teachers and for entire school districts. Educator preparation institutions and agencies can also use the standards for identifying relevant theory, research, and pedagogy for designing courses and coherent teacher preparation programs.

The Programming Standards can also acknowledge the importance that the field of gifted education places on serving underrepresented populations in the areas of assessment, curriculum planning, establishing learning environments, and programming. They reinforce the idea that diversity exists in our society and in each individual's expression of gifts and talents (Corwith & Johnsen, 2021; Johnsen, 2006).

Finally, Programming Standards can be used for advocacy and effect new initiatives at the local, state, and national levels. They may then direct educators' efforts toward adequately recognizing students with gifts and talents, developing and implementing programming, and ultimately raising the quality of services provided to gifted students and their families.

Process Used to Develop the Programming Standards

The 2019 NAGC Pre-K–Grade 12 Gifted Programming Standards are the result of many years of effort on the part of the National Association for Gifted Children (NAGC) members in collaboration with the Council for Exceptional Children, the Association for the Gifted (CEC/TAG) members and others who have sought to improve the education of gifted and talented students. The effort began more than 20 years ago with the development of the 1998 Pre-K–Grade 12 Gifted Program Standards (Landrum et al., 2001). To align the standards with the 2006 NAGC-CEC Teacher Preparation standards and recent research, the NAGC Professional Standards Committee formed a Pre-K–Grade 12 Gifted Programming Standards Revision Workgroup to update the 1998 program standards. The research support included literature/theory-based, research-based, and practice-based research (CEC, 2010, pp. 9–10; Corwith & Johnsen, 2021).

1. *Theory/literature-based*. Knowledge or skills are based on theories or philosophical reasoning. They include knowledge and skills derived from sources such as position papers, policy analyses, and descriptive reviews of the literature.
2. *Research-based*. Knowledge or skills are based on peer-reviewed studies that use appropriate research methodologies to address questions of cause and effect, and that researchers have independently replicated and found to be effective.
3. *Practice-based*. Knowledge and skills are derived from a number of sources. Practices based on a small number of studies or nomination procedures, such as promising practices, are usually practice-based. Practice-based knowledge or skills also include those derived primarily from model and lighthouse programs. Practice-based knowledge and skills include professional wisdom. These practices have been used so widely with practical evidence of effectiveness that there is an implicit professional assumption that the practice is effective. Practice-based knowledge and skills also include "emerging practice," practices that arise from teachers' classroom experiences validated through some degree of action research.

Using the recent research, the NAGC Program Standards, the NAGC-CEC Teacher Preparation Standards, state program standards, and surveys of members, the Workgroup developed a new set of Programming Standards that were approved by the NAGC and CEC-TAG Boards in 2010 (NAGC, 2010; see Johnsen, 2012, for a complete discussion of the process).

In 2017, the NAGC Professional Standards Committee was asked to update the standards to include new research, reflect updated practices and conceptions of giftedness, and focus on issues related to equity and inclusion. During this revision, the Standards Revision Workgroup (a) examined new research since the 2010 standards were published; (b) surveyed and conducted focus groups with state directors, NAGC and CEC members, and NAGC Network leaders to learn more about their knowledge and use of the standards; and (c) submitted a draft of the proposed changes to the standards to state directors, NAGC and CEC-TAG members, and the NAGC Network before submitting the final document to the NAGC Board of Directors for approval (Corwith & Johnsen, 2021; NAGC, 2019). The standards were approved by the NAGC Board of Directors in 2019.

General Principles Underlying the Programming Standards

During the process of developing the Programming Standards, the Workgroup reviewed the research base and developed the following principles to guide the revision of the 2010 program standards (NAGC, 2010, p. 4):

1. *Giftedness is dynamic and is constantly developing;* therefore, students are defined as those having gifts and talents rather than those with stable traits. Instead of a static definition of giftedness (e.g., a student is either gifted or not), more researchers have acknowledged the developmental nature of giftedness, which includes a set of interacting components such as general intelligence, domain-related skills, creativity, and non-intellective factors (Cattell, 1971; Gagné, 2010; Renzulli, 1978; Subotnik et al., 2011; Tannenbaum, 1986). A developmental perspective strongly influences identification and programming practices.

2. *Giftedness is found among students from a variety of backgrounds;* therefore, a deliberate effort was made to ensure that diversity was included across all standards. Diversity was defined as differences among groups of people and individuals based on ethnicity, race, socioeconomic status, gender, exceptionalities, language, religion, sexual orientation, and geographical area. Because the underrepresentation of diverse students in gifted education programs is well documented (Briggs et al., 2008; Ford et al., 2020; Rizza & Morrison, 2007), specific evidence-based practices needed to be incorporated to ensure that identification procedures were equitable (Ford & Harmon, 2001; Frasier et al., 1995; Harris et al., 2009; McBee et al., 2016; Siegle et al., 2016) curriculum was culturally responsive (Ford et al., 2000; Ford, 2015; Kitano & Pedersen, 2002a; Kitano & Pedersen,

2002b), and learning environments fostered cultural understanding for success in a diverse society (Harper & Antonio, 2008; Zirkel, 2008).

3. *Standards should focus on student outcomes rather than practices.* The number of practices used or how the schools used the practices were not as important as whether or not the practice was effective with students. Consequently, the Workgroup decided not to identify separate acceptable vs. exemplary standards since the distinction would be difficult to support with research.

4. *All educators are responsible for the education of students with gifts and talents.* Educators were defined as administrators, teachers, counselors, and other instructional support staff from a variety of professional backgrounds (e.g., general education, special education, and gifted education). Research suggests that collaboration enhances talent development (Gentry & Ferriss, 1999; Landrum, 2002; Olszewski-Kubilius et al., 2019; Purcell & Leppien, 1998) and improves the likelihood that gifted students with disabilities receive services in gifted education programs (Coleman & Johnsen, 2011; Mayes et al., 2019).

5. *Students with gifts and talents should receive services throughout the day and in all environments that are based on their abilities, needs, and interests.* Therefore, the Workgroup decided to use the word "programming" rather than the word "program," which might connote a unidimensional approach (e.g., a once-a-week type of program option). This emphasis is critical given the patchwork of programs and services that are currently provided to gifted and talented students, which vary from state to state and from school to school (NAGC & CSDPG, 2020).

Along with the input from a variety of sources, these principles informed both the 2010 and 2019 revisions of the program standards and assisted in maintaining consistency throughout the revision process.

Differences Between the 2010 and the 2019 Programming Standards

The differences between the 2010 Gifted Programming Standards and the 2019 Gifted Programming Standards relate to updated research, alignment with an expanded set of standards, and shared terminology (NAGC, 2019). The major differences center on the following areas:

Table 1.1 *Continued*

2019 Pre-K-12 Outcomes	2013 NAGC-CEC/TAG Initial Teacher Preparation Standards							2010 NAGC Pre-K–Grade12 Gifted Program Standards						
6.1						*								*
6.2	*					*	*							*
6.3		*												*
6.4						*								*
6.5						*								*

Note: The outcomes and evidence-based practices related to evaluation of programming and services were moved to from Standard 2. Assessment to Standard 5. Programming in the 2019 standards.

Table 1.2 Relationships Between the NAGC-CEC/TAG Initial Teacher Preparation Standards, the 2010 NAGC Pre-K–Grade12 Gifted Programming Standards, and the 2019 PreK-Grade12 Gifted Programming Standards.

2013 NAGC-CEC/TAG Initial Teacher Preparation Standards	2010 and 2019 Pre-K–Grade 12 Gifted Programming Standards (Primary Relationship to Teacher Preparation Standards)
1. Learner Development and Individual Learning Differences 2. Learning Environments 3. Curricular Content Knowledge 4. Assessment 5. Instructional Planning and Strategies 6. Professional Learning and Ethical Practice 7. Collaboration	1. Learning and Development (NAGC-CEC/TAG #1) 2. Assessment (NAGC-CEC/TAG #4) 3. Curriculum Planning and Instruction (NAGC-CEC/TAG #3, #5) 4. Learning Environments (NAGC-CEC/TAG #2) 5. Programming (NAGC-CEC/TAG #6, #7) 6. Professional Learning (NAGC-CEC/TAG #6, #7)

3. *The revised standards emphasize shared terminology across various fields, simplified language, and streamlined outcomes and evidence-based practices.* This commonality emphasizes the importance of collaboration to address the strengths and needs of all students.

An Overview of the 2019 Pre-K–Grade 12 Programming Standards

The 35 student outcomes are organized within six programming standards: Learning and Development, Assessment, Curriculum Planning and Instruction, Learning Environments, Programming, and Professional Learning (see Programming Standards in Appendix A). Each of the six standards represents an important emphasis in developing and implementing effective programming for students with gifts and talents. Practices that are based on research evidence are also included and aligned with each student outcome. These evidence-based practices provide guidance to educators in specific strategies that might be implemented to achieve the student outcomes. The following is a brief overview of each standard and its related student outcomes and evidence-based practices.

Standard 1. Learning and Development

The first standard is foundational to the remaining standards because educators must understand the population's characteristics and needs before they plan and implement assessments, curriculum, instructional strategies, learning environments, programming, and professional development. The student outcomes within this standard recognize the learning and developmental differences of students with gifts and talents, encourage the students' ongoing self-understanding, awareness of their needs, cognitive, psychosocial, and affective growth, and career development in the school, home, and community. To achieve these outcomes, educators

(a) help students identify their interests, strengths, and needs (Lee & Olszewski-Kubilius, 2006; Simonton, 2000; VanTassel-Baska, 2009);

(b) develop activities, culturally-responsive classrooms, and special interventions that match each student's characteristics (Ford, 2006; Hébert. 1991; Shade et al.,1997);

(c) use evidence-based instructional and grouping practices (Kulik & Kulik, 1992; Rogers, 1991; Vogl & Preckel, 2014);

(d) provide role models and mentors within and outside the school (Bloom & Sosniak, 1981; Feng, 2007; VanTassel-Baska, 2006);

(e) design interventions and provide accommodations for learning differences to develop cognitive and noncognitive abilities (Farrington et al., 2012; Flowers & Banda, 2016; Mofield & Parker Peters, 2019); and

(f) implement learning progressions that provide students with college and career guidance (Greene, 2003; Jung, 2014; Maxwell, 2007; Muratori & Smith, 2015).

Standard 2. Assessment

This standard incorporates two forms of assessments that include identification and the assessment of learning progress and outcomes. Evaluation of programming, which was in the 2010 Assessment Standard was moved to the Programming Standard. The student outcomes within the identification area relate to equal access, the alignment of assessments with the student's characteristics and program services, and the representation of students from diverse backgrounds. As a result of ongoing assessments, students with gifts and talents demonstrate growth commensurate with their abilities in cognitive, social-emotional, and psychosocial areas and are able to self-assess their learning progress. To achieve these outcomes, evidence-based practices include

(a) developing environments and instructional activities where students can show diverse gifts and talents (Bianco & Harris, 2014; Borland & Wright, 1994; Grantham, 2003; Hertzog, 2005);

(b) involving families in the identification process (Jolly & Matthews, 2012; Wilder, 2014);

(c) using comprehensive, cohesive, ongoing, and technically adequate procedures during the identification process that do not discriminate against any student with potential (Briggs et al., 2008; Card & Giuliano, 2015; Ford & Trotman, 2000; Johnsen, 2018; Lakin, 2018; Siegle et al., 2016);

(d) using various types of assessments from multiple sources such as off-level tests, dynamic assessments, and other types of qualitative and quantitative measures that relate to students' interests, strengths, and needs (Baker & Schacter, 1996; Baum et al.1996; Coxbill et al., 2013; Johnsen, 2009; Maddocks, 2018; Reis et al., 1992; VanTassel-Baska, 2007); and

(e) using formative and summative assessments to develop profiles for planning interventions and measuring student progress (Inman & Roberts, 2016; Johnsen et al., 2012; McCoach et al., 2013; Tieso, 2005; Tomlinson et al., 2003).

Standard 3. Curriculum Planning and Instruction

The third standard not only addresses curricular planning but also talent development, responsiveness to diversity, instructional strategies, and accessing appropriate resources to engage a variety of learners. Desired outcomes include students demonstrating academic growth commensurate with their abilities and becoming independent investigators; demonstrating social/emotional and psychosocial skills necessary for growth in talent areas or areas of interest; developing knowledge and skills for being productive in a multicultural, diverse, and global society; and accessing high-quality curricular resources. To achieve these outcomes, educators

(a) develop comprehensive, cohesive learning progressions and plans for students with a variety of gifts and talents that is based on standards (Assouline et al., 2015; Johnsen & Clarenbach, 2017; Steenbergen-Hu et al., 2016), incorporate differentiated curricula in all domains (Cho et al., 2015; Gavin et al., 2013; Hunsaker et al., 2010), use a balanced assessment system (Chappuis & Stiggins, 2020; McCoach et al., 2013; Stiggins, 2008), integrate a variety of technologies (Besnoy et al., 2012; Bouck & Hunley, 2014; Coxon et al., 2018), and consider accommodations for exceptional learners (Coleman & Hughes, 2009; Coleman & Johnsen, 2011);

(b) design learning experiences that cultivate social/emotional and psychosocial skills in the talent development process (Ferguson, 2015; Mofield & Chakraborti-Ghosh, 2010; Olszewski et al., 2015);

(c) develop and use culturally responsive curriculum (Eun, 2016; Ford, 2006; Ford et al., 2000; VanTassel-Baska, 2018);

(d) use a repertoire of instructional strategies such as critical and creative thinking, metacognitive, cognitive learning, problem solving, and research models (Anderson & Krathwohl, 2001; Hartman, 2001; Oppong et al., 2019; Paul & Elder, 2014; VanTassel-Baska & Baska, 2019); and

(e) use high quality resources to support differentiation (Periathiruvadi & Rinn, 2012; Pyryt, 2003. Siegle, 2004).

Standard 4. Learning Environments

The fourth standard focuses on the creation of safe learning environments where students are able to develop personal, social, leadership, cultural, and communication competencies. Specific student outcomes include the development of self-awareness, self-advocacy, self-efficacy, confidence, motivation, resilience, independence, curiosity, and risk taking. Students also learn how to develop positive peer relationships, social interactions, and interpersonal and technical communication skills with diverse individuals across diverse groups. In their development of leadership skills, they also demonstrate personal and social responsibility. To achieve these outcomes, educators create environments that

(a) not only have high expectations but also promote perseverance and resilience and view mistakes as learning opportunities (Cross et al., 2003; Dweck & Kamins, 1999; Kitano & Lewis, 2005; McKown & Weinstein, 2008);

(b) develop psychosocial and social and emotional skills and promote positive interactions and collaborations with artistic/creative and chronological-age peers from a variety of backgrounds (Hébert & Smith, 2018; Olszewski-Kubilius & Grant, 1994; Subotnik et al., 2010);

(c) are safe and welcoming for exploring personal and social issues (Brody, 1999; Hutcheson & Tieso, 2014; Neihart, 2002);

(d) provide opportunities for developing many forms of leadership (Frey, 1998; Hensel, 1991; Pleasants et al., 2004; Ross & Smyth, 1995);

(e) promote lifelong personal and social responsibility within and out-side of the school setting (Lee & Olszewski-Kubilius, 2006; Olszewski-Kubilius et al., 2015);

(f) model and support diverse learners (Briggs et al., 2008; Cline & Schwartz, 2000; den Brok et al., 2002; Ford, 2015); and

(g) incorporate technology in teaching communication skills that reflect the diversity of the student population (Housand & Housand, 2012; Mehta et al., 2019; Periathiruvadi & Rinn, 2012; Rizza, 2006; Siegle, 2004; Shachaf, 2008; Siefert et al., 2019).

Standard 5. Programming

The fifth standard includes a variety of programming options that are com-prehensive, cohesive, and coordinated. Educators have adequate resources and policies and procedures that enable them to collaborate with one another and stakeholders in implementing a continuum of services both within and outside of school. These services are evaluated to determine if they enhance students' performance in cognitive, psychosocial, and social-emotional areas, and assist them in identifying future postsecondary and career goals and talent development pathways. Outcomes include students demonstrating growth commensurate with their abilities in cognitive, social-emotional, and psychosocial areas, and identifying future career and talent development pathways to reach their goals. Students have access to high-quality program-ming and services that match their interests, strengths, and needs. To achieve these outcomes, educators

(a) develop and implement a comprehensive set of services that in-cludes acceleration, enrichment, grouping, individualized learning, and digital learning options that develop students' talent areas

(Allen et al., 2016; Assouline et al., 2015; Berger, 2003; Brulles et al., 2010; Colangelo et al., 2004; Horn, 2015; Johnsen & Johnson, 2007; Kulik & Kulik, 1992; Renzulli & Reis, 2003; Siegle & McCoach, 2005; Steenbergen-Hu et al., 2016);

(b) coordinate services and collaborate with families and other professionals to develop a continuum of programming and services (Boazman, 2015; Campbell & Verna, 2007; Coleman & Johnsen, 2011; Swiatek & Lupkowski-Shoplik, 2005);

(c) provide professional guidance and counseling and involve mentors and technology education to create talent development and career-oriented goals (Ackerman, 2014; Bouck & Hunley, 2014; Coxon et al., 2018; Mayes et al., 2019; Maxwell, 2007);

(d) provide sufficient human and material resources (Baker & Friedman-Nimz, 2003; NAGC & CSDPG, 2020);

(e) create policies and procedures that are aligned with laws, rules, regulations, and standards (Brown & Abernethy, 2009; Ford & Trotman, 2000; Long et al., 2015; Swanson, 2007; Swanson & Lord, 2013; Zeidner & Schleyer, 1999); and

(f) assess and evaluate programming components and disseminate and use results (Beasley et al., 2017; Callahan, 2015; Kim et al., 2014; Robinson et al., 2014).

Standard 6. Professional Learning

This standard examines the preparation of educators and the knowledge and skills needed to develop students' talent, psychosocial, and socio-emotional development. It also emphasizes high-quality educators who are committed to creating inclusive gifted education communities, lifelong learning, and ethical practice. Student outcomes include equal access to high-quality gifted programming and the full development of their talents and abilities, and social-emotional and psychosocial skills. To achieve these outcomes, educators

(a) participate in comprehensive, sustained, and research-supported forms of professional learning that models how to develop learning environments responsive to diversity and instructional activities that lead to student expression of diverse characteristics (Bianco & Leech, 2010; Chandler, 2017; Garet et al., 2001; Kitano et al., 2008; Wells, 2019);

(b) provide sufficient human and material resources for professional learning (Grantham et al., 2014; Guskey, 2000; Johnsen et al., 2002);

measures; end-of-course or AP exams; rubrics for assessing complex products and performance; critical or creative-thinking measures to assess process
skills; pre/post assessments, portfolio assessments, or student self-assessments
such as journals, written products, or surveys to examine students' performances over time. It's important that educators remember to match "the
desired outcome to the student's knowledge and skills and level of interest"
(NAGC, 2019, p. 4).

2. *Professional learning*. Following self-assessment, educators can target
   specific evidence-based practices for professional learning. For example, using the information in Table 1.3, educators across grade levels
   might select and/or design comprehensive and cohesive assessment
   tools that could be used to examine how well students are progressing in becoming independent investigators in a variety of domains.
   These assessments then might be used to drive more professional
   learning in specific practices related to research such as formulating
   questions, gathering information, analyzing data and summarizing
   information, developing products, and so on.

3. *Selection of gifted educators*. Along with the NAGC-CEC/TAG teacher
   preparation standards, these standards might also be used for selecting teachers and other educators who would be effective in planning programming and serving students with gifts and talents. For
   example: Do educators engage students in identifying their interests,
   strengths, and needs (see 1.1.)? Do they use differentiated ongoing
   product-based and performance-based assessments to measure the
   academic and social-emotional progress of students with gifts and
   talents (see 2.4.2)? Do they use critical-thinking, creative thinking,
   and problem solving strategies (see 3.4.3)? Do they establish a safe
   and welcoming climate for addressing personal and social issues
   (see 4.3.1)? Do they collaborate with other educators in planning
   and implementing programs for students with gifts and talents (see
   5.2.1)? Are they aware of how to develop learning environments
   responsive to diversity and instructional activities that lead to student expression of diverse characteristics (see 6.1.2)?

4. *Program evaluation*. The standards can help educators establish school
   or district-wide benchmarks to monitor the progress of implementing specific evidence-based practices over time. Because the Programming Standards are also written in terms of student outcomes,
   educators involved in evaluation can also assess the effect of implemented practices on students with gifts and talents. For example: To
   what degree are students demonstrating self-understanding

(Standard 1), developing critical psychosocial skills (Standards 1, 3, and 6), accessing resources to support their needs (Standards 1 and 3), demonstrating progress commensurate with their abilities (Standards 2, 3 and 5), and demonstrating skills in communicating, teaming, and collaborating with diverse individuals and across diverse groups (Standard 4)? Collecting these assessment data will not only improve programming but also will show the value added by having specialized programming for students with gifts and talents which can be used for requesting adequate human and material resources.

5. *Advocacy*. The standards can be used to inform educators, policymakers, and the community about the characteristics of effective programming for students with gifts and talents. Presentations can be made to teachers, instructional support staff, administrators, school boards, parent groups, and other community organizations in describing the important practices and related outcomes for gifted education programming. Building both grass-roots and administrative-level supports can assist in policy development at the district and state level which ultimately builds a foundation for gifted education programming that will not disappear during lean economic times.

Summary

Since the 1980s, education has been influenced by the standards movement and the need for accountability. The field of gifted education needs standards, not only to be a part of national conversations but also to provide leadership to educators who want to develop programming that is effective for gifted and talented students. The 2019 NAGC Pre-K–Grade 12 Gifted Programming Standards provide a foundation for developing consistency across schools and school districts, a structure for defining critical benchmarks, guidelines for professional learning, and a basis for advocacy efforts. Moreover, the standards' attention to underserved populations demonstrates the field's commitment to each individual's expression of gifts and talents.

Informed by national standards, research, and years of collaborative work among associations, administrators, district coordinators, full-time gifted teachers, school level gifted coordinators, state directors of gifted education, and university faculty, the Programming Standards focus on student outcomes that are organized within six areas: learning and development, assessment, curriculum planning and instruction, learning environments, programming, and professional learning. Their use in self-assessment, professional learning, selection of gifted educators, program evaluation, and advocacy will help in the development and implementation of quality programming so that students with gifts and talents have opportunities for enhancing their performance.

References

Ackerman, P. L. (2014). Nonsense, common sense, and science of expert performance: Talent and individual differences. *Intelligence, 45,* 6–17. https://doi.org/10.1016/j.intell.2013.04.009

Allen, J. K., Robbins, M. A., Payne, Y. D., & Brown K. B. (2016). Using enrichment clusters to address the needs of culturally and linguistically diverse learners. *Gifted Child Today, 39*(2), 84–97. https://doi.org/10.1177/1076217516628568

American Psychological Association, Center for Psychology in Schools and Education (2017). Top 20 principles from psychology for preK-12 creative, talented, and gifted students' teaching and learning. www.apa.org/ed/schools/teaching-learning/top-principles-gifted.pdf

Anderson, L. W., & Krathwohl, D. R. (Eds.) (2001). A *Taxonomy for learning, teaching, and assessing: A revision of Bloom's taxonomy of educational objectives*. Longman.

Assouline, S. G., Colangelo, N., VanTassel-Baska, J., & Lupkowski-Shoplik, A. (2015). *A nation empowered: Evidence trumps the excuses holding back American's brightest students* (Vol. 2). *The Belin Blank Center. www.acceleration institute.org/Nation_Empowered/Order/Default.aspx*

Avery, L. D., Van Tassel-Baska, J., & O'Neill, B. (1997). Making evaluation work: One school district's experience. *Gifted Child Quarterly, 41*(3), 124–132. https://journals.sagepub.com/doi/pdf/10.1177/001698629704100402

Bain, S. K., Bourgeois, S. J., & Pappas, D. N. (2003). Linking theoretical models to actual practices: A survey of teachers in gifted education. *Roeper Review, 25*(4), 166–172. https://doi.org/10.1080/02783190309554224

Baker, B. D., & Friedman-Nimz, R. (2003). Gifted children, vertical equity, and state school finance policies and practices. *Journal of Education Finance, 28*(4), 523–555. www.jstor.org/stable/40704183

Baker, E. L., & Schacter, J. (1996). Expert benchmarks for student academic performance: The case for gifted children. *Gifted Child Quarterly, 40*(2), 61–65. https://doi.org/10.1177/001698629604000202

Baum, S. M., Owen, S. V., & Oreck, B. A. (1996). Talent beyond words: Identification of potential talent in dance and music in elementary students. *Gifted Child Quarterly, 40*(2), 93–101. https://doi.org/10.1177/001698629604000206

Beasley, J. G., Briggs, C., & Pennington, L. (2017). Bridging the gap 10 years later: A tool and technique to analyze and evaluate advanced academic curricular units. *Gifted Child Today*, 40, 48–58. https://doi.org/10.1177/1076217516675902

Besnoy, K. D., Dantzler, J. A., & Siders, J. A. (2012). Creating a digital ecosystem for the gifted education classroom. *Journal of Advanced Academics*, 23(4), 305–325. https://doi.org/10.1177/1932202X12461005

Bianco, M., & Harris, B. (2014). Strength-based RtI: Developing gifted potential in Spanish-speaking English language learners. *Gifted Child Today*, 37(3), 169–176. https://doi.org/10.1177/1076217514530115

Bianco, M., & Leech, N. L. (2010). Twice-exceptional learners: Effects of teacher preparation and disability labels on gifted referrals. *Teacher Education & Special Education*, 33(4), 319–334. https://doi.org/10.1177/0888406409356392

Bloom, B. S., & Sosniak, L. A. (1981). Talent development vs. schooling. *Educational Leadership*, 39, 86–94. www.ascd.org/ASCD/pdf/journals/ed_lead/el_198111_bloom.pdf

Boazman, J. (2015). Important voices: Gifted children and parents share what they need. *Parenting for High Potential*, 4(7), 2–3, 22–23. www.nagc.org/sites/default/files/Publication%20PHP/PHP%20Aug%202015.pdf

Borland, J. H., & Wright, L. (1994). Identifying young, potentially gifted, economically disadvantaged students. *Gifted Child Quarterly*, 38(4), 164–171. https://doi.org/10.1177/001698629403800402

Bouck, E. C., & Hunley, M. (2014). Technology and giftedness. *Advances in Special Education*, 26, 191–210. https://doi.org/10.1108/S0270-4013(2014)0000026009

Briggs, C. J., Reis, S. M., & Sullivan, E. E. (2008). A national view of promising practices for culturally, linguistically, and ethnically diverse gifted and talented students. *Gifted Child Quarterly*, 52(2), 131–145. https://doi.org/10.1177/0016986208316037

Brody, L. (1999). The talent searches: Counseling and mentoring activities. In N. Colangelo & S. Assouline (Eds.), *Talent development III, Proceedings from The 1995 Henry B. and Jocelyn Wallace national research symposium on talent development.* (pp. 153–157). Great Potential Press.

Brown, E. G., & Abernethy, S. H. (2009). Policy implications at the state and district level with RtI for gifted students. *Gifted Child Today*, 32(3), 52–57. https://doi.org/10.1177/107621750903200311

Brulles, D., Saunders, R., & Cohn, S. J. (2010). Improving performance for gifted students in a cluster grouping model. *Journal for the Education of the Gifted*, 34(2), 327–352. https://files.eric.ed.gov/fulltext/EJ910197.pdf

Callahan, C. M. (2015). Making the grade or achieving the goal? Evaluating learner and program outcomes in gifted education. In F. A. Karnes & S. M.

Bean (Eds.), *Methods and materials for teaching the gifted* (4th ed., pp. 257–306). Prufrock Press.

Callahan, C., Cooper, C., & Glascock, R. (2003). *Preparing teachers to develop and enhance talent: The position of national education organizations.* (ERIC Document Services No. ED477882). https://eric.ed.gov/?id=ED477882

Callahan, C., & Reis, S. (2004). *Program evaluation in gifted education: Essential readings in gifted education series.* Corwin Press.

Campbell, J. R., & Verna, M. A. (2007). Effective parental influence: Academic home climate linked to children's achievement. *Educational Research and Evaluation, 13*(6), 501–519. https://doi.org/10.1080/13803610701785949

Card, D., & Giuliano, L. (2015). *Can universal screening increase the representation of low income and minority students in gifted education?* (NBER Working Paper 21519). Cambridge, MA; National Bureau of Economic Research. Retrieved from www.nber.org/papers/w21519

Cattell, R. B. (1971). *Abilities: Their structure, growth, and action.* Houghton Mifflin.

Chandler, K. L. (2017). Effective models for designing professional development in gifted education. In S. K. Johnsen & J. Clarenbach (Eds.), *Using the National gifted education standards for Pre-K–Grade 12 professional development* (pp. 89–108). Prufrock Press.

Chappuis, J., & Stiggins, R. (2020). *Classroom assessment for student learning: Doing it right—using it well* (3rd ed.). Pearson.

Cho, S., Yang, J., & Mandracchia, M. (2015). Effects of M^3 curriculum on mathematics and English proficiency achievement of mathematically promising English language learners. *Journal of Advanced Academics, 26*(2), 112–142. https://doi.org/10.1177/1932202X15577205

Cline, S., & Schwartz, D. (2000). *Diverse populations of gifted children: Meeting their needs in the regular classroom and beyond.* Prentice-Hall.

Colangelo, N. Assouline, S. G., & Gross, M. U. M. (2004). *A nation deceived: How schools hold back America's brightest students* (Vol. 2). The Connie Belin & Jacqueline N. Blank International Center for Gifted Education and Talent Development. The University of Iowa. www.accelerationinstitute.org/Nation_Deceived/ND_v2.pdf

Coleman, M. R., & Hughes, C. E. (2009). Meeting the needs of gifted students within an RtI framework, *Gifted Child Today, 32*(1), 14–17. https://doi.org/10.1177/107621750903200306

Coleman, M. R., & Johnsen, S. K. (Eds.) (2011). *RtI for gifted students.* Prufrock Press.

Collaborative for Academic, Social and Emotional Learning (2017). Social and emotional learning (SEL) competencies. https://casel.org/wp-content/uploads/2019/12/CASEL-Competencies.pdf

Copenhaver, J. (2002). *Primer for maintaining accurate special education records and meeting confidentiality requirements when serving children with disabilities—Family Educational Rights and Privacy Act (FERPA)*. Utah State University, Mountain Plains Regional Resource Center.

Corwith, S., & Johnsen, S. K. (2021). Gifted programming standards. In J. A. Plucker and C. M. Callahan (Eds.), *Critical issues and practices in gifted education* (3rd ed., pp. 229–247). Prufrock Press.

Council for Exceptional Children. (2010). *Validation study resource manual*. www.cec.sped.org/~/media/Files/Standards/Professional%20Preparation%20Standards/Specialty%20sets/Validation%20Studies%20Resource%20Manual.pdf

Council for Exceptional Children (2015). *Advanced preparation standards*. https://exceptionalchildren.org/standards/advanced-special-education-preparation-standards

Council of Chief State School Officers (2013, April). Interstate Teacher Assessment and Support Consortium InTASC *Model Core Teaching Standards and Learning Progressions for Teachers 1.0: A resource for ongoing teacher development*. https://ccsso.org/sites/default/files/2017–12/2013_INTASC_Learning_Progressions_for_Teachers.pdf

Cross, T., Stewart, R. A., & Coleman, L. J. (2003). Phenomenology and Its implications for gifted studies research: Investigating the *lebenswelt* of academically gifted students attending an elementary magnet school. *Journal for the Education of the Gifted, 26*(3), 201–220. https://doi.org/10.1177/016235320302600304

Coxbill, E., Chamberlin, S. A., & Weatherford, J. (2013). Using model-eliciting activities as a tool to identify and develop mathematically creative students. *Journal for the Education of the Gifted, 36*(2), 176–197. https://doi.org/10.1177/0162353213480433

Coxon, S. V., Dohrman, R. L., & Nadler, D. R. (2018). Children using robotics for engineering, science, technology, and math (CREST-M): The development and evaluation of an engaging math curriculum. *Roeper Review, 40*, 86–96. https://doi.org/10.1080/02783193.2018.1434711

den Brok, P., Levy, J., Rodriguez, R., & Wubbels, T. (2002). Perceptions of Asian-American and Hispanic American teachers and their students on teacher interpersonal communication style. *Teaching and Teacher Education, 18*(4), 447–467. https://doi.org/10.1016/S0742–051X(2)00009–4

Dweck, C. S., & Kamins, M. L. (1999). Person versus process praise and criticism: Implications for contingent self-worth and coping. *Developmental Psychology, 35*(3), 835–847. https://doi.org/10.1037/0012–1649.35.3.835

Eun, B. (2016). The culturally gifted classroom: A sociocultural approach to the inclusive education of English language learners. *Educational Psychology in Practice, 32*(2), 122–132. https://doi.org/10.1080/02667363.2015.1116060

Every Student Succeeds Act (ESSA). (2015). www.ed.gov/essa?src=rn

Farrington, C. A., Roderick, M., Allensworth, E., Nagaoka, J., Keyes, T. S., Johnson, D. W., & Beechum, N. O. (2012). *Teaching adolescents to become learners. The role of noncognitive factors in shaping school performance: A critical literature review.* University of Chicago Consortium on Chicago School Research.

Feng, A. (2007). Developing personalized learning experiences: Mentoring for talent development. In J. VanTassel-Baska (Ed.), *Serving gifted learners beyond the traditional classroom* (pp. 189–212). Prufrock Press.

Ferguson, S. K. (2015). Affective education: Addressing the social and emotional needs of gifted students in the classroom. In F. Karnes & S. Bean (Eds.), *Methods and materials for teaching the gifted* (4th ed., pp. 479–512). Prufrock Press.

Flowers, A. M., & Banda, R. M. (2016). Cultivating science identity through principles of self-efficacy. *Journal for Multicultural Education, 10*(3), 405–417. https://doi.org/10.1108/JME-01–2016–0014

Ford, D. Y. (2006). Creating culturally responsive classrooms for gifted students. *Understanding Our Gifted, 19*(1), 10–14. https://eric.ed.gov/?id=EJ846094

Ford, D. Y. (2015). Culturally responsive gifted classrooms for culturally different students: A focus on invitational learning. *Gifted Child Today, 38*(1), 67–69. https://doi.org/10.1177/1076217514556697

Ford, D. Y., Dickson, K. T., Davis, J. L., Scott, M. T., & Grantham, T. C. (2018). A culturally responsive equity-based bill of rights for gifted students of color. *Gifted Child Today, 41*(3), 125–129. https://doi.org/10.1177/1076217518769698

Ford, D. Y., & Harmon, D. A. (2001). Equity and excellence: Providing access to gifted education for culturally diverse students. *Journal of Secondary Gifted Education, 12*(3), 141–147. https://eric.ed.gov/?id=EJ624855

Ford, D. Y., & Harris, J. J. III (1994). *Multicultural gifted education.* Teachers College Press.

Ford, D. Y., & Trotman, M. F. (2000). The office for civil rights and non-discriminatory testing, policies, and procedures: Implications for gifted education. *Roeper Review, 23*(2), 109–112. https://doi.org/10.1080/02783190009554077

Ford, D. Y., & Trotman, M. F. (2001). Teachers of gifted students: Suggested multicultural characteristics and competencies. *Roeper Review, 23*(4), 235–239. https://doi.org/10.1080/02783190109554111

Ford, D., Tyson, C., Howard, T., & Harris, J. J. (2000). Multicultural literature and gifted black students: Promoting self-understanding, awareness, and pride. *Roeper Review, 22*(4), 235–240. https://doi.org/10.1080/02783190009554045

Ford, D. Y., Wright, B. L., & Trotman Scott, M. (2020). A matter of equity: Desegregating and integrating gifted and talented education for under-represented students of color. *Multicultural Perspectives*, 22(1), 28–36. https://doi.org/10.1080/15210960.2020.1728275

Frasier, M. M., Garcia, J. H., & Passow, A. H. (1995). *A review of assessment issues in gifted education and their implications for identifying gifted minority students*. University of Connecticut, National Research Center on the Gifted and Talented.

Frasier, M. M., Hunsaker, S. L., Lee, J., Finley, V. S., Frank, E., & Garcia, J. H. et al. (1995). *Educators' perceptions of barriers to the identification of gifted children from economically disadvantaged and limited English proficient back-grounds*. (Report RM-95216). University of Connecticut, National Research Center on the Gifted and Talented.

Frey, C. P. (1998). Struggling with identity: Working with seventh-and eighth-grade gifted girls to air issues of concern. *Journal for the Education of the Gifted*, 21(4), 437–451. https://doi.org/10.1177/016235329802100405

Gagné, F. (2010). Motivation within the DMGT 2.0 framework. *High Ability Studies*, 21(2), 81–99. https://doi.org/10.1080/13598139.2010.525341

Garet, M. S., Porter, A. C., Desimone, L., Birman, B. F., & Yoon, K. S. (2001). What makes professional development effective? Results from a national sample of teachers. *American Educational Research Journal*, 38(4), 915–945. https://doi.org/10.3102/00028312038004915

Gavin, M. K., Casa, T. M., Firmender, J. M., & Carroll, S. R. (2013). The impact of advanced geometry and measurement curriculum units on the math-ematics achievement of first-grade students. *Gifted Child Quarterly*, 57(2), 71–84. https://doi.org/10.1177/0016986213479564

Gentry, M., & Ferriss, S. (1999). StATS: A model of collaboration to develop sci-ence talent among rural students. *Roeper Review*, 21(4), 316–320. https://doi.org/10.1080/02783199909553984

Gentry, M., & Owen, S. V. (1999). An investigation of the effects of total school flexible cluster grouping on identification, achievement, and classroom practices. *Gifted Child Quarterly*, 43(4), 224–243. https://doi.org/10.1177/001698629904300402

Grantham, T. C. (2003). Increasing Black student enrollment in gifted pro-grams: An exploration of the Pulaski County special school district's advocacy efforts. *Gifted Child Quarterly*, 47(1), 46–65. https://doi.org/10.1177/001698620304700106

Grantham, T. C., Collins, K. H., & Dickson, K. (2014). Administrative leader-ship in gifted education. In J. A. Plucker, & C. M. Callahan (Eds.), *Critical issues and practices in gifted education: What the research says* (2nd ed., pp. 29–46). Prufrock Press.

Greene, M. J. (2003). Gifted adrift? Career counseling for the gifted and talented. *Roeper Review*, 25(2), 66–72. https://doi.org/10.1080/02783190309554201

Gubbins, E. J., Westberg, K. L., Reis, S. M., Dinnocenti, S. T., Tieso, C. L., & Muller, L. M., Park, S., Emerick, L. J., Maxfield, L. R., & Burns, D. E.(2002). *Implementing a professional development model using gifted education strategies with all students*. (Report RM02172). University of Connecticut, National Research Center on the Gifted and Talented. www.researchgate.net/publication/234670722_Implementing_a_Professional_Development_Model_Using_Gifted_Education_Strategies_with_All_Students

Guskey, T. R. (2000). *Evaluating professional development*. Corwin Press.

Harper, S. R., & Antonio, A. (2008). Not by accident: Intentionality in diversity, learning and engagement. In S. R. Harper (Ed.), *Creating inclusive campus environments for cross-cultural learning and student engagement* (pp. 1–18). National Association of Student Personnel Administrators. www.naspa.org/book/creating-inclusive-campus-environments-for-cross-cultural-learning-and-student-engagement

Harris, B., Plucker, J. A., Rapp, K. E., & Martinez, R. S. (2009). Identifying gifted and talented English language learners: A case study. *Journal for the Education of the Gifted*, 32(3), 368–393. https://doi.org/10.4219/jeg-2009858

Hartman, H. J. (2001). *Metacognition in learning and instruction: Theory, research and practice*. Kluwer Academic Publishers.

Hébert, T. P. (1991). Meeting the affective needs of bright boys through bibliotherapy. *Roeper Review*, 13(4), 207–212. https://doi.org/10.1080/02783199109553360

Hébert, T. P., & Smith, K. J. (2018). Social and emotional development of gifted students. *Gifted Child Today*, 41(4), 176–176. https://doi.org/10.1177/1076217518788591

Hensel, N. H. (1991). Social leadership skills in young children. *Roeper Review*, 14(1), 4–6. https://doi.org/10.1080/02783199109553370

Hertzog, N. B. (2005). Equity and access: Creating general education classrooms responsive to potential giftedness. *Journal for the Education of the Gifted*, 29(2), 213–257. https://doi.org/10.1177/016235320502900205

Horn, C. V. (2015). Young Scholars: A talent development model for finding and nurturing potential in underserved populations. *Gifted Child Today*, 38(1), 19–31. https://doi.org/10.1177/1076217514556532

Housand, B. C., & Housand, A. M. (2012). The role of technology in gifted students' motivation. Psychology in the Schools, 49(7), 706–715. https://doi.org/10.1002/pits.21629

Hunsaker, S. L., Nielsen, A., & Bartlett, B. (2010). Correlates of teacher practices influencing student outcomes in reading instruction for advanced readers. *Gifted Child Quarterly*, *54*(4), 273–282. https://doi.org/10.1177/0016986210374506

Hutcheson, V. H., & Tieso, C. L. (2014). Social coping of gifted and LGBTQ adolescents. *Journal for the Education of the Gifted*, *37*(4), 355–377. https://doi.org/10.1177/0162353214552563

Inman, T. F., & Roberts, J. L. (2016). Authentic, formative and informative assessment of advanced learning. In T. Kettler (Ed.), *Modern curriculum for gifted and advanced academic students* (pp. 205–235). Prufrock Press.

International Society for Technology in Education (2016). *Standards for Educators-Facilitator and ISTE Standards for Students-Empowered Learner*. www.iste.org/standards/for-educators; www.iste.org/standards/for-students

Johnsen, S. K. (2006). New national standards for teachers of gifted and talented students. *Tempo*, *26*(3), 26–31. https://tempo.txgifted.org/

Johnsen, S. K. (2009). Portfolio assessment of gifted students. In J. VanTassel-Baska (Ed.), *Alternative assessments with gifted and talented students* (pp. 227–257). Prufrock Press.

Johnsen, S. K. (2012). Introduction to the NAGC Pre-K–Grade 12 Gifted Programming Standards. In S. K. Johnsen (Ed.), *NAGC Pre-K–Grade 12 Gifted Education Programming Standards: A guide to planning and implementing high-quality services* (pp. 1–26). Prufrock Press.

Johnsen, S. K. (Ed.) (2018). *Identifying gifted students: A practical guide* (3rd ed.). Prufrock Press.

Johnsen, S. K., & Clarenbach, J. D. (Eds.) (2017). *Using the national gifted education standards for Pre-K–Grade 12 professional development*. Prufrock Press

Johnsen, S. K., Haensly, P. A., Ryser, G. R., & Ford, R. F. (2002). Changing general education classroom practices to adapt for gifted students. *Gifted Child Quarterly*, *46*(1), 45–63. https://doi.org/10.1177/001698620204600105

Johnsen, S. K., & Johnson, K. (2007). *Independent Study Program* (2nd ed.). Prufrock Press.

Johnsen, S. K., Sulak, T. N., & Rollins, K. (2012). *Serving gifted students within an RtI framework: A practical guide*. Prufrock Press.

Johnsen, S. K., & VanTassel-Baska, J. (2016). Introduction and background. In S. K. Johnsen, S. K., J. VanTassel-Baska, A. Robinson, A. Cotabish, D. Dailey, J. Jolly, J. Clarenbach, & C. M. Adams (Eds.), *Using the national gifted education standards for teacher preparation* (2nd ed., pp. 1–34). Prufrock Press.

Johnsen, S. K., VanTassel-Baska, J., & Robinson, A. (2008). *Using the national gifted education standards for university teacher preparation programs*. Corwin Press.

Jolly, J. L., & Matthews, M. S. (2012). A critique of the literature on parenting gifted learners. *Journal for the Education of the Gifted*, *35*(3), 259–290. https://doi.org/10.1177/0162353212451703

Jung, J. Y. (2014). Modeling the occupational/career decision-making processes of intellectually gifted adolescents: A competing models strategy. *Journal for the Education of the Gifted, 37*(2), 128–152. https://doi.org/10.1177/0162353214529045

Kim, K. H., VanTassel-Baska, J., Bracken, B., Feng, A., & Stambaugh, T. (2014). Assessing science reasoning and conceptual understanding in the primary grades using standardized and performance-based assessments. *Journal of Advanced Academics, 25*(1), 47–66. https://doi.org/10.1177/1932202X14520946

Kitano, M. K., & Lewis, R. B. (2005). Resilience and coping: Implications for gifted children and youth at risk. *Roeper Review, 27*(4), 200–205. https://doi.org/10.1080/02783190509554319

Kitano, M., Montgomery, D., VanTassel-Baska, J., & Johnsen, S. (2008). *Using the national gifted education standards for Pre-K–12 professional development.* Corwin Press.

Kitano, M. K., & Pedersen, K. S. (2002a). Action research and practical inquiry: Multicultural-content integration in gifted education: Lessons from the field. *Journal for the Education of the Gifted, 25*(3), 269–289. https://doi.org/10.1177/016235320202500304

Kitano, M. K., & Pedersen, K. S. (2002b). Action research and practical inquiry: Teaching gifted English learners. *Journal for the Education of the Gifted, 26*(2), 132–147. https://doi.org/10.1177/016235320202600204

Klein, J. P., & Lugg, E. T. (2002). Nurturing young adolescents legally and ethically. *Middle School Journal, 34*(1), 13–20. https://doi.org/10.1080/0094077.2002.11495336

Kulik, J. A., & Kulik, C-L. C. (1992). Meta-analytic findings on grouping programs. *Gifted Child Quarterly, 36*(2), 73–77. https://doi.org/10.1177/001698629203600204

Lakin, J. (2018). Making the cut in gifted selection: Score combination rules and their impact on program diversity. *Gifted Child Quarterly, 62*(2), 210–219. https://doi.org/10.1177/0016986217752099

Landrum, M. S. (2002). *Resource consultation and collaboration in gifted education.* Creative Learning Press.

Landrum, M. S., Callahan, C. M., & Shaklee, B. D. (2001). *Aiming for excellence: Gifted program standards.* Prufrock Press.

Lee, C-W., Cotabish, A., Dailey, D., Johnsen, S., Corwith, S., Guilbault, K., & Pratt, D. (2020). *Self-assess your P–12 practice or program using the NAGC gifted programming standards* (2nd ed.). National Association for Gifted Children.

Lee, S.-Y., & Olszewski-Kubilius, P. (2006). The emotional intelligence, moral judgment, and leadership of academically gifted adolescents. *Journal for the Education of the Gifted*, *30*(1), 29–67. https://doi.org/10.1177/016235320603000103

Lewis, K. D., Novak, A. M., & Weber, C. L. (2018). Where are gifted students of color? Case studies outline strategies to increase diversity in gifted programs. *The Learning Professional*, *39*(4), 50–53, 58. https://eric.ed.gov/?id=EJ1190300

Li, G. (2013). Promoting teachers of culturally and linguistically diverse (CLD) students as change agents: A cultural approach to professional learning. *Theory Into Practice*, *52*, 136–143. https://doi.org/10.1080/00405841.2013.770331

Lindsey, D. B., & Lindsey, R. B. (2016). Build cultural proficiency to ensure equity. *Journal of Staff Development*, *37*(1), 50–56. https://eric.ed.gov/?id=EJ1100652

Long, L. C., Barnett, K., & Rogers, K. B. (2015). Exploring the relationship between principle, policy, and gifted program scope and quality. *Journal for the Education of the Gifted*, *38*(2), 118–140. https://doi.org/10.1177/0162353215518279

Maddocks, D. L. S. (2018). The identification of students who are gifted and have a learning disability: A comparison of different diagnostic criteria. *Gifted Child Quarterly*, *62*(2), 175–192. https://doi.org/10.1177/0016986217752096

Maxwell, M. (2007). Career counseling is personal counseling: A constructivist approach to nurturing the development of gifted female adolescents. *The Career Development Quarterly*, *55*(3), 206–224. https://doi.org/10.1002/j.2161-0045.2007.tb00078.x

Mayes, R. D., Hines, E. M., Bibbs, D. L., Rodman, J., Bonner II, F. A., & Goings, R. B. (2019). Counselors and psychologists mentoring gifted black males with disabilities to foster college and career readiness. *Gifted Child Today*, *42*, 157–164 https://doi.org/10.1177/1076217519843150

McBee, M. T., Peters, S. J., & Miller, E. M. (2016). The impact of the nomination stage on gifted program identification, *Gifted Child Quarterly*, *60*(4), 258–278. https://doi.org/10.1177/0016986216656256

McCoach, D. B., Rambo, K. E., & Welsh, M. (2013). Assessing the growth of gifted students. *Gifted Child Quarterly*, *57*(1), 56–67. https://doi.org/10.1177/0016986212463873

McKown, C., & Weinstein, R. S. (2008). Teacher expectations, classroom context, and the achievement gap. *Journal of School Psychology*, *46*(3), 235–261. https://doi.org/10.1016/j.jsp.2007.05.001

Mofield, E. L., & Chakraborti-Ghosh, S. (2010). Addressing multidimensional perfectionism in gifted adolescents with affective curriculum.

Journal for the Education of the Gifted, *33*(4), 479–513. https://doi.org/10.1177/016235321003300403

Mofield, E., & Parker Peters, M. (2019). Understanding underachievement: Mindset, perfectionism, and achievement attitudes among gifted students. *Journal for the Education of the Gifted*, *42*(2), 107–134. https://doi.org/10.1177/0162353219836737

Muratori, M. C., & Smith, C. K. (2015). Guiding the talent and career development of the gifted individual. *Journal of Counseling & Development*, *93*(2), 173–182. https://doi.org/10.1002/j.1556–6676.2015.00193.x

National Association for Gifted Children (NAGC). (2010). *NAGC Pre-K-Grade 12 Gifted Programming Standards: A blueprint for quality gifted education programs.* www.nagc.org/sites/default/files/standards/K-12%20standards%20booklet.pdf

National Association for Gifted Children (NAGC). (2019). *NAGC 2019 Pre-K-Grade 12 Gifted Programming Standards.* www.nagc.org/resources-publications/resources/national-standards-gifted-and-talented-education/pre-k-grade-12

National Association for Gifted Children/Council for Exceptional Children-The Association for the Gifted (2013a). *Advanced standards in gifted education teacher preparation.* www.nagc.org/sites/default/files/standards/Advanced%20Standards%20in%20GT%20(2013).pdf

National Association for Gifted Children/Council for Exceptional Children-The Association for the Gifted (2013b). *Teacher preparation standards in gifted and talented education.* www.nagc.org/sites/default/files/standards/NAGC-%20CEC%20CAEP%20standards%20(2013%20final).pdf

National Association for Gifted Children (NAGC) and the Council of State Directors of Programs for the Gifted (CSDPG) (2015). 2014–2015 *State of the states in gifted education: Policy and practice data.* National Association for Gifted Children. www.nagc.org/sites/default/files/key%20reports/2014–2015%20State%20of%20the%20States%20(final).pdf

National Association for Gifted Children (NAGC) and the Council of State Directors of Programs for the Gifted (CSDPG) (2020). 2018–2019 *State of the states in gifted education.* National Association for Gifted Children. www.nagc.org/2018–2019-state-states-gifted-education

National Board for Professional Teaching Standards (NBPTS). (2016). *Exceptional needs standards* (2nd ed.). http://nbpts.org/wp-content/uploads/2017/07/ECYA-ENS.pdf

National Board for Professional Teaching Standards (NBPTS. (2016). *What teachers should know and be able to do.* http://accomplishedteacher.org/wp-content/uploads/2016/12/NBPTS-What-Teachers-Should-Know-and-Be-Able-to-Do-.pdf

National Commission on Excellence in Education. (1983). *A nation at risk: The imperatives for educational reform.* U. S. Department of Education.

Neihart, M. (2002). Risk and resilience in gifted children: A conceptual framework. In M. Neihart, S. M. Reis, N. M. Robinson, & S. M. Moon (Eds.), *The social and emotional development of gifted children: What do we know?* (pp. 113–122). Prufrock Press.

No Child Left Behind Act (2001). www2.ed.gov/nclb/landing.jhtml

Olszewski-Kubilius, P., & Grant, B., (1994). Social support systems and the disadvantaged gifted: A framework for developing programs and services. *Roeper Review, 17*(1), 20–25. https://doi.org/10.1080/02783199409553612

Olszewski-Kubilius, P., Subotnik, R. F., Davis, L. C., & Worrell, F. C. (2019). Benchmarking psychosocial skills important for talent development. In R. F. Subotnik, S. G. Assouline, P. Olszewski-Kubilius, H. Stoeger, & A. Ziegler (Eds.), The future of research in talent development: Promising trends, evidence, and implications of innovative scholarship for policy and practice. *New Directions for Child and Adolescent Development, 168,* 161–176. https://doi.org/10.1002/cad.20318

Olszewski-Kubilius, P., Subotnik, R. F., & Worrell, F. C. (2015). Antecedent and concurrent psychosocial skills that support high levels of achievement within talent domains. *High Ability Studies, 26*(2), 195–210. https://doi.org/10.1080/13598139.1015.1095077

Oppong, E., Shore, B. M., & Muis, K. R. (2019). Clarifying the connections among giftedness, metacognition, self-regulation, and self-regulated learning: Implications for theory and practice. *Gifted Child Quarterly, 63*(2), 102–119. https://doi.org/10.1177/0016986218814008

Paul, R., & Elder, L. (2014). *Critical thinking: Tools for taking charge of your professional and personal life* (3rd ed.). Prentice Hall.

Periathiruvadi, S., & Rinn, A. (2012). Technology in gifted education: A review of best practices and empirical research. *Journal of Research on Technology in Education, 45*(2), 153–169. https://files.eric.ed.gov/fulltext/EJ991843.pdf

Phelps, L. A., Durham, J., & Wills, J. (2011). Education alignment and accountability in an era of convergence: Policy insights from states with individual learning plans and policies. *Education Policy Analysis Archives, 19*(31), 1–31. https://doi.org/10.14507/epaa.v19n31.2011

Pleasants, R., Stephens, K. R., Selph, H., & Pfeiffer, S. (2004). Incorporating service learning into leadership education: Duke TIP's leadership institute. *Gifted Child Today, 27*(1), 16–21. https://doi.org/10.1177/107621750402700106

Purcell, J. H., & Leppien, J. H. (1998). Building bridges between general practitioners and educators of the gifted: A study of collaboration. *Gifted Child Quarterly, 42*(3), 172–181. https://doi.org/10.1177/001698629804200305

Pyryt, M. C. (2003). Technology and the gifted. In N. Colangelo & G. A. Davis (Eds.), *Handbook of Gifted Education* (3rd ed., pp. 582–589). Allyn & Bacon.

Reis, S. M., Burns, D. E., & Renzulli, J. S. (1992). *Curriculum compacting: The complete guide to modifying the regular curriculum for high ability students.* Creative Learning Press.

Renzulli, J. (1978). What makes giftedness? Reexamining a definition. *Phi Delta Kappan, 60*(3), 180–184, 261. https://gseuphsdlibrary.files.wordpress.com/2013/03/what-makes-giftedness.pdf

Renzulli, J. S., & Reis, S. M. (2003). The schoolwide enrichment model: Developing creative and productive giftedness. In N. Colangelo, & G. A. Davis (Eds.), *Handbook of gifted education* (3rd ed., pp. 184–203). Allyn & Bacon

Rizza, M. (2006). Computer-assisted technology for the twice exceptional. *Understanding Our Gifted, 18*(4), 11–15. https://eric.ed.gov/?id=EJ844228

Rizza, M. G., & Morrison, W. F. (2007). Identifying twice exceptional children: A toolkit for success, *Teaching Exceptional Children Plus, 3*(3). https://files.eric.ed.gov/fulltext/EJ967126.pdf

Robinson, A., Cotabish, A., Wood, B. K., & O'Tuel, F. S. (2014). The effects of a statewide evaluation initiative in gifted education on practitioner knowledge, concerns, and program documentation. *Journal of Advanced Academics, 25*(4), 349–383. https://doi.org/10.1177/1932202X14549356

Rogers, K. B. (1991). *The relationship of grouping practices to the education of the gifted and talented learner: Research-based decision making series.* University of Connecticut, National Research Center on the Gifted and Talented.

Ross, J., & Smyth, E. (1995). Differentiating cooperative learning to meet the needs of gifted learners: A case for transformational leadership. *Journal for the Education of the Gifted, 19*(1), 63–82. https://doi.org/10.1177/016235329501900105

Shade, B. J., Kelly, C., & Oberg, M. (1997). *Creating culturally responsive classrooms.* American Psychological Association.

Siegle, D. (2004). *Using media and technology with gifted learners.* Prufrock Press.

Siegle, D., Gubbins, E. J., O'Rourke, P., Langley, S. D., Mun, R. U., Luria, S. R., Little, C. A., McCoach, D. B., Knupp, T., Callahan, C. M., & Plucker, J. A. (2016). Barriers to underserved students' participation in gifted programs and possible solutions. *Journal for the Education of the Gifted, 39*(2), 103–131. https://doi.org/10.1177/0162353216640930

Siegle, D., & McCoach, D. G. (2005). Extending learning through mentorships. In F. Karnes & S. Bean (Eds.), *Methods and materials for teaching gifted* (2nd ed., pp. 473–518). Prufrock Press.

Simonton, D. K. (2000). Cognitive, personal, developmental, and social aspects. *American Psychologist, 55*(1), 151–158. https://doi.org/10.1037/0003-066X.55.1.151

Steenbergen-Hu, S., Makel, M. C., & Olszewski-Kubilius, P. (2016). What one hundred years of research says about the effects of ability grouping and acceleration on K-12 students' academic achievement: Findings of two second-order meta-analyses. *Review of Educational Research, 86*(4), 849–899. https://doi.org/10.3102/0034654316675417

Stiggins, R. (2008). *Assessment manifesto: A call for the development of balanced assessment systems.* ETS Assessment Training Institute.

Subotnik, R. F., Edmiston, A. M., Cook, L., & Ross, M. D. (2010). Mentoring for talent development, creativity, social skills, and insider knowledge: The APA Catalyst Program. *Journal of Advanced Academics, 21*(4), 714–739. https://doi.org/10.1177/1932202X1002100406

Subotnik, R. F., Olszewski-Kubilius, P., & Worrell, F. C. (2011). Rethinking giftedness and gifted education: A proposed direction forward based on psychological science. *Psychological Science in the Public Interest, 12*(1), 3–54. https://doi.org/10.1177/1529100611418056

Swanson, J. D. (2007). Policy and practice: A case study of gifted education policy implementation. *Journal for the Education of the Gifted, 31*(2), 131–164. https://doi.org/10.4219/jeg-2007–679

Swanson, J. D., & Lord, E. W. (2013). Harnessing and guiding the power of policy: Examples from one state's experiences. *Journal for the Education of the Gifted, 36*(2), 198–219. https://doi.org/10.1177/0162353213480434

Swiatek, M. A., & Lupkowski-Shoplik, A. (2005). An evaluation of the elementary student talent search by families and schools. *Gifted Child Quarterly, 49(3)*, 247–259. https://doi.org/10.1177/001698620504900306

Tannenbaum, A. (1986). Giftedness: A psychosocial approach. In R. J. Sternberg, & J. Davidson (Eds.), *Conceptions of giftedness* (pp. 21–52). Cambridge University Press.

Tieso, C. (2005). The effects of grouping practices and curricular adjustments on achievement. *Journal for the Education of the Gifted, 29*(1), 60–89. https://doi.org/10.1177/016235320502900104

Tomlinson, C. A., Brighton, C., Hertberg, H., Callahan, C. M., Moon, T. R., Brimijoin, K., Conover, L. A., & Reynolds, T. (2003). Differentiating instruction in response to student readiness, interest, and learning profile in academically diverse classrooms: A review of the literature. *Journal for the Education of the Gifted, 27*(2–3), 119–145. https://doi.org/10.1177/016235320302700203

VanTassel-Baska, J. (Ed.) (2006). *Serving gifted learners beyond the traditional classroom: A guide to alternative programs and services.* Prufrock Press.

VanTassel-Baska, J. (Ed.) (2007). *Alternative assessments with gifted and talented students.* Prufrock Press.

VanTassel-Baska, J. (Ed.) (2009). *Patterns and profiles of promising learners from poverty*. Prufrock Press.

VanTassel-Baska, J. (2018). Achievement unlocked: Effective curriculum interventions with low-income students. *Gifted Child Quarterly, 62*(1), 68–82. https://doi.org/10.1177/0016986217738565

Van Tassel-Baska, J., & Baska, A. (2019). *Curriculum planning and instructional design for gifted learners* (3rd ed.). Prufrock Press.

Vogl, K., & Preckel, F. (2014). Full-time ability grouping of gifted students: Impacts on social self-concept and school-related attitudes. *Gifted Child Quarterly, 58*, 51–68. https://doi.org/10.1177/0016986213513795

Wells, A. (2019). *Achieving equity in gifted programming: Dismantling barriers and tapping potential*. Prufrock Press.

Wilder, S. (2014). Effects of parental involvement on academic achievement: A meta-synthesis. *Educational Review, 66*(3), 377–397. https://doi.org/10.1080/00131911.2013.780009

Zeidner, M., & Schleyer, E. (1999). Evaluating the effects of full-time vs. part-time educational programs for the gifted: Affective outcomes and policy considerations. *Evaluation and Program Planning, 22*(4), 413–427. https://doi.org/10.1016/S0149–7189(99)00027–0

Zirkel, S. (2008). The influence of multicultural educational practices on student outcomes and intergroup relations. *Teachers College Record, 110*(6), 1147–1181. https://eric.ed.gov/?id=EJ825705

2

Designing Supportive School Environments for Social and Emotional Development

Thomas P. Hébert

To begin to examine the challenges of creating appropriate school environments for social and emotional development of highly intelligent young people, it is critical to define our terms. The definition of social and emotional development that informs this discussion is that proposed by Moon (2010) who defines it as "those factors from a psychological perspective that assert an affective influence on an individual's self-image, behavior, and motivation; issues such as but not limited to peer relationships, emotional adjustment, stress management, perfectionism, and sensitivity" (p. 15).

The NAGC Pre-K–Grade 12 Gifted Programming Standards (NAGC Programming Standards) driving the field of gifted education incorporate a number of student outcomes and practices that are related to the social and emotional development of students with gifts and talents. These NAGC student outcomes and evidence-based practices cut across several of the categories including learning and development, assessment, curriculum

DOI: 10.4324/9781003236863-2

planning and instruction, learning environments, programming, and professional learning. They are organized thematically and presented below followed by a succinct discussion of research support and effective practices to inform gifted education teachers and administrators. This discussion is in no way exhaustive but represents an effort to highlight the major strands of the research literature. This chapter then provides a micro-level description of one classroom to show how teachers might implement strategies to reach these outcomes and concludes with a broader description of the philosophical underpinnings that would guide such an approach in one school.

Student Outcomes and Practices

As one examines the NAGC standards it becomes evident that student outcomes in social and emotional development and the practices to support them emerge thematically and include: self-understanding, awareness of learning and affective needs, personal, social, and cultural competence, and the appreciation of talents and the recognition of ways to support their development.

Self-understanding

The first significant theme emerging in the standards related to social and emotional development is self-understanding evident in the lives of gifted young people (e.g., see Standards 1.1–1.3). Within this population there exists self-knowledge regarding their identities, interests, and strengths. Gifted students acquire a developmentally appropriate understanding of how they learn, grow, and respect similarities and differences between themselves and their peers.

The research within the field of gifted education that best informs the knowledge base on self-understanding is within the areas of identity formation in gifted individuals and their striving for self-actualization: the fulfillment of their talents and potentialities. Several studies have examined self-actualization in gifted students. Lewis et al. (1995) found that gifted elementary and middle school students scored higher on measures of self-actualization than the general population. In addition, Karnes and McGinnis (1996) reported a significant correlation between measures of self-actualization and inner locus of control in gifted teenagers. Pufal-Struzik (1999) found that gifted students reached higher levels of self-actualization than the control group did. She noted that the gifted students who had a sense of self-actualization had a higher level of self-acceptance. Moreover, a strong need for intellectual stimulation was associated with their self-acceptance. More recently, a team of researchers (Lee et al., 2018) examined the perceptions of over 1,600 gifted and typical secondary students in South Korea and the USA to identify their preferred modes of social purpose, engagement with their communities, and commitment to societal improvement. They found that gifted students identified *actualized* purpose as their preferred mode of expressing social purpose while the typically developing students favored *self-oriented* life goals. These researchers also found that the gifted students had a stronger interest in social issues and showed a greater awareness of social and civic engagement.

These findings were consistent with a qualitative research study by Hébert and McBee (2007) examining gifted college students in a university honors program. Within this population they found a strong drive to achieve self-actualization. This desire for self-actualization included valuing knowledge and education, a desire to overcome weaknesses, and a need to align one's personal behavior with ethical principles that guided their lives.

Research on identity development in gifted students supports our understanding of this need to strive for self-actualization. In a study of six gifted high-achieving males in an urban high school, Hébert (2000a) identified a strong belief in self as the most significant factor influencing the success of the young men. These males had developed a solid identity that provided them with the drive, energy, and skills they needed to deal with life's challenges in an urban environment. Similar results were found in subsequent studies conducted by Hébert on special populations of gifted males in different contexts. A strong belief in self was found to be significant in shaping the experiences of a group of gifted collegiate males pursuing careers in elementary education (Hébert, 2000b). The identities of the aspiring male teachers incorporated a sincere caring quality, and they recognized and appreciated the empathic qualities within themselves for they realized these traits would serve them well as teachers. In addition, Hébert (2002) examined gifted African-American first generation college males in a predominantly White university and discovered that their firm belief in self, combined with strong internal motivation helped to shape their identity as high achievers. Dole (2001) examined how dual exceptionalities influenced the identity formation of gifted college students with learning disabilities. Within these young adults, she found that "Knowledge of self was ongoing and led to self-acceptance and self-advocacy, not necessarily in that order" (Dole, 2001, p. 122). Their self-understanding and self-acceptance supported them in establishing realistic career goals and they tapped into their strengths and persisted in accomplishing their goals.

More recently, Wang and Neihart (2015) explored identity issues in twice-exceptional (2e) students by investigating perceptions of academic self-concepts and self-efficacy in a group of six adolescent males. Through in-depth interviews they found that academically successful twice-exceptional students possessed positive self-concepts which influenced their learning outcomes. Students were aware of their strengths and they affirmed that their positive view of their talents played an important role in achieving their goals. Moreover, positive academic self-efficacy was evident with students acknowledging their strong belief in their abilities as a psychological strength that influenced their academic performance. The researchers also found that the perceived high-academic self-efficacy of the students was positively influenced by supportive parents, teachers, and peers.

Research studies have shed light on our understanding of the critical need to support gifted and talented students in the process of coming to know and understand themselves and where they want to go in life. Educators can be trained to support them in this journey.

Awareness of Learning and Affective Needs

The second important theme emerging in the NAGC standards on social and emotional development is an awareness of learning and affective needs in gifted students (e.g., see Standards 1.4–1.6). Advanced learners recognize their preferred approaches to learning and they require meaningful and challenging school experiences that address their unique characteristics and needs. Gifted students are able to easily interact with others having similar interests, abilities, or experiences and access resources from the community to support their cognitive and affective needs. In doing so they often identify talent development opportunities to reach their future career goals.

Research literature on the important role of involvement in extracurricular activities sheds light on several of these characteristics. Gifted education scholars have found that gifted students participate actively in academic as well as athletic extracurricular activities (Bucknavage & Worrell, 2005; Olszewski-Kubilius & Lee, 2004). Such activities serve as outlets for gifts and talents and enable young people to experiment with developing them. Additionally, involvement in clubs, teams, or campaigns provides opportunities for gifted students to build a sense of self-efficacy and experience the joy of success (Calvert & Cleveland, 2006; Terry & Bohnenberger, 2007). Engaging in extracurricular activities and athletics has also served gifted adolescents as an appropriate strategy for dealing with the stressors they encounter in life and maintaining emotional well-being when faced with adversity (Hébert, 2018a; 2018b). Being a member of a group or team known for accomplishment nurtures a strong belief in self and successful and productive group experiences also support young people in raising personal aspirations for the future. Moreover, gifted students often discover significant mentors in the adults who facilitate extracurricular activities.

Researchers have also found that twice exceptional students who struggle with the challenges of being gifted with a learning disability will discover their strengths in extracurricular activities. Rather than see themselves as struggling learners in mathematics, they prefer to think of themselves as superstars on the theatrical stage or in the athletic arena (Hébert, 2018a; Mooney & Cole, 2000; Rodis et al., 2001).

Offering appropriate outlets for developing talents in gifted young people serves an important role in social and emotional development. As young people engage in talent development, they experience challenges as well as joys of success and they continue to grow in their self-understanding and self-actualization. Moreover, educators can play important roles in supporting their talent development.

Personal, Social, and Cultural Competence

The third theme emerging in the NAGC standards on social and emotional development is the personal, social, and cultural competence evident in gifted young people (e.g., see Standards 3.2, 4.1, 4.2, 4.4). Gifted students demonstrate growth in personal and social competence and dispositions for exceptional academic and creative productivity. This competence includes self-advocacy and self-efficacy, confidence, motivation, reliance, curiosity, risk taking, and leadership, which may be manifested in positive relationships with peers and in social interactions with adults. Moreover, gifted students possess skills in cultural sensitivity and are able to communicate and collaborate with diverse individuals and across diverse groups.

In order to appreciate the personal, social, and cultural competence of gifted students, educators must examine research from the 1920s when Leta Hollingworth contributed significantly to our understanding of the social and emotional development of gifted children. She was the first psychologist to systematically examine peer relationships of gifted students at differing ranges of intellectual giftedness. Hollingworth was fascinated by the differences she uncovered in the cognitive and affective development of moderately and highly gifted children. She defined the IQ range of 125–155 as "socially optimal intelligence" (Hollingworth, 1926). She pointed out that children within this range were well-adjusted, self-confident, and outgoing young people who discovered and maintained meaningful friendships with their age peers. She noted, however, that children above the 160 IQ level struggled with problems of social isolation. She discovered the more intelligent the child the less often he or she was able to find a true companion and many highly gifted children with IQs of 180 or above developed personal habits of solitary play. Since the work of Hollingworth, research has consistently confirmed Hollingworth's findings (Gallagher, 1958; DeHaan & Havighurst, 1961; Janos et al., 1985).

The work of Miraca Gross (1992; 1993; 2004) on friendships and gifted children has also added a great deal to our understanding of personal and social competence within this population. Gross conducted studies examining the longitudinal effects of acceleration and found important social and emotional benefits. She also found that gifted children's views of friendship undergo a developmental hierarchy of stages that are age-related. She noted that as children mature their expectations of friendship and beliefs about friendship become more sophisticated and complex. Through her findings, she delineated five linear stages: play partner, people to chat to, help and encouragement, intimacy/empathy, and the sure shelter. Throughout her studies Gross found that what gifted children seek in friendships is not driven by chronological age as much as mental age. It should be noted that research by Gross is consistent with studies that examined the experiences of gifted students who were accelerated and found no significant negative consequences related to personal or social competence (Assouline et al., 2015; Olszewski-Kubilius, 1995; Rinn, 2008). It remains evident that personal and social competence and the ability to search for and discover meaningful relationships with other young people will often depend on just how superior intellectually one child is over another. Moreover, with development and maturity, gifted students learn personal and social competence and become capable of enjoying important friendships.

Along with their ability to grow in developing meaningful relationships and friendships, evidence of gifted students developing other personal traits and competencies has been reported through research. Internal motivation or an inner locus of control has been highlighted. Individuals who assume control or responsibility for the events in their lives are said to display an inner locus of control. Researchers have found evidence of this trait in gifted individuals (Albert & Dahling, 2016; Goldberg & Cornell, 1998; Hébert, 2000a; McLaughlin & Saccuzzo, 1997; Phulpoto et al., 2018). Such a trait helps to explain the degree to which a student recognizes a relationship between his own behavior and the outcome of that behavior. Understanding this trait and how to develop it within young people would help educators to support gifted underachievers.

Resilience, defined by Neihart (2002) as "the ability to achieve emotional health and social competence in spite of a history of adversity or stress" (p. 114), has also been reported to be a characteristic of gifted young people. Reis et al., (1995), a team of researchers from the National Research Center on the Gifted and Talented, conducted a three-year study of high ability high school students who achieved or underachieved in an urban setting. These researchers found that many of the high achieving students demonstrated resilience by overcoming problems related to their families, their high school, and their urban community. They reported that the resilience and the courage displayed by these teenagers was remarkable, as these students quietly accepted their difficult circumstances and appreciated opportunities their school and community had to offer them. They made the best of their situations and went on to become valedictorians, school leaders, scholars, and star athletes, graduated with major scholarships and moved on to Ivy League schools or the most selective colleges in the country.

The study by Reis and her colleagues (1995) is also noteworthy in that the research team also found evidence of multicultural awareness and sensitivity within the sample of urban high school students. These young people acknowledged that appreciation for cultural diversity was an important part of their identity. They highlighted the pride they had in the culturally diverse population of their high school and how their appreciation for diversity helped them become better adults.

More recently, Hébert (2018a) conducted a study of gifted high-achieving young men who overcame serious adversity in their lives. They succeeded in overcoming difficult challenges including learning disabilities, homelessness, poverty, alcoholic family members, racism, bullying, gay bashing, dysfunctional families, and ongoing psychological and physical abuse. They overcame their difficult circumstances in adolescence and met strong success in higher education, obtaining advanced graduate degrees and moving on to productive professional careers.

Resilience enabled the men to overcome their adversity. Their resilience was influenced by several significant factors and was strengthened over time with support from others. All of the men were fortunate to have at least one teacher who recognized their promise and invested significant personal energy and time in supporting them. Talent development opportunities during the K–12 and university years provided the men with experiences in success. These experiences provided them with the positive emotional feelings that allowed them to fill their "emotional gas tanks" that fueled their resilience, enabled them to cope with their stressors, helped them develop important friendships, and influenced the development of their identities as gifted males.

The men benefitted from a number of interwoven personal characteristics that also supported them in developing resilience. Each of them maintained strong perseverance and displayed a sense of future-mindedness. Practical intelligence contributed to their survival and success. They also benefited from their intensity and having a sense of empathy.

When they entered college, they enjoyed their new independence and continued their work in developing their talents. Finding outlets for talent development in high-powered academic courses, athletic teams, musical groups, and leadership and social action projects, they were able to see themselves as capable men who could thrive intellectually, athletically, and socially. This success enabled them to view themselves as talented men capable of moving on to enjoy lives of accomplishment and fulfillment.

Hébert (2018b) later examined the experiences of 10 high-achieving first-generation college students from low-income backgrounds and found that resilience was a significant factor in their success. Family adversity and difficult personal experiences during adolescence were major themes; however, students benefited from emotionally supportive K–12 educators and academic rigor in high school. Sustained family pride helped to keep them focused on reaching their goals as well as intellectual engagement at the university, and influential mentors. The ten students developed a strong sense of purpose at the university and graduated well prepared for careers and graduate school.

The development of affective skills associated with personal, social, and cultural competence helps to prepare young people for meaningful lives. Educators may play significant roles in supporting such competencies and can do so through enriched curriculum and classroom environments designed to support social and emotional development.

Appreciation of Talents and the Recognition of Ways to Support their Development

The final theme in the NAGC standards on social and emotional development is an appreciation of talents within gifted young people and their recognition of ways to support the development of their gifts and talents (e.g., see Standards 5.1, 5.3–5.5, 5.8). Gifted students appreciate being able to develop their strengths in their domain of talent or area of interest that may be aligned with future career goals. For this reason, researchers in gifted education have long recognized the value of providing mentorship opportunities for this population.

Mentoring involves a personal relationship between a young person and an older individual who may be an expert in a field or is knowledgeable about a particular topic. In a mentoring relationship, shared interests, common passions, or career interests may bring the student and the adult together. Mentors work with their protégés in a partnership as they explore their common interest or passion. Gifted education teachers and researchers have often noted that the benefits of mentoring programs on the social and emotional development of gifted students surpass any academic or career objectives. Researchers and practitioners have reported increased self-under standing and self-confidence (Callahan and Dickson, 2014; Siegle et al., 2015); commitment, empathy, and self-trust (Tomlinson, 2001); increased responsibility (Subotnik, 2003); and positive self-image (Bruce and Bridgeland, 2014). Tomlinson (2001) celebrated the benefits of this approach as she maintained that "powerful mentorships help prepare young people to live with greater purpose, focus, and appreciation at a younger age by drawing not only on the knowledge of the past, but on its wisdom as well (p. 27).

The appreciation of diverse talents and recognition of ways to develop the strengths of gifted and talented students involves a school's effort to design appropriate mentoring opportunities. Such efforts are worthwhile and will benefit our communities in the future.

Designing a Supportive Classroom Environment: One Teacher's Approach

The following discussion presents how "Kate" a fictionalized eighth-grade teacher of gifted students incorporated multiple strategies field tested by the author to create a classroom environment designed to support the social and emotional development of her students.[1] Kate's challenge was the critical task of creating an emotional climate in her classroom that enabled her students to feel they were valued for their intelligence and creativity, and respected as individuals by both their teacher and their classmates.

Kate was a language arts teacher working with students formally identified as gifted by her school district who selected to enroll in her advanced class. She welcomed her students on the first day of school with a small brown paper sack decorated with ribbons. During the summer, Kate spent a little time at the local dollar store purchasing inexpensive items that she included in the small paper sack. She attached a simple note to the students welcoming them to her classroom and explaining the following items included in the sack:

- A blank CD—In this classroom, you will burn your own path to success.
- Laffy Taffy—Remember to always keep your sense of humor.
- A jigsaw puzzle piece—Everyone in this class is unique, but together we can make something great.
- A jumbo paper clip—In this classroom, we will all help each other keep it together.
- A free homework pass—For that one day when you will really need to cash it in.

(Hébert, 2020a)

With a little bit of preparation and creativity, Kate designed these treats for her students that helped them realize they were about to embark upon a great academic year in advanced language arts. Following the unpacking of the little brown sacks, Kate enjoyed facilitating an activity she referred to as "Little Known Facts." She asked her new students to jot down on an index card five interesting facts or items of information about themselves. She explained that within that list of five, one of the items had to be a lie. Students were then directed to exchange the cards with another classmate, enjoy conversation with each other and determine which of the items was a lie. Kate included herself in this activity. Her list of interesting bits of information were as follows:

- I enjoy dancing Zumba.
- I am a triplet.
- In my senior year I was president of my high school's drama club.
- As a young girl I enjoyed organizing my friends and putting on puppet shows in my backyard for all of the neighbors on my street.
- I once lived in Zurich, Switzerland.

Kate's students enjoyed sharing their interesting lives with each other and their teacher. They were delighted to learn that their teacher was capable of telling a lie. Although she had never lived in Switzerland, she shared with her students her dream of spending one summer backpacking across Europe. Following their conversation in dyads Kate had each student introduce his or her new friend to the class. Plenty of good-natured laughter evolved, the students quickly learned a great deal about each other, and this non-threatening activity provided Kate with plenty of conversation starters at the beginning of the year.

Later that week Kate implemented another activity she referred to as "Business Cards." She explained to her students how professionals design business cards that present an image to the world of just what they are all about. Kate then shared a collection of business cards that she had collected from her travels and helped her students to see how many of them delivered very clear messages. Kate's students enjoyed seeing how the graphic on a card from "Andrew's Lawn Care" spoke to them saying that Andrew was meticulous in his approach to mowing and landscaping. Kate's card from the "Boone Bagelry Restaurant" in Boone, NC offered a clear message that folks in Boone had a great place to enjoy a scrumptious breakfast. A card from "Lotus Sun Therapeutics" in Lexington, SC indicated to Kate's students that their teacher probably enjoyed a well-deserved massage during stressful times of the year from the therapist featured. From the colorful lotus blossom featured on the business card, Kate's students might have assumed that their teacher was in good hands.

Following the discussion of the business cards, Kate had her students reflect on "What does a business card say about you?" She distributed large sheets of art paper and crayons and provided them the time to design their personal business cards. Kate's objective behind this activity was to help each gifted student find a friend in that language arts classroom. She wanted the science fiction buffs to discover each other. She wanted the young women who designed step dance routines to find other dancers. She wanted the sports fanatics to locate others like them. She believed that through their common interests, new friendships would emerge. Kate proudly displayed their cards on the classroom walls and enjoyed watching her students as they made new friendship connections.

To reinforce the importance of those friendship connections, Kate incorporated a simple language arts activity that focused on friendships. One morning she paired her students and provided them time to get to know each other in quiet conversation. Once they had enough time to learn about each other's lives beyond their middle school, they were directed to write a two-word poem describing their new friend. She explained that each line of the poem was limited to two words. After the poets had completed their work and introduced their new friends to the class, Kate encouraged her students to accompany the poem with original artwork. The poems and illustrations were proudly displayed on a classroom bulletin board. One example of a poem that resulted from this activity is offered below:

Bakari Smith
Twin brother
Skateboard expert
Krispy Kreme lover
Basketball player

Huskies fan
Awesome guy!
  Clark Oliver

Along with strategies designed to have her students come to know each other and their teacher, Kate knew that she needed to learn more important information about her students' interests. In order to design appropriate instructional activities that would engage these bright young people, Kate conducted interest inventories with her students. Her facilitation of interest surveys enabled her to make connections with the interests of her students and the language arts curriculum she was required to deliver. By learning her students' interests, Kate was able to adjust the curriculum to address their individual needs.

Kate followed Ferguson's (2015) recommendation that teachers develop their own interest inventories by asking questions about what they enjoy doing after school, their involvement in sports, important people in their lives, family travels, reading interests, and how they feel about particular literary genres. By applying her personal creativity to the design of a Google Doc with a menu of questions for her students Kate uncovered much helpful information that would inform her language arts instruction while also creating a supportive classroom environment. Kate believed that along with planning her curriculum, having students complete the inventories sent an important message to them that said, "I care about you beyond this classroom and want to know what you're interested in." Kate used clever questions such as, "What photo is the background picture on your cell phone? Why?" and "If you could change anything about your middle school, what would it be?" and "When, where, and with whom do you feel the happiest?" Through these inventory questions Kate learned a great deal of helpful information about her students' interests, learning styles, personality traits, and lives beyond their middle school.

Realizing that her students were tech-savvy and had cell phones, Kate enjoyed utilizing their favorite technology to implement a strategy known as photo elicitation—using visual images to begin conversation (Hébert, 2020b). She provided her students with the following prompt: "Using your cell phones, shoot five pictures that represent your identity as a gifted individual." Kate asked them to write a descriptive paragraph to accompany each image and had them submit their work via email. She explained that their photographs could not include any individuals that were identifiable, helping to ensure that the focus remained centered on their identity. Kate wanted to provide them ample time for introspection and provided them one week to submit their responses.

Carson, a highly creative student, shared a photo of himself wearing a hat that covered his face, and attached to the hate was a large sketch of Wile E. Coyote, the well-known cartoon figure. He explained, "Wile E. Coyote is important to me because he represents the ideas that travel so fast through my head, my hyperactivity, and my creativity applied to my life." Jahmelia included a photo of a tall ladder pointed toward a high ceiling and explained, "I took a picture of a ladder because I'm very hard on myself. I want to go very far and high. This photo is of the bottom of the ladder. I believe you can always strive to climb higher." Kate enjoyed infusing photo elicitation into creative writing as well as crafting autobiographies with her students. She acquired helpful information through this technique, enabling her to develop supportive relationships.

As a teacher of language arts, Kate was fortunate because her content area allowed for her to address the social and emotional needs of her students through literature. Kate was a proponent of using literature to facilitate discussions with her students about their issues or concerns. Acknowledging that she was not a therapist, Kate recognized that as a classroom teacher she could facilitate good discussions with middle school students about good books. By doing so, she could help her students draw parallels between their experiences and those of the main characters in the novels, biographies, or short stories they were reading in class. Her objective was to guide gifted students to self-understanding. When she facilitated such discussions, she was always pleased to note that they were really listening to each other as they shared their feelings about personal experiences related to the central characters in the books. Kate saw this approach as her work in helping her students understand themselves and cope with developmental adolescent problems by offering literature relevant to their personal situations as gifted teenagers.

Kate agreed with Halsted (2009) who maintained that literature engages gifted students emotionally. Kate understood that the therapeutic experience began when young people enjoyed a book and discovered that the main characters were very much like themselves. This interaction is referred to as identification, and the more Kate's gifted students had in common with the characters they met in the books, the more meaningful the identification process became. When that identification process occurred, it was accompanied by a catharsis, an emotional feeling that lets gifted students know that they are not alone in tackling a problem. Kate saw that as her students enjoyed the literature, they learned vicariously through the books' characters and were often able to gain new ways of examining their troublesome issues. As a result of the sensitive manner in which she facilitated the classroom discussions, her students gained insights and they were often able to apply new problem solving strategies discussed with their classmates the next time a problematic situation occurred.

In facilitating such discussions Kate realized that she needed to incorporate meaningful follow-up activities after a class discussion of a book. She included a variety of enjoyable options such as creative writing, journaling, cartooning, blogging, writing song lyrics, writing raps, designing television commercials or self-selected options that her students generated. Kate discovered that as her students were engaged in these activities, they continued discussion among themselves about the issues they had discussed earlier with the whole class and they continued to provide each other supportive feedback. Kate smiled to herself after a class discussion when she overheard two eighth grade boys quietly chatting and one commented, "Jamal, I never knew that Sam Sherlock used to harass you in first grade. Man! It made me feel better to know that I wasn't the only kid he picked on back then."

In her work with this approach Kate also learned that follow-up activities in her classroom could be either collaborative or private. She discovered that when discussions involved students engaging in rather serious self-disclosure, private journaling as a follow-up activity provided her students the needed time to process their feelings. Kate believed that the follow-up activities were just as important to her students as the discussion of the books and she found that the more hands-on the follow-up activities, the more her eighth grade boys would talk. She found it fascinating that engaging in hands-on activities was so critical for the young men in her classroom to be more comfortable in discussing anything personal. Kate noticed that the girls had no problems with this issue.

Kate also discovered that she enjoyed facilitating discussions about social and emotional issues using movies. Kate found that this strategy referred to in the field of gifted education as guided viewing of film (Hébert & Hammond, 2006; Hébert & Sergent, 2005) offered several benefits to her students. Kate realized that movies were an important component of adolescent culture. Her students pointed out that being cool meant being knowledgeable about the most current popular films. With movies playing such an influential role in their teenage lives, Kate believed that her gifted students would be receptive to discussing sensitive topics through enjoyable films. Using movies that were aligned with her language arts curriculum she would occasionally reinforce the study of a novel with a parallel film and address affective issues such as friendship, identity development, peer pressure, and parental and family expectations. As she and her students enjoyed discussions on the films Kate was able to deliver her language arts content as well as provide healthy classroom guidance.

In her work using movies Kate found there were times when she wanted to offer guided viewing sessions with small groups of teenagers struggling with a particular issue such as underachievement, perfectionism, or gifted-ness combined with a learning disability. Other times she chose to organize single-sex groups for films that addressed gender-specific issues in a sensitive manner. Kate offered her students these opportunities during lunch or after school. These smaller groups of students found more comfort in a setting where only their classmates present shared similar challenges. Just as she incorporated follow-up activities in using literature, Kate found it helpful to assist students in processing feelings evoked by the movie through enjoyable, hands-on activities.

Along with the infusion of strategies to address affective development in her students, Kate's design of a supportive classroom environment incorpo-rated a classroom mailbox that enabled her students to communicate with her privately. Kate's mentor teacher during her year of student teaching had provided her evidence that middle school students often needed outlets for privately sharing what was going on in their lives beyond school. She saw evidence of success with this approach, and she included the mailbox in her classroom every year. She covered a shoe box in brightly colored paper, and explained to her students that if they were to leave a letter in the box, she guaranteed that they would find a letter from her in a sealed envelope the following day.

Throughout the years she implemented "Ms. Kate's Mailbox" she found that students typically communicated their thoughts on aspects of the lan-guage arts class that they were enjoying, reviews of her style of fashion, or venting about boy-girl relationships. Occasionally Kate received letters from students that were calls for help with more serious issues that she knew she was not equipped to address. Kate responded to those letters the following day with a private conversation with the student, made a point to introduce the child to the school counselor and assisted in scheduling some time with the counselor during these difficult periods in eighth grade. Kate's mailbox was an effective approach to student-teacher communication and served as a critical outlet for teenagers when they needed support, encouragement or adult guidance.

Another important component of Kate's language arts classroom was sig-nificant time dedicated throughout the year to involvement in social outreach projects. As Kate observed characteristics within her students such as moral maturity, sensitivity, and empathy, she believed that a natural approach to supporting those qualities was to encourage her students to engage in work that involved reaching out and helping others in the community. Kate believed that for gifted young people, involvement in social action projects addressed their need for consistency between their adolescent values and their actions, and such involvement enabled them to address authentic community problems and become effective voices for change (Price-Mitchell, 2015; Terry, 2003; Terry & Bohnenberger, 2007; Strobel et al., 2008).

To provide her students with such opportunities, Kate applied her personal creativity and discovered connections between the language arts curriculum and social action projects. When reading a young adult novel about the challenges faced by a teenager from a family of migrant workers, Kate's students became compelled by the difficult issues facing the family and became involved in several outreach projects to support families living in a nearby migrant community. Another novel centered on a poignant relationship between a young adolescent male and an elderly woman led Kate's students to reach out to the nearby nursing home with visits and projects that connected individual teenagers to their special friends in the senior community. With every outreach project that Kate facilitated she found that her students discovered volunteering for others less fortunate really made them feel good, and helped them to realize how their talents enabled them to make a meaningful difference in their communities.

Philosophical Underpinnings of a School that Guide Educators in Designing Supportive Classroom Environments

For school districts interested in applying the NAGC standards in gifted education to their schools, it may be time for educators and administrators to reflect on the philosophical beliefs that guide the design of classroom environments. Are the classrooms in these schools similar to Kate's? If not, what needs to be changed? Does the school district need to reflect on its philosophical beliefs related to educating gifted learners? What might that philosophy look like? Kate was fortunate to work in a middle school where her administrators and colleagues appreciated her approach to a supportive classroom environment for social and emotional development. She realized that her school's philosophical approach to middle grades education was consistent with what she valued in gifted education. Kate believed that teaching gifted middle school students required maintaining academic rigor and providing curriculum that offered intellectual challenge. She also believed that gifted young people would engage in hard intellectual work more effectively if their concomitant social and emotional needs were addressed.

Fortunately, Kate's professional colleagues took that same approach to education. As a faculty they maintained that gifted students needed appropriate levels of academic challenge and time every day to work with other students of similar abilities, interests, and motivation. They believed in a continuum of services including counseling, acceleration, enrichment, extracurricular activities, and mentorships; however, they worked hard to provide a responsive educational environment matched to the level and pace of students' learning, recognition for excellent work and persistent effort, and opportunities for choice of topics aligned with individual interests (Robinson et al., 2002).

In examining their continuum of services for gifted students, Kate's administrators and colleagues also recognized a need to develop a broad yet comprehensive approach to supporting social and emotional development by designing a scope and sequence of affective skills in educating young adolescents. To pursue such an approach educators might consider examining the NAGC standards and developing a menu of psychosocial skills to integrate into the school's curriculum. The following list of skills serves as a beginning to developing curriculum that addresses social and emotional development:

- Understanding self
- Understanding others
- Developing empathy
- Working collaboratively with others
- Peer relationships
- Parental relationships
- Moral reasoning
- Interpersonal communication
- Assertiveness training and self-advocacy
- Conflict management
- Identity development
- Celebrating your strengths
- Coping with stress
- Developing a sense of humor
- Appreciating gender differences
- Celebrating diversity
- Planning for your future

Kate's school was a model of Parker Palmer's (1993) approach to education. Palmer, a well-known educational theorist, author and activist saw teaching as creating a learning space. His poetic metaphor for a learning environment included three important characteristics that are significant in supporting the social and emotional development of young people: openness, boundaries, and a spirit of hospitality. According to Palmer, openness referred to eliminating any barriers to learning. He indicated that educators who designed learning spaces had to define and protect the boundaries of that space. They recognized that learning spaces needed structure for without it, confusion and chaos would occur. Moreover, learning spaces incorporated a spirit of hospitality that Palmer described as individuals being open to receiving each other and each other's new ideas. He maintained that learning spaces were to be hospitable to make learning enjoyable and flexible enough to provide room for young people to experience difficult challenges involved in learning such as testing one's hypotheses, questioning false information, and dealing with mutual criticism within a community of learners.

Classrooms throughout Kate's school could be viewed as what Smith and Emigh (2005) described as caring classroom communities. In a caring classroom, young people experience an orderly environment, a climate of mutual trust, honesty, and respect, and psychological protection and care in their work with others. These are family like environments in which students know one another and share a sense of purpose. From their teachers, students receive positive messages of concern, affection, and security. Students are involved in decision making and create rituals that highlight the significance of the important work they accomplish in their everyday activities. In addition, individual differences and diversity are respected and valued in caring classrooms. Clark (2013) described these responsive learning environments as "cognitively, physically, socially, and emotionally responsive" (p. 330) to students. She maintained that in such a setting young people can "learn responsibility and a sense of control when expectations and opportunities for choice, shared responsibility, and self-evaluation are a planned part of their day" (p. 333). The positive climate for learning is also supported with activities focused on social and emotional growth. Building and practicing affective skills are a consistent and significant part of the daily curriculum, and the emotional climate becomes warm and accepting. Stephanie Pace Marshall, Founding President and President Emerita of the Illinois Mathematics and Science Academy captured the essence of this approach with a simple yet thoughtful message to students in today's schools. This message is one that Kate and many more teachers of gifted students will want to post high at the front of their classrooms: "Take care of yourself. Take care of each other. Take care of this place."

Note

1. The classroom strategies and methods described are featured in Hébert (2020a). Readers are encouraged to explore that resource for further discussion and additional examples of affective educational techniques.

References

Albert, M. A., & Dahling, J. J. (2016). Learning goal orientation and locus of control interact to predict academic self-concept and academic performance in college students. *Personality and Individual Differences, 97*, 245–248. https://doi.org/10.1016/j.paid.2016.03.074

Assouline, S. G., Colangelo, N., & VanTassel-Baska (2015). *A nation empowered: Evidence trumps the excuses holding back America's brightest students* (Vol. 1). The Connie Belin & Jacqueline N. Blank International Center for Gifted Education and Talent Development.

Bruce, M., & Bridgeland, J. (2014). *The mentoring effect: Young people's perspectives on the outcomes and availability of mentoring.* Civic Enterprises with Hart Research Associates for MENTOR: The National Mentoring Partnership.

Bucknavage, L. B., & Worrell, F. C. (2005). A study of academically talented students' participation in extracurricular activities. *Journal of Secondary Gifted Education, 16*(2–3), 74–86. https://doi.org/10.4219/jsge-2005–474

Callahan, C. M., & Dickson, R. K. (2014). Mentors and mentorships. In J. A. Plucker & C. M. Callahan (Eds.), *Critical issues and practices in gifted education: What the research says* (2nd ed., pp. 413–426). Prufrock Press.

Calvert, E., & Cleveland, E. (2006). Extracurricular activities. In F. A. Dixon & S. M. Moon (Eds.), *The handbook of secondary gifted education* (pp. 527–546). Prufrock Press.

Clark, B. (2013). *Growing up gifted: Developing the potential of children at school and at home* (8th ed.). Pearson.

DeHaan, R.F., & Havighurst, R. J. (1961). *Educating gifted children* (2nd ed.). University of Chicago Press.

Dole, S. (2001). Reconciling contradictions: Identity formation in individuals with giftedness and learning disabilities. *Journal for the Education of the Gifted, 25*(2), 103–137. https://doi.org/10.1177/016235320102500202

Ferguson, S. K. (2015). Affective education: Addressing the social and emotional needs of gifted students in the classroom. In F. A. Karnes & S. M.

Bean (Eds.), *Methods and materials for teaching the gifted* (4th ed., pp. 479–509). Prufrock Press.

Gallagher, J. J. (1958). Peer acceptance of highly gifted children in elementary school. *Elementary School Journal*, *58*(8), 465–470. https://doi.org/10.1086/459677

Goldberg, M. D., & Cornell, D.G. (1998). The influence of intrinsic motivation and self-concept on academic achievement in second-and third-grade students. *Journal for the Education of the Gifted*, *21*(2), 179–205. https://doi.org/10.1177/016235329802100204

Gross, M.U.M. (1992). The use of radical acceleration in cases of extreme intellectual precocity. *Gifted Child Quarterly*, *36*(2), 91–99. https://doi.org/10.1177/001698629203600207

Gross, M.U.M. (1993). *Exceptionally gifted children*. Routledge.

Gross, M.U.M. (2004). *Exceptionally gifted children* (2nd ed.). RoutledgeFalmer.

Halsted, J. W. (2009). *Some of my best friends are books: Guiding gifted readers from preschool to high school* (3rd ed.). Great Potential Press.

Hébert, T. P. (2000a). Defining belief in self: Intelligent young men in an urban high school. *Gifted Child Quarterly*, *44*(2), 91–114. https://doi.org/10.1177/001698620004400203

Hébert, T. P. (2000b). Gifted males pursuing careers in elementary education. *Journal for the Education of the Gifted*, *24*(1), 7–45. https://doi.org/10.1177/016235320002400102

Hébert, T. P. (2002). Gifted Black males in a predominantly White university: Portraits of high achievement. *Journal for the Education of the Gifted*, *26*(1), 25–64. https://doi.org/10.1177/016235320202600103

Hébert, T. P. (2018a). *Talented young men overcoming tough times: An exploration of resilience*. Prufrock Press.

Hébert, T. P. (2018b). An examination of high-achieving first-generation college students from low-income backgrounds. *Gifted Child Quarterly*, *62*(1), 1–15. https://doi.org/10.1177/0016986217738051

Hébert, T. P. (2020a). *Understanding the social and emotional lives of gifted students* (2nd ed.). Prufrock Press.

Hébert, T. P. (2020b). Survival secrets on meeting the social and emotional needs of gifted students. In J. L. Roberts & J. R. Boggess (Eds.), *Teacher's survival guide: Gifted education* (pp. 71–74). Prufrock Press.

Hébert, T. P., & Hammond, D. R. (2006). Guided viewing of film with gifted students: Resources for educators and counselors. *Gifted Child Today*, *29*(3), 14–17. https://doi.org/10.4219/gct-2006-6

Hébert, T. P., & McBee, M. T. (2007). The impact of an undergraduate honors program on gifted university students. *Gifted Child Quarterly, 51*(2), 136–151. https://doi.org/10.1177/0016986207299471

Hébert, T. P., & Sergent, D. (2005). Using movies to guide: Teachers and counselors collaborating to support gifted students. *Gifted Child Today, 28*(4), 14–25. https://doi.org/10.1177/107621750502800405

Hollingworth, L.S. (1926). *Gifted children: Their nature and nurture.* Macmillan.

Janos, P. M., Marwood, K.A., & Robinson, N.M. (1985). Friendship patterns in highly intelligent children. *Roeper Review, 8*(1), 46–49. https://doi.org/10.1080/02783198509552929

Karnes, F. A., & McGinnis, J. C. (1996). Self-actualization and locus of control with academically talented adolescents. *Journal of Secondary Gifted Education, 7*(2), 369–372. https://doi.org/10.1177/1932202X9600700204

Lee, S.Y., Matthews, M., Shin, J., & Kim, M.S. (2018). Academically gifted adolescents' social purpose. *High Ability Studies, 31*(1), 17–42. https://doi.org/10.1080/13598139.2018.1533452

Lewis, J. D., Karnes, F. A., & Knight, H. V. (1995). A study of self-actualization and self-concept in intellectually gifted students. *Psychology in the Schools, 32*(1), 52–61. https://doi.org/10.1002/1520-6807(199501)32:1<52::AID-PITS2310320109>3.0.CO;2-P

McLaughlin, S. C., & Saccuzzo, D. P. (1997). Ethnic and gender differences in locus of control in children referred for gifted programs: The effect of vulnerability factors. *Journal for the Education of the Gifted, 20*(3), 268–283. https://doi.org/10.1177/016235329702000305

Moon, S. M. (2010, November). Socio-emotional development glossary definition. In *NAGC Pre-K–Grade12 Gifted Programming Standards: A blueprint for quality gifted education programs.* National Association for Gifted Children.

Mooney, J., & Cole, D. (2000). *Learning outside the lines.* Simon & Schuster.

Neihart, M. (2002). Risk and resilience in gifted children: A conceptual framework. In M. Neihart, S. M. Reis, N. M. Robinson, & S. M. Moon (Eds.), *The social and emotional development of gifted children: What do we know?* (pp. 113–122). Prufrock Press.

Olszewski-Kubilius, P. M. (1995). A summary of research regarding early entrance to college. *Roeper Review, 18*(2), 152–157. https://doi.org/10.1080/02783199509553712

Olszewski-Kubilius, P. M., & Lee, S. (2004). The role of participation in in-school and outside-of-school activities in the talent development of gifted students. *Journal of Secondary Gifted Education, 15*(3), 107–123. https://doi.org/10.4219/jsge-2004-454

Palmer, P. J. (1993). *To know as we are known: Education as a spiritual journey.* HarperCollins.

Phulpoto, N. H., Hussain, A., Anjum, Z., Memon, S. A., & Reham, M. U. (2018). Locus of control and its impact on self-efficacy of university graduates. *International Journal of Computer Science and Network Security, 18*(7), 1–5. http://paper.ijcsns.org/07_book/201807/20180701.pdf

Pufal-Struzik, I. (1999). Self-actualization and other personality dimensions as predictors of mental health of intellectually gifted students. *Roeper Review, 22*(1), 44–47. https://doi.org/10.1080/02783199909553997

Price-Mitchell, M. (2015). *Tomorrow's change makers: Reclaiming the power of citizenship for a new generation.* Eagle Harbor Publishing.

Reis, S. M., Hébert, T.P., Diaz, E.I., Maxfield, L.R., & Ratley, M.E. (1995). *Case studies of talented students who achieve and underachieve in an urban high school.* [Research Monograph No. 95120]. University of Connecticut, The National Research Center on the Gifted and Talented. https://nrcgt.uconn.edu/wp-content/uploads/sites/953/2015/09/rm95120.pdf

Rinn, A.N. (2008). College planning. In J. A. Plucker & C. M. Callahan (Eds.), *Critical issues and practices in gifted education: What the research says* (pp. 97–106). Prufrock Press.

Robinson, N. M., Reis, S. M., Neihart, M., & Moon, S. M. (2002). Social and emotional issues facing gifted and talented students: What have we learned and what should we do now? In M. Neihart, S. M. Reis, N. M. Robinson, & S. M. Moon (Eds.), *The social and emotional development of gifted students: What do we know?* (pp. 267–288). Prufrock Press.

Rodis, P., Garrod, A., & Boscardin, M. L. (Eds.) (2001). *Learning disabilities and life stories.* Allyn & Bacon.

Siegle, D., McCoach, D. B., & Gilson, C. M. (2015). Extending learning through mentorships. In F. A. Karnes & S. M. Bean (Eds.), *Methods and materials for teaching the gifted* (4th ed., pp. 551–587). Prufrock Press.

Smith, R. L., & Emigh, L. (2005). A model for defining the construct of caring in teacher education. In R. L. Smith, D. Skarbek, & J. Hurst (Eds.), *The passion of teaching: Dispositions in the schools* (pp. 27–39). Scarecrow Education.

Strobel, K., Kirshner, B., O'Donoghue, J., & McLaughlin, M. (2008). Qualities that attract urban youth to after-school settings and promote continued participation. *Teachers College Record, 110*(8), 1677–1705. www.colorado.edu/education/sites/default/files/attached-files/Qualities%20That%20Attract%20Urban%20Youth%20to%20After-School%20Settings%20and%20Promote%20Continued%20Participation.pdf

Subotnik, R. (2003). Through another's eyes: The Pinnacle Project. *Gifted Child Today, 26*(2), 14–17. https://doi.org/10.4219/gct-2003-100

Terry, A. W. (2003). Effects of service learning on young, gifted adolescents and their community. *Gifted Child Quarterly, 47*(4), 295–308. https://doi.org/10.1177/001698620304700406

Terry, A., & Bohnenberger, J. (2007). *Service-Learning ... by Degrees: How adolescents can make a difference in the real world.* Heinemann.

Tomlinson, C. A. (2001, December). President's column. *Parenting for High Potential, 5,* 27.

Wang, C. W., & Neihart, M. (2015). Academic self-concept and academic self-efficacy: Self-beliefs enable academic achievement of twice-exceptional students. *Roeper Review, 37*(2), 63–73. https://doi.org/10.1080/02783193.2015.1008660

Thomas P. Hébert, PhD, is professor of gifted and talented education at the University of South Carolina. Dr. Hébert has more than a decade of K-12 classroom experience working with gifted students and 25 years in higher education training graduate students and educators in gifted education. He has also conducted research for the National Research Center on the Gifted and Talented (NRC/GT) and served on the Board of Directors of the National Association for Gifted Children (NAGC). He received the 2012 Distinguished Alumni Award from the Neag School of Education at the University of Connecticut and the 2019 Distinguished Scholar Award from NAGC.

3

Addressing Gifts and Talents, Racial Identity, and Social-Emotional Learning Regarding Students of Color: Challenges and Recommendations for Culturally Responsive Practice

Donna Y. Ford, Kristina Henry Collins,
and Tarek C. Grantham

Overview

The educational needs for many of our special populations of gifted and talented education (GATE) students were and remain neglected in the standards movement and in educational policy in general. Thus, an evaluation of standards with an eye toward a culturally responsive and equity-based perspective is essential (see Ford et al., 2018; 2020, for more detail). In 2019, The National Association for Gifted Children (NAGC) updated its 2010 programming standards to further guide policy and practice to meet the evolving concept of gifts and talents, and to be more responsive to the needs of GATE

DOI: 10.4324/9781003236863-3

students from all racial and ethnic groups. Its aim was to reflect contemporary society, address students' differences and needs, and ultimately improve outcomes for such students and our nation at large.

In this chapter, we provide an updated examination of the standards and sample approaches to designing strategies and assessing students' outcomes that are culturally responsive, equitable, and efficacious. Using the alignment of NAGC's standards to the *Culturally Responsive Equity-based Bill of Rights for Gifted Students of Color* (Ford et al. 2018; 2020) as an example framework, we offer a way that GATE coordinators and educational professionals may evaluate and prioritize implementation of the standards, as indicated in an extensive figure. As an update and extension of Grantham and Ford (2003), this chapter places greater emphasis on the social-emotional learning (SEL) of students of color within both social and cultural contexts. To the point, as we update the chapter, the world is being rocked by two pandemics—COVID-19 and an upsurge in racism (especially anti-Blackness). As Collins (2020a) reinforces, both are taking a toll on the social-emotional well-being of gifted and talented Black students, resulting in increased trauma. Ford also reflects and shares her lived experiences, primarily social-emotional, as a Black GATE high school student in the hopes that it will inspire educators to do better; to do no harm (Ford, 2020).

The NAGC Board of Directors (2020) recently recognized the pervasiveness of systemic racism and called for equity and social justice in gifted and talented education:

◆ We acknowledge the injustices of structural and systemic racism and recognize the field of gifted education has historically been part of the problem by promoting these injustices, even if inadvertently. Some early researchers and thought leaders who influenced the field were involved with the eugenics movement, and early gifted identification and programming practices often became vehicles for de facto segregation. The field has made tremendous strides in addressing these historical injustices in recent years, but we have not made sufficient progress.

◆ NAGC will not endorse, support, or engage in any action that reinforces, promotes, or advances racism or racist movements, including but not limited to racial microaggressions, colorblind ideology, culture-blind policies and practices, and scientific racism in scholarship.

◆ We apologize for any past failings of NAGC that have promoted or reinforced social injustices. In order to move forward, we must be prepared for challenging conversations about our past as an association and as a field.

◆ We pledge to examine our policies, publications, practices, attitudes, and approaches to ensure alignment with our commitment to anti-racism.

This commitment extends to all NAGC stakeholders: The Board of Directors, Staff, Publication Editors, Network and Committee Leaders, Affiliates, and Members. Eliminating systemic racism begins by engaging our stakeholders in intentional conversations to envision a more just and equitable future, identifying necessary actions to eliminate racism and planning new strategies to achieve equity and justice, and facilitating action among all NAGC constituents to accomplish our goals. (NAGC Board of Directors, 2020)

The chapter is divided into four sections with subsections, posed as questions:

◆ What are some of the cultural differences and needs of GATE students of color?
◆ How are the 2019 NAGC standards responsive to the needs of GATE students of color?
◆ Why is attention to racial identity a responsive, equitable, and efficacious social-emotional learning approach for designing strategies and assessing student outcomes? and
◆ What are implications for GATE coordinators and other educational professionals (e.g., counselors, administrators, teachers)?

Before addressing the key focus of the chapter, we provide some cultural context for GATE students of color in the United States. Years of federal data trends reveal that two groups of students are frequently underrepresented in GATE and Advanced Placement courses/programs—Black and Hispanic. In the most recent data from the Office for Civil Rights, Black students represent 19% of all publicly educated students but only 10% of GATE students; Hispanic students represent 25% of all students compared to 16% of those in GATE (Ford, 2013; U.S. Department of Education, Office for Civil Rights, n.d., https://ocrdata.ed.gov).

In most U.S. schools, it has long been accepted and critiqued that access to GATE opportunities begins with referrals by educators—teachers and counselors (Baldwin, 1987; Frasier & Passow, 1994). Referrals are followed by testing. Educators are the gatekeepers to gifted and talented education; if they do not refer students, the screening and identification process often ends. Their lack of training in being culturally responsive and anti-racist often hinders them from making positive evaluations of Black and Hispanic students. As discussed later, the under-referral issue (crisis) is a function of 'deficit thinking' (Valencia, 2010) whereby cultural differences have been and still are misperceived as deficits. This can take the form of both implicit and explicit biases. Relatedly, cultural differences and gifts and talents are ignored or discounted (Baldwin, 2001; 2011; Piske et al., 2016; Torrance, 1977) under the colorblind/cultureblind philosophy—the belief that culture is inconsequential in education (teaching and learning, curriculum and instruction), testing/ evaluations, counseling, psychology, working with families, and more.

We define culture as the accumulation of beliefs, values, attitudes, habits, customs and traditions shared by a group of people. These acquired beliefs, values, etc., serve as a frame of reference and lens through which a group of people view, interpret and respond to situations. No one is born with a culture; culture is learned; culture is dynamic. As such, culture must not be devalued in our work as educators of gifted and talented students of color.

The 1993 U.S. federal definition is the most culturally responsive and equitable of all federal definitions:

> Children and youth with outstanding talent perform or show the potential for performing at remarkably high levels of accomplishment when compared with others of their age, experience, or environment. These children and youth exhibit high performance capacity in intellectual, creative, and/or artistic areas, and unusual leadership capacity, or excel in specific academic fields. They require services or activities not ordinarily provided by the schools. Outstanding talents are present in children and youth from all cultural groups, across all economic strata, and in all areas of human endeavor.
> (https://eric.ed.gov/?id=ED359743, p. 11)

As scholars of color, we maintain that educators who do not (and/or refuse to) understand and value the culture of their students have a high probability of under-referring them for GATE programs and opportunities. Dozens of studies have found that Black students, followed by Hispanic students, are seldom referred to gifted and talented education. Ford and colleagues (2008) summarized teacher referrals based on students' race and ethnicity. In every study, Black students were under-referred by teachers, the vast majority of whom are White and White females; in half of the studies, Hispanic students were under-referred. In the U.S., 79% of teachers are White in general and White females in particular (Hussar et al., 2020). Grissom and Redding (2016) conducted what we consider to be the most telling of all studies to date that expose deficit thinking and what we and others more boldly call 'anti-blackness'. (See Grantham et al. (2020) for a statement on racism in the context of gifted and talented education.) Grissom and Redding found that even when Black students are matched with White students on income, test scores, and achievement, White teachers still under-refer Black students. To reiterate, deficit thinking is operating. Further, they reported that Black students have better chances of being identified as gifted and talented when they have a Black teacher. Thus, teachers as cultural brokers matter; this also calls for more teachers of color in general education and gifted and talented education (Ford et al., 1997).

What Are Some of The Cultural Differences and Needs of Gifted and Talented Students of Color?

In the previous section, we shared our preferred definition of culture. This definition and others not shared have profound implications for GATE access and opportunities—referrals, measures adopted, interpretations of test scores, screening, eventual identification, and programming. Culturally responsive and talented education is impossible when the culture of students is not considered or when their culture is deemed inferior. This begs the question—how do different cultural groups view and value gifts and talents? How do Hispanics as a large group and then as subgroups view gifts and talents (e.g., Mexicans, Puerto Ricans, Cubans, etc.)? What views do Blacks hold about giftedness and GATE? How do culturally different groups, based on different income and educational levels, view gifts and talents?

Boykin et al. (2005) and Boykin and Cunningham (2001) conducted extensive research on the culture of Black students. In our collective works, we have adopted this Afro-centric model to help educators better understand the assets and gifts and talents of Black students, with implications for Hispanic students. This model depicts eight characteristics of gifted and talented Black students with significant GATE implications—spirituality, harmony, affect, movement, verve, communalism, expressive individualism, oral tradition, and social time perspective. Table 3.1 describes each characteristic, juxtaposes them via student and teacher lens, and provides academic and gifted and talented education outcomes. For models pertaining to other groups of color, see culturegrams (www.culturegrams.com) and Ford (2011).

Recognizing the likelihood for teaching and learning mismatches in priorities and expectations, as well as undesired academic and GATE outcomes, we proclaim that if educators approached gifted and talented education through the lens of students' race-based self-concept, they will appropriately deliver a student-centered, culturally responsive, equitable curriculum, and be better equipped to co-sign on gifted and talented students' positive racial identity development.

Table 3.1 Boykin's Afro-Centric Cultural Model with Student and Teacher Lens, and Potential Outcomes

Boykin's Afro-Centric Cultural Styles	Black Student's Lens	Teacher's Deficit Lens	Academic and Gifted and Talented Education Outcomes
Spirituality: Life's happenings are not automatic; religious and higher forces influence people's everyday lives and permeates all of life's affairs. External locus of control.	Chooses not to study and relies on existing knowledge base and talents because of their belief in God's will (i.e., if God wants me to pass, I will pass. If not, failing must have been God's will.) External orientation/ locus of control and, therefore, may exert little effort due to reliance on faith.	Dismisses spirituality and/ or misperceives students as lazy or having a low level of motivation work and work ethic.	Receives low evaluations on subjective and objective measures, resulting in under-referral to gifted education services.
Harmony: High sensitivity to the learning environment and relationships.	Prioritizes and wants to feel respected, welcomed, and valued as a student by teachers and classmates. If feels ostracized by classmates and teachers, may respond in emotional and impulsive ways.	Views students as too sensitive and not mature enough to be gifted and talented.	Experiences conflict and tension between student and teacher, resulting in under-referral to gifted education services.

(Continued)

Table 3.1 *Continued*

Boykin's Afro-Centric Cultural Styles	Black Student's Lens	Teacher's Deficit Lens	Academic and Gifted and Talented Education Outcomes
Movement: Prefers to be active or physically engaged, which emphasizes the interweaving of movement, rhythm, music, and dance.	Prefers kinesthetic and tactile learning opportunities during teaching and learning process, as well as when tested or assessed.	Modes of teaching do not allow students of color to use the styles of learning most comfortable to them.	Student learning may be stifled, resulting in academic failure and gifted under-referral and, thus, retention issues.
Verve: Tends to display a high level of energy and tends to enjoy action that is energetic and lively.	Is lively and energetic in interactions with peers and teachers.	Views students as over-excitable, off-task, and/or hyperactive.	Forced to learn in a way considered boring and irrelevant, resulting in disinterest and academic failure; possible special education referral (e.g., ADHD), and/or under-referral to gifted education services.
Affect: Sensitive to emotional cues. Feelings oriented.	Has a tendency to sense when the teacher does not care for them and may react in an emotional way deemed inappropriate (rude and/or offensive) to educators.	Considers students' responses as disrespectful and insubordinate.	Students are more likely to receive discipline referrals, which reiterates or reinforces students' belief that teacher dislikes them; reduced opportunities to learn when sent out of the classroom; academic failure; possible special education referral and/or under-referral to gifted education services.

Table 3.1 Continued

Boykin's Afro-Centric Cultural Styles	Black Student's Lens	Teacher's Deficit Lens	Academic and Gifted and Talented Education Outcomes
Communalism: A strong commitment to social connectedness. More of a cooperative learner. Extraverted.	Shows a need for affiliation and social acceptance/approval and, because of this, their communal connections and conscientiousness surpass their individual privileges. Prefers to collaborate and work with others. Dislikes individual competition.	Views students as unmotivated and immature. Views students as not competitive. Utilizes other students' individual performance as yardsticks.	Decreased opportunities for students to demonstrate what they know. Reduced likelihood of exposure to rigorous curricula, resulting in underachievement and under-referrals for gifted education services.
Oral Tradition: Prefers oral modes of communication. Blunt and direct. Likes playing with words and sayings/cliches. Great orator. Enjoys debating.	Enjoys using creative, elaborative, and exaggerated language, such as storytelling, jokes, and poetic descriptions. The direct, blunt and metaphorically colorful use of language both spoken and auditory is treated as performance.	Students viewed as loud, obnoxious, rude, off-task, lazy, and/or unmotivated. May become frustrated with students' sense of humor and embellishments, and misinterpret this as a form of disrespect, impoliteness, and/or attention-seeking behavior.	Students are more likely to receive discipline referrals and may be removed from the classroom; missed opportunities to learn, resulting in academic failure, and thus under-referral to gifted education services.

(Continued)

Table 3.1 *Continued*

Boykin's Afro-Centric Cultural Styles	Black Student's Lens	Teacher's Deficit Lens	Academic and Gifted and Talented Education Outcomes
Expressive Individualism: Seeks and develops distinctive personalities that denote a uniqueness of personal style. Creative.	Displays creative use of language (metaphors, clichés, and idioms) and dress; a risk taker with clothing/dress; flare and dramatic.	Students viewed as impulsive, eccentric, or attention seekers. Devalues students' individual and cultural creativity.	Students may receive lower grades for creative work and, thus, underachieve and/or act out. Students are more likely to be labeled with social and/or emotional behavior disorders; and, therefore, under-referred for gifted education services.
Social Time Perspective: Emphasizes what is occurring at the present—the here and now. The event is more important than the timing and the future. External locus of control. Unhurried.	Treats time, deadlines, and assignments casually, with little urgency. Misses deadlines. May not take assignments and tests seriously due to viewing them as personally and culturally irrelevant.	Believes students do not care about school. Primarily blames and places responsibility of interest and/or engagement on students.	Students are more likely to be labeled with social and/or emotional behavior disorder. Under-referral to gifted education services is likely.

Note: Adapted from Ford (2011b).

How are the 2019 NAGC Standards Responsive to the Needs of Gifted and Talented Students of Color?

In 2017, NAGC's Professional Standards Committee was tasked with revising the standards to incorporate new research, reflect updated practices and conceptions of giftedness, and focus renewed attention to issues of equity and inclusion. The principles underlying the work of the committee generally remained the same—giftedness is dynamic, and equity and inclusion are priorities (NAGC, 2019, p. 2). The purpose and goal for the revision of the NAGC Pre-K–Grade 12 Gifted Programming Standards were to provide revised programming that:

(a) is based on new research, evidence and best practices;
(b) reflects language and elements from the professional learning standards (PLS), the International Society for Technology in Education (ISTE) standards, recommendations from The Collaborative for Academic, Social, and Emotional Learning (CASEL), *Bill of Rights for Gifted Students of Color*, and the APA's Top 20 Principles from Psychology for PreK-12 Teaching and Learning; and
(c) emphasizes shared terminology across various fields (e.g., psychology, education, etc.), simplified language, and streamlined outcomes and evidence-based practices (NAGC, 2019. pp. 3–4).

Specifically, differentiating three areas of development: psychosocial (non-cognitive, psychological) skill development, social-emotional (affective) needs, and cognitive development fosters a comprehensive and responsive structure for defining important practices that are the most effective for GATE students of color.

Revisions That Show Promise for GATE Students of Color

Recruitment and identification are only the first steps in adequately serving all gifted students. Programming that develops students for maximum potential must be the goal for all GATE services. These services must prove to be appropriate, effective, and responsive. The curriculum and the pedagogy communicate the beliefs, or "official" knowledge, and practices within GATE. Revised standards that include cognitive, individual, and culturally responsive guidance fosters an environment and promise for otherwise underserved gifted students of color. The 2019 revisions that safeguards this promise are:

◆ **Standard 1:** Learning and Development incorporates new research on talent development. It included language edits, research-based in equity and inclusion, and expectations for educators to understand and explain how learner's needs differ. An important change was the removal of preferred approaches to learning that is often confused with learning styles and has no research evidence.

◆ **Standard 2:** Assessment incorporates new research on identification and clarified terminology about local norms and multiple entry points to services. Most important, student outcomes were modified to encourage identification for services that match students' strengths and needs as well as consider student self-assessment and learning progress commensurate to abilities in all three areas—psychosocial, social emotional learning, and cognitive development.

◆ **Standard 3:** Curriculum Planning and Instruction includes added practices about accommodations for equal access. The section on culturally relevant curriculum was changed to read culturally responsiveness as it relates to educators' responsibility to engage learners and to develop their knowledge and skills. Educators are now encouraged to make use of appropriate resource materials versus the more passive, and non-accountable recommendation to be familiar only with appropriate resource material.

◆ **Standard 4:** Learning Environment incorporates new research on talent development to foster use of technology to communicate and exhibit creative expression. Educators are expected to create an environment with a global perspective that fosters student development of personal and social responsibility, multicultural competence, and interpersonal and technical communications skills.

◆ **Standard 5:** Programming reference was changed from "variety of" to "comprehensiveness" with an additional emphasis on cohesiveness and evaluation as a coordinated continuum of to reflect importance holistic and responsive programming and services for students. In addition, students are also recognized as collaborators and advocates toward their own interests; this offers an important shift in offering students a sit at the table when making decisions for and about their educational experiences.

◆ **Standard 6:** Professional Learning now focuses on educator collaborative development of knowledge, skills, and evidence-based practices reflective of the three distinct areas of development. Added student outcomes related to equity and inclusion reflect more recent work in this area.

The Alignment of Updated NAGC Standards to the Bill of Rights for Students of Color

The *Culturally Responsive Equity-Based Bill of Rights for Gifted Students of Color* (Ford et al., 2018) represents a holistic approach to do what is necessary to desegregate GATE and advanced learner programs to support and advocate for students of color. Presented as rights for students of color in GATE, it also serves as an evaluation tool to assess to what extent NAGC's standards meet the needs of these students (see Ford et al., 2020, for more information). Table 3.2 lists each of the rights outlined within eight categories for the Bill of Rights' and the complementary NAGC programming standards that provide guidance (or not) toward those rights (see NAGC standards in Appendix A).

Table 3.2 Alignment of Bill of Rights for Gifted Students of Color with NAGC Standards.

Bill of Rights for Gifted Students of Color	Aligned NAGC Guidance Student Outcome and/or Brief Description of Evidence-based Practices (see full details in NAGC guidelines)
I. ADVOCACY and ACCOUNTABILITY: Gifted students of color have:	
The right to all gifted education policies and procedures grounded in equity and inclusion.	*2.3: Identification.* 2.3.2. *5.5: Resources.* 5.5.1. *5.8: Evaluation of Programming and Services.* 5.8.2. *6.1: Talent Development.* 6.1.3. *6.3: Equity and Inclusion.* *6.5: Ethics.* 6.5.2.
The right to an administrative structure committed to hiring and retaining gifted teachers of color.	*5.5: Resources.* 5.5.3.
The right to be served by educators devoted to recruiting and retaining students of color in gifted education programs.	*2.2: Identification.* 2.2.1. *2.3: Identification.* 2.3.1.
The right to be served by educators committed to removing barriers to accessing gifted education services.	*5.8: Evaluation of Programming and Services.* *6.1: Talent Development.* 6.1.3. *6.3: Equity and Inclusion.* 6.3.2. *6.5: Ethics.* 6.5.2.

(Continued)

Table 3.2 *Continued*

Bill of Rights for Gifted Students of Color	Aligned NAGC Guidance Student Outcome and/or Brief Description of Evidence-based Practices (see full details in NAGC guidelines)
The right to state and district policies that require educators to be formally prepared/trained in gifted education.	*Standard 6: Professional Learning.*
The right to state and district policies that require educators to be formally trained in culturally relevant and rigorous curriculum and pedagogy.	*2.2: Identification. 2.2.6.* *3.1: Curriculum Planning. 3.1.1, 3.1.4.* *3.3: Responsiveness to Diversity. 3.3.1.* *6.1: Talent Development.* *6.3: Equity and Inclusion. 6.3.1.*
The right to have gifted students of color communities fully engaged with educators in collaborative advocacy processes.	*1.4: Awareness of Needs. 1.4.2.* *3.6: Resources. 3.6.2.* *4.3: Responsibility and Leadership. 4.3.3.* *5.4: Collaboration. 5.4.1.* *5.8: Evaluation of Programming and Services. 5.8.2.*
The right to a family and community advocacy group that represents their culture, background, and experiences.	*5.4: Collaboration. 5.4.1.*
The right to an administrative structure that seeks funding for gifted programs and services in all federally funded programs—particularly Title I, II, III and IV.	*5.5: Resources.* *6.1: Talent Development. 6.1.4.*
The right to a guarantee that all equity data are inclusive of opportunities, access, and support within Consolidated States' plans. This includes Every Student Succeeds Act (ESSA) plans (and future legislation), as well as state level equity plans.	*2.3: Identification. 2.3.2.*
II. ACCESS to PROGRAMMING and SERVICES: Gifted students of color have:	
The right to participate in gifted education programs and services, including Advanced Placement, accelerated, magnet, early college, and other programs for advanced students/learners.	*3.1: Curriculum Planning. 3.1.1, 3.1.4, 3.1.6.* *5.1: Comprehensiveness. 5.1.1.* *5.5: Resources.* *5.6: Policies and Procedures.*

Bill of Rights for Gifted Students of Color	Aligned NAGC Guidance Student Outcome and/or Brief Description of Evidence-based Practices (see full details in NAGC guidelines)
The right to equitable access to gifted education programs and services.	1.1: Self-Understanding. 1.3: Self-Understanding. 1.4: Awareness of Needs. 1.6: Cognitive Growth and Career Development. 2.2: Identification. 2.4: Learning Progress. 2.4.4. 3.6: Resources. 4.1: Personal Competence. 4.1.2. 5.3: Career Pathways. 5.3.1, 5.3.2. 5.5: Resources. 5.7: Evaluation of Programming and Services. 6.3: Equity and Inclusion.
The right to access all district, regional, and state-level services that nurture their giftedness across all domains and content areas.	2.1: Identification. 2.1.1. 3.2: Talent Development. 3.4: Instructional Strategies. 5.2: Cohesive and Coordinated Services. 5.2.3. 6.1: Talent Development. 6.1.2.
The right to be served in their area(s) of gifts and talents.	1.1: Self-Understanding. 1.1.3. 1.2: Self-Understanding. 1.2.2. 3.2: Talent Development. 3.4: Instructional Strategies. 5.2: Cohesive and Coordinated Services. 5.2.2.
The right to access gifted and talented before school, after school, Saturday morning, and summer programs.	1.4: Awareness of Needs. 5.2: Cohesive and Coordinated Services.
The right to participate in college awareness and career development programs at institutions of higher education, including Historically Black Colleges and Universities (HBCUs).	1.6: Cognitive Growth and [College and] Career Development. 5.3: Career Pathways.

(Continued)

Table 3.2 *Continued*

Bill of Rights for Gifted Students of Color	Aligned NAGC Guidance Student Outcome and/or Brief Description of Evidence-based Practices (see full details in NAGC guidelines)
The right to the development and implementation of general and gifted program policies that are equity-based.	*Same as those identified for "The right to all gifted education policies and procedures grounded in equity and inclusion" under ADVOCACY and ACCOUNTABILITY*
The right to be assessed with tools and practices that reduce and/or eliminate bias in traditional assessment tools and practices.	*2.2: Identification. 2.2.5, .2.2.7. 2.3: Identification. 2.3.1.*
The right to be assessed for gifted education potential even if they have been referred for and served in special education (i.e., thrice exceptional: students of color who have gifted and special education needs)	*3.1: Curriculum Planning. 3.1.3, 3.1.8. 6.5: Ethics.*
The right to free or reduced fee gifted education programs and services.	No guidance.
III. GIFTED PROGRAM EVALUATION and ACCOUNTABILITY: Gifted students of color have:	
The right to district, regional, and state program assessments conducted every 3–5 years by external and culturally competent program evaluators with gifted education expertise.	*5.8: Evaluation of Programming and Services.*
The right to annual reports to the community that reveal the "equity goal" for gifted education and all advanced programs and services.	*5.7: Evaluation of Programming and Services. 5.7.1.*
The right to annual equity goals and objectives for district, regional, and state programs.	*5.8: Evaluation of Programming and Services. 5.8.2.*
The right to teachers who engage in continuous and systematic professional learning experiences in cultural competency and multicultural education.	*6.3: Equity and Inclusion. 6.3.1. 6.4: Lifelong Learning. 6.4.1.*

Bill of Rights for Gifted Students of Color	Aligned NAGC Guidance Student Outcome and/or Brief Description of Evidence-based Practices (see full details in NAGC guidelines)
The right to a program philosophy mission/belief statement that explicitly addresses the needs of gifted students of color.	No guidance.
IV. GIFTED EDUCATION EVALUATION and ASSESSMENT: Gifted students of color have:	
The right to a culturally, racially, and linguistically diverse/different gifted education assessment committee.	No guidance.
The right to general education, special education, pre-service, and current professionals trained and dedicated to recognizing and valuing their expressions of gifts and talents.	*5.2: Cohesive and Coordinated Services.*
The right to be evaluated and identified using multiple criteria.	*2.1: Identification. 2.1.3.* *2.2: Identification. 2.2.7.* *2.4: Learning Progress.*
The right to be evaluated in multimodal and multi-dimensional ways.	*2.1: Identification. 2.1.3.* *2.2: Identification. 2.2.7.* *2.4: Learning Progress.*
The right to be assessed with non-biased tests and instruments for screening and identification.	*2.1: Identification. 2.1.3.* *2.2: Identification. 2.2.8.* *2.3: Identification. 2.3.1.*
The right to be assessed with nonverbal tests for screening and identification.	*2.3: Identification. 2.3.1.*
The right to be evaluated by bilingual test examiners (e.g., school psychologists).	No guidance.
The right to be assessed by tests and instruments in their predominant or preferred language.	*2.1: Identification. 2.1.2.* *2.3: Identification. 2.3.1.*
The right to be assessed by tests and instruments translated into their primary or preferred language.	*2.1: Identification. 2.1.2.* *2.3: Identification. 2.3.1.*

(Continued)

Table 3.2 *Continued*

Bill of Rights for Gifted Students of Color	Aligned NAGC Guidance Student Outcome and/or Brief Description of Evidence-based Practices (see full details in NAGC guidelines)
The right to be assessed with culturally normed checklists.	*2.3: Identification.* 2.3.1. *2.2: Identification.* 2.2.8.
The right to be evaluated with tools re-normed to represent their cultural experiences and realities.	No guidance.
The right to be evaluated by tests and instruments normed on students of color for screening and identification.	No guidance.
The right to be assessed by tests and instructions normed locally.	*2.3: Identification.* 2.3.1.
The right to educators who adhere to official testing and assessment policies and procedures.	*2.3: Identification.* 2.3.2. *6.5: Ethics.* 6.5.2.
V. EDUCATORS: Gifted students of color have:	
The right to pre-service and current educators who are unbiased and hold culturally responsive philosophies.	*1.2: Self-Understanding.* 1.2.3. *6.3: Equity and Inclusion.* 6.3.2.
The right to pre-service and current educators who are committed to becoming culturally competent.	*6.3: Equity and Inclusion.* 6.3.3.
The right to pre-service and current educators who are committed to gifted education.	*6.4: Lifelong Learning.*
The right for pre-service and current educators to be trained in multicultural education and gifted education.	No guidance
The right to a racially diverse/different pre-service and current gifted education teaching force.	No guidance.
The right to have access to pre-service and current educators of color and members of their community who represent and can advocate for their interests, needs, and potential.	*5.4: Collaboration.*

Bill of Rights for Gifted Students of Color	Aligned NAGC Guidance Student Outcome and/or Brief Description of Evidence-based Practices (see full details in NAGC guidelines)
The right to pre-service and current educators who have bilingual training and credentials.	No guidance.
VI. CURRICULUM and INSTRUCTION Gifted students of color have:	
The right to culturally relevant curriculum and instruction.	*3.3: Responsiveness to Diversity. 3.3.1.* *6.1: Talent Development. 6.1.2.*
The right to authentic and multicultural content in all content areas.	*3.3: Responsiveness to Diversity. 3.3.1.* *4.3: Responsibility and Leadership. 4.3.3.*
The right to rigorous multicultural curriculum and materials that reflect their cultural, racial, and linguistic background and heritage.	*3.3: Responsiveness to Diversity. 3.3.1.* *4.4: Cultural Competence.*
The right to rigorous and authentic multicultural literature reflective of all cultures.	*4.5: Communication Competence. 4.5.2.*
The right to curricula that promotes cultural, racial, and linguistic pride.	*4.4: Cultural Competence.*
The right to their views being encouraged and honored rather than silenced.	*4.3: Responsibility and Leadership. 4.3.1.*
The right to curricula that will prepare them to be globally competitive and knowledgeable of world cultures.	*3.1: Curriculum Planning. 3.1.7.*
The right to program experiences that allow international travel and virtual engagement with their peers around the world.	*3.1: Curriculum Planning. 3.1.7.*
VII. SOCIAL and EMOTIONAL: Gifted students of color have:	
The right to supportive services and programs by school counselors trained in multicultural counseling (theories, methods, strategies).	*6.2: Psychosocial and Social-Emotional Development.*

(Continued)

Table 3.2 *Continued*

Bill of Rights for Gifted Students of Color	Aligned NAGC Guidance Student Outcome and/or Brief Description of Evidence-based Practices (see full details in NAGC guidelines)
The right to counselors familiar with and skilled in racial identity theories.	No guidance.
The right to counselors who understand and promote racial identity development.	No guidance.
The right to counselors and teachers who understand the unique challenges of being a gifted student of color.	No guidance.
The right to pre-service educators, current educators, and counselors formally trained in the social-emotional needs of gifted children of color.	*2.4: Learning Progress. 2.4.2.* *3.2: Talent Development. 3.2.2.* *4.2: Social Competence. 4.2.3.* *6.2: Psychosocial and Social-Emotional Development. 6.2.1.*
The right to counselors who understand the relationship between racial identity and achievement	*1.2. Self-Understanding.*
The right to interact and be educated with peers from similar cultural, racial, and linguistic backgrounds.	*1.3: Self-Understanding.*
The right to academic support when they underachieve, fail, and/or make mistakes.	*1.5: Cognitive, Psychosocial, and Affective Growth. 1.5.3.*
The right to understand the area(s) in which they are gifted and talented.	*1.3. Self-Understanding..* *1.5: Cognitive, Psychosocial, and Affective Growth.*
The right to be taught how to self-advocate to increase their access to appropriate instructional and support services.	*2.5: Learning Progress.* *3.2: Talent Development. 3.2.1.* *3.5: Instructional Strategies. 3.5.1.* *4.1: Personal Competence.*
VIII. FAMILIES and COMMUNITIES: Gifted students of color have:	
The right to educators who value the importance of their families feeling welcome in schools.	No guidance.

Bill of Rights for Gifted Students of Color	Aligned NAGC Guidance Student Outcome and/or Brief Description of Evidence-based Practices (see full details in NAGC guidelines)
The right to educators who collaborate with their families and communities.	*5.4: Collaboration.*
The right to educators who provide professional development to families to strengthen advocacy for their children.	*1.4: Awareness of Needs.* 1.4.3. *6.1: Talent Development.* 6.1.5.
The right to have community leaders (e.g., faith leaders, community center leaders) who know and understand them in different contexts involved in the referral, identification, and service delivery process.	*1.4: Awareness of Needs.*
The right to have their families assist others in the community with understanding the benefits of gifted education programs and services.	*1.4: Awareness of Needs.*
The right to have their families serve as "cultural agents" to inform educators and mediate the cultural mismatch that exists between their communities and dominant culture school personnel.	No guidance.
The right for schools to recruit and engage members of their communities who have been successful to serve in the critical role of mentoring.	*1.4: Awareness of Needs.* *1.6: Cognitive Growth and Career Development.* *4.1: Personal Competence.* 4.1.2. *5.1: Comprehensiveness.* 5.1.4. *5.3: Career Pathways.* 5.3.2. *6.1: Talent Development.* 6.1.4.
The right for administrative structures to respect the norms, traditions, and culture of communities of color when planning and conducting events.	No guidance.

Note: Bill of Rights is by Ford et al. (2018) and Ford et al. (2020).

Gaps in NAGC Standards Guidance Relative to Equity and Cultural Responsiveness

Although many of the standards provide guidance aligned with the Bill of Rights for students of color in GATE programming, there are several gaps whereby little or no significant implementation guidance is provided. For example, no guidance is offered for an administrative structure committed to: (a) hiring and retaining gifted and talented teachers of color or (b) promoting student awareness of Historically Black Colleges and Universities (HBCUs), Hispanic Serving Institutions (HSIs), and Minority Serving Institutions (MSIs), in terms of career and college planning. Both offer important reflective identity development opportunities for strong, positive scholarly identity development (Collins, 2018). Additional guidance for training as multicultural and culturally competent professionals is needed as well so that they fully understand the unique challenges that gifted students of color face. Effective training would also close gaps for the appreciation and respect of norms and cultural traditions that are valued by the families and communities. With respect comes a feeling for a more sense of belonging and empowerment for families to serve as cultural agents at school.

Why is Attention to Racial Identity a Responsive, Equitable, and Efficacious Social-Emotional Learning Approach for Designing Strategies and Assessing Student Outcomes?

While it is recognized that self-concept and self-esteem affect the academic achievement of students (Hébert, 2010), few publications have focused on the social-emotional and psychological needs of students of color (Ford et al., 2016). Our chapter addresses this void by extending the discussion of self-perception to focus on racial identity and is an update to Grantham and Ford (2003). We propose that very few efforts designed to improve the academic achievement and social-emotional well-being of gifted students of color will be successful unless educators also focus on their racial identity.

As Grantham and Ford (2003) concluded, counselors and teachers seem to focus on one body of work related to GATE students and refer to a separate body of work for culturally different students. Both matter and they are not mutually exclusive. Thus, intersectionality must be recognized and used to support students who are gifted and talented *and* culturally different (Collins, 2020b). Collins (2017a) further contended that it is the responsibility of educators to recognize and support the culture—the values and interests that families and communities instill in their members—is at the core and earliest stages of development for any individual. She proclaimed that empowerment of GATE individuals occurs when we validate, in terms of development and guidance, that which they offer through the perspective of their own social, emotional, and cultural capital. This compels an approach to learning in all other settings as extended development with continuity and culturally responsiveness, regardless of its differences.

Given that too few theories and studies have examined the psychological status of gifted and talented students of color, we explore and integrate scholarship on their social-emotional *and* psychological needs and development (Collins, 2017b; Collins & Grantham, 2017; Ford, 2 2010, 2011, 2013; Ford et al., 2003; Grantham & Ford, 1998, 2003). We contend that GATE students of color have unique needs that teachers, psychologists, and counselors must consider in their work. In doing so, we rely extensively on the most widely researched theory of racial identity development (Cross, 1971; 1995; Cross & Vandiver, 2001) as the foundation of our discussion, and offer suggestions for academic and counseling interventions appropriate for use with gifted and talented Black and Hispanic students.

Racial Identity Development Among Black Students

Racial identity, as a right within the *Bill of Rights* social and emotional support standard (Standard 7) is highlighted in four different areas related to responsibilities of counselors that work with children of color. It suggests that students of color have a right to have counselors who

(a) are familiar with racial identity theories,
(b) understand and promote racial identity development,
(c) understand the unique challenges of being gifted and a student of color, and
(d) understand the relationship between racial identity and achievement.

While the NAGC standards (1.2, Standard 4 introduction, 4.1, and Standard 6) offer guidance for student self-understanding and personal competence as well as professional learning for gifted educators, there is no specific guidance provided for developing racial identity and its importance.

Grantham and Ford (2003) asserted, racial identity theories and research about Black students dates back to the early work of Clark and Clark (1939) who used Black and White dolls to examine the extent to which Black children recognized themselves as racial beings, and how they felt about being

Black. Since then, hundreds of studies have examined some aspect of racial identity with Black adults and children. These studies contend that Blacks are more likely than White students to encounter barriers to healthy racial identity development (Helms, 1989; Hughes et al., 2009; Parham, 1989; Smith, 1989). Racial identity concerns the extent to which people of color are aware of, understand, and value their racial background and heritage. The main premise of this theory is: Do people of color recognize and value their racial background and appearance?

Smith (1989) argued that race creates a bond and feelings of peoplehood, meaning that individuals often define themselves in terms of racial membership in a particular group. She also contended that a healthy regard for one's racial status is psychologically important for people of color. Rotheram and Phinney (1987) defined self-identification as the accurate and consistent use of a racial and ethnic label, based on the perception and conception of belonging to a racial and ethnic group. Thus, for Black and Hispanic students, an important characteristic is racial identity because views about race affect their lives in meaningful ways. In short, racial identity development is a process of coming to terms with one's racial group membership as a salient reference group.

Although scholarship has examined the relationship between self-concept and achievement and between self-esteem and achievement, Ford 2010, 2011) argued that people of color have been shortchanged in theories of self-concept and self-esteem because these theories have failed to consider racial identity in the context of self-concept, self-esteem, and overall self-perceptions. Early on, researchers proposed that, for Black youth, racial identity has a significant impact on achievement, motivation, and attitudes toward school and being gifted and talented (Colangelo, 1981; Colangelo & Exum, 1979; Ford et al., 1993; Smith, 1989). For example, in the earlier stages of racial identity development, presented in the next section, Black students may deliberately underachieve and choose not to participate in GATE programs to avoid peer pressures and accusations that they are "acting White," or they may camouflage their abilities to be accepted socially by their peers (Fordham, 1988, 1991; Ogbu, 2003: Ogbu & Simmons, 1998). More recently, concepts of a *dynamic* racial identity in the context of self-concept that evolves in response to events (i.e., attachment to influences of circumstances, environments, cultural values and beliefs, and personal interactions, etc. that shape how we see ourselves) have been presented; gifted students academically develop with diverse manifestations of talents connected to the experiences and cultural values. (Baber, 2012; Collins, 2017a; Hauge, 2007; Morrison, 2013).

Specific to the development of domain-specific, academic self-concept for students of color, Collins (2018) posited that cultural context and racial identity are at the core of understanding students' science, technology, engineering, and mathematics (STEM) self-concept, which is defined as the result of reciprocal interactions among various psychological factors, individual behaviors, and the outside environment. She contended that Black students' STEM identity (BSSI) is constructed and developed as students continually evaluate their racialized sense of belonging (reflective STEM identity) and STEM interest (cultural value) along with perceptions regarding their own potential (STEM competence/ability), and necessary investment (risk vs. benefit of cultural assimilation).

One Theory of Black Racial Identity Development

The most researched theory of racial identity was first introduced by Cross in 1971. Since then, the theory has undergone three revisions, with the latest being 2001. In the most recent update, entitled Nigrescence Theory (also referred to as the process of becoming Black), Cross and Vandiver (2001) described eight identity types that are clustered into three stages: (a) pre-encounter; (b) immersion-emersion; and (c) internalization. *Pre-encounter assimilation* describes Blacks whose social identity is organized around their sense of being an American and an individual. These individuals place little emphasis on racial group identity, affiliation or salience, and consequently, are not engaged in the Black community and culture. *Pre-encounter miseducation* depicts Blacks who accept and promote the negative images, stereotypes, and historical misinformation about Black people. Some call this type a Negropean. They see little or no strength in the Black community, do not engage in solving or resolving issues in the Black community, and may even sabotage other Blacks. Relatedly, they often hold the attitude "That's the way *they* act. but *I* am different from them." The third type is called *pre-encounter racial self-hatred*. Such Blacks profoundly negative feelings and severe self-loathing due to being Black. This can include plastic surgery and other methods (e.g., skin bleaching) to appear non-Black physically. Such dysfunctionality, disassociation, and group hatred hinder Blacks' positive engagement with Black problems and social ills (e.g., racial prejudice and discrimination) and advocacy (e.g., Black Lives Matter and Say Her Name movements).

The second stage of identity, immersion-emersion comprises two identity types. In *immersion-emersion* or *anti-White*, Blacks are consumed with hating Whites (e.g., prejudice and discrimination, microaggressions, unearned privileges). They engage in tackling Black social injustices and are full rage. In *immersion-emersion intense Black involvement*, Blacks hold an obsessive dedication to all that is Black, engaging in 'blackness' in nearly a cult-like fashion. Malcolm X is often used to epitomize the stages/phases.

Internalization, the final stage, consists of three identity types. In *internalization nationalist*, Blacks stress an Afro-centric perspective in all areas of their life, such as child rearing, marriage, education, and work. They engage and invest extensively in the Black community to advance positive change. *Internalization biculturalist* are Blacks who give equal or balanced importance to being a Black *and* an American. They celebrate being both Black and American and engage in both cultures without identity conflicts, doubt, and self-questioning. *Internalization multiculturalist* are Blacks whose identity fuses three or more social categories or frames of reference. They are interested in and dedicated to resolving issues that address multiple oppressions and are confident and comfortable in multiple groups—racism, classism, sexism, ableism, and more.

Cross (1995) posited that individuals can regress or get stuck in one stage. This depends heavily on their personality, age, support systems, resources (e.g., multicultural curriculum and literature), and experiences. Cross did not place age limitations in his theory. For example, Blacks can experience a negative racial encounter as a preschool, elementary, middle, or high school student, or as an adult. Blacks and Hispanics in predominantly White settings (e.g., GATE) may experience more negative racial encounters than those in predominantly Black settings. Further, because of characteristics often associated with giftedness (i.e., insightful, perceptive, observant, intuitive, sensitivity, keen sense of justice, etc.), GATE students of color may be especially aware of and sensitive to racial injustices.

Racial identity may be directly or indirectly related to academic achievement (Ford, 2010, 2011). Specifically, Grantham and Ford (2003) propose that there may be a curvilinear relationship between racial identity and achievement, with those in the earliest stage (pre-encounter) and those in the last stage (internalization-commitment) having the highest achievement orientation. Achievement orientations and academic performance may be similar between those in the different stages (e.g., earliest vs. latest) based on the degree to which students of color are perceived as acting White. Because of their low-salience or negative Black attitudes, those in pre-encounter stage are likely to be rejected by the Black community; immersion-emersion and commitment individuals, because of their strong and positive racial identification, bicultural stance, and pluralistic perspectives, are more likely to be accepted by members of the Black community. Understanding the critical intersection of Black students' gifts and talents plus racial identity can inform appropriate strategies and impact academic achievement and persistence for all underrepresented students.

What are Implications for GATE Coordinators and Educational Professionals?

Few studies have examined the racial identities of gifted and talented Black and Hispanic students. Proactive and aggressive interventions are needed to reverse underachievement and underrepresentation among these GATE students. Black and Hispanic students, particularly those who are creatively gifted and talented (Baldwin, 2001; 2011; Torrance, 1977), may experience more psychological and social-emotional problems than students not identified as gifted and talented. Lindstrom and San Vant (1986) argued that GATE students of color find themselves in a dilemma in which they must choose between academic success and social acceptance. According to one Black student: "I had to fight to be gifted and then I had to fight because I am gifted" (p. 584). Students of color may perceive academic achievement as a pyrrhic victory (Fordham, 1988; Ogbu, 2003)—they win academically, but lose socially-emotionally and/or psychologically. Feelings of loneliness, isolation, and rejection increase, and the need for affiliation outweighs the need for achievement. When caught in this tug-of-war, some students may sabotage their achievement (e.g., procrastinate, fail to complete assignments, exert little effort, refuse to be in GATE and other advanced level classes, STEM classes, etc.) (Collins, 2018). Time and energy are devoted to seeking and securing social acceptance. Because of the many problems that can influence the overall development of Black and Hispanic students, and because of the on-going limited understanding of these problems, attention to racial identity development in all educational settings is critical.

Multicultural Counseling

Students experiencing racial identity difficulties and/or conflicts can benefit from multicultural counseling (Sue, 2016). Sessions may focus on such topics as coping with peer pressures and low teacher expectations, asking for help, and communicating effectively with educators. Counseling grounded in racial trauma from the racial pandemic is also crucial, as mentioned early in this chapter. Counseling should also include a focus on stereotype threat, which is a racialized form of test anxiety, along with test-taking skills. Counselors should become familiar with the extensive work of Steele (e.g., 1997; 1999; 2010) and others exploring race-based test anxiety. All prevention and intervention strategies must be supportive, intrinsic, and remedial strategies, providing students of color with the support they need to feel confident in their abilities, to feel motivated, to feel valued, and to overcome academic shortcomings.

Social and Communal Experiences

Counselors and teachers can also use small groups and cooperative learning experiences to facilitate communication among GATE students. These strategies provide students of color with opportunities to establish friendships and decrease feelings of isolation and alienation. Social and group experiences give Black and Hispanic students numerous opportunities to talk about their lives and concerns as racial and cultural beings. Guest speakers are recommendations. Other suggestions are described by Ford (2011), and in multicultural books and articles by such authors as James Banks, Geneva Gay, Gloria Ladson-Billings, Joyce King, and Jacqueline Irvine.

Racial Identity Counseling

Strategies and initiatives need to be designed to help Black and Hispanic students with negative racial identities (e.g., the pre-encounter and immersion-emersion stages of identity) to understand and appreciate their dual identities of being both gifted and talented and Black/Hispanic. White teachers and counselors must understand that students in the immersion-emersion stage may reject their help. These students may generalize negative perceptions of Whites in general to White counselors and teachers. A mentor may be helpful.

It is important that mentors have discussions with GATE Black and Hispanic students about the reality of life, including discrimination, such as microaggressions (Sue, 2010). Students need to know about possible sacrifices they may have to make due to participating in GATE programs (e.g., fewer Black and Hispanic classmates, more schoolwork, less time with peers, etc.). Many Hispanic and Black students face negative peer pressures when they achieve; they seldom know how to cope with these pressures and they underachieve. Anger management discussions may be especially necessary for GATE Hispanic and Black students in the immersion-emersion stage of racial identity.

Exposure to Colleges and Universities

Students who are not aware of local and national colleges and universities are less likely to have higher education aspirations. By exposing gifted and talented students to colleges, mentors are able to increase these students' awareness. College tours, including Historically Black Colleges and Universities (HBCUs; minority serving institutions), can be motivating, increasing their awareness about the critical need to do well in classes. Depending on their socio-economic status, students of color may have limited knowledge of the thousands of careers that exist, the academic courses and strengths needed to pursue certain professions, and other career-related issues and topics. Thus, students who want to be an architect can gain extensive information from shadowing a STEM professional, and learning about educational and job requirements and duties (Collins, 2017b; 2018; Collins & Grantham, 2017).

Multicultural Education

School personnel must (re)evaluate the extent to which their curriculum and instruction affirm Black and Hispanic students' racial identities, while increasing all students' knowledge and acceptance of the nation's multicultural heritage. How does the curriculum promote negative or positive images of people of color? Does the curriculum promote racial pride in GATE Black and Hispanic students? Do the lessons plans promote positive achievement orientations among these students? Do they see themselves affirmed in the lesson plans and books?

Few schools infuse multicultural content into the curriculum, which contributes to gifted and talented students of color feeling unconnected to what is being taught and read. When students—regardless of achievement level and racial background—do not see the curriculum as personally relevant, they become disinterested, unmotivated, and underachieving. We recommend that GATE teachers and counselors read the work of James Banks in order to learn how multicultural content can be infused into curriculum in at least four ways. The lowest and the most common level is the contributions approach, followed by the additive approach. At both levels, multicultural content is elementary and somewhat superficial, with a focus on multicultural heroes, holidays, foods, and fashion, and traditions. Substantive issues of diversity and inequity are ignored, minimized, or trivialized, due to the superficial nature of these levels. For example, controversial people of color and events are likely to be ignored in lesson plans (e.g., George Floyd, Tamir Rice, Sandra Bland). Further, multicultural topics tend to be reserved for special days and events (i.e., Black History Month; Hispanic Heritage Month).

The two highest and most rigorous and relevant levels are the transformation and social action approaches. In these higher levels, students are consistently exposed to substantive multicultural topics; thus, every day and every subject area is devoted to having a multicultural focus. At the transformation level, students are presented with more than one perspective on a person, topic or event; they are asked to view all issues from multiple perspectives in order to avoid polemic thinking. At the social action level, students are taught and encouraged to address social issues; to confront, for instance, discrimination in school texts, discussions, and the media.

Ford and Harris (1999) envisioned the need to ensure that GATE students were not only exposed to high levels of multicultural content, as proposed by Banks and Banks (1995, 2015), they also saw the need to ensure that such work was challenging and promoted higher level thinking skills. Thus, they included Bloom's Taxonomy (Bloom et al., 1956). The result is the Bloom-Banks Matrix for rigor and relevance, most recently updated by Ford (2011) and Ford and Trotman Scott (2016).

Relatedly, multicultural literature is powerful and empowering. It is common knowledge that many GATE students enjoy reading. Ford (2011) and Ford et al. (2000; 2005) suggested multicultural bibliotherapy as an important strategy for use with gifted and talented students of color, and provided a list of recommended multicultural books.

Multicultural Training for School Personnel

Ultimately, to work effectively with GATE Black and Hispanic students, counselors and teachers require multicultural training. Counselors require an understanding of self-perceptions that goes beyond self-esteem and self-concept when working with racially and culturally different gifted and talented students. Several professional counseling associations (e.g., American Counseling Association, Association for Multicultural Counseling and Development, and American Psychological Association) have guidelines and position statements regarding multicultural competencies. Counselors and psychologists wishing to build a positive and trusting relationship with students of color can take multicultural counseling courses offered at colleges and universities, attend multicultural workshops and conferences offered by professional associations, seek internships in urban communities, and subscribe to publications that promote culture and cultural competence. Example resources are provided at the end of the chapter (see Table 3.3).

Family Support and Collaboration

Although the majority of this chapter has addressed the role of school personnel in promoting strong racial identities among GATE Hispanic and Black students, the role of families cannot be overlooked. Families seldom have formal education and training in GATE, social-emotional needs and racial identity. Some families of color may be aware of the need to develop their children's self-concept, but they may not know that the focus on self-concept must include racial identity. Collaboration and reciprocity are important.

Counselors who have multicultural training are in the best position to provide training to families on this topic. Families can be supported and taught how to: (a) nurture gifts and talents in culturally responsive ways;

(b) discuss prejudice and discrimination with their gifted and talented children; (c) discuss negative peer pressures and resolving conflicts with their children; and (d) select books and movies that promote strong racial pride (Ford, 2011).

Conclusion

As Grantham and Ford (2003) noted earlier, GATE students of color live in a world and learn in schools that seldom affirm their dignity and worth as racial beings. Many of these students struggle at developing a healthy sense of self as racial beings. These students frequently face negative peer pressures relative to doing well in school; they are often accused of "acting white"; and they are frequently alienated and isolated from Black and White students alike. When students develop healthy racial identities (namely, the internalization state of racial identity), they are empowered to focus on the need to achieve, and are less likely to succumb to negative peer pressures. School personnel must aggressively seek to understand the powerful influence that self-perception has on students' achievement and motivation (Boaler & Dweck, 2016). When the student is a person of color, the focus must be on racial identity, not just self-esteem or self-concept.

It is vital that GATE standards, such as that by NAGC align with work that is equity focused *and* culturally responsive (eight sections), as illustrated in Table 3.2. This is clearly essential to meet the twin needs and development of students who are gifted and talented *and* have some cultural needs different from their White classmates. These differences, as we have discussed, are fundamental to supporting and advocating for underrepresented students of color. The alignment helps promote accountability and we hope a sense of urgency to do better.

References

Baber, L. (2012). A qualitative inquiry on the multidimensional racial development among first-year African American college students attending a predominantly White institution. *The Journal of Negro Education, 81*(1), 67–81. https://doi.org/10.7709/jnegroeducation.81.1.0067

Baldwin, A.Y. (1987). Undiscovered diamonds: The minority gifted child. *Journal for the Education of the Gifted, 10*, 271–285, and reprinted in T. Grantham, D.Y. Ford, M. Henfield, M.F. Trotman Scott, D. Harmon,

S. Porchér, & C. Price. (Eds.) (2011). *Gifted and advanced Black students in school: An anthology of critical works*. Prufrock Press. https://doi.org/10.1177/016235328701000406

Baldwin, A.Y. (2001). Understanding the challenge of creativity among African Americans. *Journal of Secondary Gifted Education*, 12, 121–125, and reprinted in T. Grantham, D.Y. Ford, M. Henfield, M.F. Trotman Scott, D. Harmon, S. Porchér, & C. Price. (Eds.) (2011). *Gifted and advanced Black students in school: An anthology of critical works*. Prufrock Press. https://doi.org/10.4219%2Fjsge-2001–656

Baldwin, A.Y. (2011). I'm Black but look at me, I am also gifted. In T.C. Grantham, D.Y. Ford, M.S. Henfield, M.T. Scott, D.A. Harmon, S. Porchèr, & C. Price (Eds.), *Gifted and advanced Black students in school: An anthology of critical works* (pp. 13–22). Prufrock Press.

Banks, J.A., & Banks, C.A.M. (Eds.) (1995). *Handbook of research on multicultural education*. Simon & Schuster.

Banks, J.A., & Banks, C.A.M. (Eds.) (2015). *Multicultural education: Issues and perspectives* (9th ed.). Wiley.

Bloom, B.S., Engelhart, M.D., Furst, E.J., Hill, W.H., & Krathwohl, D.R. (1956). *Taxonomy of educational objectives: The classification of educational goals*. Handbook I: Cognitive domain. David McKay Co.

Boaler, J., & Dweck, C.S. (2016). *Mathematical mindset: Unleashing students' potential through creative math, inspiring messages, and innovative teaching*. Jossey-Bass & Pfeiffer Imprints.

Boykin, A.W., Albury, A, Tyler, K.M., Hurley, E.A., Bailey, C.T., & Miller, O.A. (2005). Culture-based perceptions of academic achievement among low-income elementary students. *Cultural Diversity and Ethnic Minority Psychology*, 11(4), 339–350. https://doi.org/10.1037/1099–9809.11.4.339

Boykin, A.W., & Cunningham, R.T. (2001). The effects of movement expressiveness in story content and learning context on the analogical reasoning performance of African American children. *Journal of Negro Education*, 70(1/2), 72–83. www.jstor.org/stable/2696284

Clark, K., & Clark, M. (1939). The development of consciousness of self and the emergence of racial identification in Negro preschool children. *Journal of Social Psychology*, 10(4), 591–599. https://doi.org/10.1080/00224545.1939.9713394

Colangelo, N., & Exum, H.A. (1979). Educating the culturally diverse gifted: implications for teachers, counselors, and parents. *Gifted Child Today*, 2(1), 22–23, 54–55. https://doi.org/10.1177%2F107621757900200112

Collins, K.H. (2017a). Unpacking SENG's mission, vision, & values: A framework and standard for comprehensive support of the gifted across the lifespan. *SENGvine Newsletter: Supporting the Needs of the Gifted*, 1–2.

https://myemail.constantcontact.com/SENGVine-SENG-s-Monthly-Newsletter-is-HERE.html?soid=1102289134078&aid=CSedA6UMYJU

Collins, K.H. (2017b). From identification to Ivy League: Nurturing multiple interests and multi-potentiality in gifted students. *Parenting for High Potential*, 6(4), 19–22. https://eric.ed.gov/?id=EJ1182154

Collins, K.H. (2018). Confronting colorblind STEM talent development: Toward a contextual model for Black student STEM identity. *Journal of Advanced Academics* 29(2), 143–168. https://doi.org/10.1177/1932202X18757958

Collins, K.H. (2020a). Talking about racism in American and in education: The reflections of a gifted Black scholar and mother of a gifted Black young adult. *Parenting for High Potential*, 9(3), 5–9. www.nagc.org/sites/default/files/Publication%20PHP/bonuscontent/Collins_Talking%20About%20Racism%20in%20America%20and%20Education%20PHP.pdf?fbclid=IwAR3DcZIl2-l5RSGXcS_LdE4mGpwzLR9M7wRc_zr72qKHJ_So3hZqlrUhK_w

Collins, K.H. (2020b). Gifted and bullied: Understanding the institutionalized victimization of identified, unidentified, and underserved gifted students. In F.H.R. Piske (Ed.) *Identifying, preventing and combating bullying in gifted education*. Manuscript accepted.

Collins, K.H., & Grantham, T.C. (2017, November). Developing scholar identity: The Dr. Martin Jenkins scholars program. *Teaching for High Potential*, 6–9. www.nagc.org/sites/default/files/THP_Fall2017_Web.pdf

Cross Jr., W.E. (1971, July). Toward a psychology of Black liberation: The Negro-to-Black conversion experience. *Black World*, 20(9), 13–27. https://eric.ed.gov/?id=EJ041879

Cross Jr., W.E. (1995). The psychology of Nigrescence: Revising the Cross model. In J.G. Ponterotto, J.M. Casas, L.A. Suzuki, & C.M. Alexander (Eds.), *Handbook of multicultural counseling* (pp. 93–122). Sage.

Cross Jr., W.E., & Vandiver, B.J. (2001). Nigrescence theory and measurement: Introducing the Cross Racial Identity Scale (CRIS). In J.G. Ponterotto, J.M. Casas, L.A. Suzuki, & C.M. Alexander (Eds.), *Handbook of multicultural counseling* (2nd ed.) (pp. 371–393). Sage.

Exum, H.A., & Colangelo, N. (1981). Culturally diverse gifted: The need for ethnic identity development. *Roeper Review*, 3(4), 15–17. https://doi.org/10.1080/02783198109552543

Ford, D.Y. (2010). *Reversing underachievement among gifted Black students: Promising practices and programs* (2nd ed.). Prufrock Press.

Ford, D.Y. (2011). *Multicultural Gifted Education* (2nd ed.). Prufrock Press.

Ford, D.Y. (2013). *Recruiting and retaining culturally different students in gifted education*. Prufrock Press.

Ford, D.Y. (Producer). (2020, July 15). *Black and gifted: A trailblazer's backstory* [Audio podcast]. https://ohiostateuniversityinspire.podbean.com/e/black-and-gifted-a-trailblazers-backstory-1594747023/

Ford, D.Y., Dickson, K.T., Lawson Davis, J., Trotman Scott, M., Grantham, T.C., & Taradash, G.D. (2018). A culturally responsive equity-based Bill of Rights for gifted students of color. *Gifted Child Today*, 41(3), 125–129. https://doi.org/10.1177/1076217518769698

Ford, D.Y., & Frazier Trotman, M. (2001). Teachers of gifted students: Suggested multicultural characteristics and competencies. *Roeper Review*, 23(4), 235–239. https://doi.org/10.1080/02783190109554111

Ford, D.Y., Grantham, T.C., & Harris III, J.J. (1997). The recruitment and retention of minority teachers in gifted education. *Roeper Review*, 19(4), 213–220. https://doi.org/10.1080/02783199709553832

Ford, D.Y., Grantham, T.C., & Whiting, G.W. (2008). Culturally and linguistically diverse students in gifted education: Recruitment and retention issues. *Exceptional Children*, 74(3), 289–308. https://doi.org/10.1177/001440290807400302

Ford, D.Y., & Harris III, J.J. (1999). *Multicultural gifted education*. Teachers College Press.

Ford, D.Y., Harris III, J.J., & Schuerger, J.M. (1993). Racial identity development among gifted Black students: Counseling issues and concerns. *Journal of Counseling and Development*, 71(4), 409–417. https://doi.org/10.1002/j.1556–6676.1993.tb02657.x

Ford, D.Y., Harris III, J.J., Tyson, C.A., & Frazier Trotman, M. (2003). Beyond deficit thinking: Providing access for gifted African American students. *Roeper Review*, 24(2), 52–58. https://doi.org/10.1080/02783190209554129

Ford, D.Y., Howard, T.C., & Harris III, J.J. (2005). Using multicultural literature in gifted education. In S.K. Johnsen & J. Kendrick (Eds.), *Language arts for gifted students* (pp. 43–57). Prufrock Press.

Ford, D.Y., Lawson Davis, J., Dickson, K.T., Frazier Trotman Scott, M., Grantham, T.C., Moore III, J.L., & Taradash, G.D. (2020). Evaluating gifted education programs using an equity-based and culturally responsive checklist to recruit and retain under-represented students of color. *Journal of Minority Achievement, Creativity, and Leadership*, 1(1), 119–146. www.jstor.org/stable/10.5325/minoachicrealead.1.1.issue-1

Ford, D.Y., & Trotman Scott, M. (2016). Culturally responsive and relevant curriculum: The revised Bloom-Banks matrix. In K.R. Stephens & F.A. Karnes (Eds.), *Introduction to curriculum design in gifted education* (pp. 331–350). Prufrock Press.

Ford, D.Y., Tyson, C.A., Howard, T.C., & Harris III, J.J. (2000). Multicultural literature and gifted Black students: Promoting self-understanding.

awareness, and pride. *Roeper Review*, 22(4), 235–240. https://doi. org/10.1080/0278319009554045

Ford, D.Y., Whiting, G.W., & Goings, R.B. (2016). Biracial and multiracial gifted students: Like finding a grain of rice in a box of sand. In J.L. Davis & J.L. Moore III (Eds.), *Gifted children of color around the world: Diverse needs, exemplary practices, and directions for the future* (pp. 121–135). Bingley.

Fordham, S. (1988). Racelessness as a factor m Black students' school success: Pragmatic strategy or pyrrhic victory? *Harvard Educational Review*, *58*(1), 54–84. https://doi.org/10.17763/haer.58.1.c5r77323145r7831

Fordham, S. (1991). Peer-proofing academic competition among Black adolescents: "Acting White" Black American style. In C.E. Sleeter (Ed.), *Empowerment through multicultural education* (pp. 69–93). State University of New York Press.

Fordham, S. (1996). *Blacked out: Dilemmas of race, identity, and success at Capital High.* The University of Chicago Press.

Frasier, M.M., & Passow, A.H. (1994). *Towards a new paradigm for identifying talent potential* (Research Monograph 94112). University of Connecticut, National Research Center on the Gifted and Talented. https://nrcgt. uconn.edu/wp-content/uploads/sites/953/2015/04/rm94112.pdf

Grantham, T.C., & Ford, D.Y. (1998). A case study of the social needs of Danisha: An underachieving African-American female. *Roeper Review*, *21*(2). 96–101. https://doi.org/10.1080/02783199809553938

Grantham, T.C., & Ford, D.Y. (2003). Beyond self-concept and self-esteem for African American students: Improving racial identity improves achievement. *The High School Journal*, *87*(1), 18–29. http://dx.doi.org/10.1353/ hsj.2003.0016

Grantham, T.C., Ford, D.Y., Davis, J.L., Frazier Trotman Scott, M., Dickson, K., Taradash, G., Whiting, G.W., Cotton, C.B., Floyd, E.F., Collins, K.H., Anderson, B.N., Fox, S., & Roberson, J.J. (2020). *Get your knee off our necks: Black scholars speak out to confront racism against black students in gifted and talented education.* The Consortium for Inclusion of Underrepresented Racial Groups in Gifted Education. https://drive.google.com/file/d/1_ BMZKWTsQsIFJNaTW-UOFmmNhh-5Vha6/view?usp=sharing

Grissom, J., & Redding, C. (2016). Discretion and disproportionality: Explaining the underrepresentation of high-achieving students of color in gifted programs. *American Educational Research Association Open*. https://doi. org/10.1177/2332858415622175

Hauge, A.L. (2007). Identity and place: a critical comparison of three identity theories. *Architectural Science Review*, *50*(1), 44–51. https://doi. org/10.3763/asre.2007.5007

Hébert, T. (2010). *Understanding the social and emotional lives of gifted students.* Prufrock Press.

Helms, J.E. (1989). Considering some methodological issues in racial identity counseling research. *The Counseling Psychologist, 17*(2), 227–252. https://doi.org/10.1177/0011000089172002

Hughes, C., Manns, N., & Ford, D.Y. (2009). Racial identity attitudes and academic achievement among at-risk Black female adolescents. *Journal of At-Risk Issues, 15*(1), 25–32. https://eric.ed.gov/?id=EJ861121

Hussar, B., Zhang, J., Hein, S., Wang, K., Roberts, A., Cui, J., Smith, M., Mann, F.B., Barmer, A., Dilig, R., National Center for Education Statistics (Ed), & American Institutes for Research (AIR). (2020). *The condition of education 2020: NCES 2020–144.* National Center for Education Statistics. https://nces.ed.gov/pubsearch/pubsinfo.asp?pubid=2020144

Lindstrom, R.R., & San Vant, S. (1986). Special issues in working with gifted minority adolescents. *Journal of Counseling and Development, 64*(9), 583–586. https://doi.org/10.1002/j.1556–6676.1986.tb01210.x

Morrison, B.M.K. (2013). Development of American and foreign-national female graduate students in engineering at research universities. http://citeseerx.ist.psu.edu/viewdoc/download?doi=10.1.1.1012.2118&rep=rep1&type=pdf

National Association for Gifted Children (NAGC). (2019). *NAGC Pre-K-Grade 12 Gifted Programming Standards.* www.nagc.org/resources-publications/resources/national-standards-gifted-and-talented-education/pre-k-grade-12

National Association for Gifted Children Board of Directors (2020). *Championing equity and social justice for Black students in gifted education: An expanded vision for NAGC (Statement from the NAGC Board of Directors).* The National Association for Gifted Children. www.nagc.org/championing-equity-and-supporting-social-justice-black-students-gifted-education-expanded-vision#Plan

Ogbu, J.U. (2003). *Black students in an affluent suburb: A study of academic disengagement.* Lawrence Erlbaum.

Ogbu, J.U., & Simmons, H.D. (1998). Voluntary and involuntary minorities: A cultural-ecological theory of school performance with some implications for education. *Anthropology and Education Quarterly, 29*(2), 155–188. https://doi.org/10.1525/aeq.1998.29.2.155

Parham, T.A. (1989). Cycles of psychological nigrescence. *The Counseling Psychologist, 17*(2). 187–226. https://doi.org/10.1177/0011000089172001

Parham, T.A., & Helms, J.E. (1985). Relation of racial identity attitudes to self-actualization and affective states of Black students. *Journal of Counseling Psychology, 32*(3), 431–440. https://doi.org/10.1037/0022–0167.32.3.431

Piske, F.H.R. et al. (2016). Barriers to creativity, identification and inclusion of gifted students. *Creative Education, 7*(14), 1899–1905. http://dx.doi.org/10.4236/ce.2016.714192

Rotheram, M.J., & Phinney, J.S. (Eds.) (1987). *Children's ethnic socialization.* Sage.

Smith, E.M.J. (1989). Black racial identity development: Issues and concerns. *The Counseling Psychologist, 17*(2), 277–288. https://doi.org/10.1177/0011000089172007

Spencer, M.B., & Markstrom-Adams, C. (1990). Identity processes among racial and ethnic children in America. *Child Development, 61*(4), 290–310. https://doi.org/10.2307/1131095

Steele, C.M. (1997). A threat in the air: How stereotypes shape the intellectual identities and performance of women and African Americans. *American Psychologist, 52*(6), 613–629. https://doi.org/10.1037/0003-066X.52.6.613

Steele, C.M. (1999). Thin ice: "Stereotype Threat" and Black college students. *Atlantic Monthly, 284*(2), 50–54. https://doi.org/10.1177/108648220000500202

Steele, C.M. (2010). *Whistling Vivaldi and other clues to how stereotypes affect us.* Norton & Company.

Sue, D.W. (2010). Microaggressions in everyday life. Is subtle bias less harmful? www.psychologytoday.com/blog/microaggressions-in-everyday-life/201010/racial-microaggressions-in-everyday-life

Sue, D.W. (2016). *Race talk and the conspiracy of silence: Understanding and facilitating difficult dialogues on race.* Wiley.

Torrance, E.P. (1974). Differences are not deficits. *Teachers College Record, 75*(4), 471–487.

Torrance, E.P. (1977). *Discovery and nurturance of giftedness in the culturally different.* Council for Exceptional Children. https://eric.ed.gov/?id=ED145621

United States Department of Education. Office for Civil Rights, Civil Rights Data Collection. https://ocrdata.ed.gov

United States Department of Education and National Center for Education Evaluation. (2013). *Reducing stereotype threat in classrooms: A review of social-psychological intervention studies on improving the achievement of Black students.* https://ies.ed.gov/ncee/edlabs/projects/project.asp?ProjectID=135

Valencia, R.R. (2010). *Dismantling contemporary deficit thinking: Educational thought and practice.* Taylor & Francis.

4

The Assessment Standard in Gifted Education: Identifying Gifted Students

Susan K. Johnsen

Overview of the Assessment Standard

Assessment is a process that is used to gather information using effective tests, instruments, and techniques for a particular purpose such as identification, curriculum planning, measuring learning progress, and program evaluation. In the Gifted Programming Assessment Standard 2, two forms of assessment are included—identification and measuring learning progress (National Association for Gifted Children (NAGC), 2019b). These forms are inextricably linked to one another. Initially educators establish an environment for identifying students; students are then identified using non-biased and equitable approaches; which ultimately leads to identified students receiving individual programming based on ongoing assessments. Since the assessment of learning progress is addressed in other chapters, this chapter will focus on the identification of students with gifts and talents.

DOI: 10.4324/9781003236863-4

Foundational Principles that Inform the Standards on Identification

One of the principles that informs not only the identification standard but also all of the Pre-K–Grade 12 Gifted Programming Standards is that *gifts and talents are dynamic and are developed over time* (NAGC, 2019b). Models in gifted education recognize the importance of multiple factors that interact with one another and influence the manifestation and development of gifts and talents (Bloom, 1985; Gagné, 2010; Subotnik et al., 2011; Tannenbaum, 1983; 1986). These factors include not only general and special abilities but also environmental (e.g., family, peers, culture, social class, schooling), nonintellectual or intrapersonal (e.g., motivation, personality, mental health, self-concept), and chance (e.g., accidental events, exploratory behaviors). The assessment standard incorporates this developmental viewpoint, which results in the use of a more inclusive range and dynamic set of assessments in the identification process (Gentry et al., 2008; Lidz & Macrine, 2001; Lo & Porath, 2017; Van Tassel-Baska et al., 2007; VanTassel-Baska et al., 2002).

Another principle related to the developmental nature of giftedness is that *early identification improves the likelihood that gifts will develop into talents*. When students from diverse backgrounds are identified early and attend schools and classes for gifted and talented students, they have higher achievement than those who are placed in general education classrooms with limited or no services (Borland et al., 2000; Cornell et al., 1995; Franklin, 2009: Subotnik et al., 2011). Moreover, adverse effects may occur for some students from lower socioeconomic backgrounds who are not involved in early education opportunities and who are at a greater risk for dropping out of high achieving groups in elementary and secondary school (NAGC, 2019a; Olszewski-Kubilius & Corwith, 2018; Plucker et al., 2013). Therefore, identification needs to begin as early as pre-kindergarten and comprehensively address a diverse range of characteristics.

A third principle that influences identification is that *students exhibit their gifts and talents not only within a specific domain but also within an interest area* (Johnsen, 2018a). Subotnik et al. (2011) describe the importance of identifying these domain-specific talents and achievements so that education can be tailored to encourage each student's optimal performance. Moreover, each domain of talent requires specialized instruction in content, technical, and psychosocial skills. Consequently, assessments used in the identification process need to be aligned to students' areas of talent and interests. For example, a student with a talent in the scientific domain may have a particular interest in penguins, specifically emperor penguins. She may not show her knowledge and skills on a standardized grade-level achievement test, but might show them through teacher or parent observations or in products from independent studies that could be included in a portfolio.

The final principle emphasized in the Pre-K–Grade 12 Gifted Programming Standards is that *giftedness is found among students from a variety of backgrounds* (NAGC, 2019b). Gifted students from diverse groups are underrepresented in gifted education programs (Siegle et al., 2016). For example, 12.4% of children attending low poverty public elementary and middle schools received gifted education services, compared with 6.1% of students attending high poverty schools (Yaluma & Tyner, 2018). Moreover, regardless of economic background, race plays a significant role in gifted education identification, participation, and retention (Coronado & Lewis, 2017; Ford, 2016; Wright et al., 2017). Researchers suggest that underrepresentation is influenced by factors related to the educators involved in the identification process, specific instruments, and interpretations of assessments (Briggs et al., 2008; Ford et al., 2005; Peters & Engerrand, 2016; Siegle et al., 2010). These factors, which have a negative impact on gifted students' identification, are of serious concern to gifted education professionals and are addressed in the standards.

Each of these principles (e.g., gifts and talents are dynamic and developmental, early identification, interest-specific gifts and talents, and diversity) is foundational to the three student outcomes within the identification standards.

Student Outcome 1: Students Have Equal Access to the Identification Process

The first student outcome (2.1) within the assessment standard focuses on providing equal access to the identification process so that each building or campus is proportionally represented. To accomplish this outcome, educators must develop environments and instructional activities at school that encourage students from diverse backgrounds to express characteristics and behaviors associated with giftedness (see Standard 2.1.1). The placement of students in special education, in schools that may or may not offer gifted education services, or in classrooms where teachers do not believe in gifted education should not preclude the consideration of a student for gifted programming. To assure that all students are considered for gifted education programming, educators need professional learning in the characteristics of gifted and talented students. Without professional opportunities, teachers are more likely to refer children who reflect their conceptions of giftedness such as students who are academic achievers and independent learners (Hunsaker et al., 1997; Peters & Engerrand, 2016; Speirs Neumeister et al., 2007), are from higher socioeconomic status groups (Kitano, 2001; Swanson, 2006), have similar cultural backgrounds (Grissom & Redding, 2016; Yoon & Gentry, 2009), and are verbal and well-mannered (Dawson, 1997; Schack & Starko, 1990; Speirs Neumeister et al., 2007). Students who are economically disadvantaged (Peters & Engerrand, 2016) who are English language learners (Brulles et al., 2011), or who have disabilities (Foley Nicpon et al., 2011; Kalbfleisch, 2013) are viewed from a deficit perspective (Ford et al., 2001) and are particularly vulnerable for being excluded from the identification process.

Along with professional learning, educators also need to develop classroom environments that differentiate for individual differences (see Standard 2.1.1). Individual differences may manifest themselves in what students know and want to know (e.g., the knowledge and skills they are learning—the subject matter content), how quickly they learn the content (e.g., pacing and rate of learning), how they learn (e.g., preference for types of activities), and the environment where they learn (e.g., individual, small group, community) (Johnsen, 2018b). In differentiating content, teachers need to develop activities that emphasize depth, complexity, and creativity; ask higher level and open-ended questions; use above-grade level materials; develop problem- or concept-based units of study; and provide opportunities for independent research in an area of interest. In differentiating for rate of learning, teachers might use fewer drill and practice activities; preassessments to determine student mastery allowing students to accelerate in the curriculum; and self-checking rubrics so that students can pace themselves through assignments. In differentiating preference, teachers might vary the method of presentation allowing for discussion, experimentation, and demonstration; provide students with choices of assessments; and provide students with choices in content, process, and product. In differentiating environment, teachers might provide independent learning activities; use flexible grouping for students with similar interests and academic abilities; arrange for a mentor to work with students in an area of interest or strength; establish multi-level learning stations or centers; and integrate community-based activities. A differentiated classroom will allow all students opportunities to show diverse talents and gifts (Hertzog, 2005; Johnsen 2018b).

Along with professional learning for educators in the school setting, parents and families also need to be educated about characteristics of children with gifts and talents, how to nurture these characteristics at home, and the importance of gifted education (see Standard 2.1.2). Researchers have found that parents, particularly those from minority or lower income backgrounds, may be reticent to refer their children for gifted education programs

(Oakland & Rossen, 2005; Siegle et al., 2016). Therefore, families need to understand not only characteristics but also the importance of nurturing them at home and at school. They need to be knowledgeable about school gifted education services and the identification process. Families also need to know how to support their children's interests outside of school. Those parents who have fewer financial resources may also need assistance in finding after school and summer enrichment programs that offer scholarships (Johnsen et al., 2007).

In addition to professional learning and parent education, schools need to adopt identification practices that use universal screening and multiple indicators of potential at multiple entry points to ensure that all students have equal access (see Standard 2.1.3). Universal screening is when one or more assessments are administered to *all* of the students at one or more grade levels (McBee et al., 2016). Universal screeners may be separate assessments or be incorporated into curriculum-based measurements within a Response to Intervention (RtI) process to identify learners who are performing above level (Coleman & Shah-Coltrane, 2010; McBee et al., 2016; Sulak, 2014). These assessments are intended to bypass referral systems where teachers or parents may overlook gifted and talented students who do not fit traditional stereotypes. Multiple assessments also provide more opportunities for students to show their gifts and talents. Using both performance and nonperformance methods improve the identification of potentially gifted students (Acar et al., 2016; McBee et al., 2014; Siegle et al., 2010). Moreover, similar to the RtI process where students are monitored within and across tiers for increasing levels of service, students with potential need to be continually assessed to ensure they are identified and receive the programming necessary for developing their gifts and talents.

Student Outcome 2: Assessments Identify Students' Interests, Strengths, and Needs

The second student outcome (2.2) focuses on the use of assessments that identify students' interests, strengths and needs. The evidence-based practices focus on the comprehensiveness and cohesiveness of the identification procedures (2.2.1), alignment of the assessments with student characteristics and services (2.2.2), the variety of assessment information, (2.2.3, 2.2.4, 2.2.6), assessments that minimize bias (2.2.5), interpreting multiple assessments (2.2.7), and informing and eliciting evidence from parents (2.2.8).

Comprehensive, Cohesive, and Ongoing Identification Procedures

Comprehensive procedures require that educators align assessments across grade levels and provide programming options in all domains (e.g., math, science, social studies, English/language arts, visual and performing arts). For example, if a school district has an accelerated mathematics program for students with gifts and talents, off-level assessments might be used beginning in pre-kindergarten and aligned with end-of-course exams in various mathematics and advanced placement courses at the secondary level. In this way, assessments would not only identify students as being advanced in mathematics but also provide information regarding instructional modifications. These assessments should also be cohesive—performance on one math assessment would predict performance on a later math assessment. Moreover, equivalent difficulty levels are important in identifying students and helping them make transitions across grade levels and math courses. With these types of procedures in place, a gifted student in math could be identified at any grade level and proceed smoothly, receiving appropriate accelerated math programming.

Along with comprehensiveness and cohesion, educators need to develop policies and procedures for informed consent from families, committee reviews of assessment information, retention of identified students, reassessment of identified students if more information is needed regarding their strengths and needs, exiting from program services, and appeals for entering and exiting gifted program services (2.2.1). Details regarding these types of policies and procedures can be found in state resources (see Colorado Department of Education, 2020; Missouri Department of Elementary and Secondary Education, 2016; Texas State Plan for the Education of Gifted/Talented Students, 2019).

Alignment with Student Characteristics and Programming Services

The selection of assessments is dependent upon the characteristics of the students and available services. For example, if a school offers special programming for young artists in the field of music, then the identification instruments would most likely be different from those used for identifying students with potential in the science (e. g. auditions vs. portfolio of science experiments). In addition, if the majority of students are from diverse backgrounds (e. g., English language learners, low income, minorities), then alternative types of instruments might need to be considered such as performance assessments or those that are nonverbal or linguistically-reduced.

Variety of Assessments

Researchers and professional associations recommend the use of a variety of instruments and sources in the assessment process (American Educational Research Association et al., 2014; NAGC, 2011; Ryser, 2018; Worrell & Irwin, 2011). In selecting these assessments, educators need to attend to specific characteristics: source of information, type of assessment, levels included, and flexibility in showing growth (see NAGC Programming Standard 2.2.3, 2.2.4 and 2.2.6).

Multiple Sources

Multiple sources provide a more comprehensive view of the student's behaviors across settings. No single source of information has an opportunity to observe students at home, at school, and during after school activities. Sources may include teachers (special, general, and gifted education), coaches, counselors, psychologists, administrators, peers, parents and other family members, and the student himself or herself (Coleman & Cross, 2005; Johnsen, 2018b). Caution needs to be used in including one source of information multiple times. For example, a teacher might refer a student, might evaluate a portfolio of work, and might complete observation checklists. In this case, the teacher's information would be heavily weighted during the selection process over other sources.

Qualitative and Quantitative

Similar to a variety of sources, qualitative and quantitative information provides a broader description of students. Each type provides different information. With qualitative assessments, words are used to describe a student's strengths and needs; with quantitative, numbers are used (NAGC, 2011; Ryser, 2018b). Qualitative assessments provide flexibility and freedom while quantitative assessments provide more consistency and control. Types of qualitative assessments include portfolios, anecdotal records, interviews, methods of learning and other dynamic assessments, past educational experiences, awards and honors, and observations of performance. Types of quantitative assessments include norm-referenced, standardized tests (e.g., achievement, intelligence, creativity, aptitude), grades, and rating scales. Since quantitative assessments' uses are more restricted and generally have right or wrong answers, they may not represent the student's performance in more authentic settings like qualitative assessments. For example, as opposed to an achievement test, portfolios of work might be used to gather artifacts of students' products and performances in core subject areas that show their best work (Johnsen, 2008; Shaklee & Viechnicki, 1995). Educators in a particular field of study who have knowledge of advanced learning and development would then review the work. Ryser (2018b) adds a cautionary note to educators who assign numbers to qualitative assessments. In those cases where numbers are applied, the qualitative assessment actually becomes a quantitative assessment and loses its power in providing information about the student.

Off-Level Testing

Since students with potential in academic areas may be performing above grade level, off-level testing is needed to identify their strengths. Most diagnostic tests and state-developed assessments do not have enough ceiling so that advanced students are able to show what they know and can do. Multigrade level tests and off-level tests provide more difficult items and discriminate better among students with gifts and talents (Lupkowski-Shoplik et al., 2003; Olszewski-Kubilius & Kulieke, 2008). In fact, because assessments have more error at the upper end of a scale, students who are gifted in a particular domain may appear to perform more poorly than students who are on grade level (Johnsen, 2011).

Dynamic

To determine learning potential, teachers can use dynamic assessments in the classroom where the teacher focuses on the interaction between the student and the task to understand the student's academic strengths and needs (Swanson & Lussier, 2001). Dynamic assessment is most often administered in a test-intervene-retest format (Sternberg & Grigorenko, 2002) that focuses on improvement in student performance when an adult provides assistance on mastering the task (Kirschenbaum, 1998). Because of the interactive approach, the educator learns about the interventions that promote change, the amount of change, how quickly the student learns new information, and the students' abilities (e.g., problem solving, critical and creative thinking, metacognitive processes) (Al-Hroub & Whitebread, 2018). To examine abilities, the tasks need to be novel, problem-based, and require complex strategies (Gentry et al., 2008; Kurtz & Weinert, 1989; Lidz & Macrine, 2001; Scruggs & Mastropieri, 1985). Dynamic assessments are particularly helpful when identifying students from lower socioeconomic backgrounds, English learners, and those with disabilities. For example, when using a pre-test, teach, post-test form of dynamic assessment with a student who might have a disability in writing but an ability in math, the teacher is able to observe how quickly a student may learn the math content, the student's problem solving abilities, and variations in performance when lessons are presented in verbal vs. written formats. Similarly, a teacher might also be able to compare learning rates when an English learner is presented activities in their native language vs. English or when a student with limited knowledge about a topic learns new information quickly.

Assessments that Minimize Bias

All assessments used during the identification process need to minimize bias, increase equity, and provide information describing their technical adequacy—validity, reliability, and norming (Ryser, 2018a).

Minimize Bias and Increase Equity

Since students from diverse backgrounds are underrepresented in gifted education programs, educators need to pay close attention to whether are not assessments minimize bias and are equitable. Tests or assessment procedures are biased if they differentiate between members of various groups on some characteristics other than the one being measured. For example, an assessment in math might be biased if it measures reading ability more than mathematical problem solving. Similarly, a test that is highly verbal might be biased against students who are English language learners. In addition, items that stereotype or have knowledge that may be unknown in a particular culture may be biased against certain cultural and socioeconomic groups. For a test to minimize bias, it must accurately reflect a "true difference" on what the test is measuring (e.g., students who perform better than others on a math test know more math knowledge and skills than their peers).

To minimize bias, tests need to

(a) include groups in the sample that match national census data;
(b) show that the items discriminate equally well for each subgroup;
(c) provide separate reliability and validity information for each subgroup; and
(d) describe how the content is free of bias and aligned to a model, theory, and/or standards (Ryser, 2018a; Salvia et al., 2017).

Most test developers have professionals review the items for gender or cultural stereotyping and analyze each item statistically (e.g., differential item functioning) to ensure that every subgroup has the same probability of answering the item correctly and that the test predicts equally well for each subgroup. Content bias can also be reduced by using performance-based items, pantomimed instruction, practice items, untimed responses, abstract reasoning and problem solving, novel items, and nonverbal items (Castellano, 1998; Jensen, 1980; Joseph & Ford, 2006; VanTassel-Baska et al., 2007).

Technically Adequate

Assessments need to meet the standards outlined by professional organizations in the measurement field (American Educational Research Association, American Psychological Association, & National Council on Measurement in Education, 2014). These standards relate to validity, reliability, and norming and address these questions: What is the purpose of the test? Does the purpose of the test relate to how it will be used in the assessment process (validity)? Does the test include studies that show it actually measures what it is supposed to measure (validity)? Is the test internally consistent and consistent over time (reliability)? When was it last normed? Is the norming group representative of the national population? Educators need to research the technical adequacy of instruments they use in the identification procedure and become familiar with test review resources so that they are able to make informed decisions when selecting quantitative assessments (see Robins & Jolly, 2018, and the Buros Center for Testing for test reviews).

Interpreting Multiple Assessments

After gathering information from a variety of technically-adequate assessments that minimize bias, educators need to know how to interpret the data in determining the best programming options for students. A committee of professionals who have training in gifted education and in educational and psychological measurement should be involved in the decision-making process. NAGC suggests that educators meet national teacher preparation standards (NAGC Standard 6.1, 2019). They also need to have an understanding of the characteristics of students from special populations and factors that might influence the recognition of their gifts and talents. When organizing the information for the committee's consideration, the following guidelines should be used (Johnsen, 2018b).

Equal Weighting of Assessments

If both qualitative and quantitative assessments are technically adequate, the committee should consider them equally in making decisions. Sometimes more weight or importance is assigned to a single assessment, which undermines the multiple criteria process and eliminates opportunities for examining a student's relative strengths and needs. For example, norm-referenced, standardized tests such as intelligence and achievement might receive more weight than qualitative assessments such as portfolios or interviews. Researchers have reported that qualitative assessments such as portfolios (Johnsen & Ryser, 1997) and parent nominations (Lee & Olszewski-Kubilius,

2006) predict performance in gifted programs and relate to more quantitative measures. A second way of weighting assessments is by allowing one source, such as the teacher, to provide information for several assessments such as grades, classroom checklists, and portfolios. A third way of weighting assessments is to use a specific cut-off score on a single instrument before the rest of the data are considered. For example, a student might need to perform in the top ten percent on a statewide achievement test before being referred for gifted programming or attain a specific score on an intelligence test before the rest of the data are considered. Fourth, a single assessment's subtests might be used as separate criteria, which would weight performance on that instrument more heavily. (Do note that differences on a single test's subtests can also indicate a student's strengths and needs, and, if significant, an indication of a learning disability.) Unless required by state rules and regulations, all assessments, if they are technically adequate, should be considered in the decision-making process.

Comparable Scores

Norm-referenced, standardized instruments generate different types of scores: raw scores, percentile ranks, grade equivalent scores, and standard or index scores.

Raw scores are original numeric values before they are transformed to other scores. They do not have any meaning until they are converted. For example, a student who scores 70 on a biology test may have the "best" or "worst" score depending on the performance of the rest of the class. Scores in one teacher's class may also not be the same as scores in another teacher's class. Raw scores cannot be compared with each other in a meaningful way and should never be compared when interpreting data.

Percentile ranks are derived from raw scores and show the relative rank of how a student performed in relationship to other students who took the same test. They should not be confused with percentages, which are simply the number of items that a student passed divided by the total number of items. A student that obtained a percentile rank of 90 performed better than 90 percent of the students who took the test. While these scores are useful and easily understood, they cannot be averaged or otherwise operated on arithmetically since they are not interval data. Since percentiles cluster heavily around the mean, or 50th percentile, and are more sparsely distributed at the top and bottom of a normal curve, a difference between 50 and 55 represents a smaller difference than between 95 and 99. If percentile ranks are considered in decision making, they need to be converted to a standard or index score for comparison purposes.

Grade equivalent scores are generated from the mean raw score obtained for children at each grade level. Using interpolation, extrapolation, and smoothing, psychometrists then create a score for each of the raw score points. Researchers have criticized the use of these scores because the content of instruction and amount of knowledge gained varies from grade level to grade level and they are open to misinterpretation (Salvia et al., 2017). For example, a first grade student who received a 6.8 grade equivalent score (e.g., sixth grade, eighth month) on a reading achievement test does not mean that she is reading at a sixth grade level. It simply means that she is reading above grade level. A curriculum-based measurement is more likely to indicate the knowledge and skills she has learned. Therefore, grade equivalent scores should not be used in making placement decisions.

Standard or index scores are derived from raw scores and are transformed into a normalized score distribution (e.g., bell-shaped curve). Depending on the unit used to describe the score's distance from the mean (e.g., standard deviation [SD]) or average performance of the group, they may be called z-scores (e.g., mean is 1 and SD is ± 1), T-scores (e.g., mean is 50 and SD is ± 10), A-scores (e. g., mean is 500 and SD is ± 100), IQ scores (e.g., mean is 100 and SD is ± 15), and stanines (e.g., mean is 5 and SD is ± 1) (see Table 4.1). Because these scores are on an equal interval scale, they are more versatile than other types of scores because they can be compared to other standard scores with the same mean and standard deviation and can be added and subtracted. For example, a score of 130 on an intelligence test with a mean of 100 and a standard deviation of 15 can be compared to other tests with the same mean and standard deviation. In Table 4.1, a percentile rank of 95, the top 5 percent of students who took the test, is similar to an intelligence quotient of 125, an A-Score of 670, a T-Score of 67, a Z-score of +1.67, and a stanine score of 8, all of which are in the superior range. Since standard scores are on an equal interval scale, they should never be assigned a rank order number such as those used in matrices, which makes them less versatile and open to misinterpretation.

All types of standard or index scores represent the performance of a group of students when compared to a norm-reference group, which may be comprised of national, state, or local samples. The comparison group needs to be considered when interpreting test scores. For example, a student whose performance is compared to the performance of *only* students referred for the gifted program may score lower than when compared to *all* of the students in the school district. Similarly, a student who is compared to a national *gifted* sample may not perform as well as when compared to the *entire* national sample. Age may also make a difference when comparing performance. Young

Table 4.1 Relationships Among Various Standard or Index Scores and Percentile Ranks and Their Interpretation.

Percentile Ranks	Quotients	A-Scores	T-Scores	z-Scores	Stanines	Interpretation
99	150	830	83	+3.33	9	Very Superior
99	145	800	80	+3.00	9	
99	140	770	77	+2.67	9	
99	135	730	73	+2.33	9	
98	130	700	70	+2.00	9	
97	128	680	68	+1.75	8	Superior
95	125	670	67	+1.67	8	
94	123	650	65	+1.5	8	
84	115	600	60	+1.00	7	Above Average
81	113	580	58	+0.75	7	
75	110	570	57	+067	6	Average
63	105	530	53	+033	6	
50	100	500	50	0.00	5	
37	95	470	47	-0.33	4	
25	90	430	43	-0.67	4	
16	85	400	40	-1.00	3	Below Average
9	80	370	37	-1.33	3	

kindergarten children with summer birthdays may not do as well as children with fall birthdays or those who have spent an additional year in kindergarten. Whenever possible, ages should be used when comparing scores. For more accurate comparisons, local norms may need to be developed when schools have a dominant minority or income level group or whose score differs dramatically from the nationally normed scores.

While scores from quantitative measures can be compared using a conversion chart, qualitative information should remain descriptive.

Test Error

Many factors contribute to a student's performance on a test. Some of these relate to the test itself, the test taker and his or her background experiences, and the testing situation. Because all assessments have some error, a single test score should be viewed as an estimate of a student's actual performance. When speaking of quantitative assessments, this error is based upon the reliability and the standard deviation of the test and is called the standard error of measurement (SEM). The SEM is a way of calculating the upper and lower limits in which the student's "true score" lies. By adding and subtracting the SEM from a student's obtained score, educators can determine the likelihood that a score will fall within a particular range. For example, 68 percent of the time, a student's true score will likely fall within a range of plus or minus one SEM from the obtained test score; 95 percent of the time between plus or minus approximately two SEMs; and 99 percent of the time between plus or minus approximately two and one half SEMs. Suppose that Elena scored 115 on an intelligence test with an SEM of 4 points. One would expect that 68 percent of the time her true score would be within the range of 111–119 (adding and subtracting one SEM from 115); 95 percent of the time, within the range of 107–123 (adding and subtracting two SEMs from 115); and 99 percent of the time, within the range of 105–125 (adding and subtracting two and one half SEMS from 115). In interpreting Elena's score, if she were to take the test again, she might conceivably score within the average (e.g., 105) to superior (e.g., 125) range 99 percent of the time. Educators need to remember that having strict cut-off scores that are exceedingly high (e.g., 130) may eliminate students whose performance is affected by test error. Therefore, the SEM is very important when interpreting scores.

Best Performance

In organizing data, the committee needs to be able to examine a student's relative strengths and needs. Students don't always perform similarly across assessments or even within the same assessment because they sample different behaviors and/or different domains. Therefore, scores from each assessment should be separated to view the student's best and worst performances. The highest score is often indicative of a student's potential. Some forms that are used for organizing data such as matrices sum and average scores and collapse data into a single rating number. This approach does not help identify students with potential nor does it provide information for examining a student's talent area for needed services.

Description of the Student

Qualitative information also needs to be examined by the committee. This information might include interviews with students, anecdotal information from the classroom or home observations, students' reflections regarding their products and performances, students' responses to teaching tasks, and clinical impressions from those who administered quantitative assessments. These assessments are important in explaining the quantitative data and in providing a more holistic view of the student.

Informing and Eliciting Evidence from Parents

In their conceptual models of giftedness, Tannenbaum (2003) and Gagné (2010) identify parents as an important environmental influence in developing their child's gifts and talents. Parental support is extremely important (Briggs et al., 2008; NAGC, 2011; Olszewski-Kubilius, 2000; Yun & Schader, 2001) in providing early exposure to the talent domain (Briggs et al., 2008; Williams, 2003), special tutoring or learning outside of school (Matthews & Jolly, 2018), and quality education (Subotnik et al., 2011). Parents need training regarding the range of characteristics within the gifted population, their role in developing their child's gifts and talents, the identification process, and the benefits for their child in participating in gifted education programming. Researchers have suggested that with training, parents may be better than teachers at identifying students (Johnsen & Ryser, 1994; Jolly & Matthews, 2014; Lee & Olszewski-Kubilius, 2006; Pletan et al., 1995).

Without this training, parents/guardians may be reluctant to refer their children for assessment, particularly those from minority backgrounds (Moore et al., 2005; Siegle et al., 2016) and may not understand or approve behaviors associated with giftedness (Coleman & Cross, 2005). Consequently, special populations may be underrepresented in the first phase of the identification process. To increase the representation of special populations in the referral phase, schools need to send home flyers in multiple languages to parents of all students, include information about the gifted program at school orientations and special meetings, make announcements through public and social media, and provide professional development for parents/guardians and others who are involved in the referral process (Dawson, 1997; Johnsen &

Ryser, 1994; Reyes et al., 1996; Harris et al., 2007; Oakland & Rossen, 2005; Shaklee & Viechnicki, 1995).

Since parents can offer perspectives about their child's interests and potential outside the school setting, they need to be actively involved in gathering information throughout the identification process. For example, schools need to help parents understand how to complete student nomination forms such as checklists and rating scales and also how to contribute to their student's portfolios. Parents who are educated about gifted education are a critical component to implementing nondiscriminatory identification procedures and developing quality programming.

Student Outcome 3. Students from Diverse Backgrounds Are Identified

The third student outcome within the assessment standard focuses on the inclusion of gifted and talented students from diverse backgrounds in gifted education programming. The goal is for these students to be representative of the total school population. In addition to selecting assessments that minimize bias and using multiple assessments, researchers have identified other specific approaches that appear to increase representation of students from diverse backgrounds. Some of these approaches include more inclusive definitions, front-loading talent development activities, universal screening, locally developed norms, nonverbal assessments or assessments in preferred language, and building relationships with students (see Standard 2.3.1).

Inclusive Definitions
Narrow definitions requiring superior performance on intelligence or achievement tests (e.g., 130 or 98th percentile) may limit the number of students who are gifted, particularly those who are English language learners and those from lower income groups. Broader definitions that encompass a wider range of characteristics and include student potential similar to the federal definition of gifted and talented and use multiple assessments are more likely to identify students who exhibit their talents in a variety of ways (Passow & Frasier, 1996). For example, a cut-off score at the 90th or even the 84th percentile rank on a variety of assessments would include a more diverse group and consider measurement error. Differentiation would then occur in talent development activities or within programming for students identified as "at-potential."

Front Loading or Pre-Identification Talent Development Activities
Front loading is providing emergent talent development experiences for students from diverse backgrounds with high potential (Briggs et al., 2008;

Olszewski-Kubilius & Clarenbach, 2012; Subotnik et al., 2011; Siegle et al., 2016). These opportunities may be provided for all students or for students who have been pre-identified. When these learning experiences are meaningful, culturally-relevant and differentiated, they provide opportunities for students' talents to emerge. Teachers and families need to be provided with professional learning activities that address characteristics of gifted students in underserved populations, the rationale and importance of the program, and the program's effects. Successful pre-identification activities result in more students from diverse populations being formally identified.

Universal Screening

McBee et al. (2016) reported that referrals for testing result in a large proportion of gifted students being missed because of variability among teachers in recommending students for gifted programs. Because of misconceptions, children who have disabilities, who are economically disadvantaged or who are English language learners are referred less frequently (Harris et al., 2009; Morrison & Rizza, 2007; Peterson & Margolin, 1997; Plata & Masten, 1998). As mentioned previously, to increase this number of students referred, researchers suggest the use of universal screening or the systematic assessment of all children within a given class, grade, campus, or school district (Ikeda et al., 2008). Using longitudinal data from a large, diverse district in Florida, Card and Giuliano (2015, 2016) reported that when all students at the second grade level were tested using a nonverbal measure of cognitive ability, there was a 180% participation rate among traditionally underrepresented groups in gifted programs. Given the higher rate of inclusion and resulting achievement gains, researchers recommend this approach (Lakin, 2016; McBee, 2016)

Locally Developed Norms

While national test norms primarily reflect the population of individuals who live in the United States, they may not reflect local norms. Local norms compare students' performance on assessments with other students in their local educational setting (e.g., local building or district) rather than nationally. Some school districts with a greater number of individuals from minority or lower socioeconomic groups use local norms for comparison purposes. Local norms are particularly helpful when economic disparities exist between campuses within the same school district or when trying to find and nurture the talents of students from diverse subgroups. In this way, students who are performing beyond their local peer group can receive advanced services (Peters & Engerrand, 2016). Researchers have found that group-specific norms for low-income students will locate those who have demonstrated high achievement who often get overlooked (Peters & Gentry, 2012).

Nonverbal Assessments and Assessments in Preferred Language

Tests with high language demands may also create barriers for English learners and those from economically disadvantaged backgrounds with limited experiences. To reduce these barriers, professionals have recommended the use of nonverbal tests, tests in the preferred language, or individually administered tests (Ryser, 2018a). These types of tests not only limit linguistic requirements but also reduce the amount of previous information required in responding to the items. While some studies indicate that minority students perform similarly on verbal and nonverbal assessments (Hodges et al., 2018), other studies have indicated that minority students tend to perform better on not only nonverbal but also problem solving and performance-based types of assessments when compared to traditional forms (Pierce et al., 2007; Reid et al., 1999; VanTassel-Baska, et al., 2007; VanTassel-Baska et al., 2002).

Building Relationships with Students

Interpersonal relationships are critical to the teaching-learning process and to gifted students' psychosocial development (American Psychological Association, 2017). Sometimes students may hide their gifts and talents and even intentionally underachieve to avoid the stigma of being identified as a gifted student (Ford et al., 2008). Students may also demonstrate their talents in other contexts rather than at school (Coleman & Cross, 2005). For these reasons, teachers need to build relationships with students to learn more about their strengths and needs and identify appropriate services. These relationships are particularly important for students who are often overlooked such as students from lower socioeconomic backgrounds, minorities, and those with disabilities. For example, in their case studies of 17 Black adults who participated in New York City's gifted programs, Sewell and Goings (2019) found that teachers who developed relationships with their students took the lead in pursuing gifted education. Researchers suggest that when teachers offer a more culturally responsive curriculum and instruction that values different perspectives and have high expectations for student performance, they are more likely to build relationships and identify students from diverse backgrounds with gifts and talents (Tomlinson & Jarvis, 2014).

It is important to remember that bias may enter at any point in the identification process: notice, referral/screening, evaluation/placement, and program participation (see Table 2). The Office of Civil Rights has provided guidelines that might assist educators in evaluating the fairness of their overall system and identifying areas for improvement.

Table 4.2 Guidelines from the Office of Civil Rights.

Statistical Analysis

_____ Racial/ethnic composition of the district's student enrollment.

_____ Racial/ethnic composition of student population receiving gifted services.

_____ Determine if minority students are statistically underrepresented in gifted programs.

_____ Number (%) of students by race/ethnicity referred for evaluation for gifted eligibility.

_____ Number (%) of students by race/ethnicity determined eligible for gifted services.

_____ Number (%) of students by race/ethnicity withdrawing from, or otherwise discontinuing participation in, gifted programs/services.

Notice

_____ Notice simply and clearly explains the purpose of the program, referral/screening procedures, eligibility criteria, and identifies the district's contact person.

_____ Notice is provided annually to students, parents, and guardians, in a manner designed to reach all segments of the school community.

Referral/Screening

_____ Multiple alternative referral sources, e.g., teachers, parents, etc., are, in practice, accessible to and utilized by, all segments of the school community.

_____ Teachers and other district staff involved in the referral process have been trained and/or provided guidance regarding the characteristics of giftedness.

_____ Referral/screening criteria are applied in a nondiscriminatory manner.

_____ All referral/screening criteria/guidelines are directly related to the purpose of the gifted program.

_____ Standardized tests and cut off scores are appropriate (valid and reliable) for the purpose of screening students for gifted services.

Table 4.2 *Continued*

Evaluation/Placement

_____ Eligibility criteria are applied in a nondiscriminatory manner.

_____ Eligibility criteria are consistent with the purpose and implementation of the gifted program: Eligibility is based on multiple criteria; criteria include multiple assessments; eligibility incorporates component test scores as appropriate.

_____ Assessment instruments/measures and cut off scores are appropriate (valid and reliable) for the purpose of identifying students for gifted services.

_____ To the extent that subjective assessment criteria are utilized, those individuals conducting the assessments have been provided guidelines and training to ensure proper evaluations.

_____ Alternative assessment instruments are utilized in appropriate circumstances.

_____ If private testing is permitted as the basis for an eligibility determination, it does not have a disparate impact on minority students or, if it does, the use of such testing is legitimately related to the successful implementation of the program and no less discriminatory alternative exists which would achieve the same objective.

Program Participation

_____ Continued eligibility standards/criteria are applied in a nondiscriminatory manner.

_____ Continued eligibility standards/criteria are consistent with the purpose and implementation of the gifted program.

_____ Implementation procedures and practices facilitate equal access for all students.

Example Case Study

All of the data collected during the identification process may be organized into a case study format (see Figure 4.1). As can be seen in Figure 4.1, the assessment data is organized by qualitative and quantitative information although it might be organized by phases (e.g., nomination/referral, screening, and selection).

In this case, the gifted education teacher was responsible for collecting information from a variety of sources (e.g., parents, counselor, teacher, peers, and the student) (2.2.3). Quantitative data included achievement tests and aptitude tests and were interpreted within ranges of performance that were based on the standard error of measurement. Along with index scores, the school chose to insert percentile ranks to help with interpretation of the quantitative information. Qualitative data observations by the teacher, parent, and counselor; performances and products that were included in a portfolio of work; and interviews with the student, his parents, and peers.

The committee was comprised of the general education teacher, the gifted education teacher, the special education teacher, the parents, the counselor, and the principal. All of the members had training in gifted education. Before the committee met, each of the members reviewed the evidence for Javier, which was attached to the summary form. They learned that the parents had referred their son for the gifted education program (2.2.6). The background information indicated that Javier's first language was Spanish and he began learning English in kindergarten in the school's bilingual program. There was a discrepancy in the perspectives of the individuals regarding Javier's characteristics (e.g., the teacher's perspective vs. the parents' perspectives) and also in Javier's performance on achievement subtests. His relative areas of strength appeared to be in mathematical problem solving and reasoning with a strong interest in science. Upon reviewing all of the assessment data, the committee noted that Javier met the school district's standards on the majority of the quantitative measures, which was set at the 90th percentile or within the superior to very superior range. The qualitative data provided additional information that corroborated the earlier assessment evidence and identified specific interests (i.e., science), strengths (i.e., math and reasoning), and needs (i.e., reading). All of this information was considered in the committee's final recommendation, which was to place him in the gifted classroom for science and math, develop his interest in science, assist the general education teacher in differentiating the curriculum, assist the parent in nurturing his talents at home, and provide further support in reading. If his relative need in reading continues and he is nonresponsive to special interventions, then he will be referred for a Tier 2 intervention, which incorporates intensive instruction by a reading specialist.

Figure 4.1 Example Case Study.

Name: Javier DOB: 1–15–2014 Other: Bilingual
Campus: Clear Creek Grade: 1 Teacher: Simonton

Achievement

Test	Minimum	Subtest	Range (90%)	Date	Criterion
I. Iowa Assessments					
Reading	120	115(84th)	108–121 (6 points)	2/10/2021	No
Math	120	125 (95th)	119–131		Yes
Language	120	119 (90th)	113–125		Yes
Total	120	121 (92nd)	115–127		Yes

Aptitude

II. Screening Assessment for Gifted Elementary and Middle School Students					
Verbal	120	120 (91st)	116–126 (6 points)	3/12/2021	Yes
Nonverbal	120	135 (99th)	129–141		Yes
Total Reasoning	120	135 (99th)	130.5–139.5 (4 points)		Yes

Other quantitative measures:

Observations

Source	Comments	Date	Criterion
Teacher	With reservations: Maturity	4/7/2021	No
Parent	Highly recommends	3/21/2021	Yes

(Continued)

Figure 4.1 *Continued*

	Recommends		Yes
Other: Counselor		3/22/2021	Yes
Performance/Products			
Portfolio	math problem solving and science experiments	3/12/2021	Yes
Interviews			
Student	Likes science	4/10/2021	Yes
Parent	Discovery channel Collections of insects	4/15/2021	Yes
Other: Peers	Original; impatient	4/20/2021	Yes

See attached referral forms, products, performances, and complete interviews

Committee Decision Regarding Services:
Needed ___√___ Not Needed _____ Provisional _____

The committee's general recommendations:
• Javier should be placed in the gifted classroom for science and math and develop his interest in science.
• The general education teacher with support from the gifted education specialist will differentiate the curriculum for Javier and assist the parent in nurturing his talents at home.
• Further support in reading will be provided. If his relative need in reading continues and he is nonresponsive to special interventions, then he will be referred for a Tier 2 intervention, which incorporates intensive instruction by a reading specialist.

The case study format meets standards for organizing and interpreting multiple assessments:

multiple indicators of potential are used (2.1.3, 2.2.7);

assessments relate to services and show abilities, interests, strengths, and needs (2.2.2);

both qualitative and quantitative assessments are used from a variety of sources (2.2.3);

above-level performance and dynamic assessments were included in the observations and portfolio information (2.2.4);

parents were used as a source of information (2.2.8); and assessment tools included nonverbal formats (2.3.1).

Moreover, in interpreting the data, the committee used comparable scores, considered the standard error of measurement, and considered the student's relative strengths and needs using both quantitative and qualitative data. Using a case study format provided a broad picture of the student across contexts.

Summary

Foundational to the three NAGC student outcomes related to identification within the assessment standard are the views that

(a) gifts and talents are dynamic and are developed over time;
(b) early identification improves the likelihood that gifts will develop into talents;
(c) students exhibit their gifts and talents within not only a specific domain but also within interest areas; and
(d) giftedness is exhibited across all diverse groups.

The first student outcome addresses equal access to the identification process. To achieve this outcome requires that educators learn how to differentiate their curriculum and classroom environments and provide parents with information about the need for gifted programming. Multiple indicators and multiple entry points need to be used to ensure that gifted students can access needed services. The second outcome, which encourages the use of a variety of assessment evidence, requires the implementation of eight evidence-based practices that address these areas: designing a comprehensive, cohesive, and ongoing identification procedure; selecting and using a variety of assessments; using assessments that minimize bias; interpreting multiple assessments; and informing and eliciting evidence from parents. The final student outcome focuses on ensuring students from diverse groups, in sufficient numbers to be representative of the total school population, are considered for services. Practices that appear to be effective in increasing more gifted students from special populations in gifted education programming include developing more inclusive definitions; using pre-identification talent development activities; using universal screening; developing locally developed norms; using nonverbal assessments and assessments in preferred language; and building relationships with students. When all of these student outcomes are achieved, educators can be more assured that their identification procedure is effectively identifying each and every student who needs gifted education programming.

References

Acar, S., Sen, S., & Cayirdag, N. (2016). Consistency of the performance and nonperformance methods in gifted identification: A multilevel meta-analytic review. *Gifted Child Quarterly, 60*(2), 81–101. https://doi.org/10.1177/0016986216634438

American Educational Research Association, American Psychological Association, & National Council on Measurement in Education. (2014). *Standards for educational and psychological testing.* American Educational Research Association. www.aera.net/Publications/Books/Standards-for-Educational-Psychological-Testing-2014-Edition

American Psychological Association, Center for Psychology in Schools and Education (2017). *Top 20 principles from psychology for preK–12 creative, talented, and gifted students' teaching and learning.* www.apa.org/ed/schools/teaching-learning/top-principles-gifted.pdf

Bloom, B. J. (Ed.) (1985). *Developing talent in young people.* Ballantine Books.

Borland, J. H., Schnur, R., & Wright, L. (2000). Economically disadvantaged students in a school for the academically gifted: A post-positivist inquiry into individual and family adjustment. *Gifted Child Quarterly, 44*(1), 13–32. https://doi.org/10.1177/0016986220004400103

Briggs, C. J., Reis, S. M., & Sullivan, E. E. (2008). A national view of promising programs and practices for culturally, linguistically, and ethnically diverse gifted and talented students. *Gifted Child Quarterly, 52*(2), 131–145. https://doi.org/10.1177/0016986208316037

Brulles, D., Castellano, J. A., & Laing, P. C. (2011). Identifying and enfranchising gifted English language learners. In J. A. Castellano & A. D. Frazier

(Eds.), *Special populations in gifted education: Understanding our most able students from diverse backgrounds* (pp. 305–313). Prufrock Press.

Buros Center for Testing (n.d.). *Test reviews and information.* University of Nebraska, Lincoln. https://buros.org/test-reviews-information

Card, D., & Giuliano, L. (2015). *Can universal screening increase the representation of low income and minority students in gifted education?* (NBER Working Paper No. 21519). Cambridge, MA; National Bureau of Economic Research. www.nber.org/papers/w21519

Card, D., & Giuliano, L. (2016). *Universal screening increases the representation of low-income and minority students in gifted education.* Proceedings of the National Academy of Sciences of the United States of America. https://doi.org/10.1073/pnas.1605043113

Castellano, J. A. (1998). *Identifying and assessing gifted and talented bilingual Hispanic students* (Report No. EDO-RC-97–9). Charleston, WV: ERIC Clearinghouse on Rural Education and Small Schools. (ERIC Document Reproduction Service No. ED. 423104). https://files.eric.ed.gov/fulltext/ED423104.pdf

Coleman, L. J., & Cross, T. L. (2005). *Being gifted in school: An introduction to development, guidance, and teaching.* Prufrock Press.

Coleman, M. R., & Shah-Coltrane, S. (2010). *U-STARS~PLUS professional development kit.* Council for Exceptional Children.

Colorado Department of Education (2020). *Gifted identification guidance handbook.* www.cde.state.co.us/gt/idguidebook

Cornell, D. G., Delcourt, M. A. B., Goldberg, M. D., & Bland, L. C. (1995). Achievement and self-concept of minority students in elementary school gifted programs. *Journal for the Education of the Gifted, 18*(2), 189–209. https://doi.org/1-.1177/016235329501800206

Coronado, J. M., & Lewis, K. D. (2017). The disproportional representation of English Language Learners in gifted and talented programs in Texas. *Gifted Child Today, 40*(4), 238–244. https://doi.org/10.1177/1076217517722181

Dawson, V. L. (1997). In search of the wild bohemian: Challenges in the identification of the creatively gifted. *Roeper Review, 19*(3), 148–152. https://doi.org/10.1080/02783199709553811

Foley Nicpon, M., Allmon, A., Sieck, B., & Stinson, R. D. (2011). Empirical investigation of twice-exceptionality: Where have we been and where are we going? *Gifted Child Quarterly, 55*(1), 3–17. https://doi.org/10.1177/0016986210382575

Ford, D. Y. (2016). Desegregating gifted education for culturally different students: Recommendations for equitable recruitment and retention. In J. T. DeCuir-Gundy & P. A. Schutz (Eds.), *Race and ethnicity in the study of motivation in education* (pp. 183–198). Taylor & Francis.

Ford, D. Y., Grantham, T. C., & Whiting, G. W. (2008). Another look at the achievement gap: Learning from the experiences of gifted black students. *Urban Education, 43*(2), 216–239. https://doi.org/10.1177/0042085907312344

Ford, D. Y., & Harmon, D. A. (2001). Equity and excellence: Providing access to gifted education for culturally diverse students. *Journal of Secondary Gifted Education, 12*(3), 141–147. https://doi.org/10.4219/jsge-2001–663

Ford, D. Y., Harris III, J. J., Tyson, C. A., & Trotman, M. F. (2001). Beyond deficit thinking: Providing access for gifted African American students. *Roeper Review, 24*(2), 52–58. https://doi.org/10.1080/02783190209554129

Ford, D. Y., Moore III, J. L., & Milner, H. R. (2005). Beyond colorblindness: A model of culture with implications for gifted education. *Roeper Review, 27*(2), 97–103. https://doi.org/10.1080/02783190509554297

Franklin, R. K. (2009). *A case study of a three-year pilot program on one district's attempt to increase the gifted identification of diverse elementary school students by having a talent development program* (Unpublished doctoral dissertation). Virginia Commonwealth University, Richmond, VA.

Frasier, M. M., Garcia, J. H., & Passow, A. H. (1995). *A review of assessment issues in gifted education and their implications for identifying gifted minority students.* (RM95204). University of Connecticut, The National Research Center on the Gifted and Talented. https://nrcgt.uconn.edu/research-based_resources/frasgarc/

Gagné, F. (2010). Motivation within the DMGT 2.0 framework. *High Ability Studies, 21*(2), 81–99. https://doi.org/10.1080/13598139.2010.525341

Gentry, M., Hu, S., & Thomas, A. T. (2008). Ethnically diverse students. In J. A. Plucker & C. M. Callahan (Eds.), *Critical issues and practices in gifted education* (pp. 195–212). Prufrock Press.

Grissom, J. A., & Redding, C. (2016). Discretion and disproportionality: Explaining the underrepresentation of high-achieving students of color in gifted programs. AERA Open, 2(1), 1–25. https://doi.org/10.1177/2332858415622175.

Harris, B., Plucker, J. A., Rapp, K. E., & Martinez, R. S. (2009). Identifying gifted and talented English language learners: A case study. *Journal for the Education of the Gifted, 32*(3), 368–393. https://doi.org/10.4219/jeg-2009–858

Harris, B., Rapp, K., Martinez, R., & Plucker, J. (2007). Identifying English language learners for gifted and talented programs: Current practices and recommendations for improvement. *Roeper Review, 29*(5), 26–29. https://doi.org/10.1080/02783193.2007.11869221

Hertzog, N. B. (2005). Equity and access: Creating general education classrooms responsive to potential giftedness. *Journal for the Education of the Gifted, 29*(2), 213–257. https://doi.org/10.1177/016235320502900205

Hodges, J., Tay, J., Maeda, Y., & Gentry, M. (2018). A meta-analysis of gifted and talented identification practices, *Gifted Child Quarterly*, *62*(2), 147–174. https://doi.org/10.1177/0016986217752107

Hunsaker, S. L., Finley, V. S., & Frank, E. L. (1997). An analysis of teacher nominations and student performance in gifted programs. *Gifted Child Quarterly*, *41*(2), 19–24. https://doi.org/10.1177/001698629704100203

Ikeda, M. J., Neesen, E., & Witt, J. C. (2008). Best practice in universal screening. In A. Thomas & J. Grimes (Eds.), *Best practices in school psychology* (pp. 103–114). National Association of School Psychologists.

Jensen, A. R. (1980). *Bias in mental testing*. Free Press.

Johnsen, S. K. (2008). Using portfolios to assess gifted and talented students. In J. VanTassel-Baska (Ed.), *Alternative assessments with gifted and talented students* (pp. 227–257). Prufrock Press.

Johnsen, S. K. (2011). Using standards to design identification procedures. *Tempo*, *31*(2), 8–15, 33. https://tempo.txgifted.org/

Johnsen, S. K. (2018a). Definitions, models, and characteristics of gifted students. In S. K. Johnsen (Ed.), *Identifying students: A practical guide* (3rd ed., pp. 1–32). Prufrock Press.

Johnsen, S. K. (2018b). Making decisions about placement. In S. K. Johnsen (Ed.), *Identifying gifted students: A practical guide* (3rd ed., pp. 117–149). Prufrock Press.

Johnsen, S. K., & Corn, A. L. (2018). *Screening assessment for gifted elementary and middle school students* (3rd ed.). PRO-ED.

Johnsen, S. K., Feuerbacher, S., & Witte, M. M. (2007). Increasing the retention of gifted students from low income backgrounds in a university programs for the gifted: The UYP project. In J. VanTassel-Baska (Ed.), *Serving gifted learners beyond the traditional classroom: A guide to alternative programs and services* (pp. 55–79). Prufrock Press.

Johnsen, S. K., & Ryser, G. (1994). Identification of young gifted children from lower income families. *Gifted and Talented International*, *9*(2), 62–68. https://doi.org/10.1080/15332276.1994.11672797

Johnsen, S. K., & Ryser, G. R. (1997). The validity of portfolios in predicting performance in a gifted program. *Journal for the Education of the Gifted*, *20*(3), 253–267. https://doi.org/10.1177/016235329702000304

Jolly, J. L., & Matthews, M. S. (2014). Parenting. In J. A. Plucker, & C. M. Callahan (2014), *Critical issues and practices in gifted education: What the research says* (2nd ed., pp. 481–492). Prufrock.

Joseph, L., & Ford, D. Y. (2006). Nondiscriminatory assessment: Considerations for gifted education. *Gifted Child Quarterly*, *50*(1), 42–51. https://doi.org/10.1177/001698620605000105

Kalbfleisch, M. L. (2013). Twice-exceptional students: Gifted students with learning disabilities. In C. M. Callahan & H. L. Hertberg-Davis (Eds.), *Fundamentals of gifted education: Considering multiple perspectives* (pp. 358–368). Routledge.

Kitano, M. K. (2003). Gifted potential and poverty: A call for extraordinary action. *Journal for the Education of the Gifted, 26*(4), 292–303. https://doi.org/10.4219/jeg-2003-305

Kurtz, B. E., & Weinert, F. E. (1989). Metacognition, memory performance, and causal attributions in gifted and average children. *Journal of Experimental Child Psychology, 48*(1), 45–61. https://doi.org/10.1016/0022-0965(89)90040-4

Lakin, J. (2016). Universal screening and the representation of historically underrepresented minority students in gifted education: Minding the gaps in Card and Giuliano's research. *Journal of Advanced Academics, 27*(2), 83–102. https://doi.org/10.1177/1932202X16630348

Lee, S., & Olszewski-Kubilius, P. (2006). Comparison between talent search students qualifying via scores on standardized tests and via parent nomination. *Roeper Review, 29*(3), 157–166. https://doi.org/10.1080/02783190609554355

Lidz, C. S., & Macrine, S. L. (2001). An alternative approach to the identification of gifted culturally and linguistically diverse learners: The contribution of dynamic assessment. *School Psychology International, 22*(1), 74–96. https://doi.org/10.1177/01430343010221006

Lo, C. O., & Porath, M. (2017). Paradigm shifts in gifted education: An examination vis-à-vis its historical situatedness and pedagogical sensibilities. *Gifted Child Quarterly, 61*(4), 343–360. https://doi.org/10.1177/0016986217722840

Lupkowski-Shoplik, A., Benbow, C. P., Assouline, S. G., & Brody, L. E. (2003). Talent searches: Meeting the needs of academically talented youth. In N. Colangelo & G. A. Davis (Eds.), *Handbook of gifted education* (3rd ed., pp. 204–218). Allyn & Bacon.

Matthews, M. S., & Jolly, J. L. (2018). The learning environment at home. In J. L. Roberts, T. F. Inman, & J. H. Robins (Eds.), *Introduction to gifted education* (pp. 197–210). Prufrock Press.

McBee, M. T. (2016). What you don't look for, you won't find: A commentary on Card and Giuliano's examination of universal screening. *Journal of Advanced Academics, 27*(2), 131–138. https://doi.org/10.1177/1932202X16634141

McBee, M. T., Peters, S. J., & Miller, E. M. (2016). The impact of the nomination stage on gifted program identification: A comprehensive psychometric analysis. *Gifted Child Quarterly, 60*(4), 258–278. https://doi.org/10.1177/0016986216656256

McBee, M. T., Peters, S. J., & Waterman, C. (2014). Combining scores in multiple-criteria assessment systems: The impact of combination rule. *Gifted Child Quarterly, 58*(1), 69–89. https://doi.org/10.1177/0016986213513794

Missouri Department of Elementary and Secondary Education (2016). *Identifying and serving traditionally underrepresented gifted students.* https://files.eric.ed.gov/fulltext/ED572332.pdf

Moore III, J. L., Ford, D. Y., & Milner, H. R. (2005). Recruiting is not enough: Retaining African-American students in gifted education. *Gifted Child Quarterly, 49*(1), 49–65. https://doi.org/10.1177/001698620504900105

Morrison, W. F., & Rizza, M. G. (2007). Creating a toolkit for identifying twice-exceptional students. *Journal for the Education of the Gifted, 31*(1), 57–76. https://doi.org/10.4219/jeg-2007–513

National Association for Gifted Children (n.d.). *Identification.* www.nagc.org/resources-publications/gifted-education-practices/identification

National Association for Gifted Children (2011). *Position statement: Identifying and serving culturally and linguistically diverse gifted students.* www.nagc.org/sites/default/files/Position%20Statement/Identifying%20and%20Serving%20Culturally%20and%20Linguistically.pdf

National Association for Gifted Children (2019a). *Position statement: A definition of giftedness that guides best practice.* www.nagc.org/sites/default/files/Position%20Statement/Definition%20of%20Giftedness%20%282019%29.pdf

National Association for Gifted Children (2019b). *Pre-K–Grade 12 Gifted Programming Standards.* Washington, DC: Author. www.nagc.org/sites/default/files/standards/Intro%202019%20Programming%20Standards.pdf

Oakland, T., & Rossen, E. (2005). A 21st-century model for identifying students for gifted and talented programs in light of national conditions: An emphasis on race and ethnicity. *Gifted Child Today, 28*(4), 56–63. https://doi.org/10.1177/107621750502800413

Olszewski-Kubilius, P. (2000). The transition from childhood giftedness to adult creative productiveness: Psychological characteristics and social supports. *Roeper Review, 23*(2), 65–71. https://doi.org/10.1080/02783190009554068

Olszewski-Kubilius, P., & Clarenbach, J. (2012). *Unlocking emergent talent: Supporting high achievement of low-income, high ability-students.* National Association for Gifted Children. www.nagc.org/sites/default/files/key%20reports/Unlocking%20Emergent%20Talent%20(final).pdf

Olszewski-Kubilius, P., & Corwith, S. (2018). Poverty, academic achievement, and giftedness: A literature review. *Gifted Child Quarterly, 62*(1), 37–55. https://doi.org/10.1177/0016986217738015

Olszewski-Kubilius, P., & Kulieke, M. (2008). Using off-level testing and assessment for gifted and talented students. In J. VanTassel-Baska (Ed.), *Alternative assessments with gifted and talented students* (pp. 89–106). Prufrock Press.

Passow, A. H., & Frasier, M. M. (1996). Toward improving identification of talent potential among minority and disadvantaged students. *Roeper Review*, *18*(3), 198–202. https://doi.org/10.1080/02783199609553734

Peters, S. J., & Engerrand, K. G. (2016). Equity and excellence: Proactive efforts in the identification of underrepresented students for gifted and talented services. *Gifted Child Quarterly*, *60*(3), 159–171. https://doi.org/10.1177/0016986216643165

Peters, S. J., & Gentry, M. (2012). Group-specific norms and teacher-rating. *Journal of Advanced Academics*, *23*(2), 125–144. https://doi.10.1177/1932202X12438717

Peterson, J. S., & Margolin, R. (1997). Naming gifted children: An example of unintended "reproduction." *Journal for the Education of the Gifted*, *21*(1), 82–100. https://doi.org/10.1177/016235329702100105

Pierce, R. L., Adams, C. M., Speirs Neumeister, K. L., Cassady, J. C., Dixon, F. A., & Cross, T. L. (2007). Development of an identification procedure for a large urban school corporation: Identifying culturally diverse and academically gifted elementary students. *Roeper Review*, *29*(2), 113–118. https://doi.org/10.1080/02783190709554394

Plata, M., & Masten, W. (1998). Teacher ratings of Hispanic and Anglo students on a behavior rating scale. *Roeper Review*, *21*(2), 139–144. https://doi.org/10.1080/02783199809553946

Pletan, M. D., Robinson, N. M., Berninger, V. W., & Abbott, R. D. (1995). Parents' observations of kindergartners who are advanced in mathematical reasoning. *Journal for the Education of the Gifted*, *19*(1), 30–44. https://doi.org/10.1177/016235329501900103

Plucker, J. A., Hardesty, J., & Burroughs, N. (2013). *Talent on the sidelines. Excellence gaps and America's persistent talent underclass.* Storrs: University of Connecticut, Center for Education Policy Analyses. www.nagc.org/sites/default/files/key%20reports/Talent%20on%20the%20Sidelines%20(2013).pdf

Reid, C., Udall, A., Romanoff, B., & Algozzine, B. (1999). Comparison of traditional and problem solving assessment criteria. *Gifted Child Quarterly*, *43*(4), 252–264. https://doi.org/10.1177/001698629904300404

Reyes, E. I., Fletcher, R., & Paez, D. (1996). Developing local multidimensional screening procedures for identifying giftedness among Mexican American border population. *Roeper Review*, *18*(3), 208–211. https://doi.org/10.1080/02783199609553739

Robins, J., & Jolly, J. L. (2018). Technical information regarding assessment. In S. K. Johnsen (Ed.), *Identifying gifted students: A practical guide* (3rd ed., pp. 73–116). Prufrock Press.

Ryser, G. R. (2018a). Fairness in testing and nonbiased assessment. In S. K. Johnsen (Ed.), *Identifying gifted students: A practical guide* (3rd ed., pp. 59–72). Prufrock Press.

Ryser, G. R. (2018b). Qualitative and quantitative approaches to assessment. In S. K. Johnsen (Ed.), *Identifying gifted students: A practical guide* (3rd ed., pp. 33–57). Prufrock Press.

Salvia, J., Ysseldyke, J. E., & Witmer, S. (2017). *Assessment in special and inclusive education* (13th ed.). Cengage Learning

Schack, G. D., & Starko, A. J. (1990). Identification of gifted students: An analysis of criteria preferred by preservice teachers, classroom teachers, and teachers of the gifted. *Journal for the Education of the Gifted, 13*(4), 346–363. https://doi.org/10.1177/016235329001300405

Scruggs, T. E., & Mastropieri, M. A. (1985). Spontaneous verbal elaboration in gifted and non-gifted youths. *Journal for the Education of the Gifted, 9*(1), 1–10. https://doi.org/10.1177/016235328500900102

Sewell, J. P., & Goings, R. B. (2019). Navigating the gifted bubble: Black adults reflecting on their transition experiences in NYC gifted programs. *Roeper Review, 41*(1), 20–34. https://doi.org/10.1080/002783193.2018.1553218

Shaklee, B. D., & Viechnicki, K. J. (1995). A qualitative approach to portfolios: The early assessment for exceptional potential model. *Journal for the Education of the Gifted, 18*(2), 156–170. https://doi.org/10.1177/016235329501800204

Siegle, D., Gubbins, E. J., O'Rourke, P., Langley, S. D., Mun, R. U., Luria, S. R., Little, C. A., McCoach, D. B., Knupp, T., Callahan, C. M., & Plucker, J. A. (2016). Barriers to underserved students' participation in gifted programs and possible solutions. *Journal for the Education of the Gifted, 39*(2), 103–131. https://doi.org/10.1177/0162353216640930

Siegle, D., Moore, M., Mann, R. L., & Wilson, H. E. (2010). Factors that influence in-service and preservice teachers' nominations of students for gifted and talented programs. *Journal for the Education of the Gifted, 33*(3), 337–360. https://doi.org/10.1177/016235321003300303

Soto, L. D. (1997). *Language, culture, and power: Bilingual families and the struggle for quality education.* State University of New York Press.

Speirs Neumeister, K. L., Adams, C. M., Pierce, R. L., Cassady, J. C., & Dixon, F. A. (2007). Fourth-grade teachers' perceptions of giftedness: Implications for identifying and serving diverse gifted students. *Journal for the Education of the Gifted, 30*(4), 479–499. https://doi.org/10.4219/jeg-2007–503

Subotnik, R. F., Olszewski-Kubilius, P., & Worrell, F. C. (2011). Rethinking giftedness and gifted education: A proposed direction forward based on psychological science. *Psychological Science in the Public Interest*, *12*(1), 3–54. https://doi.org/10.1177/1529100611418056

Sulak, T. N. (2014). Using CBM to identify advanced learners in the general education classroom. *Gifted Child Today*, *37*(1), 25–31. https://doi.org/10.1177/1076217513509620

Swanson, J. D. (2006). Breaking through assumptions about low-income, minority gifted students. *Gifted Child Quarterly*, *50*(1), 11–25. https://doi.org/10.1177/001698620605000103

Swanson, H. L., & Lussier, C. M. (2001). A selective synthesis of the experimental literature on dynamic assessment. *Review of Educational Research*, *71*(2), 321–363. https://doi.org/10.3102/00346543071002321

Tannenbaum, A. (1983). *Gifted children: Psychological and educational perspectives*. Macmillan.

Tannenbaum, A. (1986). Giftedness: A psychosocial approach. In R. J. Sternberg & J. Davidson (Eds.), *Conceptions of giftedness* (pp. 21–52). Cambridge University Press.

Tomlinson, C. A., & Jarvis, J. M. (2014). Case studies of success: Supporting academic success for students with high potential from ethnic minority and economically disadvantaged backgrounds. *Journal for the Education of the Gifted*, *37*(3), 191–219. https://doi.org/10.1177/0162353214540826

Texas Education Agency (2019, April). *Texas state plan for the education of gifted/talented students*. https://tea.texas.gov/sites/default/files/GT_State_Plan_2019_1.pdf

VanTassel-Baska, J., Feng, A. X., & Evans, B. L. (2007). Patterns of identification and performance among gifted students identified through performance tasks: A three-year analysis. *Gifted Child Quarterly*, *51*(3), 218–231. https://doi.org/10.1177/0016986207302717

Yoon, S. Y., & Gentry, M. (2009). Racial and ethnic representation in gifted programs: Current status of and implications for gifted Asian American students. *Gifted Child Quarterly*, *53*(2), 121–136. https://doi.org/10.1177/0016986208330564

VanTassel-Baska, J., Johnson, D., & Avery, L. D. (2002). Using performance tasks in the identification of economically disadvantaged and minority gifted learners: Findings from Project STAR. *Gifted Child Quarterly*, *46*(2), 110–123. https://doi.org/10.1177/001698620204600204

Williams, F. (2003). What does musical talent look like to you? And what is the role of the school and its partners in developing talent? *Gifted Education International*, *17*(3), 272–274. https://doi.org/10.1177/026142940301700308

Worrell, F., C., & Erwin, J. O. (2011). Best practices in identifying students for gifted and talented education programs. *Journal of Applied School Psychology*, *27*(4), 319–340. https://doi.org/10.1080/15377903.2011.615817

Wright, B. L., Ford, D. Y., & Young, J. L. (2017). Ignorance or indifference: Seeking excellence and equity for underrepresented students of color in gifted education. *Global Education Review*, 4(1), 45–60. https://ger.mercy.edu/index.php/ger

Yaluma, C. B., & Tyner, A. (2018). *Is there a gifted gap? Gifted education in high-poverty schools*. Thomas Fordham Institute. https://edexcellence.net/publications/is-there-a-gifted-gap

Yun, D. D., & Schader, R. (2001). Parent's reasons and motivations for supporting their child's music training. *Roeper Review*, 24(1), 23–26. https://doi.org/10.1080/02783190109554121

5

The Curriculum Planning and Instruction Standard in Gifted Education: From Idea to Reality

Joyce VanTassel-Baska

This chapter presents the revised curriculum planning and instruction standards and provides a template for districts to analyze their current curriculum work for the gifted in light of those standards. Furthermore, it highlights what needs to be done in order to move toward compliance with the standards. The chapter also provides ideas for thinking about the "big picture" of curriculum planning and implementation. Finally, the chapter focuses on the use of the new standards for improving gifted programs and meeting the needs of gifted learners. The chapter concludes with a set of action steps in implementing the new standards.

An Overview of Curriculum Planning

The nature of curriculum planning for high ability learners requires the teacher and other educators to engage in several tasks somewhat simultaneously. Educators who take on the task must be able to do macro planning

DOI: 10.4324/9781003236863-5

of curriculum across years of schooling, establishing a curriculum framework that extends from early primary through the late secondary years. This framework shows the learning progressions for gifted students at each stage of development in each core area of learning. Moreover, the framework illustrates the differentiated emphases to be used consistently throughout the underlying layers of the curriculum work. At play at the same time, teachers must find, adapt or create materials for use with gifted learners. These adaptations of existing differentiated curriculum or newly designed units must attend to the principles of good curriculum design, exemplary practice in the subject area, and differentiated features of a curriculum for the gifted. Additionally, strong curriculum planning involves experts from the various subject areas to serve as collaborators and validators of the work.

Definition of Differentiation

In order to make appropriate changes in a curriculum for the gifted, educators must be clear about the meaning of differentiation for this population. It is not just providing project work on an independent or group basis. It is not just about providing choice. Rather it is about the careful incorporation of multiple approaches to make the curriculum more responsive to students who learn faster, deeper, and in more complex ways than their same-age peers. A useful definition might be:

> The process of differentiation is the deliberate adaptation and modification of the curriculum, instructional processes, and assessments to respond to the needs of gifted learners.

This definition suggests that differentiation must employ changes to curriculum, instruction, and assessment in a holistic way. It is consistent with the revised standards and has been used in the NAGC series of books on adapting curriculum in language arts, mathematics, and science (see VanTassel-Baska & Baska, 2020; Hughes et al., 2015; Johnsen et al., 2014; Adams, Cotabish & Dailey, 2015).

Revisions in the Curriculum Standard

The new curriculum standards that were developed in 2019 include some areas that differ from the 2012 standards. The evidence-based practices and student outcomes from the 2012 curriculum standards remain somewhat similar, focusing first on curriculum planning. Outcomes from curriculum planning relate to student growth commensurate with academic ability. This standard has been extended to include an emphasis on pacing and technology integration in addition to earlier areas of emphasis.

The second area of change in the revised curriculum standards relates to the topic of talent development which was contained in two standards in 2012 and is now reduced to one standard. Talent development in the revised standard focuses on the social, emotional, and psychosocial development of the gifted in their area of talent. Translation of the standard focuses on the development of self-advocacy, resilience, and monitoring of growth in an area of learning. Deleted from this standard is an emphasis on metacognition (moved to 3.5.1) and career planning, which is found in the Learning and Development Standard (1.6) and in the Programming Standard (5.3).

A third area of change in the revised standards, responsiveness to diversity (changed from culturally relevant) provides a focus on living in a diverse and global society. Evidence-based practices in this area relate to the need for honoring diverse perspectives and biases, a key idea also contained in all three of the subcategories.

The fourth and fifth standards in the 2019 revision emphasize instructional strategies, now containing two sections. The first student outcome on instructional strategies focuses on the use of diverse strategies and those that are inquiry-based. Instead of separate evidence-based practices, the specific thinking skills of critical, creative thinking and problem-solving are combined in one evidence-based practice (see 3.4.3). The second student outcome and related evidence-based practices emphasize facilitating independent learning for the gifted through teaching learning strategies and using metacognitive models which were included in a different standard in the original 2012 version.

The last standard emphasizes the use of resources, split now between those resources that are research-based and those that are school and community-based, which emphasize advanced learning for the gifted. Resources may be perceived to be materials or people. Other differences between the 2012 and 2019 standards relate primarily to changes in language that improve communication about the standard and its meaning.

Implications of these changes in the standards may account for some nuanced changes to individual district plans in the areas noted and a shift of emphasis in instructional delivery at the classroom level. The curriculum standards revisions still assume that districts may employ multiple grouping models in the implementation of the standards at all levels of the enterprise P–12, using the research base as the guidepost. These changes then may be seen as primarily a reorganization of priority areas for attention in curriculum and an attempt to employ more differentiation practices, within a clear emphasis on inquiry-based approaches. They also represent an attempt to provide a shared terminology across related fields and a simplified language. The changes noted were reviewed through survey by members of the university network as well as the Standards Committee of the organization.

Necessary Curriculum Planning Documents

In the revised NAGC Pre-K–Grade 12 Gifted Programming Standards, there is a major emphasis on establishing curriculum planning across levels of schooling. The documents that represent this macro planning effort include a curriculum framework that articulates goals, outcomes, strategies, activities, and assessment across the PK–12 levels of schooling. A second is the development of learning trajectories or progressions (i.e., scope and sequence of content curriculum) that go beyond the grade-level content standards and demonstrate reasonable outcomes for gifted learners to master at appropriate levels of learning. These documents alone would make a good starting point for meeting the revised gifted education curriculum standards.

Curriculum Framework

Curriculum planning requires a team approach where ultimately a school district publicizes its differentiated plan for gifted learners to the community and holds itself accountable for fidelity of implementation. In order to do this, the team must first identify the specific goals that it wishes to pursue for these K–12 learners. Such goals, linked to the outcomes identified in the new standards might be:

- ◆ To develop advanced skills and concepts in areas of ability at a pace consonant with capacity and readiness,
- ◆ Student outcomes might focus on accelerated content provided at each level in the relevant talent development areas.
- ◆ To develop inquiry-based learning via critical and creative thinking and problem-solving methods,
- ◆ Student outcomes might focus on the use of inquiry models like question-asking, models of thinking and problem-solving, and research methodologies.
- ◆ To internalize learning for independent applications and creative solutions to problems,

◆ Student outcomes might focus on the nature of student-initiated work products and the extent to which they meet the level of professional standards.
◆ To develop self-understanding, resilience, and self-advocacy,
◆ Student outcomes might focus on developing goals and plans for overcoming barriers and collaborating on projects that make a difference.

If a curriculum framework can be established such as the example above, then work within each content area may proceed to provide greater specificity to the framework and honor its intent. The curriculum framework of goals and outcomes then may be translated into activities, strategies, and resources for each subject.

Development of Learning Progressions (i.e., scope and sequence)

The development of learning within content areas and across levels is best effected through vertical planning groups that can tackle a given subject and suggest the differences needed in outcomes for the gifted at each level. So, for example, if Advanced Placement coursework at Grades 11–12 is desirable for gifted learners in the area of English, then what should the program of study in English/reading/language arts look like at earlier stages of development? A sample PK–12 scope and sequence chart by grade level clusters is provided in Table 5.1.

Emphases within the Curriculum Planning and Instruction Standard

Just as we can cite outcomes for gifted learners as a part of our macro planning documents, we also can recognize the importance of key features that the new standards are calling for. These features or indicators include the following:

◆ Alignment with relevant content standards
There is a need for gifted programs to ensure they are able to articulate the relationship between standards for teaching language arts, math, science, and social studies for all learners and how these standards are differentiated for the gifted. In most instances, this differentiation means going beyond the grade-level content standards and providing indicators beyond proficiency. Differentiation practices must affect the content-based curriculum documents as well as the instructional delivery system.

Table 5.1 Scope and Sequence Chart to document learning progression in ELA.

Grade Level	Outcomes: Students will be able to:	Indicators	Assessment Techniques	Comments
PK–3	Engage in advanced reading opportunities; use writing models; develop research and communication skills	Evidence of advanced behaviors in each strand	Performance-based assessment (PBA) and/or portfolios	Use of appropriate research-based materials will enhance the capacity to demonstrate outcome behaviors.
4–5	All of the above outcomes plus acquire linguistic competency in vocabulary, grammar and usage	Mastery of advanced vocabulary and basic elements of grammar and usage	Pre-post assessment of skills	Apply compacting techniques to ensure appropriate level work.
6–8	Analyze and interpret literature; design arguments in written and oral forms; research issues and present findings	Continued development of critical-thinking skills in language arts	Product Assessment; pre-post performance-based	Participation in writing competitions; second language course-taking
9–10	Evaluate multiple texts for comparative literary elements; synthesize literary concepts and themes; create literary products of merit	Evidence of critical-thinking and creative-thinking abilities	Pre-post PBA Product assessment Portfolio of work	*Concord Review* or other high quality publication outlet should be encouraged. Advanced coursework in second language.
11	AP Language course	Performance at level of 3 or higher on AP exam	AP Exam	AP coursework in a world language
12	AP Literature Course	Performance at level 3 or higher on AP exam	AP Exam	AP coursework in other subjects to be encouraged

◆ Comprehensive learning progression of opportunities in all curriculum areas

As described earlier, this planning effort represents the clear articulation of comprehensive offerings for gifted learners at each stage of development in each area of learning. The NAGC guides mentioned earlier are most helpful in translating examples of activities and strategies that are appropriate at different stages of development.

◆ Use of acceleration techniques, including preassessment, formative assessment, and pacing

This indicator calls for attention to developing consistent and ongoing acceleration approaches in determining the need for advancement within and across content areas. It also suggests the strong use of assessment to determine curriculum level and content required for curriculum to be sufficiently challenging for the most able. Finally, it suggests that the instructional approach of using a fast pace with gifted learners who can master the same material in half the time is a modality recognized in the instructional arsenal of teachers working with the gifted. The use of compacting and compression of content have been researched as effective ways to adapt the pace of the curriculum (VanTassel-Baska & Baska, 2020).

◆ Use of differentiation strategies

While differentiation has become a buzz word in general education, it is important to retain its meaning in adapting curriculum for the gifted through the deliberate use of more acceleration, complexity, depth, challenge, creativity, and abstraction (VanTassel-Baska & Baska, 2020) in activities and projects.

◆ Adaptation or replacement of the core curriculum

While the alignment to the core curriculum suggests ways to adapt it for the gifted, it is also important to clearly show how the curriculum for the gifted is related to the core. This is critical where major replacement is being recommended. For example, in the math sequence, a course in pre-algebra may be eliminated for gifted math students who can demonstrate proficiency through the concepts studied and proceed directly to Algebra I.

◆ Use of diversity approaches that acknowledge the importance of multiple perspectives in the development of global competence

Curriculum for the gifted needs to be sensitive to culturally different learners who inhabit our programs. This means that we need to select reading materials by other cultural groups, choose biographies that illustrate the contributions and role model potential of other cultural groups, and present a view of history that explores multiple perspectives, including minority viewpoints.

◆ Use of inquiry-based strategies

As research suggests (VanTassel-Baska & Brown, 2007), inquiry techniques form the backbone of differentiated instruction and its many manifestations in problem-based learning, project-based learning, and discussion strategies like Socratic seminar and shared inquiry. The indicator also suggests the power of higher-level questioning and higher-level thinking in both critical and creative areas as specific models for practicing the use of inquiry with students.

◆ Use of research-based materials

The revised standards are clear that curriculum for the gifted is not something to be created from scratch. Rather the curriculum materials developed over the past 30 years with federal funding under the auspices of the Jacob Javits Gifted and Talented Students Education Act provide an important base for curriculum development in all the core subject areas. These materials have been piloted, field-tested and researched for their effectiveness with gifted learners. As such, they provide an important resource to meeting the standards in curriculum (VanTassel-Baska & Little, 2017).

◆ Use of strategies that teach critical and creative thinking, research, and problem-solving skills

Just as inquiry is an important instructional tool, so too are the underlying higher-level process skills of thinking and problem-solving that constitute its basis as an instructional model of choice with the gifted. It is important that districts adopt models of thinking that can be used across grade levels in order to provide a common "differentiation language" around these skills. Such an approach should also target professional development to be more standardized in articulating the language of research-based instructional strategies.

◆ Use of information technologies

A strong curriculum for the gifted employs an integrated technology approach in implementing learning. Many approaches to this are possible within classrooms using mobile technologies (i.e., tablets, phones, laptops), learning management systems or cloud-based platforms, and in tandem with special computer labs. In this age of COVID-19, online learning options must be employed that are successful in transferring the skills and concepts of disciplines to different groups of learners, working in different formats and locations.

◆ Use of metacognitive strategies

All curricula for the gifted should attend to the need for gifted learners to reflect on what they have learned as well as engage in serious planning, monitoring, and assessing of that learning, especially when it applies to project work and research efforts. Engaging students in questions about their performance and activities that extend their thinking in a reflective mode all represent appropriate directions to pursue with implementing the revised standards.

◆ Use of community resources
Educators of the gifted will find ways to include community opportunities from speakers to field trips to key partnerships that result in mentorships and internships. Such opportunities should be available for gifted learners at various stages of development, often as early as middle school. It is especially critical that twice-exceptional learners have opportunities for apprenticeships early when their talent area is discerned and ready for development. These mentorship opportunities are now more readily available with multiple video conferencing applications.

◆ Talent development in areas of aptitude and interest in various domains (cognitive, affective, aesthetic)
This standard indicator suggests that schools document ways they are engaging gifted learners in multiple domains that develop the whole student. Cognitive development options may focus on advanced work in core subject domains that stress higher level thought transferred to projects and products of merit. Affective development options provide a rich array in gifted programming that can foster the independent skills of resilience and self-efficacy. Aesthetic curriculum may demonstrate reflecting about phenomena in nature, observing the elegance of mathematical formulae, and developing an appreciation for the beauty of expressions in the physical world. All of these modalities for talent development are encouraged.

Case Example: Acceleration as a Necessary but not Sufficient Differentiation Feature

Let's use the strategy of acceleration to illustrate the way that differentiation can work for gifted learners in schools. Educators know that preassessment is an important approach to find the functional level of a student and move forward with the curriculum based on results. They also know they can ask gifted learners to do fewer problems or activities in order to master a core standard. Moreover, at the secondary level, they know that a course of study can be compressed to focus on essential learnings at a higher level of organization around higher-level skills and concepts. The following example in Table 5.2 provides a carefully structured activity in the mathematics strand of statistics, demonstrating the use of preassessment, followed by a project-based set of options, followed by reflection about what has been learned from the experience and how to extend that learning. It illustrates further the use of *acceleration*, coupled with complexity, depth, challenge, and creativity to showcase differentiated activities.

Table 5.2 Differentiation Example.

Phase I
1. Pretest students' knowledge and skills of statistics.
2. Group students by results of the pretest in groups of 4. Provide streamlined (i.e., accelerated) instruction for the top group.
3. Provide differentiated task demands for the top group, using an inquiry problem-solving approach.
Phase I work has applied compacting strategies to the work of a group of heterogeneous learners, providing a data-based approach to grouping top learners together for the rest of the activity.
Phase II
Assignment of task demands to the top group:
• Use statistics (i.e., mean, median, mode, frequencies and percentages) to analyze one of the following data sets, prepare graphs to illustrate your understanding of the data, and present findings in a presentation for an appropriate group at your school.
Data Set Options for Phase II
• Health care expenses for people in each decade of life from 10 to 90 years for the years 2010–2020, or
• Auto sales in the US by car type across the last 10 years compared to world sales for those same car makes, or
• Ten-year trends in salary for different sectors of the US economy for 2010–2020.
Phase II work has differentiated the work of the gifted into activity options that require higher level thinking and problem-solving for them to complete. It is being asked within the model of conducting real world research with large databases online.
Phase III
Follow-up questions to consider:
• What would you predict would be the trend for your data over the next 5 years?
• How would you estimate it?
• What factors would influence it?

(Continued)

Table 5.2 *Continued*

Phase III
Phase III work has required gifted students to extend their learning to the level of prediction and forecasting what trends might mean for the near future. They are asked to reflect and analyze how they might make such predictions.
Product Assessment: Assess the following dimensions of the project work on a 1–5 scale, 5 being the highest level:
• Appropriate use of statistical analysis
• Articulation of trends
• Logical consistency of predictions
Performance-based Assessment: (In class response)
Using the following dataset of 10-year career trends in the US, analyze patterns of meaning by using appropriate statistics. What fields would be most open? Which ones would be the most closed? What is the evidence to support your choices? Graph your predictions of trends over the next three years? Over 5 years? What is the evidence to support your prediction?
Performance-based Rubric Dimensions: Patterns of meaning identified, evidence presented for choices, and quality of prediction graph.
Portfolio Assessment: (1 week response)
• Select three new datasets that capture trends across ten-year periods and use statistics to analyze them for patterns. Make predictions about the next three-year periods. Graph your results.
• Write a journal entry that reflects on the value of using existing datasets to understand societal trends.
Portfolio Rubric Dimensions: Quality of analysis, evidence for predictions, depth of written reflection
The last part of the case example for acceleration provides three different approaches to assessment that may be used for the activity: product assessment, performance-based assessment, and portfolio assessment. It thus illustrates choices that may be made by both students and teachers in the culminating learning module.

Review of Research Supporting the Curriculum Standards

The curriculum planning and instruction standard may be parsed into three parts. The first section addresses the macro planning tasks that must be completed in order to proceed with a district-wide planning effort in gifted education. The second part addresses core instructional strategies seen as crucial in implementing the standard. Finally, the third part suggests supportive approaches and structures that must be in place for successful implementation. The following section of this chapter reviews the literature supporting the importance of these elements in designing and implementing differentiated curriculum for the gifted.

Macro Planning

The research on macro planning approaches to curriculum for the gifted has been available to use for over 30 years yet many districts do not use the approach as it requires the involvement of many district personnel in different roles to carry it out. VanTassel-Baska (2003) and VanTassel-Baska and Baska (2020) have noted the importance of using curriculum design as a basis for all curriculum work with the gifted, modifying the structure to accommodate the characteristics and needs of the population. VanTassel-Baska and Stambaugh (2006a) illustrate the ways such modifications might work in different subject areas at different stages of development. Design products include both a curriculum framework and learning progression (scope and sequence charts) for each subject area. VanTassel-Baska and Little (2017) illustrate the application of the differentiated design model as it has been used in the College of William and Mary curriculum units of study over the past 30 years. The resulting units have demonstrated ongoing and sustained learning gains for both gifted and promising learners in the subject areas of language arts (VanTassel-Baska et al., 2002), science (VanTassel-Baska et al., 1998), and social studies (Little et al., 2007). Each of these studies employed pre- and post- assessments to calibrate the nature and extent of advanced learning as well as to decide on grouping and instructional considerations during implementation. These studies and others using a systematic framework (e. g., Gavin et al., 2007) attest to the power of macro planning curriculum, using a predetermined model for organization and structure. These developed units of study also provide a basis for district-wide curriculum implementation or modeling for further curriculum development in the common core areas of learning.

Instructional Strategies

There is a large and emergent literature on the use of specific strategies in working effectively with the gifted. Perhaps the strongest literature base exists for the use of inquiry-based approaches (VanTassel-Baska & Brown, 2007). However, other models have also been researched and found effective. Emphases on critical and creative thinking are well-supported by current research as well as older studies. Problem-solving approaches and models also have been found effective. The use of research skills to individualize curriculum and instruction for the gifted has gained much support within the field over the years, with several models organized to allow gifted students greater autonomy in learning (Betts, 2004; Reis & Renzulli, 2009). Moreover, the literature on the use of faster pacing and advanced curriculum is well supported by the 100 years of acceleration literature that includes longitudinal studies supporting the use of such strategies (Steenbergen-Hu et al., 2016).

Supportive Structures

The use of appropriate integrative technologies suggests that curriculum for the gifted may be provided in ways that increase depth and complexity in implementation (Besnoy, 2006; Siegle, 2020). For example, students may use their laptop technology to explore a real-world problem online, conversing with an expert on some aspect of the problem, obtaining an online video of the reporting of the problem in the media, and studying a three-dimensional model of the underlying aspects of the problem.

Moreover, the inclusion of a culturally relevant curriculum also enhances the learning of gifted students, especially if it is global in orientation and considers the backgrounds of the learning group to be taught (Kitano & Espinosa, 1995; Ford, 2006). The use of literature written by authors from different cultural groups, the inclusion of minority group perspectives on historical events, and the use of biographies and autobiographies of luminaries from different cultural groups all provide curriculum approaches for such inclusion.

The use of differentiation strategies and resources within gifted programs also accommodates diverse interests and needs of students from underrepresented groups. Career development opportunities such as mentorships and internships further the enhancement of diverse talent in a district as such options emphasize the real-life connections between schooling and a student's future aspirations and level of education and work (VanTassel-Baska & Baska, 2020).

The use of metacognitive strategies also enhances learning for the gifted, whether it is emphasizing reflection on learning in general or in more deliberate forms such as planning, monitoring, and assessing one's learning with regularity. To ensure such an emphasis, it should be woven into the fabric of the instructional system. For example, students may be asked to reflect on their increased understanding of important concepts they are learning and how those concepts apply to other disciplines. How does understanding systems in science enhance your understanding and application of the concept to economic policy in the United States? How does the concept of change have meaning for you personally?

The standards also call for an emphasis on talent development in discrete areas of curriculum of interest to gifted learners. The domains of cognitive, affective, aesthetic, social, and leadership are stressed as they provide a balance in the opportunities afforded gifted learners. These curriculum areas have a long history of support within the literature of the field. They suggest that school districts may want to integrate these areas for purposes of curriculum planning or to treat them as separate areas for emphasis and delivery of instruction. Thus, specialized arts curriculum for the gifted might represent a separate area for learning progression development as well as a leadership curriculum. Social and affective curriculum might be viewed as a separate strand also to be addressed differentially at each stage of development, although several curriculum models provide avenues for inclusion of these strands within a common core curriculum (e. g., The Parallel Curriculum Model).

Two Curriculum Models that Respond to the Demands of the Programming Standards

While new curriculum may be designed using the standards as the basis, it may be more prudent to consider existing models that have already designed curriculum that employs the features discussed thus far in this chapter. Two such models are discussed in respect to the features employed and the extent to which they are responsive to the revised (2019) national standards for curriculum planning and instruction.

Parallel Curriculum Model

The Parallel Curriculum Model (PCM) is a model for curriculum planning based on the composite work of Tomlinson et al. (2008). The heuristic model employs four dimensions, or parallels that can be used singly or in combination. The parallels are the core curriculum, the curriculum of connections, the curriculum of practice, and the curriculum of identity. PCM assumes that the core curriculum is the basis for all other curricula, and it should be combined with any or all of the three other parallels. It is the foundational curriculum that is defined by a given discipline. National, state, and/or local school district's standards should be reflected in this dimension and are used as the basis for understanding relevant subjects within and across grade levels. The second parallel, the curriculum of connections, supports students in discovering the interconnectedness among and between disciplines of knowledge. It builds from the core curriculum and has students exploring those connections for both intra- and interdisciplinary studies. The third parallel, the curriculum of practice, also derives from the core curriculum. Its purpose is to extend students' understandings and skills in a discipline through application and promote student expertise as a practitioner of a given discipline. The last parallel, the curriculum of identity serves to help students think about themselves within the context of a particular discipline; to see how a particular discipline relates to their own lives. The curriculum of identity uses curriculum as a catalyst for self-definition and self-understanding. The authors suggest that the level of intellectual demand in employing all elements of the Parallel Curriculum Model should be matched to student needs. Units have been developed based on the model for use across content areas K-12 (Tomlinson et al., 2006).

Integrated Curriculum Model

The VanTassel-Baska (1986) Integrated Curriculum Model (ICM) was developed specifically for high-ability learners, based on research evidence of what works with the gifted in classroom contexts. It has three dimensions: (a) advanced content, (b) high-level process and product work, and (c) intra- and interdisciplinary concept development and understanding. VanTassel-Baska, with funding from the Jacob Javits Gifted and Talented Students Program, used the ICM to develop specific curriculum frameworks and underlying units of study in language arts, social studies, and science. The model was designed to demonstrate a way to use the content standards but go beyond them, using differentiation practices for the gifted.

The content dimension is the first component of the model and represents, in the unit development process, a total alignment with national and state standards. However, it also represents the use of appropriate advanced content that goes beyond the standards, often calibrating unit activities or reading choices to what typical students can do at higher grade levels in the content area. In addition to being aligned with standards, the content dimension was designed to represent the most exemplary curriculum in that subject area by using the research-based pedagogical practices that are effective and national reports emanating from the various subject areas. Thus, the content of the standards is the core area for beginning the differentiation process with respect to acceleration, adding complexity and depth, incorporating creativity demands, and increasing the challenge level.

The process-product dimension of the ICM focuses on the importance of designing curriculum that incorporates higher-level processing skills as a part of the challenge for students. Units of study systematically use a reasoning model, a research model, and some use a problem-solving model to ensure that students can manipulate these thinking skills within specific subject areas. In some instances, like science and literature, the subject area already incorporates higher-level thought in the use of the scientific research model and the study of literary elements that move from the concrete elements of character, plot, and setting to the abstract elements of theme, motivation, and structure. As students manipulate these skills, they are encouraged to generate a meaningful product that demonstrates their capacity to apply these higher-level skills effectively. In most units of study, the product or series of products are research oriented.

The third dimension of the model emphasizes the use of a higher-level macro concept that has meaning within and across subject areas and provides an interdisciplinary pathway to bind the curriculum together. It is the integrative glue that allows the model to be cohesive in design and implementation. The concepts used in the unit development process were those identified by scientists as the most critical for today's students to understand—concepts like change, systems, models, and scale. These concepts and their underlying generalizations guide the learning of specific content and amplify the use of higher-level skills and processes. Students continue to apply these concepts to their learning across subject areas and across grades, and to see ways they apply to their own lives.

A Comparison of the Two Models

The ICM was conceived to be integrative in design and implementation while the PCM has deliberately put the components on parallel tracks. They also diverge with respect to the treatment of affective development. In the PCM, the affective emphasis in the curriculum is a separate focus with respect to identity development and other aspects of affective development. In the ICM, the affective emphasis is woven into the fabric of the design using activities, questions, and assessments that stress student reflection and establishing personal relevance of the curriculum for one's life. By choosing books for discussion that employ gifted characters who face problems and issues similar to gifted students, the ICM curriculum also promotes affective understanding in the context of the real world. Both models employ multiple approaches and opportunities for social learning through collaborative project work and discussion.

Assessing Student Outcomes

Differentiating the assessment approaches in curriculum for the gifted is an essential part of the new standards, both in assessment and curriculum elements. Why is such differentiation required? Because typical assessment, usually defined as results on the state assessment test, is not sufficiently advanced to assess real learning of gifted students. Even though most state tests contain an "advanced level", it is not discriminating enough to discern the level of performance of gifted learners within a given domain. Moreover, there is often a misalignment between what is tested and what is taught in programs for the gifted. Often these tests, for example, do not assess higher-level thinking or problem-solving, both key features of such programs. Thus, a differentiated approach to assessment is required that employs a combination of the following approaches:

Preassessment—the use of assessments to understand what gifted learners already know before a unit of study begins in order to calibrate the appropriate level for curriculum intervention. These assessments may be end of year or semester tests on the current year curriculum in common core areas like spelling, vocabulary, math skills and concepts, and science concepts.

Off-level assessment—the use of achievement tests and ability-aptitude measures at one or two grade levels above recommended use to provide sufficient ceiling for gifted student performance. These tests then allow teachers to discriminate effectively gifted performance in a domain (e.g., identify what a gifted student does and does not know).

Portfolio assessment—the use of a collection of student work over time to make judgments about growth gains in one or more areas.

Performance-based assessment—the use of products or extended activities within or across domains to demonstrate higher-level thinking and problem-solving of gifted students.

Pre-post assessment of thinking—the use of an assessment that directly assesses the elevation of critical or creative thinking skills in gifted learners.

Research in gifted education indicates that curriculum-embedded performance-based assessments are reliable measures of student learning (Moon et al., 2005) and provide a means to assess higher-level thinking in content areas (VanTassel-Baska et al., 2002). Pre- and post-experiment concept maps have provided a valid and reliable measure for assessing changes in conceptual understanding (Nafiz, 2008). Curriculum-embedded science performance-based assessments were found to foster critical thinking with middle grade gifted students (Tali Tal & Miedijensky, 2005). Further, VanTassel-Baska et al. (2002) developed a process to construct valid and reliable measures of performance where the performance measures also have been found to be successful at identifying gifted students of color (VanTassel-Baska, Feng, & de Brux, 2007; VanTassel-Baska, Feng, & Evans, 2007).

Product-based assessments have proven useful in demonstrating gifted students' inventive qualities in constructing and implementing Type III activities (Renzulli & Callahan, 2008), and portfolio approaches have been employed as especially useful tools in schools for the gifted where integrative learning is stressed (Johnsen & Johnson, 2007). Because product development encompasses so many critical elements of differentiation for gifted learners, creation and assessment of products are important components of gifted education curriculum and instruction (Moon, 2015, Roberts & Inman, 2015).

Off-level assessment has been most strongly applied in the talent search literature both to identify advanced-level functioning but also to assess outcomes of learning using College Board Achievement tests with younger populations (see Webb et al., 2012). The use of Advanced Placement exams represents an off-level assessment approach, calibrated to first-year college. The International Baccalaureate Program and Talent Searches also use a similar off-level approach (Olszewski-Kubilius & Kulieke, 2008). The importance of getting an accurate picture of what individual students are capable of doing academically cannot be overestimated. Thomson and Olszewski-Kubilius (2014) have noted that the use of these measures enhances our understanding of how to counsel students and parents in the talent development process as well as provide educators cognitive profiles useful for curriculum planning in estimating learning levels of this population.

All of these assessment approaches are viable ways to gain insight into gifted student learning as a result of using a differentiated curriculum and instructional template. Choosing a suitable approach may depend on several factors such as availability of tests, familiarity with the approach, desire to create performance-based tools, or relevance to the nature of the curriculum outcomes selected for the program.

How Might the Curriculum Planning and Instruction Standard be Employed?

Most gifted programs will not be starting from scratch in using the revised Curriculum Planning and Instruction Standard. Thus, there is a need to think about how to go about the process of alignment to the standard, including the student outcomes and evidence-based practices. In the area of curriculum planning and instruction, there are several ways they might be employed. A few ideas follow:

1. To create coherent curriculum documents that include a curriculum framework and learning progressions for each subject area.
   The task of creating such documents constitutes the heart of curriculum development work in a school district and sets the stage for

the nature of the programs to unfold. The revised standards offer an opportunity to revisit your existing curriculum framework and update it as necessary.

2. To design new curriculum.

The revised curriculum planning and instruction standards may call for new curriculum to be developed in order to close a gap revealed by a discrepancy analysis. This may take the form of units or syllabi that respond to need areas such as in the social emotional areas of self-advocacy and resilience.

3. To revise existing curriculum.

Sometimes districts have curriculum in place that needs to be upgraded for better alignment and differentiation with revised standards. A review of your curriculum provides a chance to consider how well it is responding to the needs of your gifted students and what revisions might need to be made.

4. To provide exemplars of differentiated curriculum.

Educators from general and special education backgrounds need to have a sense of what a differentiated curriculum for the gifted looks like. Published research-based materials used with the gifted provide good exemplars to share with educators not trained in gifted education.

5. To train teachers in differentiated curriculum, instruction, and assessment.

Curriculum development is always followed by professional development of educators responsible for implementing it. In this way, assurance of fidelity of implementation is made. New standards call for adaptation in the curriculum at various stages of development which in turn calls for extension of professional learning in key areas such as project-based learning and independent project learning.

Recommendations for Getting Started

1. Do a gap analysis of current curriculum and revisions needed. Work with a district team to determine priorities across a three-year period as changes cannot be done quickly. The following Yes/No checklist may be a good place to start the analysis.

The curriculum currently addresses:

__Y/N Alignment with relevant content standards?

__Y/N Comprehensive scope and sequence (i.e., learning progressions) of opportunities in common core curriculum areas?

__Y/N Use of acceleration techniques, including preassessment, formative assessment, and pacing?

__Y/N Use of differentiation strategies?

__Y/N Adaptation or replacement of the core curriculum?

__Y/N Use of culturally sensitive curriculum approaches leading to cultural competence?

__Y/N Use of inquiry-based strategies?

__Y/N Use of research-based materials?

__Y/N Use of strategies that teach critical and creative thinking, research, and problem-solving skills?

__Y/N Use of information technologies?

__Y/N Use of metacognitive strategies?

__Y/N Use of community resources?

__Y/N Talent development in areas of aptitude and interest in various domains (cognitive, affective, aesthetic)?

2. Tackle the big-picture items first. Most districts will need to engage in developing a curriculum framework, designing scope and sequence charts in common core areas, and aligning the gifted curriculum with the common core. Consequently, these tasks should be undertaken as a first priority as they provide the frame for other modifications to be made.

3. Develop a vertical planning task force who can undertake the curriculum changes most efficiently and effectively. By engaging teachers from relevant grade-level clusters, gifted education staff, and administrators relevant to the curriculum areas in the district, progress can be made more rapidly on the macro tasks.

4. Integrate the needed changes into the School Improvement Plan (SIP) model so that the gifted curriculum receives appropriate attention within a school setting and so that general and special educators have an understanding of the differentiation features required for gifted learners that go beyond the simple feature of choice.

5. Disseminate the developed documents through various professional development venues, including webinars, school-based workshops, and faculty discussions at relevant meetings. The sessions may be conducted by different members of the vertical planning team as appropriate. Provide educators with the knowledge, skills, and concepts in order to implement the changes effectively.

6. Monitor the progress of implementation through using school-based instructional specialists, mentor teachers, peer coaches, and administrative staff as appropriate. Trying out new practices precedes changing attitudes to institutionalize change (Guskey, 2000); thus,

the monitoring of such changes is crucial to gauging what needs to be done next.

7. Assess student outcomes for value-added benefits of the changes. As is suggested by the revised standards, student assessment tactics must be changed in order to understand authentic learning of the gifted. The coordinator of gifted education programming or whoever is designated in charge of the program must see this piece as a critical part of the role of managing the program.

8. Develop workshops for parents on the changes made in the gifted curriculum, instruction, and assessment features of programming. Celebrate the changes through a family night that emphasizes the strategies used and the student products that have resulted. In this way, the approaches can be diffused into the homes of gifted learners where strategies and projects can be replicated in home settings.

These steps must be viewed as action steps to be implemented across a multi-year period lest the tasks be seen as overwhelming. Some of them like program monitoring and assessment, however, should be undertaken annually.

Conclusion

This chapter has presented several ideas for implementing the revised curriculum standards at P–12 levels. It has provided models for incorporating curriculum planning tools such as a curriculum framework and learning progressions on which to build a sound curriculum base. It has also provided the research support for the suggestions made along with ideas for implementation. The work needed to meet these standards is ongoing as school districts recognize the primacy of a strong curriculum in building a powerful program emphasis for gifted education. The effort, however, is worth it in regard to the importance of the enterprise for our best learners.

References

Adams, C. M., Cotabish, A., & Dailey, D. (2015). *A teacher's guide to using the next generation science standards with gifted and advanced learners.* Prufrock Press.

Besnoy, K. (2006). How do I do that? Integrating web sites into the gifted education classroom. *Gifted Child Today, 29*(1), 28–34. https://doi.org/10.4219/gct-2006-191

Betts, G. (2004). Fostering autonomous learners through levels of differentiation. *Roeper Review, 26*(4), 190–191. https://doi.org/10.1080/02783190409554269

Ford, D. Y. (2006). Creating culturally responsive classrooms for gifted students. *Understanding Our Gifted, 19*(1), 10–14. https://eric.ed.gov/?id=EJ846094

Gavin, M. K., Casa, T. M., Adelson, J. L., Carroll, S. R., Sheffield, L. J., & Spinelli, A. M. (2007). Project M3: Mentoring mathematical minds—a research-based curriculum for talented elementary students. *Journal of Advanced Academics, 18*(4), 566–585. https://gifted.uconn.edu/wp-content/uploads/sites/961/2015/02/Project_M3.pdf

Guskey, T. R. (2000). *Evaluating professional development.* Corwin Press.

Hughes, C. E., Kettler, T., Shaunessy-Dedrick, E., & VanTassel-Baska, J. (2015). *A teacher's guide to using the Common Core State Standards with gifted and advanced learners in the English language arts.* Prufrock Press.

Johnsen, S. K., & Johnson, K. (2007). *Independent study program* (2nd ed.). Prufrock Press.

Johnsen, S. K., Ryser, G. R., & Assouline, S. (2014). *The practitioner's guide for using the common core state standards for mathematics.* Prufrock Press.

Kitano, M. K., & Espinosa, R. (1995). Language diversity and giftedness: Working with gifted English language learners. *Journal for the Education of the Gifted, 18*(3), 234–254. https://doi.org/10.1177/016235329501800302

Little, C., Feng, A., VanTassel-Baska, J., Rogers, K., & Avery, L. (2007). A study of curriculum effectiveness in social studies. *Gifted Child Quarterly, 51*(3), 272–284. https://doi.org/10.1177/0016986207302722

Moon, T. R. (2015). Alternative assessment. In J.A. Pucker & C.M Callahan (Eds.), *Critical issues and practices in gifted education* (pp. 45–55). National Association for Gifted Children.

Moon, T. R., Brighton, C. M., Callahan, C. M., & Robinson, A. (2005). Development of authentic assessments for the middle school classroom. *Journal of Secondary Gifted Education, 16*(2/3), 119–133. https://doi.org/10.4219/jsge-2005–477

Nafiz, K. (2008). A student-centered approach: Assessing the changes in prospective science teachers' conceptual understanding by concept mapping in a general chemistry classroom laboratory research. *Science Education, 38*(1), 91–110. https://doi.org/10.1007/s11165-007-9048-7

Olszewski-Kubilius, P., & Kulieke, M. J. (2008) Using off-level testing and assessment for gifted and talented students. In J. VanTassel-Baska (Ed.), *Alternative assessments with gifted and talented students* (pp. 89–106). Prufrock Press.

Reis, S. M., & Renzulli, J. S. (2009). The schoolwide enrichment model: A focus on students' strengths and interests. In J. S. Renzulli, E. J. Gubbins, K. S.

McMillen, R. D. Eckert, & C. A. Little (Eds.), *Systems and models for developing programs for the gifted and talented* (2nd ed., pp. 323–352). Creative Learning Press.

Renzulli, J., & Callahan, C. (2008) Product assessment. In J. VanTassel-Baska (Ed.), *Alternative assessments with gifted and talented students* (pp. 259–283). Prufrock Press.

Roberts, J. L., & Inman, T. F. (2015) *Assessing differentiated student products: A protocol for development and evaluation* (2nd ed). Prufrock Press.

Siegle, D. (2020). I have an idea I need to share: Using technology to enhance brainstorming. *Gifted Child Today*, 43(3), 205–211. https://doi.org/10.1177/1076217520919967

Steenbergen-Hu, S., Makel, M. C., & Olszewski-Kubilius, P. (2016). What one hundred years of research says about the effects of ability grouping and acceleration on K–12 students' academic achievement: Findings of two second-order meta-analyses. *Review of Educational Research*, 86(4), 849–899. https://doi.org/10.3102/0034654316675417

Tali Tal, R., & Miedijensky, S. (2005). A model of alternative embedded assessment in a pull-out enrichment program for the gifted. *Gifted Education International*, 20(2), 166–186. https://doi.org/10.1177/026142940502000208

Thomson, D., & Olszewski-Kubilius, P. (2014). The increasingly important role of off-level testing in the context of the talent development perspective. *Gifted Child Today*, 37(1) 33–40. https://doi.org/10.1177/1076217513509619

Tomlinson, C. A., Kaplan, S. N., Purcell, J. H., Leppien, J. H. Burns, D. E., Strickland, C. A. (Eds.) (2006). *The parallel curriculum in the classroom, Book 2: Units for application across the content areas, K-12*. Corwin Press.

Tomlinson, C. A., Kaplan, S. N., Renzulli, J. S., Purcell, J. K., Burns, D. E., Strickland, C. A., & Imbeau, M. B. (2008). *The parallel curriculum: A design to develop learner potential and challenge advanced learners*. Corwin Press.

VanTassel-Baska, J. (1986). Effective curriculum and instructional models for talented students. *Gifted Child Quarterly*, 30(4), 164–169. https://doi.org/10.1177/001698628603000404

VanTassel-Baska, J. (2003). *Curriculum planning and instructional design for gifted learners*. Love Publishing.

VanTassel-Baska, J., & Baska, A. (2020) *Curriculum planning and instructional design for gifted learners*. Prufrock Press.

VanTassel-Baska., J., Bass., G., Ries, R., Poland, D., & Avery, L. D. (1998). A national study of science curriculum effectiveness with high ability students. *Gifted Child Quarterly*, 42(4), 200–211. https://doi.org/10.1177/001698629804200404

VanTassel-Baska, J., & Brown, E. (2007). Towards best practice: An analysis of the efficacy of curriculum models in gifted education. *Gifted Child Quarterly*, 51(4), 342–358. https://doi.org/10.1177/0016986207306323

VanTassel-Baska, J., Feng, A., & deBrux, E. (2007). A longitudinal study of identification and performance profiles of Project STAR performance task-identified gifted students. *Journal for the Education of the Gifted*, *31*(1), 7–34. https://doi.org/10.4219/jeg-2007–517

VanTassel-Baska, J., Feng, A., & Evans, B. (2007). Patterns of identification and performance among gifted students identified through performance tasks: A three year analysis. *Gifted Child Quarterly*, *51*(3), 218–231. https://doi.org/10.1177/0016986207302717

VanTassel-Baska, J., Johnson, D., & Avery, L. D. (2002). Using performance tasks in the identification of economically disadvantaged and minority gifted learners: Findings from Project STAR. *Gifted Child Quarterly*, *46*(2), 110–123. https://doi.org/10.1177/001698620204600204

VanTassel-Baska, J., & Little, C. (Eds.) (3rd ed.). (2017). *Content-based curriculum for gifted learners*. Prufrock Press.

VanTassel-Baska, J., & Stambaugh, T. (2006a). *Comprehensive curriculum for gifted learners* (3rd ed.). Allyn & Bacon.

VanTassel-Baska, J., & Stambaugh, T. (2006b). Developing key curriculum products. In J. VanTassel-Baska & T. Stambaugh (Eds.), *Comprehensive curriculum for gifted learners* (3rd ed., pp. 17–30). Allyn & Bacon.

VanTassel-Baska, J., & Stambaugh, T. (2006c). Using technology to supplement gifted curriculum. In J. VanTassel-Baska & T. Stambaugh (Eds.), *Comprehensive curriculum for gifted learners* (3rd ed., pp. 290–308). Allyn & Bacon.

VanTassel-Baska, J., Zuo, L., Avery, L., & Little, C. (2002). A curriculum study of gifted-student learning in the language arts. *Gifted Child Quarterly*, *46*(1), 30–43. https://doi.org/10.1177/001698620204600104

Webb, R. M., Lubinski, D., & Benbow, C. P. (2012) Mathematical facile adolescents with math-science aspirations: New perspectives on their educational and vocational development. *Journal of Educational Psychology*, *94*(4),785–794. https://doi.org/10.1037/0022–0663.94.4.785

6

Differentiation: Standards Inform Best Practice

Julia Link Roberts

"Differentiation provides the arena for children to show what they know" (Kaplan, webinar, May 19, 2020). Differentiation allows students to demonstrate what they know and are able to do—what they have learned and at what levels they are ready to perform. In order to do just that, differentiation must be more than different; rather, it must be different with a purpose. Differentiation is "the match of the curriculum and learning experiences to learners ... to facilitate ongoing continuous progress for all students" (Roberts & Inman, 2015a, p. 5). In the broadest sense, differentiation includes acceleration and enrichment as strategies that allow curriculum to be matched to learners. Modification to the curriculum may address readiness, interests, and profiles of learners. Differentiation includes modifications to the content, process, product, assessment, and the learning environment (Tomlinson, 2014, p. 198).

Perhaps it would seem that the Programming Standard 3: Curriculum Planning and Instruction would be the only standard to examine for a chapter on differentiation; however, this standard cannot stand alone for planning and implementing defensible differentiation. Instead, it is important for educators to review and consider all of the standards as each includes elements that are important as teachers make accommodations to facilitate students

DOI: 10.4324/9781003236863-6

learning at optimum levels. Effective differentiation requires that educators understand all six of the standards and how they intertwine and support each other.

Examples from various standards in the 2019 Pre-K–Grade 12 Gifted Programming Standards that tie to differentiating include the following:

- Standard 1 highlights the need for "cognitive growth and psychosocial skills that support their talent development" (1.5., p. 7).
- Standard 2 states that "students with gifts and talents demonstrate growth commensurate with abilities in cognitive, social-emotional, and psychosocial areas" (2.4., p. 9).
- Standard 3 points out the need to "demonstrate growth commensurate with their abilities each school year" (3.1., p. 10).
- Standard 4 emphasizes the importance of developing "self-awareness, self-advocacy, self-efficacy, confidence, resilience, independence, curiosity, and risk taking" (4.1., p. 12).
- Standard 5 includes the phrase "to continuously advance their talent development and achieve their learning goals" (5.4., p. 15).
- Standard 6 states, "Students develop their gifts and talents as a result of educators who are lifelong learners, participating in ongoing professional learning and continuing education opportunities" (6.4., p. 17).

These standards combine to establish the underpinnings for differentiating as well as to set individual and group goals for students with gifts and talents.

Rationale for Differentiation

Students differ in many ways no matter what their ages are, and these differences require opportunities for learning to match those differences if learning is optimal. When the one-size-fits-all approach to learning is used, opportunities for learning are missed for those who need more complex content as well as for those who need more basic content. Students also require different paces for their learning if learning potential is optimal. Students need an appropriate level of challenge—not too much and not too little. The appropriate level of challenge to promote learning is the Zone of Proximal Development (ZPD) which is the level at which one can perform without support and the potential level of performance (Vygotsky, 1997). The appropriate level of challenge is above the ZPD, but not too far above that level. Most of all, learning experiences must engage the students in learning with the realization that there is "no finish line for learning" (Tomlinson & Moon, 2013, p. 4).

Wide Range of Student Differences in Classrooms

Differentiation is necessary in order to be free from expectations imposed by age and grade. There is a wide range of readiness levels among children and young people of any particular age or grade in heterogeneous classrooms.

> [R]esearch suggests that instructional differentiation is difficult to accomplish and thus is rarely implemented well, likely due to the enormous distribution of student ability in elementary school classrooms (e.g., up to 11 grade levels of reading performance in Grade 4 and 5 classrooms). Although a good idea in theory, the nature of our age-based, grade-level-focused system prevents differentiation from being implemented consistently or effectively.
>
> (Makel et al., 2016, p. 10)

Teachers recognize the wide range of differences that is present in any classroom. Differences in levels of readiness (prior knowledge related to a topic), interest in a specific topic, and learner preferences vary among children and young people. Thus, it is important to differentiate in all classrooms, including those in which children who are advanced in one or more content areas are homogeneously grouped.

Current Practice

The current picture on differentiation is mixed. Although it is offered as the most frequently used service for gifted students, the implementation is less often observed in classrooms.

When surveyed, state officials responded that the most frequently offered service was differentiation (Rinn et al, 2020). Differentiation in the general education classroom was the number one service reported in 33 states regarding Pre-Kindergarten and Kindergarten, 34 states regarding Grades 1–3, 33 states regarding Grades 4–5 or 6, and 33 states regarding Grades 6 or 7–8 (pp. 22–23). The preponderance of differentiation as the major service offered gifted students emphasizes the importance of differentiation in classrooms across the United States.

VanTassel-Baska and Hubbard (2018) reported a study of differentiation practices in which 329 elementary, middle, and high school classrooms in 57 schools were observed. They found "Most strategies that are markers of differentiated practice were not evident in the majority of classrooms and schools across the districts studied" (p. 2). "Whole class instruction or small group work without differentiation for advanced learners was the norm for elementary and middle school cluster-grouped classes" (p. 3). VanTassel-Baska et al. (2020) described their findings from classroom observations as "a portrait of the underutilization of differentiated strategies and materials" (p. 162).

Peters et al. (2017) published a study entitled "Should Millions of Students Take a Gap Year? Large Numbers of Students Start the School Year Above Grade Level." This study found "among American elementary and middle school students, 20% to 49% in English Language Arts and 14% to 37% in mathematics scored 1 year or more above grade level" (p. 229). These results highlight the need for assessing the starting point for students in English Language Arts and mathematics and then differentiating instruction to allow all students to be learning every day in school.

Differentiating to facilitate continuous progress for all students has not been the prevailing message in many schools across the United States. "Bringing students to grade-level proficiency has been a focus of U.S. education policy and practice for well over a decade, but little attention has been devoted to addressing the learning needs of those students who already have achieved this proficiency target before setting foot in the classroom" (Makel et al., 2016, p. 9). Emphasis in schools has often been on getting students ready to perform on the state assessment. Johnsen et al. (2020) found that "both teachers and administrators were concerned about covering the content related to state tests. These concerns inhibited implementation of more differentiated practices" (p. 216). Thinking about addressing the instructional needs of children with gifts and talents, Pfeiffer stated, "Gifted students in the schools are among the most underserved special needs population in American schools" (2020, p. 1511).

Learning Requires Appropriate Challenge

Classroom instruction that is one-size-fits-all for students of a particular grade lacks challenge for students who already know the material or would remember it when it is presented once and it provides too much challenge for children who need more time and less complexity. The appropriate level of challenge is the ZPD (Vygotsky, 1997), but it would not be teaching too far above that level. The learning experiences need to require effort and thinking in order to successfully complete them. Easy A's do not help children develop a work ethic or create the feeling of succeeding due to important thinking and effort.

Grouping for Instructional Purposes

1.5.1. Educators use evidence-based approaches to grouping and instruction that promote cognitive growth and psychosocial and social-emotional skill development for students with gifts and talents.

5.1.3. Educators use multiple forms of evidence-based grouping, including clusters, resource rooms, special classes, or special schools.

In order to provide the appropriate levels of instruction to match learner readiness to learn in a specific content, it is important to narrow the range of readiness levels in the class. Grouping can accomplish this task, and, even then, differentiating is important to do.

Grouping for instructional purposes takes many forms, some of which are flexible and some of which are in place for the year. The reason to group must always tie to instruction. Sometimes the instructional purpose may be to group students by interests. For example, implementing this type of grouping might involve putting together students who are interested in arts, economics, or politics of the 1920s in U.S. history. At other times, students might be grouped within a class by those who already know more than the basic information about cells, those who know the basic information, and those who have little background or understanding of the basics of cells. Rogers and Hay (2020) state:

> If we group high-talent students in any form to extend the depth, breadth, and complexity of their learning, they will thrive, improve in their motivation, and form social relationships that result from the sharing of their interests and talents. Grouping becomes an effective vehicle that is the starting point for teachers to begin their differentiation for talent development.
>
> (p. 139)

Grouping makes it possible to address the readiness of students to learn new content and enhance their skills.

Special programming placements can enhance learning for children with interest and readiness to learn in a particular area. For example, a magnet program one day a week can build expertise in science and mathematics or the arts. Students may be clustered in classrooms with teachers who are knowledgeable about differentiation strategies to ensure that differentiation occurs, or they may learn in self-contained classrooms where students learn with other gifted and talented peers throughout the school day. Students may receive services through pull-out classes, where gifted and talented students are grouped for a portion of the day or a portion of the week. It is very important to ensure that children from all backgrounds have opportunities to participate in all placement options; and all backgrounds include children from all economic levels, all ethnic and racial groups as well as children for whom English is an additional language and those who are twice exceptional. An important consideration for grouping is to find children who share interests and have advanced ability. Having time to spend with "idea-mates" helps young people build positive self-concepts (Roberts & Boggess, 2011, p. 62).

Planning

3.1. *Curriculum Planning. Students with gifts and talents demonstrate academic growth commensurate with their abilities each school year.*

3.1.2. *Educators design a comprehensive and cohesive curriculum and use learning progressions to develop differentiated plans for Pre-K through grade 12 students with gifts and talents.*

The first step for differentiation begins with planning—planning the classroom climate and then planning the unit of study. Neither can be overlooked if differentiation is to be effective.

Planning the Classroom Climate to Support Differentiation

Program Standard 1 *Learning and Development*

Description. Educators understand the variations in learning and development in cognitive, affective, and psychosocial areas between and among individuals with gifts and talents, creating learning environments that encourage awareness and understanding of interest, strengths, and needs; cognitive growth, social and emotional, psychosocial skill development in school, home, and community settings.

Program Standard 4 *Learning Environments*

Description. Learning environments foster a love of learning, personal and social responsibility, multicultural competence, and interpersonal and technical communication skills for leadership to ensure specific student outcomes.

A classroom climate for effective differentiation must support variations in assignments based on interests, strengths, and readiness related to the topic/concept being studied. Students must understand that everyone in the class is not ready for identical learning experiences, so they cannot expect to always be completing the same assignments on the same time schedule. Students ready for advanced learning do not need to do what all others in the class do and then more, but rather they need to be engaging in learning at levels at which they are ready to learn.

Educators must communicate with parents to let them know not to expect all young people to be completing the same assignments on the same schedule. Parents must understand that differentiation promotes learning which, of course, is the goal of school.

Planning the Unit of Study

Planning is the first step in developing curriculum, and meaningful preassessment is possible only after the intended outcomes are established and connections are made to the content standards. Only after that initial step has been taken can the teacher preassess to determine which students have similar levels of readiness and/or interests in the content to be studied. Planning needs to include "(a) advanced content, (b) high-level process and product work, and (c) intra- and interdisciplinary concept development and understanding" (VanTassel-Baska, 2018, p. 352). It is important to plan for the highest level of instruction first rather than doing that as an additional responsibility.

Roberts and Inman (2015b) place planning at the top of the list for teachers who implement effective differentiation. The question that accompanies the planning process is "What do I want students to know, understand, and be able to do?" (p. 47).

Content

> 3.1.4. *Educators design differentiated curriculum that incorporates advanced, conceptually challenging, in-depth, and complex content for students with gifts and talents.*

Outcomes for the unit of study provide the starting point for planning. Only when the outcomes are planned can learning experiences be designed to focus on the stated outcomes rather than selected because they are favorite or already planned learning experiences.

The first element of effective differentiation is solid content that is important to learn. Content must be organized for students to be introduced to major concepts, themes, and problems that offer complexity and in-depth study. State standards provide guidance in the choice of content. Content must include basic concepts in various content areas and also abstract concepts that are necessary for problem solving and delving into issues. Content knowledge provides the necessary background to allow students to engage in complex problem solving.

Children and young people have opportunities to enhance their learning when a universal theme ties the learning to generalizations that cut across disciplines (Kaplan, 2009; Roberts & Roberts, 2015).

> The use of universal concepts as a theme or organizing element allows for curriculum to be inclusive of a broader and larger scope of content, processes, and products. The theme provides the overarching construct under which a variety of topical areas of study can be subsumed.
>
> (Kaplan, 2009, p. 240)

For example, the universal theme of patterns has key connections in science, music, history, language arts, art, mathematics, and languages. The universal theme of patterns can be highlighted as students learn about weather, life cycles, dances, periods of art, poetry, and immigration. Generalizations to accompany any study of patterns include patterns repeat, patterns predict, and patterns maintain order. Complex content emphasizes issues and problems related to the concept/content and tied to interdisciplinary themes. It is so important to have knowledge and understanding of concepts prior to using that information in creative ways.

Figure 6.1 illustrates the basics of learning experiences—content, process, and product. Each component of learning experiences has implications for differentiating to address learners' levels of readiness and interests in the topic/concept as well as interests in ways to demonstrate learning.

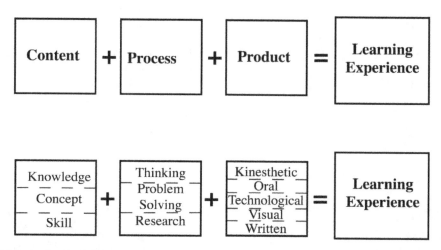

Figure 6.1 Learning Experiences

Note: From Writing units that remove the learning ceiling in *Methods and Materials for Teaching the Gifted* (3rd ed., p. 233). By J. L. Roberts and R. A. Roberts, 2015, Prufrock Press. Copyright 2015 by Prufrock Press. Reprinted with permission.

Process

3.4.3. Educators use models of inquiry to engage students in critical thinking, creative thinking, and problem-solving strategies, particularly in their domain(s) of talent, both to reveal and address the needs of students with gifts and talents.

Learning experiences for effective differentiation must be designed with opportunities to engage in high-level thinking, preparing students to think from different perspectives about content, problem solve, and generate new knowledge. Creative and critical thinking combine and serve key roles when students are engaged in problem solving. Higher-level thinking is the necessary component of engaging learning tasks. Deeper learning often is seeded in problem-based approaches.

Thinking skills have been central in designing learning experiences for gifted learners for decades. Figure 6.2 highlights the skills that are recognized as a priority for those who will succeed in 21st century careers.

in 2020

1. Complex Problem Solving
2. Critical Thinking
3. Creativity
4. People Management
5. Coordinating with Others
6. Emotional Intelligence
7. Judgment and Decision Making
8. Service Orientation
9. Negotiation
10. Cognitive Flexibility

in 2015

1. Complex Problem Solving
2. Coordinating with Others
3. People Management
4. Critical Thinking
5. Negotiation
6. Quality Control
7. Service Orientation
8. Judgment and Decision Making
9. Active Listening
10. Creativity

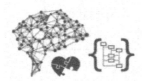

Figure 6.2 Top 10 Skills
Note: Future of Job Reports, World Economic Forum, 2020.

Product

Products provide students with opportunities to demonstrate what they have learned, and they offer various choices that capitalize on student strengths and interests. Choice of products may provide motivation, yet a high-level cognitive process is the necessary component to make the learning experience challenging. The choice of learning experiences without being a match to the students' readiness to learn is not effective differentiation if they lack challenge even though they are allowed choice. The learning experiences with no cognitive challenge could be compared to working on building strength with only two-pound weights.

There are times teachers want students to demonstrate learning and the specific product does not matter. In these cases, it is useful to offer a variety of products that tap interests in art, technology, drama, or writing with the goal of capturing interest with the product choices. A choice of three written products is not the same as providing product choices with a variety of types of products. For example, students who are so engaged in technology may put maximum effort into creating products using technology even with luke-warm interest in the topic.

Products can be categorized in various ways. Roberts and Inman (2015a) categorize products as kinesthetic, oral, technological, visual, and written (pp. 9–11). There are other ways to categorize products, and it is important for teachers to have categories of products in mind as it alerts them when product choices offered are limited to one or two categories, usually the teacher's most comfortable choices for completing and/or assessing products. The Developing and Assessing Product Tool (DAP Tool; Roberts & Inman, 2015a) is a protocol for developing and assessing products, eliminating the need for developing numerous rubrics when choice of products is offered. The DAP Tool also provides guidance for students when developing products. Figure 6.3 provides a list of potential products.

Diverse Perspectives

3.3.1. Educators develop and use curriculum that is responsive and relevant to diversity that connects to students' real-life experiences and communities and includes multiple voices and perspectives.

3.3.3. Educators use high-quality, appropriately challenging materials that include multiple perspectives.

In order to engage learners with a range of experiences, it is important to plan content that addresses multiple perspectives. Diversity is present in every classroom, whether it is found in economic background, cultural experiences,

Advertisement (online)
Advertisement (print)
Advertisement (radio)
Advertisement (television)
Biography
Blog
Blueprint
Board Game
Book Cover
Bulletin Board
Cartoon
Case Study
Chart
Children's Book
Choral Reading
Collage
Collection
Column
Commercial
Computer Graphic
Computer Program
Costume
Dance
Debate
Demonstration
Diagram
Dialogue
Diorama
Document-Based Question
Documentary
Dramatic Presentation
Drawing
Editorial
Essay
Exhibit/Display
Experiment
Feature Article
Game
Graph

Graphic Organizer
Greeting Card
Illustrated Story
Interview (live)
Interview (recorded)
Interview (written)
Invention
Journal
Lesson
Letter (business)
Letter (friendly)
Letter to Editor
Mask
Matrix
Mathematical Formula
Mentorship
Mime
Mock Trial (attorney)
Mock Trial (defendant)
Mock Trial (judge)
Mock Trial (plaintiff)
Model
Monologue
Movie
Mural
Museum Exhibit
Musical
News Article
Newscast
Newsletter
Op Ed Article
Open Response
Oral History
Oral Presentation
Outline
Painting
Pamphlet
Peer Evaluation
Photo
Photo Essay

Plan
Play
Podcast
Poem
Political Cartoon
Poster
PowerPoint
Presentation
Prezi
Press Release
Public Service
Announcement (radio)
Public Service
Announcement (television)
Puppet
Puppet Show
Questionnaire/Survey
Research Paper
Review (Film, Book, etc.)
Science Fair Project
Sculpture
Scrapbook
Script
Service Learning Project
Short Story
Simulation
Skit
Song
Speech (oral)
Speech (written)
Story Telling
Technical Report
Timeline
Venn Diagram
Video Game
Volunteer Activity
Web Page
Wiki
Workshop
Written Report

Product List

Figure 6.3 Possible Products

Note: Adapted from *Assessing Differentiated Student Products: A Protocol for Development and Evaluation* (2nd ed., p. 12). By J. L. Roberts and T. F. Inman, 2015, Prufrock Press. Copyright 2015 by Prufrock Press. Adapted with permission.

and familial structures. Planning curriculum to engage students in learning content from multiple perspectives prepares students to think at high levels as well as to be citizens of their communities, state, country, and world. "The curriculum must not only be rigorous, but also provide students with the ability to see the world from the viewpoints of others, and it must be relevant to students' lives—their interests and experiences" (Wright et al., 2020, p. 22). It is important for educators to recognize that

> [G]ifted students (and all students) need to be engaged in learning that invites their cultural preferences into the classroom and tasks them with hands-on, experiential learning that requires them to be critical about the world around them. Critical and culturally relevant experiential education accomplishes these goals, especially for those historically underrepresented in gifted education.
>
> (Anderson & Coleman-King, 2020, p. 53)

The Culturally Responsive Equity-Based Bill of Rights for Gifted Students of Color (Ford et al, 2018) presents important expectations for the curriculum:

> Gifted students of color have the right to culturally relevant curriculum and instruction; authentic and multicultural content in all content areas; rigorous multicultural curriculum and materials that reflect their cultural, racial, and linguistic background and heritage; rigorous and authentic multicultural literature reflective of all cultures, and curricula that promotes cultural, racial, and linguistic pride.
>
> (p. 128)

Preassessment

3.1.5 Educators regularly use pre-assessments, formative assessments, and summative assessments to identify students' strengths and needs, develop differentiated content, and adjust instructional plans based on progress monitoring.

Perhaps the statement that supports preassessment so well is the title of an article by Julian Stanley (2000), "Helping Students Learn Only What They Don't Already Know." That is what learning is all about—learning new things on an ongoing basis.

While the first step in effective differentiation is planning, the second step is preassessment. The questions to be answered are "Who already knows, understands, and/or can use the content or demonstrate the skills? Who needs additional support in order to know, understand, and/or demonstrate the skills?" (Roberts & Inman, 2015b, p. 11).

"Diagnostic assessment is as important to teaching as a physical exam is to prescribing an appropriate medical regimen" (McTighe & O'Connor, 2005, p. 141). Not gathering information about what students know and are able to do in regard to an upcoming unit of study is very much like driving a car at night without the lights turned on. Responsible drivers would not do that.

Why Preassess?

The goal of preassessing is to provide the teacher with information needed to determine the levels of student knowledge and skills related to the outcomes of the unit of study. "Preassessment makes differentiation strategies defensible" (Roberts & Inman, 2015b, p. 48). Information from preassessing students helps the teacher put students into groups in order to tailor learning experiences to students' levels of readiness (what do they already know about the topic and what degree of skill development do they have related to the outcomes planned) as well as interests in the topic being studied that can be incorporated into projects or project choices. Teachers who want to see that all students make continuous progress will gather information about what students know and are able to do as well as their interests in the topic to be studied and then use that information to differentiate for students or clusters of students.

Students who already know the material being studied find it difficult to stay engaged in learning. The situation can be compared to the driver who is slowed down in heavy traffic, perhaps stopped for a while. The feeling generated is one of frustration. The same is true for students who know the content. Differentiated learning experiences can eliminate that frustration by elevating the thinking that students engage in as other students are learning at levels at which the preassessment indicates they are ready to proceed.

Ways to Preassess

Preassessment offers the information teachers need to analyze the appropriateness of learning experiences for individual learners and clusters of learners. Once the teacher has the preassessment information, it is imperative to use it. Not using what is gleaned during the preassessment misses the opportunity to relate to students, learning about their interests related to the concept or topic being studied as well as what they know and are able to do in relation to what they are soon to be studying.

Preassessment strategies are numerous, and they do not need to be long and time consuming to administer. The type of preassessment used depends on what information will be useful in grouping the students based on readiness and interest in the topic/concept to be studied. Discerning what students know about a topic or concept can be as simple as a four or five-minute opportunity to write about the topic or concept. Another way to gather information about what students know, want to learn, and how they want to learn is a T-W-H Chart (Roberts & Boggess, 2020) (see Figure 6.4). The T column provides the opportunity for students to tell what they think about the topic/concept to be studied, the W allows a place to tell what they want to learn about the topic/concept, and the H is the time to share how they would want to learn about the topic/concept. Other appropriate information to preassess relates to what types of products would be motivating to specific students. Such information can be gained with a form about interests in the topic and ways in which students would like to engage in learning about the topic and how it will be presented (Roberts & Boggess, 2020; see Figure 6.5).

T - W - H CHART		
Topic/Unit_____	name_____	
What do you **Think** about this topic?	What do you **W**ant to learn about this topic?	**H**ow do you want to learn about this topic?

Figure 6.4: T-W-H Chart

Note. From *Teacher's Survival Guide: Gifted Education* (p. 105), by J. L. Roberts and J. R. Boggess, 2020, Prufrock Press. Copyright 2020 by Prufrock Press. Reprinted with permission.

Preassessment for a Project on COVID-19

The coronavirus changed lives dramatically in 2020. A pandemic had been predicted and written about previously; however, the preparation for such a pandemic varied a lot from country to country. This time was a defining moment for individuals across the globe - a time to remember and share with your children.

In preparation for conducting a study of one aspect of the pandemic, please respond to the following.

◆ Circle all that apply:
   1) I was most interested in the statistical projections related to the spread of the coronavirus.
   2) I was very interested in the social distancing required to slow the pandemic and the changes to life that social distancing required.
   3) My time and attention during the pandemic was focused on learning remotely.
   4) I didn't pay much attention to COVID-19.
◆ Circle the response that best applies to you.
   1) I enjoy interviewing to learn.
   2) I have no experience interviewing for a project but think I would like to give it a try.
   3) I have interviewed for a project but would prefer getting information another way.
◆ I would prefer to show my results in a:
   1) Video
   2) Series of illustrations or charts to accompany a report
   3) Project of my choice (with teacher approval)

Figure 6.5. Preassessment for a Project on COVID-19

Note: From *Teacher's Survival Guide: Gifted Education* (2nd ed., p. 108). By J. L. Roberts and J. R. Boggess, 2020. Copyright 2020 by Prufrock Press. Reprinted with permission.

Strategies to Differentiate

3.5.2. Educators select, adapt, and use a repertoire of instructional strategies to differentiate instruction for students with gifts and talents.

With the first step in effective differentiation relating to planning and the second step directed towards preassessment, the third step is to ask the differentiating question: What can I do for him, her, or them so they can make continuous progress and extend their learning? (Roberts & Inman, 2015b, p. 11).

Effective differentiation depends on students and parents understanding that all students will not always be engaging in the same learning experiences because their starting points with learning about a particular topic differ as do their interests in the specific topic being studied. What parents and students must also realize is that everyone learns from each other as the various aspects learned about the topic are shared. For example, in a study of World War II, some students had the most interest in patterns on the various fronts while others were more intrigued by the leadership and others in life on the Home Front during this time period or the politics during this time in U.S. history.

Although there are no specific strategies that are a "must" to master for differentiation, there are strategies that will facilitate all students learning what they are ready to learn. Preassessment results will help the teacher match learning experiences to students and clusters of students. No matter the strategies selected, "all students participate in respectful work" (Tomlinson, 1999, p. 12).

Passow (1982) offered a set of three questions to determine if curriculum is appropriate for all students or for some students. *Would* all children want to be involved in such learning experiences? *Could* all children participate in such learning experiences? *Should* all children be expected to succeed in such learning experiences? (p. 12). These three questions provide criteria for assessing whether learning experiences should be available to all children or for children who are advanced and ready for that particular learning experience at this time. Remember, coaches do not wait until all eighth graders have the requisite skills to play varsity ball, rather they offer ongoing opportunities for those with advanced skills to make continuous progress.

Tiering

Tiering provides the opportunity for all students in the class to be studying one topic and engaging in respectful learning experiences yet approaching the topic or concept from different perspectives. Learning experiences are matched to the students' readiness to learn about the topic or their preferred way to demonstrate what they know.

A study of the heart provides an example of tiering based on readiness with a specific content (Roberts & Boggess, 2012). Students who are early in their knowledge of the heart are asked to create a diagram of the human heart tracing the flow of blood through the heart and lungs. Another cluster of students is ready to study two diseases that affect the heart and write a blog or article about one of them. Other students are given the opportunity to design an apparatus to detect a human heartbeat. As with all effective differentiation, students have the opportunity to learn from each other as they have studied the topic or concept from different perspectives, learning at a level matched to one's readiness to learn that specific content.

Choice With Challenge

Choice of learning experiences related to a specific topic or concept can be motivating to students; however, choice without challenge does not lead to continuous progress. Effective differentiation is designed to offer a choice of learning experiences that would all provide challenge. Beware of giving choices in hopes that students will make the choice that would be challenging as it is likely that some or many students will select the easiest choice.

Open-endedness allows for children to demonstrate what they know and can do. Right-answer questions don't allow for that opportunity for children to present their knowledge based on their experiences in their cultures.

Differentiating With Interests

An example of differentiating that addresses preferred ways of knowing relates to the concept of forces and motion. After the class works together in the lab on an experiment demonstrating forces and motion, the teacher passes out the next assignment based on what is

known about students' interests. One group is asked to use the principles of forces and motion in writing an essay describing a sports car coming down a mountain (they are the writers). Another group is tasked with designing a different experiment from the one they completed in the lab and implementing the experiment (they enjoy thinking up solutions). Still another group is to describe examples of forces and motion in their environment and take photos or make illustrations (they are the practical thinkers). Everyone is studying the same concept yet will have different perspectives to add to the discussion when they share what they learned.

Formative Assessment

2.4.1. *Educators use differentiated formative assessments to develop learning experiences that challenge students with gifts and talents.*

Preassessment is one type of formative assessment, yet it was separated in this discussion as it comes as the first step beyond the planning while other types of formative assessment are ongoing throughout the unit as learning proceeds.

Formative assessment is essential to the learning process. Formative assessment comes from the teacher, peers, and the learner. Black and Wiliam (2009) state that formative assessment consists of five strategies:

1. Clarifying and sharing learning intentions and criteria for success;
2. Engineering effective classroom discussions and other learning tasks that elicit evidence of student understanding;
3. Providing feedback that moves learners forward;
4. Activating students as instructional resources for one another; and
5. Activating students as the owners of their own learning. (p. 8)

Feedback, Feedforward, and Coaching

4.1.4. Educators provide feedback that promotes perseverance and resilience and focuses on effort, on evidence of potential to meet high standards, and on mistakes as learning opportunities.

Feedback to feed forward to coaching provides a trajectory that leads to the development of elite talent. Feedback allows for making corrections at a timely point to enhance learning. After all, feedback is the breakfast of champions. Feedback provides the information for improving and eliminating incorrect information or enhancing skill development. Feedforward is a different term for feedback as it focuses on what happens next to promote learning. Coaching is often done individually optimizing opportunities for reaching advanced or elite levels of performance. At each level—feedback, feedforward, and coaching—the goal is to improve learning or performance in order to be prepared for the future (see Figure 6.6).

The follow-up to feedback, feedforward, and coaching is what matters the most. Just taking one's temperature with no follow-up makes little difference to one's health. Formative assessment is the action that informs the student of what it takes to promote learning.

FEEDBACK ➡ **FEED FORWARD** ➡ **COACHING**

Figure 6.6 Feedback-Feed Forward-Coaching

Reflection

2.5. Students self-assess their learning progress.

Reflection requires skills that are essential both for enhancing learning in the present and for creating lifelong learners. Reflection is key to ensuring learning has occurred and for moving thoughts forward with questions that remain unanswered and questions that take thinking beyond present questions and promote forward thinking. "All curricula for gifted students should attend to the need of gifted learners to reflect on what they have learned as well as engage in serious planning, monitoring, and assessing of that learning, especially when it applies to project work and research efforts" (VanTassel-Baska, 2018, p. 358).

Without reflection, performance the next time the student encounters a similar learning experience is likely to show no improvement over the former experience. Students who make a habit of reflecting on their learning experiences are empowered to be lifelong learners.

Professional Learning

6.4. Students develop their gifts and talents as a result of educators who are lifelong learners, participating in ongoing professional learning and continuing education opportunities.

"Given the heavy emphasis on differentiation in the general education classroom for pre-K through Grade 8, the importance of professional learning for general education teachers regarding gifted students and gifted education cannot be understated" (A. N. Rinn, personal communication, November 17, 2020).

> Despite common acceptance of the concept of differentiation, however, it is likely that preservice teacher education and professional development practices are not currently robust enough to support the broad changes necessary for teachers to implement comprehensive differentiation in ways that incorporate best practices and address the learning needs of contemporary student populations.
>
> (Tomlinson, 2014, p. 198)

Recommendations for professional learning in regard to differentiation are numerous. Professional learning to facilitate differentiation should:

- Include administrators as well as teachers in order to identify school goals in the area of differentiation (Johnsen et al., 2020),
- Target expectations of what teachers will do to differentiate in the classroom so it will focus on what is practical (Jolly & Jarvis, 2018; Van Tassel-Baska et al., 2020),
- Be differentiated for teachers with varying levels of experience and expertise with differentiating in their classrooms,
- Offer opportunities for coaching to practice in classrooms with no tie to teacher evaluation, and
- Receive "support from school administrators" (Little & Paul, 2017, p. 464).

Assessing Appropriateness of Curriculum for Advanced Learners

VanTassel-Baska (2017) offers important questions to judge appropriateness for differentiated curriculum for advanced learners:

- Is the curriculum sufficiently advanced for the strongest learners in the group?
- Is the curriculum complex enough for the best learners, requiring multiple levels of thinking, use of resources, and/or variables to manipulate?
- Is the curriculum sufficiently in-depth to allow students to study important issues and problems related to the topic under study?
- Is the curriculum sufficiently encouraging of creativity, stimulating open-ended responses and providing high-level choices?

(p. 16)

Conclusion

Differentiation for all cannot exclude children who are ready to learn at a more advanced pace and more complex levels than age-mates. Instead, opportunities must be planned and implemented that allow all students to make continuous progress. Remember, differentiating is not new as teachers have been expected to differentiate for students who need additional time and more basic content to reach proficiency or grade-level outcomes.

Providing differentiation for students who have already achieved grade-level standards and move on to advanced levels of learning is equally important. The end goal for effective differentiation is for all students to enjoy learning, make continuous progress, and become life-long learners.

The classroom climate to support effective differentiation needs to be in place at the beginning of the year and must be more than asking high-level questions occasionally. Rather, effective differentiation starts with students understanding that the classroom teacher supports each student learning every day in school; consequently, students will not be doing the same assignments on the identical schedule. Effective differentiation can be implemented to allow all students to learn what they are ready to learn, and all students include those who are gifted and talented.

The 2019 NAGC Pre-K–Grade 12 Gifted Programming Standards work together to guide teachers as they enhance their experiences differentiating in classrooms from the time children enter school until they graduate from high school. Differentiation is essential for creating life-long learners, ones who continue to be curious and enjoy challenges. The standards help educators as they collaborate with other educators and families. When everyone knows the guiding principles (i.e., the standards), it enhances opportunities of implementing them in providing quality gifted programming for young people throughout their school careers.

References

Anderson, B. N., & Coleman-King, C. (2020). Exploring critical and culturally relevant experiential learning for underserved students in gifted education. In J. H. Robins, J. L Jolly, F. A Karnes, & S. M. Bean (Eds.), *Methods & Materials for Teaching the Gifted* (5th ed., pp. 37–60). Prufrock Press.

Black, P., & Wiliam, D. (2009). Developing the theory of formative assessment. *Educational Assessment, Evaluation and Accountability*, 21(1), 5–31. https://doi.org/10.1007/s11092-008-9068-5

Ford, D. Y., Dickson, K. T., Davis, J. L., Scott, M. T., & Grantham, T. C. (2018). A culturally responsive equity-based bill of rights for gifted students of color. *Gifted Child Today*, 41(3), 125–129. https://doi.org/10.1177/1076217518769698

Jolly, J. L., & Jarvis, J. S. M. (Eds.) (2018). *Exploring gifted education: Australian & New Zealand perspectives*. Routledge.

Johnsen, S. K., Fearon-Drake, D., & Wisely, L. W. (2020). A formative evaluation of differentiation practices in elementary cluster classrooms. *Roeper Review*, 42(3), 206–218. https://doi.org/10.1080/02783193.2020.1765921

Kaplan, S. N. (2009). The grid: A model to construct differentiated curriculum for the gifted. In J. S. Renzulli, E. J. Gubbins, K. S. McMillen, R. D. Eckert, & C. A. Little (Eds.), *Systems & models for developing programs for the gifted & talented* (2nd ed., pp. 235–252). Prufrock Press.

Little, C. A., & Paul, K. A. (2017). Professional development to support successful curriculum implementation. In J. Van Tassel-Baska & C. A. Little (Eds.), *Content-based curriculum for high-ability learners* (3rd ed., pp. 461–481). Prufrock Press.

Makel, M., Matthews, M., Peters, S., Rambo-Hernandez, K., & Plucker, J. (2016). How can so many students be invisible? Large percentages of American students perform above grade level. https://edpolicy.education.jhu.edu/wpcontent/uploads/2016/08/Studentsinvisiblemasthead-FINAL.pdf

McTighe, J., & O'Connor, K. (2005). Seven practices for effective learning. *Educational Leadership*, 63(3), 10–17. www.ascd.org/publications/educational-leadership/nov05/vol63/num03/Seven-Practices-for-Effective-Learning.aspx

National Association for Gifted Children (2019). *Pre-K–Grade 12 Gifted Programming Standards*. Author. www.nagc.org/sites/default/files/standards/Intro%202019%20Programming%20Standards%281%29.pdf

Passow, A. H. (1982). Differentiated curricula for the gifted /talented: A point of view. In S. Kaplan, A. H. Passow, P. H. Phenix, S. Reis, J. S. Renzulli, I. Sato, L. Smith, E. P. Torrance, & V. Ward, *Curricula for the gifted: Selected proceedings of the First National Conference on Curriculum for the Gifted and Talented* (pp. 4–20). Ventura County Superintendent of Schools Office.

Peters, S. J, Rambo-Hernandez, Makel, M. C., Matthews, M. S., & Plucker, J. A. (2017). Should millions of students take a gap year? Large numbers of students start the school year above grade level, *Gifted Child Quarterly*, 6(3), 229–238. https://doi.org/10.1177/0016986212460084

Pfeiffer, S. I. (2020). Introduction: Psychology in the Schools special issue on the gifted. *Psychology in the Schools*. https://doi.org/10.1002/pit.22407

Rinn, A. N., Mun, R. U., & Hodges, J. (2020). *2018–2019 State of the states in gifted education*. National Association for Gifted Children and the Council for State Directors of Programs for the Gifted. www.nagc.org/2018–2019-state-states-gifted-education

Roberts, J. L., & Boggess, J. R. (Eds.) (2012). *Differentiating instruction with centers in the gifted classroom*. Prufrock Press.

Roberts, J. L., & Boggess, J. R. (2011). *Teacher's survival guide: Gifted education*. Prufrock Press.

Roberts, J. L., & Boggess, J. R. (2020). *Teacher's survival guide: A first-year teacher's guide to gifted education* (2nd ed.). Prufrock Press.

Roberts, J. L., & Inman, T. F. (2015a). *Assessing differentiated student products: A protocol for development and assessment* (2nd ed.). Prufrock Press.

Roberts, J. L., & Inman, T. F. (2015b). *Strategies for differentiating instruction: Best practices in the classroom* (3rd ed.). Prufrock Press.

Roberts, J. L., & Roberts, R. A. (2015). Writing units that remove the learning ceiling. In F. A. Karnes & S. M. Bean (Eds.), *Methods and materials for teaching the gifted* (4th ed., pp. 221–255). Prufrock Press.

Rogers, K. B., & Hay, P. (2020). Survival secrets for grouping gifted and talented children for talent development and socialization. In J. L. Roberts & J. R. Boggess (Eds.), *Teacher's survival guide: Gifted Education* (2nd ed., pp. 136–141). Prufrock Press.

Stanley, J. C. (2000). Helping students learn only what they don't already know. *Psychology, Public Policy, and Law, 6*(1), 216–222. https://doi.org/10.1037/1076–8971.6.1.216

Tomlinson, C. A. (1999). *The differentiated classroom: Responding to the needs of all learners.* Association for Supervision and Curriculum Development.

Tomlinson, C. A. (2014). Differentiated instruction. In J. A. Plucker & C. M. Callahan (Eds.), *Critical issues and practices in gifted education: What the research says* (2nd ed., pp. 197–210). Prufrock Press. https://doi.org/10.1177/0014402914527244

Tomlinson, C. A., & Moon, T. R. (2013). *Assessment and student success in a differentiated classroom.* Association for Supervision and Curriculum Development

VanTassel-Baska, J. (2018). Considerations in curriculum for gifted students. In S. I. Pfeiffer, E. Shaunessy-Dedrick, & M. Foley-Nicpon (Eds.), *APA handbooks in psychology®. APA handbook of giftedness and talent* (pp. 349–369). American Psychological Association. https://doi.org/10.1037/0000038–023

VanTassel-Baska, J., & Hubbard, G. F. (2018, November 15–18). *A study of teacher use of differentiation practices in classrooms for gifted learners* [Conference Session]. National Association for Gifted Children 65th Annual Convention, Minneapolis, MN.

VanTassel-Baska, J., Hubbard, G. F., & Robbins, J. L (2020). Differentiation of instruction for gifted learners: Collated evaluative studies of teacher classroom practices. *Roeper Review, 42*(3), 153–164. https://doi/full/10.1080/02783193.2020.1765919

VanTassel-Baska, J. (2017). Introduction to the Integrated Curriculum Model. In J. Van Tassel-Baska & C. A. Little (Eds.), *Content-based curriculum for high ability learners* (3rd ed., pp. 13–32), Prufrock Press.

Vygotsky, L. S. (1997) Interaction between learning and development. In M. Gauvain & M. Cole (Eds.), *Readings on the development of children* (pp. 29–36). Worth.

Wright, B. L., Ford. D. Y., Scott, M. F. T., & Moore III, J. L. (2020). Cultural differences and early access matter: Increasing gifted and talented education participation for underrepresented students. *Tempo, 40*(2), 18–25. https://tempo.txgifted.org/category/equity/

7

Programming Models and Program Design

Cheryll Adams

Educators use evidence-based practices to promote (a) the cognitive, social-emotional, and psychosocial skill development of students with gifts and talents, and (b) programming that meets their interests, strengths, and needs. Educators make use of expertise systematically and collaboratively to develop, implement, manage, and evaluate services for students with a variety of gifts and talents to ensure specific student outcomes. (National Association for Gifted Children (NAGC), 2019a, Description)

Introduction

According to the NAGC Pre-K–Grade 12 Gifted Programming Standards, Standard 5, "programming refers to a continuum of services that address the interests, strengths, and needs of students with gifts and talents in all settings" (2019a, Introduction). This definition is supported by professionals in the field of gifted education who advocate for a continuum of services rather than a single program to meet the needs of students with gifts and talents (Callahan, 2009; Callahan et al., 2017; Rogers, 2006; Tomlinson, 2009; Treffinger et al.,

DOI: 10.4324/9781003236863-7

2004). To ensure that this continuum of services is in place and appropriately implemented, policies and procedures to guide and sustain the necessary service components must be developed. In order that gifted education is considered a vital and critical component of Pre-K–12 education, the services that are developed must be aligned with both general education and special education (NAGC, 2014a). Thus, educators must have the necessary knowledge and skills to choose appropriate programming options such as acceleration and enrichment, provide varied grouping arrangements (e.g., cluster grouping, special classes) and offer individualized learning options (e.g., independent study, mentorships) to increase students' performance academically as well as socially and emotionally (Johnsen et al., 2016). Through the use of technology to enhance performance or increase access to additional learning opportunities and collaboration with persons within the family, school and community, the diverse learning needs of these students have a better chance of being met. Although there are a number of services that can be provided for little additional cost to the district (Adams, 2009; Assouline et al., 2015; Gentry, 2014; Gentry & Mann, 2008; Tomlinson, 2017; Winebrenner & Brulles, 2008), some districts cite lack of funding as a reason for not providing services to these students. Even the most well-conceived and appropriately designed range of services cannot be implemented without the continued support of administrators and policymakers who determine the level of human and material resources that are allocated to students with gifts and talents.

Despite many years of research, including a landmark study by the National Research Center on the Gifted and Talented (Delcourt et al., 1994; Delcourt et al., 2007), researchers have yet to determine programming or services that allow all academically gifted students to reach their full potential. At one time schools may have had specific programming such as self-contained classes or a resource room, but over the last several years programming for gifted learners has been frequently eliminated in favor of an inclusionary model that places all students in the general education classroom. Reasons for this phenomenon include a lack of funding and an appropriate infrastructure for gifted services (Hodges, 2018; VanTassel-Baska, 2006) as well as the passing of the No Child Left Behind Act (2002) and its policies which focused on struggling learners and not those who are above proficiency (Scot et al., 2009). According to Plucker and his colleagues, the passage of a law or policy "is best viewed as a milestone in a much longer journey. Implementation of the policy, careful review of its intended and unintended consequences, and revision of that policy are part of a never-ending cycle" (2017, p. 214). When the reauthorization of the Elementary and Secondary Education Act at the federal level, often called the Every Student Succeeds Act (ESSA, 2015) passed, there was a general feeling of optimism in the field of gifted education because many of the changes could potentially benefit advanced learners, particularly those who were traditionally underserved. Unfortunately, there were no advocates for gifted students appointed to the committee that would provide the U.S. Department of Education guidance for implementing these new regulations (Plucker et al., 2017). Ultimately, Title II, Part A (Supporting Effective Instruction) of the Act addressing improving skills of teachers, principals, or other school leadership to identify students with specific learning needs was the only section that directly mentioned gifted learners. The U.S. Department of Education did require states to include gifted education in this section of the Consolidated State Plans that they submitted, but without specific guidance to states concerning implementation, the initial hope that ESSA's focus on the academic growth of all children would specifically include those with gifts and talents faded. Thus, the default program still often becomes differentiation of instruction in the general education classroom rather than a continuum of services. Without a deep understanding of differentiation, particularly with respect to gifted learners, educators may only provide minimal services at best to these students.

The purpose of this chapter, then, is to provide information that will allow school personnel to make appropriate choices for programming for gifted students. These choices are predicated on educators' awareness of empirical evidence to guide their understanding of gifted students' cognitive, affective, and creative development. Understanding the development of students with gifts and talents is the foundation necessary for choosing appropriate programming options and services. By using Standard 5 to focus on evidence-based practices and the corresponding student outcomes, educators can make informed choices to select programming that meets the specific learning needs of their students.

Program Design

Standard 5 specifically addresses these questions:

◆ Does a properly funded continuum of services offer a variety of programming and learning options that are collaboratively developed and implemented and that enhance student performance in cognitive and affective areas?

◆ Has a system been implemented, including articulated policies and procedures, that allows for educators to develop multiyear plans, plan and coordinate programming and services with the school's professional service providers, evaluate program outcomes, and communicate with family and community members to meet student needs and program goals?

These guiding questions imply that the programming options selected are viable, effective, thoughtfully considered, and proactively designed with advanced learner needs in mind. Merely providing programming or a set of services for students with gifts and talents does not indicate the quality of that programming. Too often programming may be operating as a patch to cover weak general education programming (Tomlinson, 2009, 2017, 2018) or an add-on that does not align with the general education curriculum (Reis & Gubbins, 2017; Robinson, 2009; VanTassel-Baska, 2009). Moreover, in a recent survey conducted by Callahan et al. (2017) of 1566 school district personnel, about a third reported that there was no framework chosen to guide their gifted programming. Of 50 state directors of gifted programs reporting, only 24 indicated a law or rule mandating gifted programing options or services. Fifteen states reported that programs or services were not required, and 11 responded that it was decided by each Local Education Agency (LEA). Additionally, of 48 respondents, 23 indicated their state had state program standards or guidelines for gifted education, but 25 answered they did not. (National Association for Gifted Children & Council of State Directors of Programs for the Gifted & National Association for Gifted Children (NAGC & CSDPG), 2020).

Before any discussion of various types of services or programming options can occur, educators must first look at the criteria for exemplary programming. Effective programming and services have the following well-defined elements: a philosophy, goals, definition, identification plan, coherent curriculum, scope and sequence, professional learning programs, teacher and administrator selection, and an evaluation plan (Callahan, 2020; Eckert & Robins, 2017; NAGC, 2019b). Furthermore, the services are aligned with the general curriculum; there is administrative support, oversight by qualified personnel, and communication among all stakeholders (Adams, 2009; Tomlinson, 2009). When these elements are in place and working effectively, the cognitive and affective needs of students with gifts and talents can be met. Evidence of students' needs being met includes yearly growth in cognitive and affective areas commensurate with their abilities through a variety of programming options that allow them to progress without administrative barriers.

When I was in graduate school, my professor, Dr. Carolyn Callahan, often reminded us, "You cannot evaluate that which you cannot describe!" Thus, it is paramount that programs for students who are gifted and talented be described in detail so that they may be evaluated to determine which components effectively influence the student outcomes. Thus, beginning with this end in mind is a good strategy.

Philosophy

The philosophy gives a broad overview of the vision for programming. It may be helpful to think of this as a "This we believe" statement about students who are gifted and talented and the manner in which a continuum of services may be provided for them. It is in this statement that the alignment to special education and general education can be initially affirmed. For example, "We believe that all students require a program of study that provides choice, challenge, and a response to their individual needs." This statement implies that the needs of *all* children, including the gifted and talented, will be met and their learning strengths and limitations will be considered. The next statement may be one that addresses gifted students specifically, such as: "There are some students whose performance or potential for performance exceeds what is generally expected at their grade level. Our district believes that these students need to be offered a continuum of services that meet their academic, psychosocial, and social and emotional needs." Other statements may further address particular beliefs of the school district.

Goals

Goals are the road maps for programming; without a clear idea of the outcomes of the services provided, educators will not know when (or if) they have succeeded. High quality goals must be aligned with best practices in the field, valid and worthy of attaining, comprehensive, and clear (Adams, 2006). For example, look at this goal: "All gifted students in our district will reach their full potential." When measured against the above criteria, this goal has little evidence of alignment, is lacking in validity, provides little guidance in how the programming would be developed, and is neither measurable nor unambiguous. In contrast, the following goal is more closely aligned with the criteria for high quality programming goals: "Gifted students demonstrate progress as a result of programming that provides a variety of appropriate types and levels of acceleration and enrichment that are based on students' learning needs in Grades K–12."

Definition

There is currently no universal definition of giftedness, but the field of gifted education does have many definitions that identify this population based on particular behaviors, habits of mind, potential, and/or facility for learning.

Some theorists ascribe to a more conservative definition (e.g., Stanley, 1980; Terman, 1922) and some to a more liberal one (e.g., Gagné, 1995; Renzulli, 1986). More recently, the focus has shifted toward a more domain-specific view of giftedness (e.g., Olszewski-Kubilius et al., 2018; Subotnick et al., 2011; Worrell et al., 2019). The Board of Directors of the National Association for Gifted Children convened a task force in late 2017 to redefine "gifted-ness" for the 21st century. Note that this definition has a student outcome component:

> Students with gifts and talents perform—or have the capability to perform—at higher levels compared to others of the same age, experience, and environment in one or more domains. They require modification(s) to their educational experience(s) to learn and realize their potential. Student with gifts and talents:
>
> ◆ Come from all racial, ethnic, and cultural populations, as well as all economic strata.
> ◆ Require sufficient access to appropriate learning opportunities to realize their potential.
> ◆ Can have learning and processing disorders that require specialized intervention and accommodation.
> ◆ Need support and guidance to develop socially and emotionally as well as in their areas of talent.
> ◆ Require varied services based on their changing needs.
>
> (NAGC, 2019c, para. 2).

It is vital that an appropriate definition be chosen that adequately describes the group for whom the programming is being designed. If the definition puts an emphasis on cognitive skills and programming aimed at visual and performing arts is designed, then educators have a mismatch between the programming options and the students who will be provided those options.

Identification Plan

Once a definition has been selected the school must provide a clearly articulated plan to determine who is eligible for services based on that definition. If the definition focuses on mathematics and language arts, for example, then the instruments chosen will be those that identify students who are gifted in mathematics and language arts, and the programming options will focus on those two content areas. Selecting appropriate reliable and valid instruments that provide both quantitative and qualitative data, ensuring all students have an opportunity to demonstrate their gifts and talents, recognizing potential as well as performance, determining placement options, and providing procedures for due process are critical issues that must be considered when designing an identification plan.

Curriculum

Ludicrous as it may seem, a number of schools and districts spend time carefully crafting a gifted education program's philosophy and goals, choosing a research-based definition, and selecting appropriate instruments for identification only to place identified students in the general education classroom using the same curriculum that all other students of that grade use. Conversely, in a study of the impact of using cluster grouping and specific curriculum to support gifted learners' math achievement in urban elementary schools, teachers were rated as either "implementers" (implemented the gifted curriculum as directed) or "non-implementers" (did not implement the gifted curriculum as directed). Some of those teachers rated as non-implementers actually were trying to teach the gifted curriculum to the whole class with the results that gifted learners made fewer gains in these classrooms compared to the implementers' classrooms because the gifted curriculum had to be simplified to enable non-gifted learners to access it (Pierce et al., 2011).

Issues and outcomes related to curriculum and instruction are discussed in detail in other chapters in this volume; I make mention of them here to underscore their importance as vital pieces of comprehensive programming for gifted learners.

Teacher Selection, Professional Learning, and Program Administration

Teachers assigned to provide an appropriately differentiated curriculum that addresses advanced learner needs within a particular program model or service option do not necessarily possess the knowledge and skills crucial for this task. According to a recent survey, 18 of 46 states responding did not require teachers of students with gifts and talents to be certified or endorsed in gifted education (NAGC & CSDPG, 2020). The remaining states required a range of credentials including professional learning. Only 14 out of 46 reporting states required districts to have a gifted coordinator/ administrator, but there was no evidence to indicate whether they were required to be full time. Only five states required this administrator to have gifted education preparation. Of 48 states responding, three indicated that preservice teachers are required to take coursework in gifted education. In four out of 47 states, administrators, counselors, and special education professionals must take a course in the nature and needs of gifted learners. In 11 states, it is left up to the LEAs to decide, and 29 states do not require such coursework. To this regard, NAGC identifies three knowledge and skills standards that all teachers should be able to meet:

1. recognize the learning differences, developmental milestones, and cognitive/affective characteristics of gifted and talented students, including those from diverse cultural and linguistic backgrounds, and identify their related academic and social-emotional needs;
2. design appropriate learning and performance modifications for individuals with gifts and talents that enhance creativity, acceleration, depth and complexity in academic subject matter and specialized domains; and
3. select, adapt, and use a repertoire of evidence-based instructional strategies to advance the learning of gifted and talented students.

(NAGC, 2014b)

Although there may be pockets of excellence where all teachers receive professional learning opportunities in gifted education and all teachers and program administrators of gifted and talented students are certified, the results of the survey suggest this is not the norm.

Evidence-based Programming Options

I generally receive a variety of responses when I conduct professional learning or program evaluations and ask the question, "What is your gifted program?" Reponses range from the name of a particular set of curriculum units, such as the CLEAR units (Callahan et al., 2015), the name of a specific program option, such as a pull-out program, or an indication that the teacher for the gifted learners simply decides what students will learn each semester. Clearly, there is not a consistent understanding of what we mean when we ask, "What is your gifted program?" Unified Program Design (UPD) is a framework conceived by Rubenstein and Ridgley (2017) to address how to provide a clear response to the question "What is your gifted program?" They argue that to describe a program one must include information about the delivery method, the curriculum, and any underlying theory or philosophy of gifted learners. This distinction is consistent with the program standards which address both curriculum (Standard 3) and programming (Standard 5) (NAGC 2019a). A schema for categorizing programming options and curriculum can help districts determine whether components are missing. For example, the CLEAR curriculum model (Callahan et al., 2015) by itself is not a gifted program, but when it is used as the basis for the curriculum used in an elementary pull-out program option, the district can now answer the question, "What is your gifted program?" Next, I examine a variety of programming options with the understanding that without a clearly articulated curriculum model, the choice of a program or service option itself does little to provide students who are gifted with opportunities for growth academically.

To meet the advanced learning needs of students with gifts and talents, schools must choose programming options that have amassed a body of empirical evidence (e.g., acceleration, cluster grouping) suggesting they are appropriate for this population, which result in students making gains commensurate with their abilities. There are other popular options that have practice-based evidence of effectiveness, generally through action research. This chapter will examine programming options that have been shown to be effective with students with gifts and talents and that recent reports indicate encompass the range of available offerings most often chosen by school districts to meet the needs of their gifted learners (Callahan et al., 2017; NAGC & CSDPG, 2020). Regardless of the programming options being used, research demonstrates that it is beneficial to keep students who are gifted together for a major part of their academic day (Delcourt et al., 2007; Delcourt et al., 1994; Kulik, 2003; Rogers, 2007; Steenbergen-Hu et al., 2016). Additionally, it should be noted that the responsibility of developing and implementing programming options for gifted students is best undertaken by qualified personnel who have the appropriate knowledge and skills to accomplish these tasks effectively.

Acceleration

Section 5.1.1 of NAGC Programming Standard 5, Programming, provides guidance for the use of acceleration which allows the pace of the instruction to be adjusted for the learners to a degree that dramatically affects the pace of their instruction (NAGC 2019a). According to VanTassel-Baska and Sher (2011):

> Acceleration of gifted students is the first consideration in planning an appropriate curriculum for them....[Their] higher level of functioning demands that the level of curricular challenge be raised to ensure a good match to the child's readiness pattern for learning. Thus, acceleration has to precede enrichment within core areas of learning.
>
> (pp. 49–50)

In general, the flexibility needed to allow a third-grade student to accelerate into middle school math, for example, has not had strong support in schools. The Templeton Report, *A Nation Deceived*, compiled by Colangelo and his colleagues (2004) sought to change negative attitudes and beliefs about acceleration by providing empirical evidence about 18 different forms of acceleration going far beyond grade skipping and clearly setting the record straight on the advantages of each in an easily understood manner, demonstrating that acceleration is an inexpensive, viable option for gifted students.

The most recent update, *A Nation Empowered*, still stresses that acceleration is the most effective and low-cost academic intervention for students who are gifted (Assouline et al., 2015). Despite the publicity surrounding these reports and other research on the benefits of acceleration (Neihart, 2007; Steenbergen-Hu & Moon, 2011; Steenbergen-Hu et al., 2016), many school administrators still discourage the use of acceleration as a programming option. Recent surveys of school district personnel (Callahan et al., 2017) and state directors of K–12 gifted education (NAGC & CSDPG, 2020) reported that acceleration did not rank at the top of options selected by respondents in the former study and only ranked in the top three options in Grades 1–6 in the latter.

An often-mentioned reason for not accelerating students is the long-held belief about the certainty of social and emotional problems for students who have been subject-skipped, although recent research shows positive social and psychological effects across many studies (Bernstein et al., 2020; Rogers, 2015; Wai, 2015). Because having an acceleration policy is key to any set of programming options, teachers, administrators, and other school personnel would benefit from reading these reports and designing one based on the *Developing Academic Acceleration Policies: Whole Grade, Early Entrance, & Single Subject* document (Lupkowski-Shoplik et al., 2018). Two common forms of acceleration offer schools low cost, viable options for students with gifts and talents.

Content-based Acceleration

Content-based acceleration or subject skipping is most often employed when students have demonstrated outstanding growth in and understanding of the curriculum for a subject or performance area at their grade levels. Providing enrichment and extension activities for these students no longer results in progress commensurate with their abilities. Accelerating these students may simply involve placing them in the particular subject or performance area at the next grade or level. Other forms of content-based acceleration include compacting, dual enrollment, credit by examination, Advanced Placement, independent learning programs and taking classes through Talent Search programs (Rogers, 2015; Southern & Jones, 2015). Although content-based acceleration that occurs within the school generally does not involve additional expense, classes at Talent Search sites, distance learning programs, Advanced Placement, and dual enrollment may require out-of-pocket expenses on the part of the student's family, the school, or both. The results of Rogers' (2015) recent synthesis of about 108 research studies on acceleration and their academic effects from 2008 to 2013, an update to her previous meta-analyses (Rogers, 1992; 2004), included strong academic effect sizes for gifted participants in accelerated high school classes and AP classes, moderate academic effects for dual/concurrent enrollment, single subject acceleration, and participation in talent search programs, and slight but positive effects for curriculum compacting. Across all options, grades and subjects, the summary academic effect size was moderately positive, .51, indicating that students who were accelerated in specific subjects were ahead of nonaccelerated students by about five months.

Much of the research on content-based acceleration focuses on mathematics instruction (Johnsen & Sheffield, 2013; Johnsen et. al., 2014; Lubinski & Benbow, 2006; Lubinski et al., 2001; Swiatek & Lupkowski-Shoplik, 2003), although recent works have included science (Adams et al., 2014; Adams et al., 2015; Ihrig & Degner, 2015) and English Language Arts (Hughes et al., 2014; VanTassel-Baska, 2013). This should not preclude choosing acceleration as an option for those students whose performance in another area requires it. One important caveat: Once content acceleration has been implemented, it is too late to worry about what happens the next year and in the future! A discussion about having a 4th grade student take 5th grade science needs to include a thoughtful conversation about the student the next year when, as a 5th grader, she may have to be transported to the middle school for 6th grade science.

Grade-based Acceleration

Grade-based acceleration or grade skipping, involves taking classes generally a year or more ahead of age mates. Early entrance to school (e.g., entering first grade when their age mates are entering kindergarten) and early entrance to college (e.g., skipping the senior year and proceeding to college after Grade 11) are included. In its simplest form, grade acceleration entails moving from one grade to another but skipping the grade between the two (e.g., completing grade two and entering grade four the next year rather than grade three). Gifted students whose achievement measures indicate they are performing several years above their grade level peers are good candidates for grade skipping, but researchers encourage choosing grade skipping as an option as early in the child's school career as possible (Assouline et al., 2015; Coleman & Cross, 2005; Peters et al., 2014; Rogers, 2001). Research indicates that early acceleration may prevent potential behavior or social issues and concerns about gaps in academic content (Behrens & Lupkowski-Shoplik, 2020). Some states may not allow early acceleration. For example, in Florida all students who are five years old by August 31 must attend kindergarten, and state policy forbids both early entrance to kindergarten and skipping kindergarten. The only exception is for a child who moves to Florida from a state with a later birth date cut-off, providing the student was in a public school (Florida Statutes, 2019a). However, students may skip any other grade if academic ability warrants it (Florida Statutes, 2019b).

As reported in Rogers' (2015) recent summary of acceleration options, grade-skipping had a strong academic effect size while early entrance to school and college had slight but positive effects on achievement compared to students' same-age peers. Across all studies of grade-based acceleration regardless of grade level, there was a moderate academic effect size of .50. Because the students join an already intact class and thus no additional materials or teachers are needed, this form of acceleration is cost effective. See Southern and Jones (2015) and Rogers (2015) for definitions of types of acceleration and Rogers for research statistics on effect sizes of specific forms of acceleration.

Enrichment

Enrichment may be defined as "modifications a teacher makes to go above and beyond the regular curriculum for a student or cluster of students who need advanced learning opportunities" (Roberts, 2005, p. 6). When students have mastered the grade level material and acceleration is not a viable option, the teacher may choose to offer options for them to study the topic in depth, breadth, or at a more complex level while other students needing more practice continue to work with the general education or grade-level curriculum. Section 5.1.2 of NAGC Programming Standard 5, Programming, encourages the use of enrichment: "Educators use enrichment options to extend and deepen learning opportunities within and outside the school setting" (NAGC, 2019a). The key to providing appropriate enrichment options is predicated on the view that the activities have substance, are meaningful, respectful, and provide a level of challenge commensurate with the student's ability.

There are several studies that look at curriculum developed specifically to deepen or extend the learning for gifted students (e.g., Callahan et al., 2015; Gavin et al., 2007; Kaplan, 2009; Reis et al., 2011; VanTassel-Baska et al., 2002). These may be used as replacement units (i.e., using a geometry unit designed for gifted learners to replace their general education unit on geometry) or as stand-alone units within a particular programing option (i.e., using a unit on fairy tales as the language arts focus in a pull-out program).

In his study of grouping, Kulik (1992) reported significant learning gains for students when they were ability-grouped and when the curriculum was adjusted to reflect the performance level of the students. Tieso (2005) noted gains in academic performance in math in a study of flexible grouping practices, and Gentry and Owen (1999) found greater gains in reading in their focus on flexible cluster groups. Similarly, Rogers (1991) found an effect size of .65 when students were grouped by ability in a pull-out program using a curriculum extension approach. Clearly enrichment is supported by empirical research, but one must not forget that in these studies, enrichment extended and complemented the general education curriculum. According to Adams and Boswell (2012):

> To be clear, enrichment for the sake of providing fun activities for those who have finished their work or who already understand the material being presented is not what we are advocating. Although the enrichment may be in content, process, or product, substantial content must be involved. Simply having students engage in an exciting project such as making a piñata is best situated within a discussion of cultures whose celebrations include piñatas, the science involved in making papier-mâché, or the origins of papier-mâché.
>
> (pp. 43–44)

Hence enrichment must be carefully planned and clearly articulated so that students can enhance their performance through higher level critical and creative thinking skills as they complete the activities so that hands-on learning is simultaneous with minds-on learning.

Differentiation

Differentiation is a mindset that takes into account the variety of learner needs and characteristics that students bring to the classroom (Tomlinson, 2018). In response to these characteristics and needs, teachers modify the content, process, product, learning environment and affect to meet the needs of all learners, including gifted learners. The emphasis is on developmentally appropriate lessons that provide students with choice and a moderate challenge. A fundamental principle is that students should not be required to continually repeat something they have already learned. Instead, the teacher employs a variety of instructional strategies that are engaging, meaningful, and worthy of the time students spend completing these activities.

Differentiation is perhaps the most widely employed programming option because it does not require that students be pulled into a resource room, special class, or special school. Students with gifts and talents are placed in the general education classroom with their age mates. The teacher must constantly assess students academically, socially, and emotionally to select suitable materials to advance their learning. Based on this knowledge, the teacher modifies one or more aspects according to the student's interest, learning profile, or readiness level for the task. Much of the evidence researchers have about differentiation is based on observational data or action research from practitioners (Adams & Pierce, 2006; Renzulli & Reis, 2008; Tomlinson, 2003, 2009, 2018, VanTassel-Baska, Hubbard, & Robbins, 2020) or about particular strategies (Gavin et al., 2009; Pierce et al., 2011). Although differentiation is quite popular as a programming option, many schools that choose this option have great difficulty putting it into practice appropriately. Implementing differentiation runs the whole gamut from providing individual spelling lists or novels based on reading levels to constantly arranging and rearranging students into flexible configurations based on the teacher's data from continuous assessments using exit cards, informal dialog, observation, and formal testing.

A critical component of differentiation is time. Time is needed to pre-assess students, determine appropriate content and activities based on that assessment, and modify the materials in depth, pace, and complexity. If time and effort to design and implement these tasks are not considered in the differentiation plan, there is little chance that the learning needs of the gifted students will be met in the regular classroom (Tomlinson, 2018). For differentiation to be a viable and effective programming option, teachers and administrators must embrace it wholly, and administrators must ensure that teachers have proper professional learning, time, and support to consistently put it into practice.

Individual Options

Mentorships, internships, and independent study are options that may be selected on a case-by-case basis for individual students who need these opportunities to enhance their learning or refine their knowledge and skills in a particular area of study. For example, a student may want to pursue a subject such as the nest building habits of the cerulean warbler. Generally, a topic like this is beyond the realm of expertise of the regular classroom teacher. A field study might be arranged with a university professor who has a similar research interest. Internships for students who want an opportunity to acquire real-world experience in a specific field such as medicine or accounting may be arranged with members of the community who work in the field of interest. Independent studies are often completed in the classroom or resource room under the guidance of the teacher. Many teachers and students may see independent study as simply writing a research paper, but according to Johnsen and Johnson (2007), "Independent studies may be used for solving community problems; uncovering new questions; writing histories; and, most importantly, helping a student create a lifelong love affair with learning" (p. 379). For a meaningful independent study experience both the teacher and the students must set out a clear plan with checkpoints along the way, particularly for younger students. Just assigning the topic and sending students off to work on their own until the due date is neither appropriate nor effective as an alternative to regular assignments. No matter which individual option is presented to students as a learning opportunity, it is vital that a study plan be developed so that all those involved know the expectations and responsibilities involved.

Grouping Options

Delcourt and her colleagues (1994) undertook one of the first empirical studies that looked at students in a variety of grouping options. Focusing on achievement, the study compared students enrolled in gifted programs (special school, separate class, pull-out, within-class), high-achieving students from districts in which no program was available at the designated grade levels, and nongifted students in regular classrooms. Several recommendations from this study are worth noting:

1. Decisions about programming implementation should be based on research about learning outcomes for specific program types (Special School, Separate Class, Pull-Out, Within-Class).
2. Gifted children who were provided specific programming options performed better than their gifted peers not in programs. Specifically, children in Special Schools, Separate Class programs, and Pull-Out programs for the gifted showed substantially higher levels of achievement than both their gifted peers not in programs and those attending Within-Class programs.
3. Students from the Separate Class program scored at the highest levels of achievement.

(p. xxi)

Although time spent receiving services in each configuration was provided, there was no way to determine the exact strength of dose needed for achievement to be significant. However, the outcomes indicate the longer students were in their homogeneous group per day, the larger the gain in achievement.

In the qualitative extension of this study, Delcourt and Evans (1994) sought to determine what attributes separated the exemplary programs from the rest. Regardless of the overall results about a particular programming option, to be effective, the school district using the model must demonstrate effectiveness in the following areas: Leadership, Atmosphere and Environment, Communication, Curriculum and Instruction, and Attention to Student Needs (pp. 76–79). Thus, there is not one programming option that works for all students with gifts and talents; instead, student outcomes are dependent on both the match of the program to the student's needs and the quality of implementation of the programming option.

Cluster Grouping

Cluster grouping is a widely recommended and frequently used strategy for meeting the needs of high achieving students in the regular classroom. Originally, clustering was the intentional placement of four to ten identified gifted students in a heterogeneous classroom with a teacher who possesses both desire and expertise in working with gifted children. Many variations in the total number within the cluster appear in the literature (Gentry, 2014; 2018; Gentry & Mann, 2008; Rogers, 2001) and practice. The students in the cluster are then provided appropriate materials and learning experiences beyond what is offered in the general education curriculum to enhance their performance in the cognitive, creative, and/or affective areas.

The rationale underlying this programming model suggests that it provides opportunities for gifted students to interact with intellectual peers on a full-time basis and expedites the classroom teacher's capacity to address the needs of a group of gifted students. Cluster grouping presents a cost-effective option, and evidence suggests it improves achievement across all levels by allowing students not identified as academically gifted to emerge as leaders and achievers in non-clustered classrooms (Brulles, 2005; Delcourt & Evans, 1994; Gentry & Owen, 1999; Rogers, 1991).

Several misconceptions may impact whether school districts choose cluster grouping because it is sometimes confused with tracking students and the negativity surrounding this practice. With state-wide mandates for frequent testing (e.g., benchmark tests, end -of-year tests) and the use of test scores as a measure of teacher quality, many teachers cite the perception that cluster teachers' test scores will be higher than non-cluster teachers as a reason for not advocating for the use of cluster grouping as an option for gifted programming. Teachers may also believe that clustering gifted learners in several classes diminishes learning opportunities for students in non-clustered classrooms, although research indicates the opposite (Gentry, 2018; Gentry & Owen, 1999; Schuler, 1997). In a study by Pierce et al. (2011), both identified and non-identified students in the cluster classrooms performed better on measures of math achievement than their age-mates in non-cluster classrooms, demonstrating a spillover effect that was advantageous to all students in the cluster classrooms. In a survey of district personnel by Callahan and colleagues (2017), cluster grouping was among the top three chosen program options in elementary and middle school, lending support to the view that cluster grouping benefits not only elementary but also older students.

There are challenges to the effective use of clustering, including the need to provide ongoing professional learning to support cluster teachers; otherwise, the academic challenge in a cluster classroom is no greater than in a non-clustered classroom (Gentry, 2018: Gentry & Owen, 1999; Kulik 1992; Kulik & Kulik, 1992; Pierce et al., 2011; Rogers, 1991; Tieso, 2005). Moreover, without an appropriate level of challenge for the cluster, cluster grouping becomes camouflage for no gifted program at all. When designed and implemented with fidelity, cluster grouping can simultaneously address the needs of gifted students *and* the needs of other students (Gentry, 2018; Gentry & MacDougall, 2009; Pierce et al., 2011).

Self-contained Classes

Self-contained classes are used to group students with gifts and talents into a separate classroom at a particular grade (Rogers, 2001). In this grouping arrangement students' learning activities are planned to be qualitatively different from the regular grade level instruction. The implications are that these classes would have learning experiences that would not be appropriate for less able students and use materials that provide a higher level of depth and complexity. Thus, self-contained classrooms are best suited for students who have strong academic and intellectual profiles in all academic areas. Rogers (2007) found an effect size of .49 at the elementary level for the self-contained classrooms option. In a recent survey of state directors of gifted programming, self-contained classes were one of the top five options at the elementary level, but not at the middle or high school levels (NAGC & CSDPG, 2020). Elementary students are assigned to their self-contained classroom on a full-time basis. A few states indicated that they served middle school students in self-contained classes. However, unlike elementary students, most middle and high school students change classes for each subject rather than staying with one teacher for the day. Top choices tended to be AP or honors classes for those students.

When students with gifts and talents are placed in self-contained classrooms without changing what occurs differently in that classroom, educators should not expect them to make academic gains commensurate with their abilities. It is not just the configuration that makes the difference; it is what happens in the configuration that allows gains to be made. Depending on staffing and classroom availability, there may be a need to hire additional staff and dedicate additional classrooms to the program. Furthermore, the teachers assigned to the self-contained classrooms must have the ability to provide advanced instruction on a full-time basis. Additional expense comes from the need to purchase specialized materials that are not being used by other students at that grade.

Special Schools

The most expensive grouping option is the special school configuration. Because of the expense involved in creating a separate school, many special schools that currently exist are laboratory schools connected to a university, state-supported residential or day schools, or private schools. In addition to all the expenses incurred in the day-to-day maintenance of a building, teaching staff must be hired, materials must be ordered, and, in the case of a residential program, students must have dormitory space, residence counselors must be hired, and a plan for dealing with students who are high school age and living away from home must be developed. Some schools currently focus on particular content areas such as the performing arts or science and mathematics. Despite the expense involved in setting up and maintaining a special school, there are decided advantages of such an arrangement. Students with gifts and talents spend the majority of their day surrounded by other such students; students have access to curriculum and instruction that is not available in their regular school; and teachers generally are content specialists with advanced degrees. For these reasons, students may be able to move faster from competency to expertise or have easier access to mentorships and apprenticeships (Olszewski-Kubilius, 2010). For students who want a challenge that is above what is generally offered in a regular classroom, a special school may be a viable choice (Kolloff, 2003).

Pull-out/Resource Room

Pull-out programs, sometimes called resource rooms, are a part-time service option for students who are gifted and talented. Usually, a group of students leave their regular classrooms to receive instruction in a resource room within the school with a special teacher for a set amount of time, after which they return to their regular classroom. The amount of time spent in the pull-out class may vary from 30 minutes once a week to several hours every day, and the time is generally spent engaged in enrichment or extension activities that may or may not be connected to the regular curriculum.

Pull-out programs have been the mainstay of gifted education, particularly at the elementary level, for years. One of the earliest studies of gifted programs found that more than 80% of them used the pull-out model (Cox et al., 1985). More recently, over 50% of 1,566 school districts surveyed responded that a part-time pull-out program was their program option (Callahan et al., 2017). Similarly, a survey of state directors of gifted programs listed the pull-out model as their state's third choice of service option in Grades 1 to 6 after differentiation of instruction and acceleration (NAGC & CSDPG, 2020). Many are being eliminated due to lack of funding, and there are expenses associated with this model, such as the need for an additional teacher, a separate classroom or place for the program to be housed, and enrichment or extension materials.

Exemplary programs of this type are carefully aligned to the regular curriculum and extend it vertically or horizontally. A good example would be a third-grade pull-out program for math. When the third-grade class has math, those identified as high ability in math would go to the resource room and work on math at a higher level of depth and complexity than the regular class. Conversely, pulling out the gifted students to go to the resource room and work on critical thinking puzzles without a context that is centered in a content area is not a good use of anyone's time. Vaughn et al. (1991) found when the curriculum used in the pull-out was aligned with the regular classroom, there were positive effects. The Delcourt et al. study (2007) saw positive academic gains in achievement when the pull-out program had a strong academic focus, and Rogers' (2007) synthesis of research on educational practices noted an effect size of .65 for pull-out programs with strong academic focuses. Hence, pull-out programs that favor strong, sustained academic emphasis should be chosen rather than those that provide a plethora of unrelated activities focusing on processes without content.

Often pull-out programs are difficult to schedule around the activities of several classrooms at the same grade level. Thirty minutes once a week will not greatly affect the learning needs of these students with gifts and talents, thus the pull-out program needs to extend over a significant amount of time each week. The onus for meeting these students' needs when they are not in the resource room falls on the classroom teacher, making it vital for the regular classroom teacher to have training to meet those needs. Furthermore, it is not appropriate to insist students make up all the work that was missed when they were pulled out, to start new material, or to provide a special treat such as a video or an extra recess when students who are gifted are out of the room receiving services. Those developing pull-out programs may want to look at some guidelines for establishing and evaluating these programs (Adams, 2018).

Delivery of Services

It's clear that there are a variety of effective, evidence-based programming options and service delivery models that will support students with gifts and talents. Additionally, appropriate curriculum and instructional strategies must be chosen to ensure continuous delivery and fidelity of implementation of the option or model chosen. Hence, how do educators ensure consistent implementation of programming that leads to student outcomes commensurate to their abilities and talents? Standard 5 provides guidance on these matters.

In terms of student outcomes, there are six critical components to providing a systematic and continuous delivery of services:

- ◆ Comprehensive, cohesive, and coordinated services (Student Outcomes 5.1 & 5.2)
- ◆ Career pathways (Student Outcome 5.3)
- ◆ Collaboration to Advance Talent Development (Student Outcome 5.4)
- ◆ Resources (Student Outcome 5.5)
- ◆ Policies and procedures (Student Outcome 5.6)
- ◆ Evaluation of Programming and Services (Student Outcomes 5.7 & 5.8)

Comprehensive, Cohesive, and Coordinated Services

Comprehensiveness

To this point I have discussed the research, strengths, and weaknesses of a variety of individual, grouping, and service options that may be chosen as the basis for providing comprehensive services to students who are gifted and talented. Reis and Gubbins (2017) define a comprehensive program design as "a thoughtful, unified service delivery plan that has a singular purpose: to identify the many, varied ways that will be used to meet the needs of high-potential students" (p. 58). Hence, this is not a pick one-and-done situation as it is highly unlikely that any one option will serve the needs of all students with gifts and talents in a particular district (Callahan & Davis, 2018; Delcourt et al., 2007). A comprehensive program design based on the needs of the students in each particular school or district must be provided at all levels, Pre-K to Grade 12 to provide continuous services, and Standard 5, Student Outcome 5.1 offers guidance for accomplishing that goal (NAGC, 2019a). Thus, by reviewing the various options provided to this point and examining each in light of the students with gifts and talents in your particular situation, you have the opportunity to create a comprehensive program design that will support these students in demonstrating growth commensurate to their abilities.

Cohesive and Coordinated Services

Similar to the notion that it takes a village to raise a child, it takes all educators and relevant professional personnel to provide cohesive and coordinated gifted services and programming to ensure positive student outcomes from PreK to Grade 12. For example, to ensure the needs of twice-exceptional students are being met, collaboration must exist among the general, gifted, and special education teacher; for students who are English language learners, the ELL teacher must be included on the team. Adams et al. (2013) argue that educators can no longer establish programs that are associated with a label; instead, they need to examine the educational needs of the whole child. Educators can no longer exist in separate silos.

To provide coordinated learning activities across and within specific grade levels, content areas, classes, or programming options, all educators must be at the planning table to ensure vertical and horizontal alignment as well as any accommodations needed for students who are twice-exceptional or who are from underserved populations. Otherwise, there is little chance for cohesive and coordinated services to occur. Deitz (2019) uses the analogy of the "all for one" attitude of the French musketeers to underscore the type of attitude needed for successful collaboration as teachers work together to accomplish a task, such as developing a continuum of services and programs that is responsive to the needs of a variety of gifted learners. According to Deitz, "Most importantly, they worked together to identify challenges and specific strategies that could help them address issues" (p. 13). For these collaborations to be successful, an administrator or other decision-maker must consistently provide expectations and the support necessary to meet them (Bauml, 2016). Guidance is provided in Student Outcome 5.2.

Career Pathways

Collaboration to support growth in academic and affective domains is necessary to help determine how students' strengths, interests, and values might contribute to developing their talent areas and to making career decisions. Callahan (2007) suggested the creation of a "Master Adult Triad" consisting of parent, teacher, and mentor to support and nurture students who are gifted and from underserved populations. Mathematics educators know that the strongest support comes from the triangle, and this three-legged stool can be the foundational support needed by their students. Extending this triad metaphor to all students with gifts and talents and adding the school counselor in a pivotal role as a member to coexist with or take the place of one of these triad members advocating for and supporting the needs of gifted students adds one more adult to provide professional guidance as students consider their future career pathways. Educators, parents, and counselors can work together to help students identify their own strengths and interests. Goal setting, as early as middle school and revisiting those goals often for realigning as needs and challenges change, is vital to support students with gifts and talents as they become successful adults. Greene Burton (2016) describes this as a cyclical process rather than a linear one and emphasizes the importance of offering training in career education to teachers and parents rather than having career counseling resting solely on the shoulders of the school counselor.

Mentorships, internships, and shadowing practicing professionals offer opportunities for students to investigate options that align with their current strengths and interests. Moreover, counselors, teachers, and parents are critical partners when students must make decisions about what courses to take and when. For example, students who have an interest in pursuing a career in a science or math field must make that decision at middle school to plan for the advanced coursework needed before entering college. Adams et al. (2014), Johnsen and Sheffield (2013), and VanTassel-Baska (2013) offer suggestions for talent trajectories in advanced coursework in science, mathematics, and English language arts, respectively that are helpful in making decisions about what course to take when.

Collaboration to Advance Talent Development

Parents and other family members often can provide unique perspectives on the abilities of their children. They frequently recognize and nurture talent at an early age before students even enter school. Community institutions and organizations can provide support in the form of supplemental services such as educational programs, youth groups, and psychological services. A plethora of supplemental programs within or outside of the school day offer students with gifts and talents opportunities to engage in activities with other students with the same interests and talents (Olszweski-Kubilius, 2020). These programs may include offerings such as chess club; Saturday and summer programs at colleges, universities, and museums; contests such as Science Olympiad or Destination Imagination; art camp; and local theater productions, to name a few. Furthermore, those individuals who teach or direct these programs "provide insider knowledge about who can assist them further with job opportunities, internships, or other mentors" (Olszewski-Kubilius, 2020, p. 442). For students to take advantages of these opportunities to advance talent development, it is essential that educators engage families, advocates, and the community in identifying student needs, talents, and goals and matching them with appropriate opportunities or in developing programs and services when those opportunities do not yet exist.

Resources

While policy helps ensure a seamless delivery of services, it also "creates the rules and standards by which scarce resources are allocated to meet almost unlimited social needs" (Gallagher, 1994, p. 337). Educational institutions are not exempted from this competition for resources. The current reform movement focuses on bringing all students to a minimal level of proficiency and uses high-stakes testing and standards-based accountability systems to achieve that goal. In the minds of many, this concentrates resources to remediate those that are "falling behind" and takes away the ability to "'do the right thing' by gifted students" (Scot et al., 2009, p. 50). Students with gifts and talents have specialized needs. To support their continued cognitive, creative, and affective growth, adequate resources must be provided. This includes staff time, funds, and administrative support.

In a survey of state directors of gifted programs, only 24 of 50 respondents indicated that their state mandated gifted services, 15 indicated no mandates, and 11 indicated mandates were determined by the LEAs. Interestingly, four of the 38 states with mandates to identify gifted students have no mandate to serve them. Twenty-three of 46 respondents indicated the state provided funding to support gifted education, but the interpretation of what that means varied by state. Only 28 of 48 states reported that teachers of students with gifts and talents are required to have some type of credential in gifted education. (NAGC & CSDPG 2020). According to Kaul and Davis' (2018) study on the use of Title II funds for professional learning in state plans, only 16 states mention gifted and talented explicitly and 3 states had no mention of gifted services. Thus, programs and services are rarely fully funded, and teachers of students with gifts and talents do not necessarily have to obtain certification to teach them. Although Student Outcome 5.5, Resources, states that programs should be adequately staffed and funded, in reality, that is not consistently happening.

Policies and Procedures

To provide a comprehensive, coordinated delivery of services and thus promote student growth, schools must have clear policies and procedures in place to guide gifted education (Callahan, 2017; McIntire, 2017). Brown et al. (2003) point out that strong policy is a basic foundation of comprehensive gifted program development. They find that policy for identifying students' needs is often strong, but that policies related to curriculum, program, and service provisions often need strengthening. As a result, they suggest giving particular attention to these areas, including details on grouping arrangements, differentiation methods, and options for acceleration, with special attention to counseling and guidance services. Specific policies regarding weighted grades, testing out of standards, acceleration and dual enrollment are also relevant to include (Adams et al., 2012). Moreover, those policies and procedures must be transparent and easily accessible to all stakeholders. Hence, having an acceleration policy is commendable, but it is of little help if it is buried deep in legal documents within a department of education's website and difficult to find.

Evaluation of Programming and Services

Unfortunately, many programs have never been evaluated. In fact, there may be no evaluation plan in place, no plans for evaluations, and/or no consideration that evaluation is an important component of programming. As mentioned earlier in this chapter, evaluation is a vital piece of program development. Program evaluation must be frequent and ongoing, including both summative and formative assessment, to get beyond the results that provide little information beyond, "We liked it." All aspects of the program, from identification for services to student outcomes as a result of receiving those services must be frequently monitored to ensure the effectiveness of the program (Callahan, 2017; 2020). When not prohibited by state policies, yearly standardized tests should be used rather than the grade level ones to provide a high enough ceiling for gifted learners to show growth.

Revising the selection process, improving the curriculum, assessing the various programming options, and guaranteeing fidelity of implementation are all vital processes necessary to ensure the learning needs of students with gifts and talents are being met. Both qualitative and quantitative data should be gathered and analyzed to provide a more informed evaluation of their effectiveness (Callahan, 2017; 2020). Because programming for gifted students comes in a variety of options and no single program can serve the differences recognized in gifted populations, fidelity of implementation is often best measured by observing what happens in individual classrooms.

When the curriculum for gifted learners is based on advanced content, process, and products, assessments given by the teacher must reflect more than grade level knowledge and skills; otherwise, it will be difficult to determine how much progress gifted learners are making as a result of receiving special programming. Hence, on-going professional learning and teachers' commitment to serve these students are critical to successful fidelity of implementation of any programming option (Azano et al., 2011). Evaluations, including student assessment of learning, need to have support from all school personnel, including the school administrator. Otherwise, the lack of necessary time and resources to implement any degree of program evaluation or differentiated assessments may impede this process. The results of any program evaluation should be distributed in multiple formats to all stakeholders, including an action plan for how the results will be used for program improvement.

Standard 5 at the District Level: Oceanview Public Schools

Oceanview Public Schools (OPS) is an above average, public school district located in a medium sized city, situated in a county that includes urban, suburban, and rural schools. OPS believes there are some students whose performance or potential for performance exceeds what is generally expected at their grade level. OPS believes that these students need to be offered a continuum of services that meet their academic, social and emotional needs. By state law, all policies and procedures at the district level must align with state policies that impact gifted learners.

Oceanview Public Schools identifies students who demonstrate exceptional academic aptitude in science and/or mathematics (Grades K–5) and in English, mathematics, science, and/or social studies (Grades 6–12). A student is determined eligible for gifted education program services in a specific academic area(s) based upon both quantitative and qualitative indicators. Multiple criteria are utilized in the identification and placement process. Program and service options include pull-out programs, K–5, at all elementary schools; one magnet school with special classes for students with gifts and talents in Grades 3–5, and one for Grades 6–8; special advanced content classes in English language arts, math, science, and social studies in middle and high school; and dual enrollment, Advanced Placement, International Baccalaureate, and the Cambridge Advanced Program at the high school level. There is a state-wide K–12 virtual school that offers individual advanced programming for gifted students that they may access to replace any coursework in the regular classroom. Except for early entrance into kindergarten, acceleration is permitted as part of state policy and may be considered at any time during the school year.

All teachers who teach gifted learners in OPS must be certified in gifted education from a nationally recognized teacher education program that is aligned with the NAGC-CEC Teacher Preparation Standards in Gifted Education. Thus, they have a repertoire of evidence-based practices from which to choose to provide comprehensive and cohesive services to meet the needs of their students who are gifted and talented. Because most students are served using a pull-out model, all teachers at each specific grade level in each school have a common planning time. This allows general, special, and gifted education teachers to communicate and coordinate the educational plans of all learners. The general education teacher, in collaboration with the special and gifted education teachers, can differentiate instruction for these students based on the input of their other teachers. Hence, students with gifts and talents and those who are twice-exceptional have their needs met throughout the school day rather than just during their daily one-hour pull-out program.

Moreover, there is a counselor in each school whose primary job is to monitor the progress of each gifted learner through an Education Plan, schedule assessments, meet with gifted learners and their parents when there is concern about their cognitive, social, emotional, or psychological welfare, and provide career and college guidance. The counselor coordinates mentorships, internships, and shadowing opportunities for gifted students who are interested in participating in these in their areas of interest. Assessments to ensure students who are gifted are making adequate yearly progress are coordinated by the counselor. Every other year, the students take the state-mandated tests above grade level, and in alternate years, the students are given the Iowa Assessments out of level in the content areas in which they have been served. Hence, the district can better gauge actual student progress by lowering the chance that they are hitting the ceiling of the grade level assessments.

There is a broad-based planning committee for the district that includes parents, teachers, community leaders, gifted specialists, and school board representatives that collaborates to advocate for students who are gifted and talented. This includes meeting with law and policy makers at the state level to ensure that the needs of gifted learners are considered in all applicable legislation or when new legislation is necessary. For example, based on research presented in *A Nation Empowered* (Assouline et al., 2015), local OPS advocates for gifted education along with those in other districts succeeded in getting the legislature to institute a state-wide evidenced-based acceleration policy.

All administrators in OPS must provide opportunities for professional learning that focus on gifted education three times per year. Furthermore, they must have completed the state's series of three administrator modules on gifted education: Nature and Needs, Differentiation, and Programming. OPS fully funds gifted programming through a combination of grants, state funds, and district funds. The district superintendent ensures that each OPS school completes an annual internal evaluation of its gifted services and every five years undergoes an external evaluation by a nationally recognized expert in gifted education. Thus, every year an evaluation report is presented to the broad-based planning committee and each building level advisory board. Following that, the report is presented at a school board meeting and posted on each school's website. Because OPS teachers of gifted learners must be certified in gifted education, all other educators must participate in professional learning opportunities focusing on gifted learners, and administrators must have training in gifted education, gifted programs and services have a better chance of being implemented with fidelity.

Standard 5 at the School and Classroom Levels: Low Country Elementary School

Low County Elementary School is located in the Oceanview Public Schools district and uses the pull-out model to serve gifted learners in Grades K–5. The principal, Mr. Williams, has completed the district modules in gifted education for administrators and is a strong supporter of gifted education. In conjunction with the counselor and assistant principal, he has approved a schedule that causes minimal disruption when the gifted students leave their classroom to receive services through the pull-out program. For example, all second grades teach math and science at the same time. When Mr. Michaels teaches his second-grade science class, any students identified as gifted in science leave and go to Ms. Anderson's gifted science class; thus, the gifted students miss only the subject that is being replaced.

In addition to her master's degree, Ms. Anderson has her gifted endorsement from a nationally recognized program in gifted education. She is required by state law to use the grade level curriculum and pacing guide as the basis of instruction, but she has a repertoire of instructional strategies and replacement curriculum units developed specifically for gifted learners that she can use once she has ensured the students know the grade level standards. For example, she pre-assesses each science unit to determine who has already mastered the unit standards and content. She compacts the instruction and accelerates the pace of instruction where gaps exist, grouping and regrouping students as needed to ensure mastery. With the remainder of her time allotted for that particular chapter, she chooses above grade level state standards to develop content and activities that will enrich and accelerate her students' learning in science based on their strengths and interests. These learning experiences allow students to work like practicing scientists as she provides opportunities for them to develop expertise in the field. In addition to the unit tests that are provided in the state textbook, she creates assessments that provide student outcome data aligned with the advanced content, process, and products that have engaged her students. During her weekly collaboration time, Ms. Anderson updates the rest of the second grade teachers and the special education teacher about what their students have been learning in science, apprises them on any academic or social/emotional issues that have arisen during her time with the students, and addresses any modifications for 2e students that have been necessary. She suggests ways to differentiate for her students when they are back in the regular classroom, particularly in language arts. Although students are not identified in this area, Ms. Anderson's gifted background raises her awareness of students whose gifts may go beyond science or math and their need to work above grade level in additional subjects. Ms. Anderson finds time to discuss what she is doing in science with the counselor responsible for students with gifts and talents that might require changes to their EP.

Ms. Anderson has designed and implemented a Super Scientists after-school club, a Saturday Science program and a summer STEM camp for eligible students to ensure there are options for gifted science students outside the school day. She chairs the school's Gifted Advisory Committee, composed of the two teachers of gifted students, the school counselor, the assistant principal, and one teacher and one parent from each grade level. Once a quarter, the Advisory Committee meets with the district's Broad-based Planning Committee to ensure comprehensive and ongoing services for students with gifts and talents are in place and if any changes need to be made. In her leadership role on the Advisory Committee, Ms. Anderson assists with internal and external evaluations by delineating areas that may need to be evaluated, helping to create appropriate questions to gather the necessary data, encouraging all stakeholders to respond to surveys or volunteer for focus groups, and determining next steps for the program based on the data gathered. Hence, gifted services at Low Country Elementary School are regularly adjusted based on data to ensure that students with gifts and talents have access to programming that meets their needs, addresses their strengths and interests, and fosters adequate yearly progress commensurate with their abilities.

Conclusion

Standard 5, Programming, of the *NAGC Pre-K–Grade 12 Gifted Programming Standards* (2019a) underscores the need for educators to use empirical evidence when seeking to design, develop, and implement programming for students with gifts and talents. Understanding their needs from a student outcomes perspective allows educators to match learner needs with appropriate programming options. No matter which practice educators may choose to use for a specific learner or group of learners, educators must keep in mind that no one practice works for every student. Some learners may need multiple accommodations, and others may just need a few simple modifications to the general curriculum for challenging, meaningful learning to occur. To enhance student outcomes at a level commensurate to their needs, some learners may need access to material at a faster pace or at a higher level of complexity. Others may require in-school and out-of-school enrichment opportunities or specific individualized internships or mentorships. In summary, to ensure that specific, measurable student outcomes are attained, educators must have expertise in gathering these data and systematically using them in collaboration with other educators, parents, and community members to "develop, implement, manage, and evaluate services for students with a variety of gifts and talents" (NAGC, 2019b, p. 14).

References

Adams, C. M. (2006). Articulating gifted education program goals. In J. Purcell & R. Eckert (Eds.), *Designing services and programs for high ability learners: A guidebook for gifted education* (pp. 62–72). Corwin Press.

Adams, C. M. (2009). Waiting for Santa Clause. *Gifted Child Quarterly*, 53(4), 272–273. https://doi.org/10.1177/0016986209346942

Adams, C. M. (2018). Pull-out programs as a service delivery option. In C. M. Callahan & H. L. Hertberg-Davis (Eds.), *Fundamentals of gifted education: Considering multiple perspectives* (2nd ed., pp. 187–199). Routledge.

Adams, C. M., & Boswell, C. A. (2012). *Effective practices for gifted students from underserved populations*. Prufrock Press.

Adams, C. M., Cotabish, A., & Dailey, D. (2015). *A teacher's guide to using the Next Generation Science Standards with gifted and advanced learners.* Prufrock Press.

Adams, C. M., Cotabish, A., & Ricci, M.C. (2014). *Using the Next Generation Science Standards with gifted and advanced learners.* Prufrock Press.

Adams, C. M., Mursky, C. V., & Keilty, B. (2012). Programming models and programming design. In S. K. Johnsen (Ed.), *NAGC Pre-K–Grade 12 Gifted Education Programming Standards: A guide to planning and implementing high-quality services* (pp. 141–174). Prufrock Press.

Adams, C. M., & Pierce, R. L. (2006). *Differentiating instruction: A practical guide to tiering lessons in the elementary grades.* Prufrock Press.

Adams, C. M., Yssel, N., & Anwiler, H. (2013). Twice exceptional gifted learners and RTI: Targeting both sides of the same coin. In M. R. Coleman & S. K. Johnsen (Eds.), *Implementing RtI with gifted students: Service models, trends, and issues* (pp. 229–252). Prufrock Press.

Assouline, S. G., Colangelo, N., VanTassel-Baska, J., & Lupkowski-Shoplik, A. E. (2015). *A nation empowered: Evidence trumps the excuses that hold back America's brightest students* (Vol. I). The Connie Belin & Jacqueline N. Blank International Center for Gifted Education and Talent Development. www.accelerationinstitute.org/nation_empowered/

Azano, A., Missett, T. C., Callahan, C. M., Oh, S., Brunner, M., Foster, L. H., & Moon, T. R. (2011). Exploring the relationship between fidelity of implementation and academic achievement in a third-grade gifted curriculum: A mixed-methods study. *Journal of Advanced Academics* 22(5), 693–719. https://doi.org/10.1177/1932202X11424878

Bauml, M. (2016). The promise of collaboration. *Educational Leadership, 74*(2), 58–62. https://eric.ed.gov/?id=EJ1116568

Behrens, W. A., & Lupkowski-Shoplik, A. (2020). Acceleration: It's about time! In J. H. Robins, J. L. Jolly, F. A. Karnes, & S. M. Bean (Eds.), *Methods & materials for teaching the gifted* (5th ed., pp. 231–257). Prufrock Press.

Bernstein, B. O., Lubinski, D., & Benbow, C. P. (2020). Academic acceleration in gifted youth and fruitless concerns regarding psychological well-being: A 35-year longitudinal study. *Journal of Educational Psychology.* Advance online publication. https://doi.org/10.1037/edu0000500

Brulles, D. (2005). *An examination and critical analysis of cluster grouping gifted students in an elementary school.* (Unpublished Doctoral Dissertation, Arizona State University).

Brown, E., Avery, L., & VanTassel-Baska, J. (2003). *Gifted policy analysis study for the Ohio Department of Education.* The Center for Gifted Education.

Callahan, C. M. (2007). What can we learn from research about promising practices in developing the gifts and talents of low income students? In J. VanTassel-Baska & T. Stambaugh (Eds.), *Overlooked gems: A national perspective on low income promising learners* (pp. 53–56). The National Association for Gifted Children.

Callahan, C. M. (2009). A family of identification myths: Your sample must be the same as the population. There is a "silver bullet" in identification. There must be "winners" and "losers" in identification and programming. *Gifted Child Quarterly, 53*(4), 239–241. https://doi.org/10.1177/0016986209346826

Callahan, C. M. (2017). Developing a plan for evaluating services provided to gifted students. In R. D. Eckert & J. H. Robins (Eds.), *Designing services and programs for high-ability learners: A guidebook for gifted education* (2nd ed., pp. 225–238). Corwin.

Callahan, C. M. (2020). Gifted programming standards: Understanding their role in program design and evaluation. In J. H. Robins, J. L. Jolly, F. A. Karnes, & S. M. Bean (Eds.), *Methods & materials for teaching the gifted* (5th ed., pp. 127–144). Prufrock Press.

Callahan, C. M., & Hertberg-Davis, H. L. (2018). Contexts for instruction: An introduction to service delivery options and programming models in gifted education. In C. M. Callahan & H. L. Hertberg-Davis (Eds.), *Fundamentals of gifted education: Considering multiple perspectives* (2nd ed., pp. 169–172). Routledge.

Callahan, C. M., Moon, T. R., & Oh, S. (2017). Describing the status of programs for the gifted: A call to action. *Journal for the Education of the Gifted, 40*(1), 20–49. https://doi.org/10.1177/0162353216686215

Callahan, C. M., Moon, T. R., Oh, S., Azano, A. P., & Hailey, E. P. (2015). What works in gifted education: Documenting the effects of an integrated curricular/instructional model for gifted students. *American Educational Research Journal, 52*(1), 137–167. https://doi.org/10.3102/0002831214549448

Colangelo, N., Assouline, S. G., & Gross, M. U. M. (2004). *A nation deceived: How schools hold back America's brightest students.* The Connie Belin & Jacqueline N. Blank International Center for Gifted Education and Talent Development. www.accelerationinstitute.org/nation_deceived/Get_Report.aspx

Coleman, L., & Cross, T. L. (2005). *Being gifted in school.* Prufrock Press.

Cox, J., Daniel, N., & Boston, B. O. (1985). *Educating able learners: Programs and promising practices.* University of Texas Press.

Deitz, C. (2019, May). All for one: The essential art of collaboration. *Teaching for High Potential,* 12–13.

Delcourt, M. A. B., Cornell, D. G., & Goldberg, M. D. (2007). Cognitive and affective learning outcomes of gifted elementary school students. *Gifted Child Quarterly, 51*(4), 359–381. https://doi.org/10.1177/0016986207306320

Delcourt, M. A. B., & Evans, K. (1994). *Qualitative extension of the learning outcomes study* (Report No. RM94110). The National Research Center on the Gifted and Talented. https://nrcgt.uconn.edu/wp-content/uploads/sites/953/2015/04/rm94110.pdf

Delcourt, M. A. B., Loyd, B. H., Cornell, D. G., & Goldberg, M. D. (1994). *Evaluation of the effects of programming arrangements on student learning outcomes.* The National Research Center on the Gifted and Talented. https://nrcgt.uconn.edu/wp-content/uploads/sites/953/2015/04/rm94108.pdf

Eckert, R. D., &. Robins, J. H. (Eds.) (2017). *Designing services and programs for high-ability learners: A guidebook for gifted education* (2nd ed). Corwin.

Every Student Succeeds Act, 20 U.S.C. § 6301 (2015). https://congress.gov/114/plaws/publ95/PLAW-114publ195.pdf

Florida Statutes, Title XLVII.K-20 Education code § 1003.21. School attendance (2019a). www.leg.state.fl.us/Statutes/index.cfm?App_mode=Display_Statute&URL=1000–1099/1003/Sections/1003.21.html

Florida Statutes, Title XLVII.K-20 Education code § 1002.3105. Student and Parental Rights and Educational Choices (2019b). www.leg.state.fl.us/Statutes/index.cfm?App_mode=Display_Statute&URL=1000–1099/1002/Sections/1002.3105.html

Gagné, F. (1995). From giftedness to talent: A developmental model and its impact on the language of the field. *Roeper Review, 18*(2), 103–111. https://doi.org/10.1080/02783199509553709

Gallagher, J. J. (1994). *Policy designed for diversity: New initiatives for children with disabilities.* In D. Bryant and M. Graham (Eds.), *Implementing early interventions* (pp. 336–350). Guilford Publications.

Gavin, M. K., Casa, T. M., Adelson, J. L., Carroll, S. R., & Sheffield, L. J. (2009). The impact of advanced curriculum on the achievement of mathematically promising elementary students. *Gifted Child Quarterly, 53*(2), 188–202. https://doi.org/10.1177/0016986213479564

Gentry, M. L. (2014). *Total school cluster grouping & differentiation: A comprehensive, research-based plan for raising student achievement & improving teacher practices* (2nd ed.). Prufrock.

Gentry, M. L. (2018). Cluster grouping. In C. M. Callahan & H. L. Hertberg-Davis (Eds.), *Fundamentals of gifted education: Considering multiple perspectives* (2nd ed., pp. 213–224). Routledge.

Gentry, M., & MacDougall, J. (2009). Total school cluster grouping: Model, research, and practice. In J. S. Renzulli, E. J. Gubbins, K. S. Mc Millen, R. D. Eckert, & C. A. Little (Eds.), *Systems and models for developing programs for the gifted & talented* (2nd ed., pp. 211–234). Creative Learning Press.

Gentry, M., & Mann, R. L. (2008). *Total school cluster grouping & differentiation: A comprehensive, research-based plan for raising student achievement & improving teacher practices*. Creative Learning Press.

Gentry, M., & Owen, S. V. (1999). An investigation of total school flexible cluster grouping on identification, achievement, and classroom practices. *Gifted Child Quarterly, 43*(4), 224–243. https://doi.org/10.1177/001698629904300402

Green Burton, M. J. (2016). Career and life planning for gifted adolescents. In M. Neihart, S. I. Pfeiffer, & T. L. Cross (Eds.), *The social and emotional development of gifted children* (2nd ed., pp. 259–268). Prufrock Press.

Hodges, J. (2018). Assessing the influence of No Child Left Behind on gifted education funding in Texas: A descriptive study. *Journal of Advanced Academics, 29*(4), 321–342. https://do1.org/10.1177/1932202X18779343

Hughes, C. E., Kettler, T., Shaunessy-Dedrick, E., & VanTassel-Baska, J. (2014). *A teacher's guide to using the Common Core State Standards with gifted and advanced learners in the English language arts*. Prufrock Press.

Ihrig, L. M., & Degner, K. M. (2015). Acceleration and STEM education. In S. G. Assouline, N. Colangelo, J. VanTassel-Baska, & A. Lupkowski-Shoplik (Eds.), *A nation empowered: Evidence trumps the excuses holding back America's brightest students* (Vol. 2, pp. 123–135). The Connie Belin & Jacqueline N. Blank International Center for Gifted Education and Talent Development.

Johnsen, S. K., & Johnson, K. (2007). *Independent study program* (2nd ed.). Prufrock Press.

Johnsen, S. K., Ryser, G., & Assouline, S. G. (2014). *A teacher's guide to using the Common Core State Standards in mathematics with gifted and advanced learners*. Prufrock Press.

Johnsen, S. K., & Sheffield, L. (Eds.) (2013). *Using the Common Core State Standards in mathematics with gifted and advanced learners*. Prufrock Press.

Johnsen, S. K., VanTassel-Baska, J. L., Robinson, A., Cotabish, A., Dailey, D., Jolly, J., Clarenbach, J., & Adams, C. M. (2016). *Using the national gifted education standards for teacher preparation* (2nd ed.) Prufrock Press.

Kaplan, S. K. (2009). The Grid: A model to construct differentiated curriculum for the gifted. In J. S. Renzulli, E. J. Gubbins, K. S. Mc Millen, R. D. Eckert, & C. A. Little (Eds.), *Systems and models for developing programs for the gifted & talented* (2nd ed., pp. 235–251). Creative Learning Press.

Kaul, C. R., & Davis, B. K. (2018). How the state education agencies addressed gifted education in the Title II sections of their ESSA state plans. *Gifted Child Today, 41*(1), 159–167. https://doi.org/10.1177/1076217518769700

Kolloff, P. B. (2003). State-supported residential high schools. In N. Colangelo & G. A. Davis (Eds.), *Handbook of gifted education* (3rd ed., pp. 238–246). Allyn & Bacon.

Kulik, J. A. (1992). *An analysis of the research on ability grouping: Historical and contemporary perspectives.* National Research Center on the Gifted and Talented. https://nrcgt.uconn.edu/wp-content/uploads/sites/953/2015/04/rbdm9204.pdf

Kulik, J. A. (2003). Grouping and tracking. In N. Colangelo & G. A. Davis (Eds.), *Handbook of gifted education* (3rd ed., pp. 268–281). Allyn & Bacon.

Kulik, J. A., & Kulik, C-L. C. (1992). Meta-analytic findings on grouping programs. *Gifted Child Quarterly, 36*(2), 73–77. https://doi.org/10.1177/001698629203600204

Lubinski, D., & Benbow, C. P. (2006). Study of Mathematically Precocious Youth after 35 years: Uncovering antecedents for the development of math-science expertise. *Perspectives on Psychological Science, 1*(4), 316–345. https://doi.org/10.1111/j.1745–6916.2006.00019.x

Lubinski, D., Webb, R. M., Morelock, M. J., & Benbow, C. P. (2001). Top 1 in 10,000: A 10-year follow-up of the profoundly gifted. *Journal of Applied Psychology, 86*(4), 718–729. https://doi.org/10.1037/0021–9010.86.4.718

Lupkowski-Shoplik, A., Behrens, W. A., & Assouline, S. G. (2018). *Developing academic acceleration policies: Whole grade, early entrance, & single subject.* The Connie Belin & Jacqueline N. Blank International Center for Gifted Education and Talent Development. www.accelerationinstitute.org/Resources/Policy_Guidelines/Developing-Academic-Acceleration-Policies.pdf

McIntire, J. (2017). Developing local policies to guide and support gifted programs and services. In R. D. Eckert & J. H. Robins (Eds.), *Designing services and programs for high-ability learners: A guidebook for gifted education* (2nd ed., pp. 212–224). Corwin.

National Association for Gifted Children (2014a). *Position statement: Collaboration among all educators to meet the needs of gifted learners.* www.nagc.org/sites/default/files/Position%20Statement/Collaboration%20Among%20Educators.pdf

National Association for Gifted Children (2014b). *Knowledge and skills standards in gifted education for all teachers.* www.nagc.org/resources-publications/resources/national-standards-gifted-and-talented-education/knowledge-and

National Association for Gifted Children (2019a). *The NAGC Pre-K to Grade 12 Gifted Programming Standards: Programming standard 5: Programming.* www.nagc.org/sites/default/files/standards/Programming%20Standard%205%20Programming.pdf

National Association for Gifted Children (2019b). *The NAGC Pre-K to Grade 12 Gifted Programming Standards.* www.nagc.org/sites/default/files/standards/Intro%202019%20Programming%20Standards%281%29.pdf

National Association for Gifted Children (2019c). *Position statement: A definition of giftedness that guides best practice.* www.nagc.org/sites/default/files/Position%20Statement/Definition%20of%20Giftedness%20%282019%29.pdf

National Association for Gifted Children & Council of State Directors of Programs for the Gifted (2020). State of the states in gifted education 2018–2019. www.nagc.org/sites/default/files/Revised%20-%20NAGC_CSDPG_2018–2019%20State%20of%20the%20States%20in%20Gifted%20Education%20Report-Final.pdf

Neihart, M. (2007). The socioaffective impact of acceleration and ability grouping: Recommendations for best practice. *Gifted Child Quarterly, 51*(4), 330–341. https://doi.org/10.1177/0016986207306319

No Child Left Behind (NCLB) Act of 2001, Pub. L. No. 107–110, § 101, Stat. 1425 (2002). www2.ed.gov/policy/elsec/leg/esea02/107–110.pdf

Olszweski-Kubilius, P. (2010). Special schools and other options for gifted STEM students. *Roeper Review, 32*(1), 61–70. https://doi.org/10.1080/02783190903386892

Olszweski-Kubilius, P. (2020). Programming for talent development beyond the classroom. In J. H. Robins, J. L. Jolly, F. A. Karnes, & S. M. Bean (Eds.), *Methods & materials for teaching the gifted* (5th ed., pp. 439–455). Prufrock Press.

Olszewski-Kubilius, P., Subotnik, R. F., & Worrell, F. C. (Eds.) (2018). *Talent development as a framework for gifted education: Implications for best practices and applications in schools.* Prufrock Press.

Peters, S. J., Matthews, M. S., McBee, M. T., & McCoach, D. B. (2014). *Beyond gifted education: Designing and implementing advanced academic programs.* Prufrock Press.

Pierce, R. L., Cassady, J. C., Adams, C. M., Speirs Neumeister, K., Dixon, F. A., & Cross, T. L. (2011). The effects of clustering and curriculum on the development of gifted learners' math achievement. *Journal for the Education of the Gifted, 34*(4), 569–594. https://doi.org/10.1177/016235321103400403

Plucker, J. A., Makel, M. C., Matthews, M. S., Peters, S. J., & Rambo-Hernandez, K. E. (2017). Blazing new trails: Strengthening policy research in gifted education. *Gifted Child Quarterly 61*(3), 210–218. https://doi.org/10.1177/0016986217701838

Reis, S. M., & Gubbins, E. J. (2017). Comprehensive program design. In R. D. Eckert & J. H. Robins (Eds.), *Designing services and programs for high-ability learners: A guidebook for gifted education* (2nd ed., pp. 58–75). Corwin.

Reis, S. M., McCoach, D. B., Little, C. A., Muller, L. M., & Kaniskan, B. (2011). The effects of differentiated instruction and enrichment pedagogy on reading achievement in five elementary schools. *American Educational Research Journal, 48*(2), 462–501. https://doi.org/10.3102/0002831210382891

Renzulli, J. S. (1986). The three-ring conception of giftedness: A developmental model for creative productivity. In R. J. Sternberg & J. Davidson (Eds.), *Conceptions of giftedness* (pp. 53–92). Cambridge University Press.

Renzulli, J. S., & Reis, S. M. (2008). *Enriching curriculum for all students* (2nd ed.). Corwin Press.

Roberts, J. L. (2005). *Enrichment opportunities for gifted learners.* Prufrock Press.

Robinson, A. (2009). Examining the ostrich: Gifted services do not cure a sick program. *Gifted Child Quarterly, 53*(4), 259–261. https://doi.org/10.1177/0016986209346935

Rogers, K. (1991). *The relationship of grouping practices to the education of the gifted and talented learner.* National Research Center on the Gifted and Talented. https://nrcgt.uconn.edu/wp-content/uploads/sites/953/2015/04/rbdm9102.pdf

Rogers, K. B. (1992). A best-evidence synthesis of research on acceleration options for gifted students. In N. Colangelo, S. G. Assouline, & D. L. Ambrose (Eds.), *Talent development: Proceedings of the 1991 Henry B. and Jocelyn Wallace National Research Symposium on Talent Development* (pp. 406–409). Trillium Press.

Rogers, K. (2001). *Reforming gifted education.* Gifted Potential Press.

Rogers, K. (2004). The academic effects of acceleration. In N. Colangelo, S. G. Assouline, & M. Gross (Eds.), *A nation deceived: How schools hold back America's brightest students* (Vol. 2, pp. 47–57). The Connie Belin and Jacqueline N. Blank International Center for Gifted Education and Talent Development. .

Rogers, K. B. (2006). *A menu of options for grouping gifted students.* Prufrock Press.

Rogers, K. B. (2007). Lessons learned about educating the gifted and talented: A synthesis of research on educational practice. *Gifted Child Quarterly, 51*(4), 382–396. https://doi.org/10.1177/0016986207306324

Rogers, K. B. (2015). The academic, socialization, and psychological effects of acceleration: Research synthesis. In S. G. Assouline, N. Colangelo, J. VanTassel-Baska, & A. Lupkowski-Shoplik (Eds.), *A nation empowered: Evidence trumps the excuses holding back America's brightest students* (Vol. 2, pp. 19–29). The Connie Belin & Jacqueline N. Blank International Center for Gifted Education and Talent Development.

Rubenstein, L. D., & Ridgley, L. M. (2017). Unified program design: Organizing existing programming models, delivery options, and curriculum. *Gifted Child Today, 40*(3), 163–174. https://doi.org/ 10.1177/1076217517707234

Schuler, P. (1997, Winter). Cluster grouping coast to coast. *The National Research Center on the Gifted and Talented Newsletter.* www.gifted.uconn.edu/nrcgt/newsletter/winter97/wintr974.html

Scot, T. P., Callahan, C. M., & Urquhart, J. (2009). Paint-by-number teachers and cookie-cutter students: The unintended effects of high-stakes testing on the education of gifted students. *Roeper Review, 31*(1), 40–52. https://doi.org/10.1080/02783190802527364

Southern, W. T., & Jones, E. D. (2015). Types of acceleration: Dimensions and issues. In S. G. Assouline, N. Colangelo, J. VanTassel-Baska, & A. Lupkowski-Shoplik (Eds.), *A nation empowered: Evidence trumps the excuses holding back America's brightest students* (Vol. 2, pp. 9–18). The Connie Belin & Jacqueline N. Blank International Center for Gifted Education and Talent Development.

Stanley, J. C. (1980). On educating the gifted. *Educational Researcher, 9*(3), 8–13. https://doi.org/10.3102/0013189X009003008

Steenbergen-Hu, S, Makel, M. C., & Olszewski-Kubilius, P. (2016). What one hundred years of research says about the effects of ability grouping and acceleration on K–12 students' academic achievement: Findings from two second order meta-analyses. *Review of Educational Research, 86*(4), 849–899. https://doi.org/10.3102/0034654316675417

Steenbergen-Hu, S., & Moon, S. M. (2011). The effects of acceleration on high ability learners. *Gifted Child Quarterly, 55*(1), 39–53. https://doi.org/10.1177/0016986210383155

Subotnik, R. F., Olszewski-Kubilius, P., & Worrell, F. C. (2011). Rethinking giftedness and gifted education: A proposed direction forward based on psychological science. *Psychological Science in the Public Interest, 12*(1), 3–54. https://doi.org/10.1177/1529100611418056

Swiatek, M., & Lupkowski-Shoplik, A. (2003). Elementary and middle school student participation in gifted programs: Are gifted students underserved? *Gifted Child Quarterly, 47*(2), 118–130. https://doi.org/10.1177/001698620304700203

Terman, L. M. (1922). A new approach to the study of genius. *Psychological Review, 29*(4), 310–318. https://doi.org/10.1037/h0071072

Tieso, C. L. (2005). The effects of grouping practices and curricular adjustments on achievement. *Journal for the Education of the Gifted, 29*(1), 60–89. https://doi.org/10.1177/016235320502900104

Tomlinson, C. A. (2003). *Fulfilling the promise of the differentiated classroom.* Association for Supervision and Curriculum Development.

Tomlinson, C. A. (2009). The "patch on" approach to programming is effective. *Gifted Child Quarterly, 53*(4), 254–256. https://doi.org/10.1177/0016986209346931

Tomlinson, C. A. (2017). *How to differentiate instruction in academically diverse classrooms* (3rd ed.). Association for Supervision and Curriculum Development.

Tomlinson, C. A. (2018). Differentiated instruction. In C. M. Callahan & H. L. Hertberg-Davis (Eds.), *Fundamentals of gifted education: Considering multiple perspectives* (2nd ed., pp. 279–292). Routledge.

Treffinger, D. J., Young, G. C., Nassab, C. A., & Wittig, C. (2004). *Talent development: The levels of service approach.* Prufrock Press.

VanTassel-Baska, J. (2006). A content analysis of evaluation findings across 20 gifted programs: A clarion call for enhanced gifted program development. *Gifted Child Quarterly, 50*(3), 199–210. https://doi.org/10.1177/001698620605000302

VanTassel-Baska, J. (2009). Gifted programs should stick out like a sore thumb. *Gifted Child Quarterly, 53*(4), 266–268. https://doi.org/10.1177/0016986209346938

VanTassel-Baska, J. (Ed.) (2013). *Using the Common Core State Standards for English language arts with gifted and advanced learners.* Prufrock Press.

VanTassel-Baska, J., Hubbard, G., & Robbins, J. (2020). Differentiation of instruction for gifted learners: Collated evaluative studies of teacher classroom practices, *Roeper Review, 42*(3), 153–164. https://doi.org/10.1080/02783193.2020.1765919

VanTassel-Baska, J., & Sher, B. T. (2011). Accelerated learning experiences in core content areas. In J. VanTassel-Baska & C. A. Little (Eds.), *Content-based curriculum for high-ability learners* (2nd ed., pp. 49–69). Prufrock Press.

VanTassel-Baska, J., Zuo, L., Avery, L. D., & Little, C. A. (2002). A curriculum study of gifted student learning in the language arts. *Gifted Child Quarterly, 46*(1), 30–44. https://doi.org/10.1177/001698620204600104

Vaughn, V. L., Feldhusen, J. F., & Asher, J. W. (1991). Meta-analysis and review of research on pull-out programs in gifted education. *Gifted Child Quarterly, 35*(2), 92–98. https://doi.org/10.1177/001698629103500208

Wai, J. (2015). Long-term effects of educational acceleration. In S. G. Assouline, N. Colangelo, J. VanTassel-Baska, & A. Lupkowski-Shoplik (Eds.), *A nation empowered: Evidence trumps the excuses holding back America's brightest students* (Vol. 2, pp. 73–83). The Connie Belin & Jacqueline N. Blank International Center for Gifted Education and Talent Development.

Winebrenner, S., & Brulles, D. (2008). *The cluster grouping handbook: How to challenge gifted students and improve achievement for all.* Free Spirit Publishing.

Worrell, F. C., Subotnik, R. F., Olszewski-Kubilius, P., & Dixson, D. D. (2019). Gifted students. *Annual Review of Psychology, 70,* 551–576. https://doi.org/10.1146/annurev-psych-010418-102846

8

Professional Learning Standards

Sandra N. Kaplan, Jessica Manzone,
and Julia Nyberg

The importance of professional learning is acknowledged as a fundamental contribution to the performance of both students and teachers. Yet, often the practices of professional learning are not consistently commensurate to the underlying principles that have defined their purposes and practices. The fundamental issues of professional learning for educators of the gifted relate to key elements that underscore the purposes and justification of professional learning in general: *relevance, support, continuity*, and *visibility*. The purpose of this chapter is to introduce alternative practices and the variables that facilitate or impede professional learning.

Key Elements for Professional Learning

Relevance
Relevance in terms of professional learning refers to the degree of alignment between the content, skills, and instructional strategies presented during the professional learning and the actual needs of the audience for whom the professional learning is intended. The gap between what is intended and what is actualized is critical. The construction of relevant professional learning is

DOI: 10.4324/9781003236863-8

accomplished through an analysis of the needs of the participants related to building capacity in their content knowledge or skills, motivational awareness, and/or organizational structures (Clark & Estes, 2008). Questions such as the ones listed below can be used to ascertain how relevant the professional learning will be, is, or was for the people in attendance.

- ◆ What are the needs (content, knowledge, skills, materials, motivational emphasis) of the group and are those needs being directly addressed through the professional learning?
- ◆ How receptive is the group to the idea of professional learning? Do they value the content and see it as a means of improving their practice/institution?
- ◆ What are the organizational structures currently in place at the institution? Do they facilitate or hinder the content presented during the professional learning?

Support

Support for effective professional learning is defined as the mechanisms in place within an institution that provide teachers with the best possible chance for successful implementation. According to Ball and Cohen (1999), this is the power to "immunize teachers" against the regression to the norm related to ineffective practice, cynicism, and institutional barriers. Support for teachers, administrators, and coaches can embody many forms—planning time, materials and resources, mentors, opportunities to engage in goal setting, webinars, funding for continuing education, substitute support. The following questions can be asked to target the types of support needed and how those supports can enhance any professional learning experience.

- ◆ What opportunities are available (or could become available) to teachers to assist with the implementation of professional learning?
- ◆ How can support for teachers be individualized and/or customized for each teacher in a school setting?

Continuity

Continuity in relationship to professional learning relates to the set of experiences as a whole. Effective professional learning is not singular in nature. It requires intensive opportunities for teachers to engage over time and through a variety of aligned activities. Professional learning that is isolated and sporadic will never have the same degree of transfer as those constructed with purposeful continuity in mind. Bransford and Schwartz's

(1999) seminal work on transfer theory suggests that the manner in which information is learned impacts the degree to which it is internalized and transferred to other situations and settings. If the ultimate goal of a professional learning is application and deep levels of meaning on the part of the participant, the construction of the professional learning must contain continuity.

- ◆ What follow-up opportunities exist for teachers to engage in the knowledge and skills learned during the professional learning?
- ◆ What are the overarching goals and competencies for the professional learning? Have they been clearly articulated and defined?
- ◆ What are the short and the long term goals for the professional learning?

Visibility

Out of all of the key terms related to professional learning, visibility is one of the last discussed. Visibility is an extension of awareness and is impacted by a variety of factors both inside and outside the field of education. Trends in political agendas, social norms, economic interests, and educational mandates encompass and affect the *visibility* of professional learning. The ability of a professional learning to address current and contemporary issues of best practice and to translate those issues to the various stakeholder groups is a construct of visibility. Visibility is a distinctly different issue than relevance (as defined above). *Relevance* refers to the need for the professional learning. *Visibility* translates that need to others.

- ◆ What is the relationship between seminal and contemporary educational landscape?
- ◆ Who does the professional learning impact? How can the impact (short term and long term) of the professional learning be articulated to various stakeholder groups?
- ◆ How can various stakeholder groups advocate for professional learning opportunities?

The National Association for Gifted Children Professional Learning Standards addresses the essence of these terms within and across the defined standards. Table 8.1 exemplifies the relationships between the key words that define the purpose and disposition of professional learning conceptually and the professional learning standards that guide their practical application.

Table 8.1 Relationship between Key Elements and NAGC Professional Learning Standards.

Key Elements	Relationships between Key Words and elements of the NAGC Professional Learning Standards
Relevance	Ethical principles (6.5) Equal opportunity (6.3) Compliance with rules and responsibilities (6.1, 6.1.1)
Support	Curriculum and instruction responsive to gifted students and diverse populations (6.3.1) Response to social, emotional development of gifted students (6.2, 6.2.1) Research-based (6.1.1) Budgetary allocations and release time (6.1.4)
Continuity	Sustained opportunities for professional learning (6.4, 6.4.2)
Visibility	Responses to past and present issues affecting gifted education (6.3.3)

Practical application and the transfer of knowledge and skills related to professional learning opportunities are critical to their success. A literature review on professional learning over time uncovers numerous studies articulating the features necessary for effective professional learning. This list includes, but is not limited to: contextually situated instruction, mentoring, coaching, continuous assessment, feedback, time for reflection, modeling, study groups, and systemic, on-going follow up. Guskey's (1994) seminal work on effective professional learning encompasses this list by highlighting the symbiotic relationship that exists between the needs of the organization and the need for individual development. These concentric circles of influence approach to professional learning aligns with the key terms of *relevance*, *support*, *continuity*, and *visibility* defined above. Table 8.2 highlights the areas of overlap that exist between the seminal features of effective professional learning as defined in the literature and the dispositions for professional learning articulated in this chapter. Many items appear in multiple categories. The cross-population of items between the different categories evidences the interconnections between the NAGC professional learning standards and the nuances involved in creating effective professional learning experiences.

Of great importance are discussions about recognizing the varied practices employed by districts and school sites that have thwarted rather than

Table 8.2 Features of Effective Professional Learning.

Relevance	Support	Continuity	Visibility
Contextually situated instruction Continuous assessment Time for reflection On-going follow-up	Mentoring Coaching Feedback Modeling Study groups On-going follow-up	Contextually situated instruction Coaching Continuous assessment Modeling Study groups	Continuous assessment Feedback Time for reflection On-going follow-up

promoted the intended outcomes of professional learning. The lack of discussion surrounding the barriers to effective professional learning are multi-faceted and are tangled up in a web of policy, political, and economic variables. If *relevant*, *support*-based, *continuous*, and *visible* professional learning is to exist, the following barriers must be addressed.

Professional Learning Barriers

Barrier 1
Emphasis on the requirement of credit *for* attendance at a professional learning rather than credit for acquired practices implemented *from* the professional learning.

In 2009, Klein and Riordan coined a term called SSW or "single shot workshop" (p. 63) to describe professional learning experiences that were singular in presentation and driven by the number of hours one spent in their seat rather than what was learned and applied. As a result, teachers became more focused on acquiring the required number of hours to obtain a certificate or letter of completion then on internalizing and transferring the content back to their classrooms. To be clear, this was not the fault of the teacher, rather the result of a system of professional learning that valued compliance and completion over true learning. The beliefs, norms, and values of the system itself must be altered if effective professional learning is to take place.

Barrier 2
Focus on a current *"popular"* topic of education rather than addressing a *relevant* issue or problem of practice related to the school, district or state's standards for gifted education.

A popular children's book provides the perfect analogy for this issue. In the story, the fish are enamored with the glitz and glamour of the scales of one fish in the ocean. They are convinced that they want these scales…that their lives will be much improved if they possessed these scales. Just like the fish, educators are enamored with "glittery" topics for professional learning. These topics contain a "wow factor" and have usually been selected because they represent the current "buzzwords" of the times. But, just like the fish in the story, these "hot topics" have in shine, they lack in substance. Professional learning experiences enacted to meet the NAGC standards must have a connectedness to three things: (a) the conceptual constructs of gifted education, (b) the context in which they are implemented, and (c) the current research on identification and services.

Barrier 3

Attendance as a *requirement to teach the gifted rather than becoming more adept at becoming an advocate* to share with colleagues to inform peers and to improve education for all learners.

The requirements needed to teach gifted learners vary from state to state, district to district, and even school site to school site. The *State of the States in Gifted Education* (NAGC, 2020) conducted a survey to determine the level of requirements needed to teach gifted learners across the country. Although their survey found that 29 states required endorsements or certifications in gifted education for teachers working in specialized programs for gifted learners, 36 states offered professional learning in gifted education. This becomes problematic because depending on location and belief system, the allocation of classes for gifted learners can be based more on the seniority of the teacher rather than on the disposition of that teacher. The authors advocate for professional learning that includes a focus on teacher dispositions rather than just a checklist of competencies. These dispositions can include the identification of personal bias regarding who is gifted, the willingness to engage (and allow students to engage) in open-ended exploration of content, the courage to challenge the status-quo of curriculum implementation, and the ability to serve as a model for peers.

Barrier 4

Expectation to absorb and exit as a consequence of attending a professional learning without clearly defined follow-up processes for assistance to implement *in the classroom*. The idea that teachers are supposed to generate deep levels of understanding from the content presented during a professional learning might be unrealistic. Since the mid-1950s cognitive and educational psychologists have argued that the formation of higher-level concepts required a sequence of experience related to the practice and application of those knowledge and skills (Bruner et al., 1956). Mathematics professor Van Engen said it best—"The best way to teach problem solving is to give them lots of problems to solve" (1959, p. 74). These researchers and others advocated for learning experiences that were purposefully designed, strategically organized, and spiral-based in nature. The learning experiences that encompass effective professional learning should be no different. A scope and sequence to professional learning must be constructed so that it provides opportunities for teachers to learn about and engage in the practice of knowledge and skills. Content should be chunked and organized with a developmental process in mind, with systems in place for feedback, assistance, and reflection. This trajectory moves professional learning from a static, stand-alone experience, to a fluid and flexible approach to changing classroom and instructional practice.

Barrier 5

Design professional learning that is not merely responsive to the immediacy of gifted education and services rather responsive to gifted students and services over time.

This issue requires an examination of both the content and structure of professional learning. Contemporary theories of professional learning move away from the static model and employ one that views the teacher as an "active agent" in the learning process (Gutierez, 2019, p. 1181). This shift in paradigm from a traditional "sit and listen" model encourages teachers to examine their own lessons and context as the means of building sustainable capacity. Teachers are not only solving current problems of practice, but are taught to hypothesize and explore solutions to potential and future problems. The transferability of the content presented during a professional learning is meant to have both immediate and long-standing implications and applications. For example, teachers would learn about an instructional strategy as it applies to their classroom today and address how it could potentially benefit learners in the future.

Translating the Elements of Professional Learning

Professional learning encompasses various levels and means of *translation* from what educators need to know to what and how educators are provided with the opportunities to know. These forms of *translation* include stakeholders at all levels of the education profession: from novice to expert teachers, and from coaches and coordinators to administrators and superintendents. These groups are inclusive of anyone responsible for the education of individual gifted learners within a classroom or groups of gifted students in a program. Stakeholders such as community members, school board members, and parents concerned with and/or related to gifted education and gifted students are also included in this description.

Translation related to professional learning is defined as the ability to collect and utilize information as the basis for planning a single or series of professional learning experiences. The *translation* process is dependent on the collection and analysis of various types of data:

(a) observations of teacher and student performances in classroom settings,
(b) statistically-based research and quantitative outcomes of the teaching/learning processes,
(c) portfolios and case studies of individual or small groups of gifted learners,
(d) anecdotal notes taken from teachers during faculty meetings, and
(e) survey results from parents and community members as a consequence of board meetings and back-to-school night events.

Such analysis also is inclusive of responses to queries about the efficacy of the principles and/or philosophies that underscore gifted education for the state, community, school district, and/or classrooms. The focus of a professional learning responsive to the needs of various stakeholders is representative of a Community of Practice model. Under this paradigm, teachers, administrators, parents/guardians, and support personnel in the same school create a shared professional culture based on a shared set of experiences (Ufnar & Shepherd, 2019). The co-construction of knowledge based on similar needs sustains the relevancy, importance, and value of the professional learning experience.

The rationale for articulating and conducting professional learning needs to be applicable in some manner and to some degree to multiple populations composed of individuals directly and indirectly involved with gifted education and services. The inclusion of multiple individuals representing multiple roles directly or indirectly related to the gifted program or services provides the generalizability of the professional learning experiences and helps to target the goal of lasting effects. This concept of generalizability underscores the *relevance, continuity* and *support* that sustains and furthers qualifies expectations for gifted education and services. The concept of generalizability is inherently connected to the idea of developing teacher efficacy and capacity. The objectives for a generalizable professional learning include both short and long term knowledge retention, application, and transfer. Teachers are engaged in thoughtful and meaningful work that helps them solve problems of practice today and to develop the skill-set to "frame future actions" for the problems of tomorrow (Gutierez, 2019).

Central to school reform and teacher development is the ability of different individuals to work collaboratively towards a common goal (Darling-Hammond & McLaughlin, 2011). Professional learning experiences that *translate* and *generalize* to the many individuals involved in gifted education and services has the potential to affect practices over time. The inclusion of many and varied personnel attending the same purposeful professional learning serves three main purposes: (a) the reinforcement of collegiality within, between, and across educators and the community, (b) the transmission of a shared message, and (c) the solidification of a common set of goals, values, and missions. A hallmark of a professional learning community is the concept of shared leadership (Hord, 1997). Members of various stakeholder groups come together to actively engage in the critical examination of problems of practice related to the learners in the community. Figure 8.1 depicts how an analysis of the same recognized need, issue and/or problem is used as the central focus of professional learning experiences. This model provides an

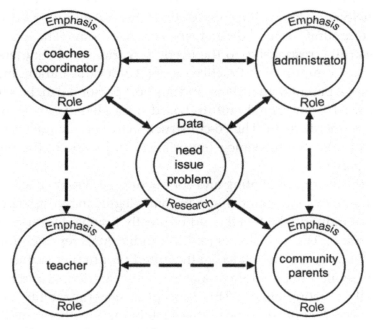

Figure 8.1 Voices Affecting Professional Learning Decisions.

orientation to how different perspectives and expectations for those in attendance can be used to recognize and resolve the same educational issue, concept, and topic.

A Continuum of Professional Learning

Since the 1980s professional learning has been defined as any activity or set of activities designed to "prepare educators for improved performance" (Desimone, 2009, p. 182). Purpose, resources, and time are among the many factors that help to determine the structure of the set of activities offered to educators and community members. The organization of activities and experiences into *A Continuum of Professional Learning* can provide a guide for deciding the appropriate match between the intent of the professional learning activity and its connection to an option for implementation. Table 8.3 illustrates the range of options from simple to complex: Informal to Formal, Single to Multiple Provisions, and Few to Many Participants.

Implementing a Continuum of Professional Learning

The following questions can serve as guide for any/all stakeholder groups regarding the decisions for implementing various types of professional learning activities:

- ◆ What is the urgency of the "topic" for the professional learning?
- ◆ What individuals should participate in the professional learning in order to resolve or attend to the topic?

Table 8.3 A Continuum of Professional Learning.

Informal	Hybrid	Formal
Read and discuss articles Teacher-to-teacher sharing	Classroom observations and feedback Consultant workshops Lesson planning and feedback loop	Regularly scheduled, purpose-focused meetings A cycle of implementation and feedback

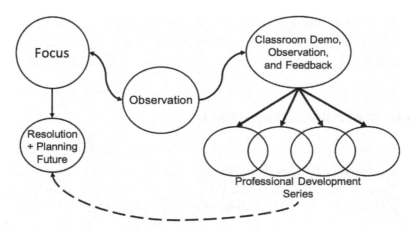

Figure 8.2 Forms of Professional Learning: The Connections.

◆ What factors and organizational systems (people, budget, setting, etc.) need to be considered to plan and implement the selected professional learning?

◆ What are the expectations needed to assess professional learning?

Professional learning experiences can be represented and enacted through many different patterns of implementation. The literature is replete with suggestions describing such patterns. However, the concept of developing and implementing professional learning as a series of learning experiences that range from informal to formal has the potential to yield greater and lasting outcomes for teachers and gifted students. Torff and Sessions (2008) refer to a group (or series) of activities designed to enhance the knowledge of teachers as a "professional learning initiative" (p. 124). Figure 8.2 depicts the series of events that comprise a continuum, or initiative for professional learning rather than single experiences for teachers.

Several factors are necessary for the implementation of this model of professional learning:

◆ Convene a group of individuals representative of the school, district, and community. This group should also include the voices of gifted students as a key stakeholder constituent. The goal of this group threefold: (a) to identify the FOCUS or central topic and scope of the professional learning, (b) to conduct a needs assessment based on an analysis of existing data, and (c) to determine data sets to be collected over time to provide assessment and feedback to the professional learning.

- Observe teachers and gifted students in classroom settings to provide a context for discussing the relevant and potential FOCUS of the professional learning experiences. The actual classroom examples that support the FOCUS or topic of the professional learning highlight the degree of alignment between the reality of gifted education and services in the school, district and community and the intended goals. Note that these observations are not intended to indict or to be viewed as punitive, but to inform the reality of a need to learn, improve, and implement as a consequence of professional learning.

- Conduct professional learning inclusive of a series of learning experiences that reinforce the same topic from simple to complex and incorporate the perspectives of the student, the classroom, the school, and the district. A continuum approach to professional learning experiences advocates the analysis of the topic from various instructional delivery methods: demonstrations, literature, discussions, examples, curriculum and instruction planning time, etc.

- Define opportunities for classroom visits that could either provide a consultant or peer teacher to demonstrate the skill using the students as we model. These classroom visits can also serve as a means of providing targeted and specific feedback to individual teachers regarding their practice and anticipated students' responses.

- Conduct intermittent related professional learning opportunities regarding the progress and alternative needs and questions that emerge over time. Importantly, use prior experiences of the professional learning series to define and initiate next steps for additional professional learning. This level of alignment to ensure the continuity between topics and increase the level of teacher capacity originally defined by the group. The concept of in-depth learning rather than sporadic learning is the primary outcome of this type of professional learning continuum.

Professional Learning Delivery Formats: Technology Use

Technology has expanded the mediums available for professional learning delivery formats. Professional learning can either be in-person with embedded technology use or a hybrid of online and in-person enrichment (see Figure 8.3). The decision to design online professional learning as the basis or dominant structure of the professional learning experience differs from the decision to utilize technology as a feature within the structure of the professional learning experience.

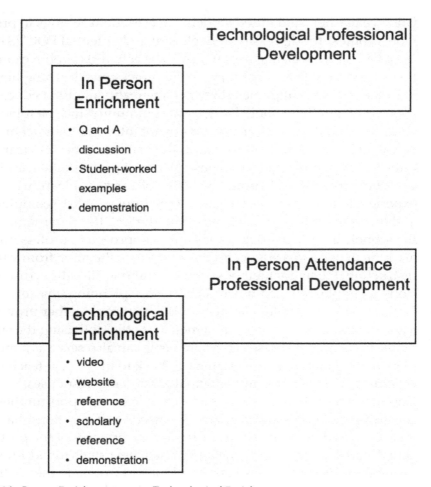

Figure 8.3 In Person Enrichment versus Technological Enrichment.

Several factors dictate the use of technology as either the source of or a feature within the structure of the professional learning opportunity. Taking into consideration either delivery format, the following factors should be considered in the before, during, and after stages of the planning process: *pedagogical emphasis, engagement strategies, participant evaluation of the professional learning experience,* and *transfer into practice* (Dede, 2006).

Technology use in professional learning may become what Papert (1987) described as technocentric, as the medium has the potential to detract from the converging elements of content knowledge, pedagogy, and context with technology implementation, thereby clouding the ability to facilitate problem-solving, inquiry, critical, and creative thinking in the classroom in response to the differentiated instructional needs for gifted learners (Harris, Mishra & Koehler, 2009). The *pedagogical emphasis* ensures the professional learning session does not place the technological tool as dominant, with a focus solely on the implementation of a technology application as an aid or extension device to respond to the needs of gifted students. Instead, the technology application intersects with pedagogical strategies, content knowledge, and the context of the instructional environment. The *engagement strategies* monitor the needs of the adult learners, allowing them to be active participants or contributors throughout the experience, which may be overlooked in an exclusively online format. The *participant evaluation of the professional learning experience* emphasizes the degree to which the professional learning strategies transfer to classroom practice. The evaluation should not focus on the medium in which the professional learning occurred nor the technology used as a means to enrich the experience. Pairing the online professional learning experience with in-person enrichment can further reinforce *transfer into practice*.

The quality of the pedagogical strategies for learners who are gifted and talented, design considerations in the before, during, and after stages of the planning process, and instruction as measured by engagement, participant evaluation, and the transfer of strategies into classroom practice determines the value of the professional learning experience, not the delivery format (Kleiman & Treacy, 2006).

A Concluding Charge for Action

Educators and community members have basically accepted the general purposes defining the needs and structures of opportunities for professional learning. However, what is often challenged is the relationships between these purposes and the implementation practices and outcomes of professional learning opportunities. The NAGC Professional Learning Standards guide decisions and experiences for those responsible for designing and implementing professional learning as well as those who benefit from it. The major issue facing all stakeholder groups is how to utilize the NAGC Standards as guides to respond to plan and execute successful professional learning. An analysis and responses to these global and essential questions is fundamental to a successful professional learning experience:

- ◆ How will the design of the professional learning opportunities directly affect both the teachers of the gifted and gifted students?
- ◆ What formal and/or informal short and long-term evidence will be identified that exemplifies and validates the outcomes of the implemented professional learning?

References

Ball, D.L., & Cohen, D.K. (1999). Developing practice, developing practitioners: Toward a practice-based theory of professional education. In G. Sykes & L. Darling-Hammond (Eds.), *Teaching as the learning profession: Handbook of policy and practice* (pp. 3–32). Jossey Bass.

Bransford, J.D., & Schwartz, D. (1999). Rethinking transfer: A simple proposal with multiple implications. In A. Iran-Nejad & P.D. Pearson (Eds.), *Review of Research in Education, 24*(1), 61–100. American Educational Research Association. https://doi.org/10.3102/0091732X024001061

Bruner, J.S., Goodnow, J., & Austin, G. (1956). *A study of thinking*. Wiley.

Clark, R.E., & Estes, F. (2008). *Turning research into results: A guide to selecting the right performance solutions.* Information Age Publishing, Inc.

Darling-Hammond, L., & McLaughlin, M.W. (2011). Policies that support professional development in an era of reform. *Phi Delta Kappan, 92*(6), 81–92. http://dx.doi.org/10.1177/003172171109200622

Dede, C. (2006). *Online professional development for teachers: Emerging models and methods.* Harvard Education Press.

Desimone, L.M. (2009). Improving impact studies of teachers' professional development: Toward better conceptualizations and measures. *Educational Researcher, 38*(3), 181–199. https://doi.org/10.3102/0013189X08331140

Guskey, T.R. (1994). Results-oriented professional development: In search of an optimal mix of effective practices. *Journal of Staff Development, 15*(4), 42–50. https://eric.ed.gov/?id=EJ497011

Gutierez, S.B. (2019). Learning from teaching: Teacher sense-making on their research and school-based professional development. *Issues in Educational Research, 29*(4), 1181–1200. www.iier.org.au/iier29/gutierez.pdf

Harris, J., Mishra, P., & Koehler, M. (2009). Teachers' technological pedagogical content knowledge and learning activity types: curriculum-based technology integration reframed. *Journal of Research on Technology in Education, 41*(4), 393–416. https://doi.org/10.1080/15391523.2009.10782536

Hord, S.M. (1997). *Professional learning communities: Communities of continuous inquiry and improvement.* Southwest Educational Development Laboratory. www.sedl.org/pubs/catalog/items/cha34.html

Kleiman, G., & Treacy, B. (2006). EdTech leaders online: Building organizational capacity to provide effective online professional development. In C. Dede (Ed.), *Online professional development for teachers: Emerging models and methods* (pp. 31–48). Harvard Education Press.

Klein, E.J., & Riordon, M. (2009). Putting professional development into practice: A framework for how teachers in expeditionary learning schools implement professional development. *Teacher Education Quarterly*, *36*(4), 61–80. www.jstor.org/stable/i2347906

National Association for Gifted Children & Council of State Directors of Programs for the Gifted (2020). *State of the states in gifted education 2018–2019*. www.nagc.org/sites/default/files/Revised%20-%20NAGC_CSDPG_2018–2019%20State%20of%20the%20States%20in%20Gifted%20Education%20Report-Final.pdf

Papert, S. (1987). Computer criticism vs. technocentric thinking. *Educational Researcher*, *17*(1), 22–30. https://doi.org/10.3102/0013189X016001022

Torff, B., & Sessions, D. (2008). Factors associated with teachers' attitudes about professional development. *Teacher Education Quarterly*, *35*(2), 123–133. www.jstor.org/stable/i23479148

Ufnar, J.A., & Shepherd, V. L. (2019). The scientist in the classroom partnership program: An innovative teacher professional development model. *Professional Development in Education*, *45*(4), 642–658. https://doi.org/10.1080/19415257.2018.1474487

Van Engen, H.V. (1959). Twentieth century mathematics for the elementary school. The Arithmetic Teacher, *6*(2), 71–76. https://doi.org/10.5951/AT.6.2.0071

9

Using the NAGC Standards for Program Development and Improvement

Keri M. Guilbault and Alicia Cotabish

The field of education is guided by common standards that serve to establish student performance goals. Standards support accountability measures and can be used to monitor student growth and evaluate programming. Programming standards serve as a roadmap to educators and administrators and are often used to guide programs, policies, and procedures. Without programming standards, educators of students with gifts and talents may struggle to document the effects of their teaching and programming on student performance.

The 2019 NAGC Pre-K–Grade 12 Gifted Programming Standards (PK–12 Standards; NAGC, 2019) were developed with input from diverse stakeholder groups and a review of current research on best practices in the field. They provide important benchmarks for student outcomes and for using evidence-based practices that are the most effective for students with gifts and talents. With a focus on diversity and collaboration, these standards can be used to identify and document gaps in programs and services and provide

DOI: 10.4324/9781003236863-9

direction for the development of action plans for the district or at the school level. Grounded in theory and evidence-based research, the PK–12 Standards provide an important base for all educational efforts on behalf of students with gifts and talents at all ages and stages of development.

This chapter will introduce you to a Self-Study tool and provide guidance on how to use the 2019 NAGC Pre-K–Grade 12 Gifted Programming Standards to make critical decisions related to program development.

How Might the Standards be Used?

The Venn Diagram represented in Figure 9.1 suggests seven ways in which state department personnel, gifted education program coordinators, and classroom teachers can use the 2019 NAGC Pre-K–Grade 12 Gifted Programming Standards.

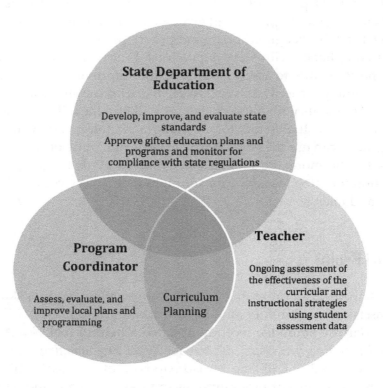

Figure 9.1 Using the 2019 NAGC Pre-K–Grade 12 Gifted Programming Standards.

Note: Adapted with permission from Cotabish, A., & Krisel, S. (2012). Action plans: Bringing the program standards to life! In S. K. Johnsen (Ed.), *NAGC Pre-K–Grade 12 Gifted Education Programming Standards: A guide to planning and implementing high-quality services* (pp. 231–253). Prufrock Press.

Specifically, these uses include the following:

1. To assess, evaluate, and improve local policies, administrative rules, and procedures.
2. To select and plan curriculum.
3. To provide appropriate professional learning experiences.
4. To advocate for students with gifts and talents.
5. To develop, improve, and evaluate state gifted education standards.
6. To approve district gifted education plans and programs and monitor these plans for compliance with state regulations.
7. To continually assess and evaluate the effectiveness of curricular and instructional strategies.

State Department personnel, gifted education coordinators, administrators, advocates, and educators of the gifted can use the Gifted Programming Standards. State Department personnel may use the Gifted Programming Standards to develop, improve, and evaluate their state policies or standards, to approve local district gifted plans and programs, and to monitor local programs for compliance with state regulations. District program coordinators may use the standards to assess, evaluate, and improve local plans, policies, and programming. School administrators, district program coordinators, and educators of students with gifts and talents will find the Gifted Programming Standards to be a valuable tool for curriculum planning and evaluation, and all three groups can use the standards to inform and guide professional learning plans. Furthermore, the standards may also provide language, rationale, and direction for effective advocacy for high-quality services for all students with gifts and talents.

Where Do I Begin?

Using the standards for program design or improvement requires skillful planning. To assist in this careful planning, a workgroup from the NAGC Professional Standards Committee recently updated a helpful tool: *Self-Assess Your P–12 Practice or Program Using the NAGC Gifted Programming Standards, 2nd Edition* (NAGC, 2020). Utilizing a roadmap-type of approach, this tool will help you evaluate current programming services, set goals, and strategically plan to meet those goals. This Self-Study tool provides a checklist and supporting materials based on the PK–12 Standards to assist gifted education program coordinators, administrators, and educators of students with gifts and talents in assessing programmatic and professional learning needs so that they may implement effective classroom practice and programming for these students. In using the tool, you will assess the degree to which your staff engages in evidence-based practices that positively affect student outcomes.

The Self-Study checklist is intended for two primary audiences: (a) educators of students with gifts and talents, whose focus is on student outcomes, and (b) gifted program coordinators or administrators whose responsibilities include not only addressing student outcomes throughout the school or district, but also on providing resources and support to educators so that they can implement best practices in gifted education. The Self-Study checklist is designed to be quick and easy to use and can provide a visual indication of priorities and needs when planning for students with gifts and talents.

Why Should I Engage in Self-Study?

Self-study involves systematically investigating one's own practice. Grounded in critical theory and concerned with addressing challenging issues (Berry, 1998; Giroux, 1997; McLaren, 1997), self-study is similar to action research in that systematic processes are employed to identify and explore problems in authentic educational contexts (Hong & Lawrence, 2011). Self-study is undertaken not only by administrators, but also by practitioners who have an administrative focus at the program level. The practice is commonly seen in professional learning activities, strategic planning, and programmatic accreditation processes (Attard, 2017; Garin & Harper, 2016; Rincones-Gómez, et al., 2016). The self-study approach has become salient in planning, developing, and implementing educational programs and interventions (Dombek, et al., 2016; Phillips, et al., 2016; Smith, et al., 2016a; 2016b; Smith & Foorman, 2015). The adoption of the self-study approach in the field of education merits our continuous use of this Self-Study tool as a means for K–12 gifted education practitioners and administrators to generate knowledge to inform and improve their practices and programming for advanced learners. The self-study process found within this document will also assist in:

- ◆ planning programs in the early stages of development,
- ◆ conducting an internal analysis,
- ◆ documenting the need for the program,
- ◆ justifying the programming approach,
- ◆ identifying each program's strengths and weaknesses,
- ◆ determining new directions or components, and
- ◆ evaluating each program's alignment with state and national standards.

By examining one's role in teaching and learning and the factors that impact practice, gifted education personnel can increase their awareness of each program's strengths and weaknesses. Through a reflective process that includes an examination of supportive evidence, program personnel may have a better understanding of practices, student outcomes, and barriers that may impede services to students with gifts and talents, including those from underrepresented groups, as well as gain greater insight into students' perspectives as learners.

Using the Self-Study Checklist

There are six steps in this Self-Study process (Figure 9.2). After completing them, you will be confident in your strengths and have a plan in place to address the components of your classroom practice or program that need adjustment or additional data to better serve your advanced learners.

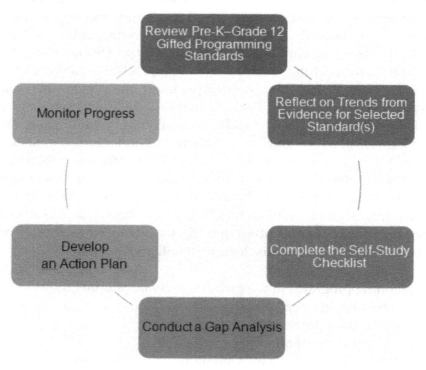

Figure 9.2 Six Steps in the Self-Study Process.

Note: Reprinted with permission from National Association for Gifted Children (2020). *Self-assess your P–12 practice or program using the NAGC gifted programming standards* (2nd ed.).

The student outcomes and evidence-based practices in the programming standards can be used as evaluation criteria to provide data on which to base informed decisions about the effectiveness of gifted education programming. There are six steps recommended in the Self-Study process:

1. Stakeholders or an evaluation committee reviews the six NAGC Pre-K–Grade 12 Gifted Programming Standards to become familiar with each standard and student outcome.
2. Identify data sources that can be used to assess student outcomes, practices, and professional learning information found in the standards.
3. Complete the Self-Study checklist.
4. Conduct a gap analysis.
5. Create an action plan.
6. Monitor progress.

Step 1: Review Pre-K–Grade 12 Gifted Programming Standards

The self-study begins with a review of the 2019 Pre-K–Grade 12 Gifted Programming Standards. There are six programming standards:

Standard 1: Learning and Development
Standard 2: Assessment
Standard 3: Curriculum Planning and Instruction
Standard 4: Learning Environments
Standard 5: Programming
Standard 6: Professional Learning

Cotabish et al. (2020) provide a detailed overview and a description of each of the six PK–12 standards. A total of 35 student outcomes and specific evidence-based practices associated with the student outcomes within the six standard areas are also enumerated. These student outcomes and corresponding evidence-based practices provide readers with information that will be revisited at various junctures during the self-study process described in this chapter.

Step 2: Identify Data Sources to Assess Selected Student Outcomes

Following the review of the six standards, begin to identify available data to assess student outcomes, evidence-based practices, and professional learning information found in the standards. The task of assessing student outcomes must be completed using appropriate and varied measures that minimize bias. Table 1 provides examples of the types of documents that might provide student outcome information needed to complete the next step, the checklist.

Table 9.1 Examples of Data Sources.

P–2 Standard	Educators of Students with Gifts and Talents	Gifted Education Program Administrators
Learning and Development	Observations; student journals; Socratic seminars; student self-reflections; learner profiles and portfolios; dynamic learning activities; interviews with family	Curriculum in place to address affective growth; student surveys; records of out-of-school resources used; parent conferences; learning inventories; district program design for all levels; counselor-led professional learning modules
Assessment	Formative and summative assessments; ability and achievement data; assessments related to interests and talent domain; local student assessments; learner profiles and portfolios; retention in gifted education services; above-grade-level testing and/or talent search data	Reviewed and updated district assessment procedure; formative and summative assessments; referrals for gifted services by school; demographic data for gifted education vs. school district; data of annual progress measurement; retention in gifted education services by school; Talent Search participation; differentiated assessment tools; professional learning for classroom teachers on classroom indicators of giftedness and program identification; website with identification information
Curriculum Planning and Instruction	Formative and ongoing assessments; documented student growth (knowledge and skills) commensurate with aptitude; talent development in student's area of interest and/or multiple talent areas across the dimension of learning; high articulation of and engagement with advanced curriculum	Curriculum maps/scope and sequence; differentiated lesson plans; district acceleration plan; use of Depth of Knowledge; observations; evaluator walk-throughs; program evaluation results; collaboration between gifted education specialists and classroom teachers on differentiated instructional practices that meet the needs of gifted students; gifted education specialists share resources that will assist with differentiated learning for general classrooms; strength-based Response to Intervention (RtI) support provided by the gifted education professional; professional learning on culturally responsive curriculum

Table 9.1 *Continued*

P-2 Standard	Educators of Students with Gifts and Talents	Gifted Education Program Administrators
Learning Environments	Dispositions toward academic and creative productivity; positive peer relationships and social interactions; responsible behavior and leadership; collaboration with diverse individuals and across diverse groups; employment of strategies to address social justice issues; advanced oral and written communication skills and creative expression	Student surveys; student and teacher classroom observations; examples of using formative feedback; classroom groupings; before/after school groups/clubs; leadership projects; evidence of collaboration with classroom and English language learners (ELL) teachers; Socratic seminars with students; results of program evaluation; guest lectures on underrepresented groups in gifted education and related diversity issues
Programming	Parent-teacher conferences; anecdotes; meeting logs with classroom teachers; vertical articulation of program; curriculum maps; district policy guides; career curriculum; collaboration between gifted education specialists and classroom teachers that results in accommodating gifted learners in the regular classroom setting (RtI, differentiation, MTSS, etc.); conversations/feedback/indicators from students, counselors, classroom teachers, parents that indicate the level of social/ emotional/behavioral health of the student	Parent conferences; district gifted education budget; district programming scope and sequence; district policies; acceleration addressed along with identification and programming procedures; identification procedures match the definition of giftedness used by the school/ district; participation in Advanced Placement, International Baccalaureate, postsecondary enrollment options, etc.; professional learning opportunities; collaboration with special and general education teachers that allows gifted students to continue pursuit of learning that originates in the gifted classroom; participation of gifted education professionals on district/building RtI teams; program design and implementation responsibility assigned to trained personnel; consistency between state definition and program guidelines; description of roles of key gifted education personnel; established schedule for gathering RtI or Multi-Tiered System of Support (MTSS) data (e.g., program evaluation plan) and information about school/district-level decision-making

(Continued)

Table 9.1 *Continued*

P–2 Standard	Educators of Students with Gifts and Talents	Gifted Education Program Administrators
Professional Learning	Gifted education endorsement or certification; peer coaching; department meetings; meetings with classroom teachers; webinars; online classes; conference attendance; conference presentations; advanced degrees; participation in professional learning communities	Evidence of an annual professional learning plan; participation in conferences/webinars/classes; attainment of gifted education endorsement or certification; degree in gifted education; participation in professional learning communities; gifted education leadership roles within the district/region/state/nation; professional learning linked to gifted education teacher's identification of areas for personal growth

Note: Adapted with permission from National Association for Gifted Children (2020). *Self-assess your P–12 practice or program using the NAGC gifted programming standards,* 2nd ed. Author.

Step 3: Complete the Self-Study Checklist

Informed by previously reviewed data sources, complete the Self-Study Checklist which consists of four guiding questions posed for each of the student outcomes within a given standard. The four guiding questions are:

1. To what degree do we address this student outcome?
2. To what degree have current practices improved this student outcome?
3. How high of a priority do we place on meeting this standard element?
4. Is support readily available in our district?

Reflect on the availability of sufficient data to inform a response, and if such data exist, then proceed to the response options for each guiding question. Responses range from *"Not at all"* (1) to *"To a great extent"* (4). Checklists for each standard are provided in to allow for ease of use, scoring and ranking priorities, and dissemination.

After indicating a response for each of the guiding questions on the Self-Study Checklist, sum points across each row, and then sort the scores calculated in the "Total points" column for each student outcome in increasing value, with items receiving lower point values deemed higher priorities than those with higher scores and lower priorities.

Based on the point values indicated in the column labeled "Total points," rank-order the priorities to be addressed. When choosing programming areas on which to focus, you should prioritize the evidence-based practices that are not currently addressed or are only minimally addressed. Addressing every single one would be too overwhelming during a single school year; therefore, it is better to choose a limited number of evidence-based practices to tackle first. To help you prioritize your selection, consider these three questions:

1. Will addressing the evidence-based practice positively and significantly affect student outcomes?
2. Is it doable this academic year or do other components need to be in place first?
3. Is it worth the time and effort at this time or would addressing another evidence-based practice first have a greater impact?

After considering these questions, you should choose several evidence-based practices to address.

Table 9.2 Gap Analysis Chart.

1	2	3	4	5
Standard/ Desired student outcome	Evidence-based practices	What do we do to support this practice?	What evidence do we have that current practices are leading to the desired student outcome?	Gaps: What additional information or change in practice is needed?

Note: Adapted with permission from National Association for Gifted Children (2010). *NAGC Pre-K–Grade 12 gifted programming standards: A blueprint for quality gifted education programs.* Author. https://bit.ly/2YLzvUA

Step 4: Conduct a Gap Analysis

After using the Self-Study Checklist to identify the student outcome priorities warranting further attention, the next step is to explore gaps between current and evidence-based practices that improve outcomes for gifted students. A gap analysis requires gathering information, interpreting the trends the information suggests, and determining the additional information and/or changes in practice needed to yield the desired outcomes. The completion of a gap analysis chart will assist educators and program coordinators in determining the next steps in ensuring that classroom practice supports the desired student outcomes for gifted and talented students. To use the chart (see Table 9.2) follow these steps:

1. Place the highest priority student outcomes from the Self-Study Checklist results in Column 1. List the evidence-based practices in Column 2 that correspond to each outcome. The specific evidence-based practices linked to individual outcomes for each standard are part of the PK–12 Standards document. Be sure to keep in mind any district policies or state administrative rules that must be addressed.

2. After completing Columns 1 and 2, list in Column 3 the current efforts (e.g., classroom practices in which a teacher engages, or strategies a district coordinator employs) that support this practice.

3. Next, indicate in Column 4 the efforts that have occurred in each selected Standard area as well as evidence indicating desired student outcomes are being achieved. Do not forget to consider those efforts made in collaboration with general and special education classroom teachers. Although limited evidence might be available at this time, give credit for work that may serve as the foundation for continuous program improvement.

4. Finally in Column 5, consider what additional evidence or information is needed to determine if there is a gap between current procedures and practices and those that are based on research.

The last two columns identify specific issues or gaps in programming practice(s).

Step 5: Develop an Action Plan

An action plan highlights the steps that must be taken or activities that must be performed well, for a strategy to succeed. The Action Plan Chart (see Table 9.3) components include:

◆ the desired student outcome,
◆ evidence-based practices aligned to a specific P–12 Standard,
◆ the identified gap,
◆ supporting and opposing forces that could affect change,
◆ action to close the identified gap,
◆ the person(s) responsible for carrying out the action, and
◆ a timeline to bring the action to fruition.

Consider the following open-ended questions (e.g., supporting evidence, forces, resources) that impact implementation of change to improve practice and student outcomes under each standard:

◆ What are two or three actions we could implement to improve student outcomes and teacher practices in each standard?
◆ What supporting factors promote the implementation of this standard (including those that may exist in general education classrooms)?
◆ What resisting forces or obstacles hinder the implementation of this standard (including those that may exist in general education classrooms)?
◆ To what degree will the suggested change in the practice affect current district policy(ies)?

Table 9.3 Action Plan Chart.

Standard/ Desired student outcome	Evidence-based practices	Identified gaps	Supporting forces	Opposing forces	Action(s) to address the identified gap (Practice or Research)	Person(s) responsible	Timeline

Note: Adapted with permission from National Association for Gifted Children (2010). *NAGC Pre-K–Grade 12 Gifted Programming Standards: A blueprint for quality gifted education programs.* Author. https://bit.ly/2YLzvUA

To use the Action Plan Chart:

1. List the desired student outcome in Column 1.
2. List the corresponding evidence-based practices in Column 2.
3. In Column 3, record the gap identified on the Gap Analysis Chart.
4. Columns 4 and 5 document the supporting and opposing forces that impact services for gifted learners. These may include district or state-level policies, district or state-level funding, personnel or other resources, parental support (or lack of), as well as localized or situational considerations (e.g., community, partnerships, etc.).
5. Column 6 lists the action(s) needed to address the gap and implement the evidence-based practice or need for further information. *Note to program administrators: Remember to include actions that may result from the gifted education professional's role as a collaborator with classroom teachers and special educators or specialists.*

The last two columns allow you to designate the person(s) responsible and set a timeline during which you plan to act. Educators of students with gifts and talents and program coordinators will most likely identify program "gaps" and carry out an action plan quite differently due to the nature of their roles in gifted programming. To illustrate this variance in program planning, Table 5 provides examples of action plans based on the roles of the educators.

Step 6: Monitor Progress

After finalizing the action plan, periodically, revisit and modify the plan according to environmental changes—new personnel, change in leadership, or new information gained based on research. Additionally, frequent charting of progress towards instituting the evidence-based practices ensures the desired student outcomes are reached.

As you work through the examples, we encourage you to review the resources located on the NAGC website and in the appendices of the *Self-Assess your PK–12 Program or Practice Using the NAGC Gifted Programming Standards*, 2nd ed. (NAGC, 2020) to support you in improving gifted and talented student outcomes.

Putting the Standards into Practice

You will now be presented a scenario that will illustrate use of the three planning documents. This scenario is an example of how a gifted program coordinator might address Standard 2: Assessment.

Program Coordinator Scenario

The Juniper School District is located in a low-income suburban community. Seventy-four percent of the district's students qualify for free or reduced lunches; however, only 10% of the students identified for gifted programming services qualify for free or reduced lunches. Ms. Jones, the district's gifted program coordinator, wants to find ways for students to reveal their exceptionalities or potential through assessment evidence so that an increased number of low-income students will be identified for programming services and appropriate instructional accommodations and modifications can be made. Currently, the district utilizes standardized test scores as well as a gifted behavior checklist completed by classroom teachers to inform program placement. Locally developed norms or assessment tools in nonverbal formats are not considered. Although the program coordinator accepts referrals from multiple sources, most of the student referrals are received from teachers. An identification committee is in place and is made up of the elementary principal, the school counselor, one elementary teacher, one middle school teacher, and one high school teacher. Program guidelines were developed about 12 years ago and include procedures for identifying students, committee guidelines, and appeal procedures for both entry and exit.

Ms. Jones completed the Self-Study Your P–12 Practice or Program Using the NAGC Gifted Programming Standards document for Standard 2 (see Table 9.4). A partial listing of her ratings can be found in Table 5. Ms. Jones combed through the student outcomes and marked the extent to which she engaged in evidence-based practices associated with each outcome, assessed the extent to which a change in the evidence-based practice would improve student outcomes, examined how high of a priority was placed on meeting the standard, and determined if administrator support was readily available. As you can see, she felt that she minimally addressed Student Outcome 2.1, All students in Pre-K through Grade 12 with gifts and talents have equal access to the identification process and proportionally represent each campus. Upon closer examination, Ms. Jones realized that although the identification committee went through the motions of identifying students for services at each campus, the Juniper School District's program procedures were outdated and did not reflect the latest research or practice. She acknowledged her committee's failure to utilize multiple identification assessments addressing different domains and recognized her committee's lack of understanding of how to interpret assessments, including assessment uses and limitations in identifying the needs of students with gifts and talents. She admitted that she and her committee never considered using locally developed

Table 9.4 Self-Study Checklist: Programming Standard 2.

Programming Standard 2: Assessment	Question 1 — To what degree do we address the student outcome?				Question 2 — To what degree have current practices improved this student outcome?				Question 3 — How high of a priority do we place on meeting this standard element?				Question 4a — Is support readily available in my district? (check 4b to indicate a need to address with the coordinator or other administrator)				Question 4b	Total points	Rank order of priorities to address
	Not at all 1	2	3	To a great extent 4	Not at all 1	2	3	To a great extent 4	Low 1	2	3	High 4	Not at all 1	2	3	To a great extent 4			
Student Outcomes																			
2.1. Identification. All students in Pre-K through grade 12 with gifts and talents have equal access to the identification process and proportionally represent each campus.	X				X							X		X				8	1

(Continued)

Table 9.4 Continued

Programming Standard 2: Assessment	Question 1 To what degree do we address the student outcome?		Question 2 To what degree have current practices improved this student outcome?		Question 3 How high of a priority do we place on meeting this standard element?		Question 4a Is support readily available in my district? (check 4b to indicate a need to address with the coordinator or other administrator)		Question 4b	Total points	Rank order of priorities to address
	Not at all	To a great extent	Not at all	To a great extent	Low	High	Not at all	To a great extent			
2.2. Identification. Students with gifts and talents are identified for services that match their interests, strengths, and needs.	X			X	X			X		14	5
2.3. Identification. Students with identified gifts and talents represent diverse backgrounds.	X		X			X	X			9	2

Table 9.4 Continued

Programming Standard 2: Assessment	Question 1 To what degree do we address the student outcome?			Question 2 To what degree have current practices improved this student outcome?			Question 3 How high of a priority do we place on meeting this standard element?			Question 4a Is support readily available in my district? (check 4b to indicate a need to address with the coordinator or other administrator)			Question 4b	Total points	Rank order of priorities to address
	Not at all		To a great extent	Not at all		To a great extent	Low		High	Not at all		To a great extent			
2.4. Learning Progress. As a result of using multiple and ongoing assessments, students with gifts and talents demonstrate growth commensurate with abilities in cognitive, social-emotional, and psychosocial areas.	X			X					X			X		10	3
2.5. Learning Progress. Students self-assess their learning progress.			X	X			X					X		11	4

norms (including campus norms), nor added nonverbal testing to the mix of identification assessments. She acknowledged that a change in the practice would increase access to services including identifying more diverse students across the district and individual campuses. Furthermore, she indicated that it would not require a great amount of effort to change the practice, however, it would require her to coordinate with the program administrator.

Now, let us look at how Ms. Jones plotted her selected Student Outcome 2.1 on a Gap Analysis Chart (Table 9.5).

As you can see in Table 9.6, Ms. Jones drilled down to the specific evidence-based practice. She listed the identified gap as "Teachers need to understand the characteristics of giftedness to guide classroom instruction and activities." She also recognized her building principal as a supporting force, and state requirements being a possible opposing force. To remedy the problem, she chose to provide school-wide professional learning activities to increase understanding about the characteristics of giftedness, and to tie the professional learning activities to state educational priorities. She allotted herself one month to carry out the task.

Bringing it All Together

Implementing the programming standards effectively requires thoughtful planning and careful consideration. There are several NAGC resources available that can assist you in your quest to bring the standards to life. These include a full glossary of terms available on the NAGC website as well as links to references for many of the strategies recommended in the 2019 programming standards. The early stages of program planning and development are ideal times to use the three planning documents: Self-Study Checklist, Gap Analysis Chart, and Action Plan Chart. These may also be used periodically to evaluate your programs and services and to identify focus topics for professional learning in your school or district. Evidence-based practices provide the most compelling support for effective programming. Regardless of whether you are a novice or an experienced pro, utilizing district action plans are a smart way to organize data collection and resources, and put informed judgments into practice.

Table 9.5 Gap Analysis Chart Example.

Standard/Desired student outcome	Evidence-based practices	What do we do to support this practice?	What evidence do we have that current practices are leading to the desired student outcome?	Gaps: What additional information or change in practice is needed?
2.1. All students in Pre-K through Grade 12 with gifts and talents have equal access to the identification process and proportionally represent each campus.	2.1.1. Educators develop environments and instructional activities that prepare and encourage students from diverse backgrounds to express characteristics and behaviors that are associated with giftedness.	We currently collect learner profiles and portfolios, formative and summative assessment measures, student program evaluations, demographic data, ability and achievement data, data analysis, local student assessments. We do not use this information to differentiate types of activities.	We have evidence of students' progress but have no mechanism in place to assess for giftedness.	Teachers need to understand the characteristics of giftedness to guide classroom activities. Need a tool to assess.

Note: Adapted with permission from Cotabish, A., & Krisel, S. (2012). Action plans: Bringing the program standards to life! In S. K. Johnsen (Ed.), *NAGC Pre-K–Grade 12 Gifted Education Programming Standards: A guide to planning and implementing high-quality services* (pp. 231–253). Prufrock Press.

Table 9.6 Action Plan Example.

Standard/ Desired student outcome	Evidence-based practices	Identified gaps	Supporting forces	Opposing forces	Action(s) to address the identified gap (Practice or Research)	Person(s) responsible	Timeline
2.1. All students in Pre-K through Grade 12 with gifts and talents have equal access to the identification process and proportionally represent each campus.	2.1.1. Educators develop environments and instructional activities that prepare and encourage students from diverse backgrounds to express characteristics and behaviors that are associated with giftedness.	Teachers need to understand the characteristics of giftedness to guide classroom instruction and activities.	Building principal makes identifying students from diverse populations a priority.	State requires professional learning activities to be linked to the state's educational priorities.	Provide school-wide professional learning activities to increase understanding about the characteristics of giftedness. Tie to state educational priorities.	Program Coordinator	One month

Note: Adapted with permission from Cotabish, A., & Krisel, S. (2012). Action plans: Bringing the program standards to life! In S. K. Johnsen (Ed.), *NAGC Pre-K–Grade 12 Gifted Education Programming Standards: A guide to planning and implementing high-quality services* (pp. 231–253). Prufrock Press.

References

Attard, K. (2017). Personally driven professional development: Reflective self-study as a way for teachers to take control of their own professional development. *Teacher Development*, 21(1), 40–56. https://doi.org/10.1080/13664530.2016.1218363

Berry, K. S. (1998). Nurturing the imagination of resistance: Young adults as creators of knowledge. In J. L. Kincheloe, & S. R. Steinberg (Eds.), *Unauthorized methods: Strategies for critical teaching* (pp. 43–58). Routledge.

Cotabish, A., Dailey, D., Corwith, S., Johnsen, S. K., Lee, C. W., & Guilbault, K. (2020). Ushering in the 2019 Pre-K to Grade 12 Gifted Programming Standards. *Gifted Child Today*, 43(2), 135–140. https://doi.org/10.1177/1076217519898226

Cotabish, A., & Krisel, S. (2012). Action plans: Bringing the program standards to life! In S. K. Johnsen (Ed.), *NAGC Pre-K–Grade 12 Gifted Education Programming Standards: A guide to planning and implementing high-quality services* (pp. 231–253). Prufrock Press.

Dombek, J. L., Foorman, B. R., Garcia, M., & Smith, K. G. (2016). *Self-study guide for implementing early literacy interventions* (REL 2016–129). U.S. Department of Education, Institute of Education Sciences, National Center for Education Evaluation and Regional Assistance, Regional Educational Laboratory Southeast. https://ies.ed.gov/ncee/edlabs/projects/project.asp?projectID=4520

Garin, E., & Harper, M. (2016). A self-study investigation of using inquiry groups in a professional development school context. *School-University Partnerships*, 9(1), 54–63. https://eric.ed.gov/?id=EJ1107081

Giroux, H. (1997). *Pedagogy and the politics of hope: Theory, culture, and schooling.* Westview.

Hong, C. E., & Lawrence, S. A. (2011). Action research in teacher education: Classroom inquiry, reflection, and data-driven decision making. *Journal of Inquiry & Action in Education*, 4(2), 1–17. https://eric.ed.gov/?id=EJ1134554

McLaren, P. (1997). *Revolutionary multiculturalism: Pedagogies of dissent for the new millennium.* Routledge.

National Association for Gifted Children (2019). *NAGC 2019 Pre-K–Grade 12 Gifted Programming Standards.* www.nagc.org/sites/default/files/standards/Intro%202019%20Programming%20Standards%281%29.pdf

National Association for Gifted Children (2010). *NAGC Pre-K–Grade 12 Gifted Programming Standards: A blueprint for quality gifted education programs.* www.nagc.org/sites/default/files/standards/K-12%20standards%20booklet.pdf

National Association for Gifted Children (2020). *Self-assess your P–12 practice or program using the NAGC gifted programming standards* (2nd ed.).

Phillips, B. M., Mazzeo, D., & Smith, K. (2016). *Self-study guide for Florida VPK provider improvement plan development.* U.S. Department of Education, Institute of Education Sciences, National Center for Education Evaluation and Regional Assistance, Regional Educational Laboratory Southeast. https://files.eric.ed.gov/fulltext/ED574650.pdf

Rincones-Gómez, R., Hoffman, L., & Rodríguez-Campos, L. (2016). The model for collaborative evaluations as a framework for the accreditation self-study. *Journal of Emerging Trends in Economics and Management Sciences,* 7(5), 335–341.

Smith, K. G., Dombek, J. L., Foorman, B. R., Hook, K. S., Lee, L., Cote, A.-M., Sanabria, I., & Stafford, T. (2016a). *Self-study guide for implementing high school academic interventions* (REL 2016–218). U.S. Department of Education, Institute of Education Sciences, National Center for Education Evaluation and Regional Assistance, Regional Educational Laboratory Southeast. https://ies.ed.gov/ncee/edlabs/projects/project.asp?projectID=4505

Smith, K. G., Dombek, J. L., Foorman, B. R., Hook, K. S., Lee, L., Cote, A.-M., Sanabria, I., & Stafford, T. (2016b). *Self-study guide for implementing literacy interventions in Grades 3–8* (REL 2016–224). U.S. Department of Education, Institute of Education Sciences, National Center for Education Evaluation and Regional Assistance, Regional Educational Laboratory Southeast. https://ies.ed.gov/ncee/edlabs/projects/project.asp?projectID=4543

Smith, K. G., & Foorman, B. R. (2015). *Summer reading camp self-study guide* (REL 2015–070). U.S. Department of Education, Institute of Education Sciences, National Center for Education Evaluation and Regional Assistance, Regional Educational Laboratory Southeast. https://ies.ed.gov/ncee/edlabs/projects/project.asp?projectID=463

10

State Models for Implementing the Standards

Wendy Behrens and Mary L. Slade

Introduction

In 1998, the National Association for Gifted Children (NAGC) published the initial version of the Pre-K–Grade 12 gifted education programming standards, which are followed by two subsequent editions in 2010 and 2019 respectively. The intent of the NAGC standards (1998, 2010, 2019) is to present desired student outcomes that align with high quality services to prospective stakeholders. Because research, theoretical constructs, and best practice frameworks substantiate the NAGC standards, they serve to form the foundation of effective gifted education programming at local and state levels. The NAGC standards translate into effective policies, procedures, and systematic programming to meet the needs of Pre-K–Grade 12 gifted students (Center for Talent Development, 2017; NAGC, 2019). Current revisions of the standards documents are formatted as student outcomes (NAGC, 2010; 2019).

The utility of the current NAGC standards (stands for 2019 edition unless otherwise specified) in serving gifted learners varies, encompassing

DOI: 10.4324/9781003236863-10

a wide range of purposes. For example, the standards have importance concerning the appraisal of existing programming in order to examine equity and guide the ongoing progression of a comprehensive set of services. Additionally, regarding accountability purposes, the NAGC standards serve the roles of milestones and criteria in rubrics for evaluation (New Jersey Department of Education, n.d.; Thomas Fordham Institute, 2016). In fact, these standards are benchmarks against which to measure the effectiveness of gifted education programming (Callahan et al., 2017). Given that each revision of the NAGC standards reflects research-based practices in gifted education aligning with current knowledge about empirically-supported practices for gifted students (NAGC, 2019); the standards provide the necessary direction and focus to designing services for gifted students on the frontline at the state and local levels of education (CTD, 2017).

The purpose of this chapter is to discuss the utility of the NAGC standards' implementation at the state level, including pre-collegiate schools, universities, and state departments of education. To determine the real-time implementation of the NAGC standards as well as to illustrate their impact on states, localities, and universities; we conducted a brief survey of state directors of gifted education in spring 2020. Survey responses tabulated depict the type and frequency of impacts. To further explain implementation at the state level the chapter includes exemplary NAGC standards implementation scenarios in the form of vignettes and an in-depth case study. Therefore, vignettes and a case study from local, state, and higher education perspectives are provided in order to identify commendable practices worthy of mention and replication.

Review of Literature

Over two decades, three different versions of the NAGC Pre-K–Grade 12 Gifted Programming Standards (1998, 2010, 2019) have been readily welcomed and used by practitioners, researchers, and evaluators (NAGC, 2019). The NAGC standards serve as guideposts for best practice that substantiate or focus practice at the local and state levels of education. Recommended practices for implementing the most recent version of the NAGC standards includes assessing, evaluating, and improving local policies, rules, and procedures; planning curriculum; providing professional learning; advocating; developing, improving, and evaluating state standards; approving gifted plans and programs and monitoring for compliance with state regulations (NAGC, 2019, p.1).

Standards Rationale

The NAGC standards are prescriptive in that their intent is to inform every school district in the delivery of effective services that address the learning needs of advanced learners are met (Johnsen, 2012). Consequently, they contain student outcomes in both academic and socio-emotional realms. Relatedly, the NAGC standards act as criteria for program evaluation and other accountability tasks. Over time, the purpose of the NAGC standards has expanded in practice at state and local levels.

A comprehensive list of the purposes for implementing the NAGC standards at the school and local levels encompass

(a) documenting programming necessity;
(b) justifying services;
(c) identifying programming strengths and weaknesses;
(d) determining directions for programming improvement;
(e) providing a rationale for the continuation of services;
(f) indicating progress in program development; and
(g) providing a framework for programming evaluation (Cotabish, et al., 2017).

Educators engage with the NAGC standards most frequently when developing local plans, conducting curriculum planning, and designing professional learning initiatives.

Increasingly, school districts are being held accountable for gifted education programming, which necessitates documenting effectiveness, which gives rise to additional purposes for NAGC standards implementation. Not only are services called into question in terms of need, but also to prove their worth or value (Cotabish & Krisel, 2012). Perhaps most commonly, accountability efforts are expected to include documentation of effectiveness as well as measures of the impact of the services on students and the community. Stakeholders interested in this information are likely to include parents, community members, local administrators, school board members, and state department personnel. Therefore, the NAGC standards expanded capacity for implementation includes programming accountability in addition to programming development.

Impact on State and Local Needs

Perhaps the most descriptive manner for depicting the role of the NAGC standards is that of a "blueprint" for building appropriate gifted programming services that support gifted students (Roberts, 2011). However, most often the NAGC standards are described as benchmarks in the practice of effective gifted education programming (Callahan et al., 2017; Cotabish et al., 2017; Landrum et. al., 2000; NAGC, 1998; 2010; 2019). Other descriptors include milestones and exemplars, which indicate the evolutionary process of educational programming, and the need for both formative and summative assessments based on the NAGC standards (Callahan, 2011).

The NAGC Standards are critically important in dictating how gifted students should be identified and served by school, district, and state level educational endeavors. Informing programming is accomplished by using the standards as a framework from which policies, regulations, and procedures emerge (Johnsen, 2011). Additionally, the NAGC standards represent benchmarks for best practice, a yardstick for program evaluation, and a set of beliefs that guide decision-making at the local, district, and state levels (Johnsen, 2011; Callahan et al., 2017; NAGC, 2019). The initial revision of the NAGC standards (2010) emphasized curriculum (VanTassel-Baska, 2011), which directly speaks to the day-to-day practice of addressing the academic needs of gifted students. Perhaps most noteworthy, however, is the emphasis on consistency (Johnsen, 2011) and equity of services provided to all gifted students across the NAGC standards.

Biennial reports of the nature of gifted education services developed collaboratively by NAGC and the Council of State Directors of Gifted Education (CSDPG) collect and report data regarding gifted education programming by states (Callahan et al., 2017). These reports outline how Pre-K–Grade 12 gifted education programming is regulated and supported by the state. Information pertaining to key areas such as funding, definitions, identification, programs and services, personnel, and accountability provide a "national portrait" of guiding principles, policies, and practices that represent gifted education programming (NAGC & CSDPG, 2011; 2013; 2015; 2020).

The NAGC standards provide a "toolbox" for planning, implementing, and enhancing programming offered to gifted students (Callahan, 2011), however, the translation of the standards to action in individual schools and across districts is dependent upon consideration of the context and unique aspects of any entity. For example, the resources, demographics, curricular emphasis, and other variables influence how the standards are translated from best practice to action (Callahan, 2011). Thus, the NAGC standards remain consistent across school districts; however, the implementation must consider the environment, circumstances, and distinctive qualities of the locality or state during related decision-making.

Impact on Research and Evaluation

In addition to guiding programmatic decision-making, the implementation of the NAGC standards provides a framework for the evaluation of gifted education programming. A critical evaluation will determine the effectiveness of services and address gaps to guide future development, thus, the NAGC standards serve as a means to document program effectiveness and impact on students (Cotabish & Krisel, 2012). Research and other inquiries into gifted education programming can be positively impacted by use of the NAGC standards for data collection and analysis. The NAGC standards have been used as a research framework or for evaluating programs in the following studies.

More than 1500 schools in separate school districts participated in a study (Callahan et al., 2017) using the 2010 NAGC standards as a framework for data collection in the investigation of the status of gifted education programming in our county. Only a little more than half of the participants at the elementary level reported using the 2010 NAGC standards to guide gifted education programming, and the percentage decreased substantially at the middle and high school levels. Therefore, findings reveal that typical gifted education programming does not reflect best practices as dictated by either the existing knowledge base or the 2010 NAGC standards.

A study was conducted to examine how teacher beliefs regarding research-based practices in gifted education influenced the implementation in the classroom (Johnsen & Kaul, 2019). The belief statements were based on the 2010 NAGC standards. Results indicated that teachers' acceptance of belief statements did not necessarily lead to action in the classroom. Despite the determination that a majority of the teachers agreed with the belief statements grounded in research-based practices, fewer actually implemented the beliefs as action in the classroom on a consistent basis. Further, these teachers indicated that obstacles prevented action, including limited resources, training, skill level, and the focus on the general education curriculum (Johnsen & Kaul, 2019).

Explanations for the gap between teachers' beliefs and action in the classroom include consistent barriers and obstacles. For example, the lack of teacher's acquisition of knowledge and skills specific to gifted education serves as an obstacle to the implementation of the standards (Johnsen & Kaul, 2019; NAGC & CSDPG, 2015, 2020). Specifically, national reports (NAGC & CSDPG, 2015, 2020) attribute teacher's lack of awareness and understanding of the needs of gifted students to the exclusion of this knowledge in most traditional initial licensure teacher preparation programs as well as school-based professional learning. Additionally, limited access to resources and administrator support is often the cause for the lack of translation of standards into action (Hertberg-Davis & Brighton, 2006). Finally, local district policies and procedures related to curriculum development and implementation can limit teacher's translation of standards to classroom practice (Latz et al., 2009).

Comparable to the use of the standards in research, the NAGC standards are invaluable to programming evaluation. In an evaluation of eight gifted programs, VanTassel-Baska and Hubbard (2019) used the 2010 version of the NAGC standards including all six components including learning and development, assessment, curriculum planning and instruction, learning environments, programming, and professional development. The degree to which each district implemented each standard was assessed. They reported that only 50% of the indicators were met for three of the standards, and only about 33% of them were met in the three remaining standards. This example illustrates a significant utility of NAGC standards implementation, to evaluate the effectiveness of Pre-K–Grade 12 gifted education programming as well as acknowledge gaps that exist that should be addressed in the continued evolution of services (Landrum et al., 2001). VanTassel-Baska and Hubbard (2019) refer to the NAGC standards as a yardstick against which one measures the effectiveness of gifted education programming in Pre-K–Grade 12.

The 2010 NAGC standards, specifically the student identification component, were used to guide the development of an instrument used for data collection in the study of 43 locally developed plans for identifying diverse gifted learners (Matthews & Shaunessy, 2010). In reporting study findings, the authors provide guidance in how the 2010 NAGC standards could be revised in order to function more effectively in the use of gifted education program evaluation. Given that decision-makers at the local levels are responsible for the policies and procedures that operationalize the standards, their utility should be intelligible to practitioners and readily transferable from print to action. In fact, Matthews and Shaunessy (2010) concluded that if standards play an integral role in the development and evaluation processes, standards should be written in formats that are readily usable for implementing recommendations.

When considering how the NAGC standards are used in the gifted programming evaluation process, two types of assessments are possible. First, the NAGC standards can serve in the formative assessment of gifted education programming in terms of reflecting best practice. Second, the NAGC standards can inform summative assessment when the student outcomes of best practices are measured against them (Callahan, 2011).

Survey of State Implementation of NAGC Standards

In order to determine the current status of the implementation of standards at the state level, we conducted a survey of state directors. During spring 2020, surveys were emailed to 54 offices of education, including Guam, Puerto Rico, the Virgin Islands and the Department of Defense. However, seven of the 54 offices were vacant. Another four offices declined to participate on the basis that the standards are not used in their state. Of the remaining 43 offices, twenty-two respondents (51%) completed the surveys. Not all state offices of gifted education responded to the survey query given other priorities related to Covid-19. It should be noted that rarely do all states and territories in the USA concurrently have appointees as state directors in gifted education, nor are all the positions that exist filled at any given time.

The survey items included contact information for the respondent as well as questions about NAGC standards and implementation of best practices. Respondents answered multiple-choice questions aligned with the six categories identified in the introduction to the gifted programming standards document under the heading, How may the standards be used? The standards document authors note (Corwith et al., 2019):

> There are a variety of ways in which the 2019 Pre-K–Grade 12 Gifted Programming Standards may be used in schools and districts across the country.
>
> The uses fall into six categories:
>
> ◆ Assess, evaluate, and improve local policies, rules and procedures
> ◆ Plan curriculum
> ◆ Provide professional learning
> ◆ Advocate
> ◆ Develop, improve, and evaluate state standards
> ◆ Approve gifted plans and programs and monitor for compliance with state regulations.
>
> (p. 1)

The state directors were also asked which set of NAGC standards (1998, 2010, or 2019) were being implemented. Follow-up interviews were conducted with four persons representing positions in state departments of education, two university professors, and a local-level gifted education administrator in order to ask follow-up questions to obtain descriptive information regarding survey results.

Results

Most, but not all, respondents indicated some use of the standards. Of those who had implemented the standards, not all used the most current revision. We agree that expecting states to implement the standards within six months of their revision may not be realistic. This is particularly true given the devastating impact of the Coronavirus pandemic on state and local education agencies during the 2019–2020 school year.

Frequency of States that Implement the Standards

Twenty-two state directors of gifted education indicated currently implementing the state standards at the state or local level. The directors also indicated the degree that standards were being used at the school district and higher education levels. Six of the 22 coordinators specified that their state did not implement any of the NAGC standards in their gifted education initiatives. The remaining 16 coordinators used either the 2019 or the 2010 version of the NAGC standards. The rate of implementation (approximately 30%-50% of the 43 coordinators) is consistent with published research studies over the past ten years (Callahan et al., 2017; Matthews & Shaunessy, 2010).

Frequency of Uses at State and Local Levels

State level. Survey respondents indicated that the NAGC standard implementation serves four primary purposes (see Table 10.1). Most often, state directors used the standards to plan professional learning (60%). Almost as many respondents (55%) indicated that the standards were used at the state level to inform program design initiatives for their state. Finally, 46% of the state directors reported using the standards for gifted education programming advocacy and 41% for monitoring for compliance.

Table 10.1 Rationales for Implementing the NAGC Standards.

	State (%)	District (%)	Higher Education (%)
Provide Professional Learning	60	55	43
Approve Gifted Plans & Programs	55	59	43
Advocate	46	50	43
Monitor for Compliance	41	41	29

Local level. Respondents indicated the same primary purposes for the NAGC standards implementation at the local level; however, fewer states reported use at this level. While the majority of states specified that district's used the NAGC standards to inform professional learning (55%) and program design (59%), 50% noted their impact on gifted education advocacy and 41% for monitoring compliance.

Frequency of Uses at Institutions of Higher Education Level

The survey asked respondents whether institutions of higher education in their state implemented the NAGC standards. Respondents reported these primary uses of the NAGC standards by colleges and universities, including informing

(a) the design of their educational programs and course content in gifted education (43%);
(b) the development of professional learning experiences (43%); and
(c) advocacy (43%).

Case Study and Vignettes of State Implementation of NAGC Standards

In addition to determining the extent to which the NAGC standards are being implemented, a secondary purpose of the study was to collect illustrative exemplars of the NAGC Standards execution at state and local levels as well as in institutions of higher education. The descriptions reveal the most common uses of the NAGC standards implementation and provide accounts that articulate how the applications transpired. It is hoped that the case study and vignettes will support the replication of such initiatives across local and state levels as well as by higher education programs. The experiences presented vary in the nature and the context of the circumstances and environments in which standards were employed.

Although the exemplars embrace diverse implementation methodologies, the educators reporting them shared common themes or trends in standards utility. These tendencies parallel those found in the survey results. Specifically, the NAGC standards provide structure and organization to gifted education programming. Further, the standards initiate conversations in support of program expansion, evaluation, and refinement. Finally, the NAGC standards inform professional learning initiatives relative to design and content.

State directors and administrators of local programming alike note that the NAGC standards provide a framework or infrastructure for comprehensiveness and consistency of services. Similarly, gifted education leaders report that the NAGC standards serve as a catalyst for dialogue about the provision of programming to gifted learners. At all levels of the provision of educational services, administrators referred to the use of the NAGC standards as a means for discussing programming alignment with educational initiatives, the basis for requesting the expansion of services, as well as the impetus for advocacy efforts. University, state, and local educators rely on the NAGC standards for the designing the format, content, and evaluation of professional learning activities for pre-collegiate educators and parents. Individuals designing and offering university course work concur that the NAGC standards inform necessary content. The standards themselves are often part of the content included in graduate-level courses in gifted education.

In this next section, we will explore how three state agencies, two universities and one school district use the NAGC standards to guide their work. Table 10.2 illustrates how each vignette and case study reflects the implementation of specific standards.

Case Study: Using the NAGC Standards to Build Capacity
Wendy A. Behrens, M.A. Ed., Gifted and Talented Education Specialist
Minnesota Department of Education

The Minnesota K–12 Academic Standards define expectations for the educational achievement of public-school students across the state in Grades K–12. Academic standards are in place for English language arts, mathematics, science, social studies and physical education; and those in the arts are available although districts may choose to develop their own. Districts and charter schools also are required to develop local academic standards for health, world languages, as well as career and technical education.

In addition to academic standards development in specified areas, Minnesota districts and charter schools are encouraged to incorporate the NAGC Standards into their service design, assessment of students for services, evaluation of services and curriculum selection. Professional learning opportunities sponsored or provided by the Minnesota Department of Education (MDE) align with the standards. Workshops consistently reinforce the dynamic and developing nature of giftedness; diversity in gifted characteristics and individuals; a focus on outcomes rather than practices; a responsibility among all staff to educate students with gifts and talents; and the need for services throughout the day. As a result, MDE uses the standards to inform the development of resources, selection of workshop content, and the research-based strategies and enrichment activities shared at the annual Hormel Foundation Gifted and Talented Education

Table 10.2 Case Study and Vignette Summary: Implementation of the NAGC Program Standards.

Institution	Assess, evaluate, and improve local policies, rules, and procedures	Plan Curriculum	Provide professional learning	Advocate	Develop, improve, evaluate state standards	Approve gifted plans and programs, monitor for compliance
Eastern Carolina University		✓	✓	✓	✓	
Georgia Department of Education	✓	✓	✓	✓	✓	✓
Maryland Department of Education	✓	✓	✓	✓	✓	
Minnesota Department of Education	✓	✓	✓	✓	✓	
Richardson ISD	✓	✓	✓	✓		
Towson University		✓	✓	✓		

Symposium. Not only do the standards provide a structure for defining benchmarks and establishing best practices, they serve as a reminder of what gifted education can and should be. Further, they align with MDE's goal of providing an outstanding education for Minnesota students by striving for excellence, equity, and opportunity. NAGC's standards define the same in gifted education.

Building capacity among practitioners and school leaders is critical to creating an infrastructure of support for gifted learners. Unfortunately, many educators responsible for educating the gifted or planning services have had little or no training to prepare them for the task. In fact, the *2014–2015 State of the States Report in Gifted Education*, concluded, "Most general education teachers were unlikely to be required to receive any training or professional development in gifted and talented education" (p. 39). In Minnesota, and in other states where gifted education credentials are not required, practitioners frequently rely on state agencies to provide high-quality professional learning opportunities. For this reason, MDE offers a series of training events for coordinators, workshops that focus on timely topics during the school year, and a multi-day symposium each summer.

In 2015, a Jacob K. Javits grant was awarded to the state of Minnesota. *Project North Star* elevates culturally responsive identification and services and provides for underserved gifted rural populations by preparing educators, administrators and families to understand the unique needs of gifted and talented learners. Through the project, MDE created three two-year training modules: one for teachers, another for school leaders, and a third for family and community. Each on-demand module is aligned with the NAGC Standards and is now available in Learning Management System format for use by individuals or in a cohort setting. The materials created include:

In 2019, MDE received a second Jacob K. Javits grant. *Universal Plus: A Two-Step Process for Equitably Identifying Computer Talent* affords MDE an opportunity to collaborate with Minnesota elementary schools to further equity in gifted and talented identification systems and services toward a global goal of providing access and opportunity for all students, including gifted and talented learners. Universal Plus provides identification and enrichment opportunities for students who are often overlooked for gifted and talent development services. While the grant primarily focuses on increasing the number of identified gifted learners, and on the development of computer science talent there is a significant professional learning component that requires teachers from participating districts to complete selected *Project North Star* training modules and attend the Hormel Symposium.

Table 10.3 On-demand Module Content and Resources.

Supporting Gifted and Talented Students	Four professional learning modules focusing on the pedagogical underpinnings of gifted education and practical instructional strategies that support gifted and talented learners from rural locations and diverse populations.
Introduction to Gifted and Talented for Administrators	This professional development offers two professional learning modules focusing on intentional school leadership with gifted and talented learners from rural locations and diverse populations.
School-Wide Professional Learning	While not specific to gifted education, these modules are research-based and aligned with best practices. They reinforce the importance of cultural competence for educators and administrators so that they have knowledge of the attitudes, background, and beliefs of cultures other than their own through the use of culturally responsive instructional practices, leadership skills and resources.
Other resources created	Literature resources, materials for community forums and a searchable database for student programs and enrichment opportunities.

Vignette 1: Georgia Department of Education Implementation of Standards

Mary Jean Banter, E.Ds., NBCT
College Readiness and Talent Development
Department of Curriculum and Instruction
Georgia Department of Education

Gail Humble, Program Manager
College Readiness and Talent Development
Georgia Department of Education

Georgia embraced the first revision of the NAGC standards by revisiting the standards used in Georgia. In 2010, the Georgia Department of Education (GaDOE) collaborated with the Georgia Association for Gifted Children (GAGC) to develop state standards for gifted education programming. In addition to the state-level standards, a rating scale of emergent, operational, and exemplary ratings of each was added to provide school district leaders a tool to evaluate their progress in standards implementation.

The NAGC standards also were used in the development of Georgia's Gifted Program Guidelines that require districts' self-evaluation of the effectiveness of its gifted programming every three years. The State Board of

Education Rule 160–4–2-.38 Education Program For Gifted Students states that Georgia districts shall evaluate their gifted programming at least every three years using criteria established by the Georgia Department of Education. Many of the items included in the evaluation are based on the NAGC standards. To illustrate how these standards and goals could be implemented in schools, classrooms, and in statewide meetings with district gifted leadership, state leaders included alternating activities based on the NAGC Standards. Additionally, the standards have been used as a means to initiate small-group discussions among educational leaders sharing implementation strategies.

Since 2018, a shift in district leaders occurred as many of the district leaders retired. In fact, more new gifted district coordinators with less than five years of experience were in roles of a gifted district leader. With a shift in district-level gifted education leadership, GaDOE realized the need to include the programming standards in the initial training sessions for new district-level administrators. Professional learning activities included the jigsaw strategy whereby participants collectively studied the various gifted programming standards and indicators. Other activities included explaining the standards to one another in various forms such as role-play and graphic organizers. Follow-up activity included webinars, conference calls, and other sessions to explain statewide procedures that reflect the standards. At the most recent new coordinators' meetings, the new NAGC standards (2019) were presented for participant review and comparison with the current Georgia programming standards. Plans to review and revise state gifted programming standards to align with the 2019 NAGC standards are underway.

Vignette 2: Maryland State Department Education Implementation of Standards
Dr. Bruce D. Riegel, Lead Specialist for Gifted and Talented Education Division of Curriculum, Instructional Improvement, and Professional Learning Maryland State Department of Education

Maryland state law contains a long-standing definition for gifted and talented students, potential for identification, and provision of programs and services, as well as a legal requirement to provide local school systems (LSSs) funding, should it be available and endorsed by the legislature. Special education law does not cover gifted education, and there has been no line item funding since before the start of the last decade. Regulations suggesting the need to identify, provide programs and services, and require LSSs to train educators in gifted and talented education were developed in the early part of this decade. Still, it was not until last year that the leadership was able to change the Regulations to mandate identification, provision of programs and services, and training of educators directly involved with gifted and talented students. The new mandate is strong, yet it is unfunded, and there is no substantial consequence for non-compliance. There is also a strong regulation for specific endorsement in gifted and talented education based on the National Standards, which is not required for licensing or hiring teachers or administrators. The state also does not have local gifted standards, nor does the State Board of Education officially endorse the NAGC standards for gifted and talented educational programming.

Even though the NAGC standards are not in the Regulations, they are used every day. All of the LSS GT Supervisors have a copy, and their use is encouraged when developing programs, curriculum, and educator training, lessons, student assessments, and educator evaluations. The NAGC standards are referenced and were used in the development of many critical documents, including a State Guidance that is required by Regulations. The Maryland State Schools Award of Excellence is heavily based on the NAGC standards, meaning that schools earning this designation are utilizing programs and practices that were developed using the NAGC standards. Every LSS GT Supervisor knows that the NAGC standards should play a vital role in all decision making.

On a State level, the NAGC standards are used as the basis for statewide teacher certification, as well as the basis for the IHE program certification process. In 2019, the new version of the NAGC standards quickly replaced the older version in the program certification guidelines. A lesson learned is that even though a state has not officially adopted the NAGC standards, it can still incorporate them directly or in spirit into every aspect of program development, instruction, and student support.

Vignette 3: Richardson Independent School District Implementation of Standards
Monica Simonds, M.Ed., Director of Advanced Learning
Richardson Independent School District Richardson, Texas

Richardson Independent School District is a large, urban and suburban school district with almost 40,000 students. It also is one of the most diverse districts in the state of Texas. Texas requires districts and campuses to use the *Texas State Plan for the Education of Gifted/Talented Students* (Texas Education Agency, 2019),, making it the priority document utilized for gifted service guidance; however, the NAGC standards provide an overarching set of guidelines for planning and delivering gifted services in any context and they correlate closely with much of the state document. Therefore, the standards are used in two broad applications: service fidelity and aspirational forecasting.

Relationships exist between the services provided along with the NAGC standards and the Texas State Plan, the district strategic plan, and district goals. With a focus on personalized learning, collaboration with other departments was initiated to broaden the multi-tiered systems of support to include interventions for students who need more challenge. A shift occurred away from a single gifted program model, meaning all students who qualified for gifted services received the same treatment option, to a gifted service design model, a systematic approach to personalized learning, to ensure that students' instructional needs were the focus of the decisions. Now students who qualify for services are matched to the level and type of support they need.

While focusing on the Texas State Plan at a district level, gifted education services are based on the NAGC standards as a way of forecasting next steps in a continuous improvement model. By looking to long-term aspirations while implementing more immediate innovations, decisions now lead to smooth transitions and progress later. An example of this model of implementation includes providing the gifted population in the district with Social-Emotional Learning symposium opportunities so they can learn more about the challenges they may face and receive guidance from a certified coach. This enhancement is an extension of the currently embedded SEL components within the curriculum.

Vignette 4: Towson University Implementation of Standards
Mary Slade, Ph.D., Professor and FACET Teaching Fellow
Towson University

Recently, the College of Education at Towson University in Towson, Maryland initiated a new master's degree in Gifted, Talented, and Creative Education (GACE). The new GACE certificate and degree program options include five new graduate courses supported by the Early Childhood Education Department. Given that the intent of the course work is to prepare Pre-K–Grade 12 educators for the development, implementation, and evaluation of educational programming for pre-collegiate learners, the NAGC standards impact course content. Not only is the NAGC standards document included in the content of one or more courses, but also dictates the content of each course.

In addition to the delivery of professional education courses in gifted education, Towson faculty engage in the provision of professional learning aimed at educators in Pre-K–Grade 12. The NAGC standards guide the content and delivery of professional learning initiatives. The professional learning component of the standards guides the nature, delivery, and evaluation of related activities. However, the remaining NAGC standards components command the nature and context of these endeavors.

Lastly, the GACE faculty at Towson University engage and support pre-collegiate gifted education programming initiatives at local, state, and national levels. For example, consultative activities include curriculum development and program evaluation. The NAGC standards emphasis on curriculum and instruction can be used to measure gaps in existing curriculum, guide expansion or refinement, as well as guide the alignment of differentiated curricula for gifted learners. The NAGC standards serve as benchmarks for programming evaluation. As exemplars representing best practice, the NAGC standards can be used to demonstrate the effectiveness and well as deficiencies in current programming options for individual schools, districts, and across the state.

Vignette 5: Eastern Carolina University Implementation of Standards,

Angela M. Novak, Ph.D., Eastern Carolina University
Assistant Professor of Elementary and Middle Grades Education
Greenville, North Carolina

In the 2019–2020, the gifted program (termed Academically and Intellectually Gifted, or AIG in North Carolina) at East Carolina University (ECU) in rural eastern North Carolina was reconfigured to have a greater emphasis on equity, have classes at both the undergraduate and graduate level, and align with several iterations of the NAGC standards. When written, the courses were designed to align with the NAGC-CEC Teacher Preparation Standards in Gifted Education (NAGC & CEC, 2013). Additionally, embedded in many of the courses' authentic assessments are connections to the NAGC standards focused on Pre-K–Grade 12 gifted programming.

The university courses are taught predominantly through a lens of equity firmly embedded in each of the courses, versus a stand-alone course, or as a topic or module in a course. For example, ECU's first course in the series is purposefully titled The Diverse Gifted Learner, not Characteristics of the Gifted Child; it is taught through a series of modules, starting with characteristics, then students explore giftedness through a series of lenses: culture, place, economics, exceptionalities, and beyond academics. Each module asks students to apply their learning to a challenge, differentiated for the undergraduate and graduate level. It is in these challenges that students are asked to integrate the NAGC standards.

In the first module of the Diverse Gifted Child, students are asked to reflect on myths and stereotypes of gifted students; in the cultural lens module, students recognize that culturally, linguistically and ethnically diverse gifted students push the definitions and conceptions of gifted and challenge teachers to see beyond one image of a gifted child. Thus, their challenge is to reflect on and analyze the stories of two gifted children and the ways their giftedness manifests based on their culture or ethnicity, and how these attributes might not be recognized as gifted by an untrained teacher. Challenges tend to be open-ended, and as long as the objective of the challenge is met and the criteria are achieved, products can be submitted in any form of the students' choosing; they are encouraged to consider what an authentic product would be for their desired goal: an administrator of an AIG program, an AIG pull-out teacher, a resource teacher, an AIG classroom teacher, and gear their products for that role, and whatever real world audience might fit that role. Additional guidance and criteria are provided for the assignment; however, a key component is the connection to the NAGC standards.

With standard 4.4, Cultural Competence under Learning Environments, the student outcome refers to student growth in valuing, communicating, and collaborating with members of their own and others' cultures, while also encouraging social activism. The evidence-based practices for educators include modeling appropriate strategies for such activism, and providing opportunities for communication and collaboration, while modeling soft skills in appreciating and valuing their own and others' language and heritage. In this assignment, students integrate this standard through the description of the case study of the children, utilizing the student outcomes. The evidence-based practices are a better fit for the teacher recognition aspect of the challenge, in which they reflect on how the manifested gifts are seen by trained vs. untrained teachers.

With NAGC standard 1.2, Self-Understanding under Learning and Development, the student outcome focuses on how students' self-awareness of their identities and values affects their learning and behavior. The teachers' evidence-based practices include modeling respect for all students while using data-informed instructional and grouping practices, differentiated materials and learning activities, and facilitating the interaction and collaboration of diverse students. In the challenge assignment for the culture lens module, both graduate and undergraduate students at ECU reflect on their case studies' self-awareness, connecting to this standard, and interpreting this standard in a real-world example. Moreover, they can connect the teacher perspective both to their own reflections and awareness, as well as to the teacher's response in the challenge.

How the NAGC standards are embedded in each challenge is left up to the student. If they decide to write a typical paper, they cite the standards as examples and apply them accordingly. However, students may record a podcast, create paper slides, perform a stop-go animation, record a video log, create a series of blog entries, design a professional learning experience for their school, and the list goes on. The form of integration of the NAGC standards can vary based on the product, and it can be as a reflection, or a direct part of the assignment, as long as it is included. This assignment is just one example of how the standards overall are one way to continually embed equity in the courses.

Case Study and Vignette Summary

The similarities and differences in the implementation of the NAGC standards in the examples previously provided reflect a variety of approaches to education in the USA. While each of the three states employs the standards in planning professional learning, advocacy, evaluation and improvement of policy, Georgia is one of the few states using the standards as a tool for program evaluation. Georgia, known for robust programming and resources, has equally rigorous standards for gifted education programming. Though Maryland does not evaluate district programs, the standards guide the work of the state director and are included in the rubric used to determine which schools qualify for exemplary gifted education awards. In contrast, Minnesota, with its strict adherence to local control, neither reviews nor evaluates LEA plans. Instead, the state embeds the standards within all gifted and talented professional learning opportunities and creation of district guidance documents. In Minnesota, the state director is a member of the academic standards team and collaborates with various internal and external advisory groups.

Towson University and Eastern Carolina University illustrate the important role universities play in preparing educators to recognize and respond to the unique needs of gifted learners. With an equity perspective, the standards provide university personnel with exemplars representing best practice, and are used to demonstrate the effectiveness as well as deficiencies in current programming options for schools and districts. Each of the two universities profiled embeds authentic assessments focused on the NAGC standards within their coursework, ultimately preparing teachers to use the standards, recognize and respond to the needs of gifted and talented learners.

Richardson Independent School District, a Texas district known for its comprehensive level of services, uses the standards for service fidelity and for aspirational forecasting. In doing so, the district sets both short-term and long-term goals for the provision equitable services and a robust array of student opportunities. The process of using the standards in aspirational forecasting (e.g., setting goals, deciding on actions to achieve those goals, and mobilizing the resources needed to take those actions) distinguish Richardson Independent School District from other districts of similar size.

Recommendations

The standards act as guideposts for the planning, implementation, and evaluation of professional learning initiatives related to gifted education. The greatest utility of the NAGC standards for district, state, and university implementation is clearly professional learning as reported by survey respondents and illustrated across real-world applications contained in the vignettes. For example, Vignette 1 discusses the need for extensive professional learning following a statewide turnover in district-level gifted education leadership. In planning professional learning initiatives led by the state department of education, the standards served to set parameters for training activities as well as to constitute their content. Specifically, the NAGC standards dictated the content of a statewide needs-assessment of local gifted education coordinators, many of whom possessed less than five years of job experience in the field. Similarly, another state director in gifted education who is represented in Vignette 2, notes that a statewide course in gifted education facilitated by his office was informed using the NAGC standards when developing content. Vignette 4, which depicts district-level implementation of the NAGC standards, discusses integration of their content in local professional learning initiatives led by district leadership outside of gifted education. Both higher education vignettes consist of examples of NAGC standards implementation in providing the parameters for professional learning activities conducted on behalf of local and state agencies in gifted education.

The NAGC standards provide a means for gifted programming design, enhancement, and expansion at local, state, and higher-education levels. With equal frequency to informing professional learning, survey results illustrate the impact of the NAGC standards on educational programming. Examples from the case study and vignettes illustrate the utility of the NAGC standards in programming enterprises. Vignette 1 portrays a statewide effort that uses the standards to inform the content of a widely used local programming documentation plan. The NAGC standards are used to guide self-examination of existing gaps in current programming efforts and in order to set goals for programming enhancement that will improve shortcomings. Similarly, the local district gifted education coordinator in Vignette 3 summarizes her experience in using the NAGC standards as correlates for local and state programming planning. Specifically, the author of the vignette notes that the NAGC standards are a means to enable the planning of gifted education programming and to close gaps between current efforts and best practices in the field. Nearly every vignette denotes the implementation of NAGC standards specifically to create and fulfill local and state level planning documents.

The NAGC standards support diverse advocacy endeavors at the district, state, and higher education levels. The third most frequent use of the NAGC standards as reported by the survey results is gifted education advocacy. For example, the state director who authored Vignette 2 describes the use of the standards to create a gifted education programming recognition program that annually distinguishes gifted programming that reflects excellence. The standards serve as benchmarks of distinction to denote programming efforts across all school districts. This type of state department sponsored recognition program serves to advocate for excellence across districts and to support the continuation of programming of high quality. Similarly, state directors representing Vignette 1 discuss the need for local district advisory boards and related task force members to advocate for the expansion of gifted education programming by emphasizing alignment with NAGC standards' outcomes. Finally, the NAGC standards provide best practice and intended outcomes of evidence-based practice that higher education gifted education leaders can use to inform local and state levels consultancies and advocacy tactics.

Summary

The release of the most recent edition of the NAGC standards prompted a query into their implementation at local and state levels in pre-collegiate education as well as for universities. The results of a survey of state directors of gifted education programming revealed consistent patterns in the execution of the standards across local and state domains. In addition, findings reflect consistent rationales for use of the standards across pre-collegiate and university programming focusing on gifted education. Primarily, the NAGC standards inform professional learning for localities, states, and universities. Further, the educational programming for pre-collegiate and collegiate learners is driven by the standards. Finally, the NAGC standards guide advocacy for gifted education for localities, states, and universities.

The results of the current survey of state-level leaders in gifted education consistently report on the general purposes if not needs for the NAGC standards in informing professional learning initiatives and programming content, as well as comprising the basis for advocacy in gifted education. Moreover, these needs are similarly important at local and state levels of Pre-K–Grade 12 education. Perhaps most interesting is that universities' purposes for standards implementation are aligned with those of pre-collegiate entities. The NAGC standards serve multiple purposes including shaping policy and providing a framework for the evaluation of gifted education programming. However, clearly three primary rationales—professional learning, educational programming, and advocacy—for the utility of the NAGC standards standout at all levels of implementation.

References

Callahan, C. M. (2011). Evaluation of programming: Student outcomes. *Tempo*, *31*(2), 21–24.www.txgifted.org/files/Tempo/2011/2011–2.pdf

Callahan C. M., Moon, T., & Oh, S. (2017). Describing the status of programs for the gifted: A call for action. *Journal for the Education of the Gifted*, *40*(1), 20–49. http://dx.doi.org/10.1177/0162353216686215

Corwith, S., Johnsen, S., Lee, C-W, Cotabish, A., Dailey, D., & Guilbault, K. (2019). *2019 Pre-k–Grade 12 Gifted Programming Standards*. National Association for Gifted Children. www.nagc.org/sites/default/files/standards/Intro%202019%20Programming%20Standards%281%29.pdf

Cotabish, A., Dailey, D., & Jackson, N. (2017). Aligning programs and services with national and state standards. In R. D. Eckert and J. H. Robins (Eds.), *Designing services and programs for high-ability learners: A guidebook for gifted education* (revised; pp. 1–17). Corwin Press.

Cotabish, A., & Krisel, S. (2012). Action plans: Bringing the program standards to life. In S. K. Johnsen (Ed.), *NAGC Pre-K–Grade 12 Gifted Education Programming Standards: A guide to planning and implementing high-quality services* (pp. 231–253). Prufrock Press.

Cotabish, A., & Krisel, S. (2012). Action plans: Bringing the program standards to life. In S. K. Johnsen (Ed.), *NAGC Pre-K–Grade 12 Gifted Education Programming Standards: A guide to planning and implementing high-quality services* (pp. 231–253). Prufrock Press.

Center for Talent Development (2017). *Applying gifted education standards: The what, the who, and the how*. Northwestern University: CTD. www.ctd.northwestern.edu/blog/applying-gifted-education-standards-what-who-and-how

Hertberg-Davis, H. L., & Brighton, C. M. (2006). Support and sabotage: Principal's influence on middle school teachers' responses to differentiation. *The Journal of Secondary Gifted Education*, *17*(2), 90–102. https://doi.org/10.4219/jsge-2006–685

Johnsen, S. K. (2011). A comparison of the Texas state plan for the education of gifted/talented students and the 2010 NAGC Pre-K–Grade 12 Gifted

Programming Standards. *Tempo, 31*(1), 10–20. www.txgifted.org/files/Tempo/2011/2011–1.pdf

Johnsen, S. K. (Ed.) (2012). *The NAGC Pre-K–Grade 12 Gifted Education Programming Standards: A guide to planning implementing high-quality services.* Prufrock Press.

Johnsen, S. K., & Kaul, C. R. (2019). Assessing teacher beliefs regarding research-based practices to improve services for GT students. *Gifted Child Today, 42*(4), 229–239. https://doi.org/10.1177/1076217519862332

Landrum, M. S., Callahan, C. M., & Shaklee, B. (2000). *Aiming for excellence: Gifted Program Standards Annotations to the NAGC preschool–Grade 12 gifted program standards.* Prufrock Press.

Latz, A. O., Speirs-Neumeister, K. L., Adams, C. M., & Pierce, R. L. (2009). Peer coaching to improve classroom differentiation: Perspectives from Project CLUE. *Roeper Review, 31*(1), 27–39. https://doi.org//10.1080/02783190802527356

Matthews, M. S., & Shaunessy, E. (2010). Putting standards into practice: Evaluating the utility of the NAGC Pre-K–Grade 12 gifted program standards. *Gifted Child Quarterly, 54*(3),159–167. https://doi.org/10.1177/0016986209356708

National Association for Gifted Children (1998). *Pre-K–Grade 12 gifted program standards.* http://hamburgschool.com/wp-content/uploads/2016/12/Gifted-Program-Standards.pdf

National Association for Gifted Children (2010). *Pre-K–Grade 12 Gifted Programming Standards.* www.nagc.org/sites/default/files/standards/K-12%20programming%20standards.pdf

National Association for Gifted Children (2019). *Pre-K–Grade 12 Gifted Programming Standards.* www.nagc.org/resources-publications/resources/national-standards-gifted-and-talented-education/pre-k-grade-12

National Association for Gifted Children (2013). NAGC-CEC Teacher Preparation Standards in Gifted Education. www.nagc.org/sites/default/files/standards/NAGC-%20CEC%20CAEP%20standards%20(2013%20final).pdf

National Association for Gifted Children & Council of State Directors of Programs for the Gifted (2011). *The state of the states in gifted education.*

National Association for Gifted Children & Council of State Directors of Programs for the Gifted (2013). *The state of the states in gifted education.* www.nagc.org/sites/default/files/State%20of%20the%20Nation.pdf

National Association for Gifted Children & Council of State Directors of Programs for the Gifted (2015). *The state of the states in gifted education.* https://www.nagc.org/sites/default/files/key%20reports/2014–2015%20State%20of%20the%20States%20summary.pdf

National Association for Gifted Children (NAGC) and the Council of State Directors of Programs for the Gifted (CSDPG) (2020). 2018–2019 *State of the states in gifted education.* National Association for Gifted Children. www.nagc.org/2018–2019-state-states-gifted-education

New Jersey Department of Education (n.d.). *The New Jersey student learning standards: Gifted education.* www.state.nj.us/education/aps/cccs/gandt/

Roberts, J. L. (2011). Implementing the NAGC Pre-K–Grade 12 Programming Standards in the classroom. *Tempo, 31*(2), 25–29. www.txgifted.org/files/Tempo/2011/2011-2.pdf

Thomas Fordham Institute (2016). Gifted education standards to guide teaching and deepen student learning. Thomas Fordham Institute. https://fordhaminstitute.org/national/commentary/gifted-education-standards-guide-teaching-and-deepen-student-learning

VanTassel-Baska, J. (2011). The logic of the design and development of curriculum for gifted learners. *Tempo, 31*(1), 10–20. www.txgifted.org/files/Tempo/2011/2011–1.pdf.

VanTassel-Baska, J., & Hubbard, G. F. (2019). A review of the national gifted standards implementation in eight school districts: An uneven picture of practice. *Gifted Child Today, 42*(4), 215–228. https://doi.org/10.1177/1076217519862336

11

Aligning Gifted Programming Standards with ISTE Standards for Enhanced Student Outcomes

Debbie Dailey, Jason Trumble, and Michelle Buchanan

To address the importance of technology in the teaching and learning of gifted students, the revised Pre-K–Grade 12 Gifted Programming Standards (NAGC, 2019) include elements from the International Society for Technology in Education (ISTE) standards. Whereas the Pre-K–Grade 12 Gifted Programming Standards are presented as student outcomes and evidence-based practices, the ISTE presents separate standards for educators, students, coaches, and administrators. In this chapter, we will focus on the ISTE Standards for Students and the ISTE Standards for Educators (ISTE, 2016).

All of the ISTE standards focus on the development of learners as digital citizens in technology-rich environments, and the implications of the ISTE standards impact the practice of teaching including those strategies that promote active, collaborative, and self-directed learning. Additionally, the ISTE standards support the design of student-centered activities that accommodate learner variability. The ISTE standards are structured with the standard descriptor which describes the standard. Each standard has multiple standard

DOI: 10.4324/9781003236863-11

indicators that clarify and indicate the expected action needed to achieve the standard. The ISTE Standards for Educators view educators as empowered learners who engage in learning and using evidence-based practices, collaborate to learn from and lead local and global communities, and advocate for opportunities for students to become empowered learners. The ISTE Standards for Educators also encourage teachers to become learning catalysts who utilize technology to innovatively design and expertly facilitate lessons with a focus on thoughtful data-driven decision making. ISTE Standards for Students prepare students to thrive in a constantly evolving technological landscape by using technology to empower students to become digital citizens, build knowledge, design solutions using a variety of technologies, and communicate clearly using multiple platforms.

This chapter connects the revised Pre-K–Grade 12 Gifted Programming Standards to the ISTE Standards for Educators and Students. A discussion of each gifted standard will begin with a comparison of gifted student outcomes and the ISTE Standards for Students. The focus will then shift to the recommended educator and program practices needed for the desired student outcomes (NAGC evidence-based practices and ISTE Standards for Educators). Each section also provides practical classroom or program applications that can be used to improve student outcomes and promote achievement in technology-rich environments. Table 11.1 presents a comparison of the standards.

Standard 1: Learning and Development

The Learning and Development Standard addresses student outcomes in the areas of self-understanding, awareness of needs, and cognitive, psychosocial, and affective growth; and cognitive growth and career development. Furthermore, this standard promotes self-understanding of how students learn and how their identity, culture, beliefs, traditions, and values influence their learning and behavior. In a similar focus on student self-awareness and understanding, the ISTE Standard for Students-Empowered Learner encourages students to take ownership of their learning goals and outcomes with students actively choosing how to demonstrate competency. In particular, students should set learning goals, customize their learning environments to meet their particular needs, use technology as an instructional and learning tool, and demonstrate learning in a variety of ways.

To facilitate these student outcomes, the evidence-based practices from the Standard 1 (Learning and Development) encourage educators to acknowledge and understand gifted students' learning and developmental differences, provide opportunities for students to identify their interests, talents,

Table 11.1 Comparison of Standards: Pre-K–Grade 12 Gifted Programming, ISTE for Educators, and ISTE for Students.

Pre-K–Grade 12 Gifted Programming Standards Descriptions	ISTE Standards for Students	ISTE Standards for Educators
Standard 1: Learning and Development Educators understand the variations in learning and development in cognitive, affective, and psychosocial areas between and among individuals with gifts and talents, creating learning environments that encourage awareness and understanding of interest, strengths, and needs; cognitive growth, social and emotional, and psychosocial skill development in school, home, and community settings.	Standard 1: Empowered Learner Students leverage technology to take an active role in choosing, achieving, and demonstrating competency in their learning goals, informed by the learning sciences.	Standard 6: Facilitator Educators facilitate learning with technology to support student achievement of the ISTE Standards for Students.
Standard 2: Assessment Assessments provide information about identification and learning progress for students with gifts and talents.	Standard 1: Empowered Learner Students leverage technology to take an active role in choosing, achieving, and demonstrating competency in their learning goals, informed by the learning sciences.	Standard 7: Analyst Educators understand and use data to drive their instruction and support students in achieving their learning goals.

(Continued)

Table 11.1 *Continued*

Pre-K–Grade 12 Gifted Programming Standards Descriptions	ISTE Standards for Students	ISTE Standards for Educators
Standard 3: Curriculum Planning and Instruction Educators apply evidence-based models of curriculum and instruction related to students with gifts and talents and respond to their needs by planning, selecting, adapting, and creating curriculum that is responsive to diversity. Educators use a repertoire of instructional strategies to ensure specific student outcomes and measurable growth.	Standard 3: Knowledge Constructor Students critically curate a variety of resources using digital tools to construct knowledge, produce creative artifacts, and make meaningful learning experiences for themselves and others. Standard 4: Innovative Designer Students use a variety of technologies within a design process to identify and solve problems by creating new, useful, or imaginative solutions.	Standard 5: Designer Educators design authentic, learner-driven activities and environments that recognize and accommodate learner variability. Standard 6: Facilitator Educators facilitate learning with technology to support student achievement of the ISTE Standards for Students.

Table 11.1 Continued

Pre-K–Grade 12 Gifted Programming Standards Descriptions	ISTE Standards for Students	ISTE Standards for Educators
Standard 4: Learning Environments Learning environments foster a love for learning, academic, personal, and social responsibilities competence in working with diverse people, and interpersonal and technical communication skills to ensure specific student outcomes.	Standard 2: Digital Citizen Students recognize the rights, responsibilities, and opportunities of living, learning, and working in an interconnected digital world, and they act and model in ways that are safe, legal, and ethical. Standard 6: Creative Communicator Students communicate clearly and express themselves creatively for a variety of purposes using the platforms, tools, styles, formats, and digital media appropriate to their goals. Standard 7: Global Communicator Students use digital tools to broaden their perspectives and enrich their learning by collaborating with others and working effectively in teams locally and globally.	Standard 2: Leader Advocate for equitable access to educational technology, digital content, and learning opportunities to meet the diverse needs of all students Standard 3: Citizen Educators inspire students to positively contribute to and responsibly participate in the digital world. Standard 4: Collaborator Use collaborative tools to expand students' authentic, real-world learning experiences by engaging virtually with experts, teams, and students, locally and globally.

(Continued)

Table 11.1 Continued

Pre-K–Grade 12 Gifted Programming Standards Descriptions	ISTE Standards for Students	ISTE Standards for Educators
Standard 5: Programming Educators use evidence-based practices to promote (a) the cognitive, social-emotional, and psychosocial skill development of students with gifts and talents and (b) programming that meets their interests, strengths, and needs. Educators make use of expertise systematically and collaboratively to develop, implement, manage, and evaluate services for students with a variety of gifts and talents to ensure specific student outcomes.		Standard 4: Collaborator Educators dedicate time to collaborate with both colleagues and students to improve practice, discover and share resources and ideas, and solve problems. Standard 5: Designer Educators design authentic, learner-driven activities and environments that recognize and accommodate learner variability.

Table 11.1 *Continued*

Pre-K–Grade 12 Gifted Programming Standards Descriptions	ISTE Standards for Students	ISTE Standards for Educators
Standard 6: Professional Learning All educators (administrators, teachers, counselors, and other instructional support staff) build their knowledge and skills using the NAGC-CEC Teacher Standards for Gifted and Talented Education, NAGC-CEC Advanced Standards in Gifted Education Teacher Preparation, and the Standards for Professional Learning. Institutions of higher education utilize these standards and the NAGC Faculty Standards to ensure quality professional learning experiences in pre-service, initial, and advanced educator preparation programs. Educators frequently assess their professional learning needs related to the standards, develop and monitor their professional learning plans, systematically engage in coaching and learning to meet their identified needs, and align outcomes with educator performance and student curriculum standards. Administrators assure educators have access to sustained, intensive collaborative, job-embedded, and data-driven learning and assure adequate resources to provide for release time, fund continuing education, and offer substitute support. The effectiveness of professional learning is assessed through relevant student outcomes.		Standard 1: Learner Educators continually improve their practice by learning from and with others and exploring proven and promising practices that leverage technology to improve student learning. Standard 2: Leader Educators seek out opportunities for leadership to support student empowerment and success and to improve teaching and learning.

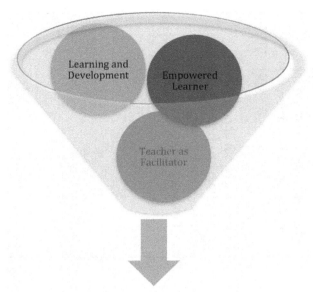

Empowered, Invested, and Engaged Learner

Figure 11.1 Empowered, Invested, and Engaged Learner.

strengths, and needs, and design learning experiences tailored to their students' developmental and cultural learning needs. To aid in students identifying resources for their learning, educators should provide role models that match student interests, strengths, and needs and identify out-of-school and community resources to facilitate student talent development. Whereas ISTE for Educators-Facilitator promotes environments where students develop individual learning goals and are provided choices to customize their learning process. A prevalent theme across the NAGC and ISTE standards is student ownership of learning. To create a classroom where students take ownership of their learning requires an educator to provide opportunities for student self-discovery, identify support structures to help students determine and achieve their goals, and take a back seat when needed in the teaching and learning process. A learner in a student-centered classroom will be empowered, invested, and engaged in the learning process (see Figure 11.1).

Standard 1: Learning and Development—Practical Application

To address these standards, student interests should be identified so that a learning plan can be tailored to students' interests and cultural learning needs. Educators know that interest is instrumental in talent development, persistence, and achievement in a domain (Maltese & Tai, 2010; Subotnik et al., 2011). Data from informal observations, discussions with parents and families, and interest inventories can be used to determine student interest and cultural learning needs. Young children may not be aware of their interests; so, it is important to provide them multiple enrichment opportunities across various domains. The National Research Center on the Gifted and Talented (NRCGT, n.d.) recommends two interest inventories to help students find the types of enrichment they would like to pursue. "If I Ran the School" (Reis & Siegle, 2002) asks students to identify 10 things from a list that they would like to learn more about. The list is divided into items related to science, technology/ audiovisual, social studies, language arts, and art. Although the technology section needs updating, this tool contains important information necessary to design an instructional plan for individual students. "Secondary Interest-A-Lyzer" (Hébert et al., 1997) is a questionnaire that asks scenario-based or hypothetical questions to help identify secondary students' areas of interest.

When interests are identified, students should be given choices in their learning plan. For example, if the CCSS.ELA-Literacy.RH.6–8.8 standard "Distinguish among fact, opinion, and reasoned judgment in a text" is the focus of the lesson, and students have an interest in science, the standard can be met through a science investigation. Students could investigate an authentic problem in science that differentiates fact, opinion, and reasoned judgment. For example, there were many controversial arguments on the occurrence, spread, control, and treatment of the virus in the COVID-19 pandemic. Presented with a statement or statements regarding the topic, students would investigate scientific evidence that supports the statement as a fact, opinion, or reasoned judgment. Using technology, such as approved websites, virtual and augmented reality applications, and virtual conversations with mentors and peers, students develop their arguments and present their evidence using analog or digital tools. An example learning plan is provided in Table 11.2.

Standard 2: Assessment

The Assessment Standard encourages student outcomes in the areas of identification, access, and academic and affective growth. Students from all backgrounds should be represented in the identification process and gifted programming. Students' interests, strengths, and needs should be addressed in assessments created or selected for identification and learning progress, and programming services. Students' growth should be commensurate with their cognitive, social-emotional, and psychosocial abilities. Students should also self-monitor their progress by setting personal goals and recording their progress toward meeting their goals. Similarly, ISTE for Students-Empowered

Table 11.2 Individual Student Learning Plan.

Standard: CCSS.ELA-Literacy.RH.6–8.8: Distinguish among fact, opinion, and reasoned judgment in a text.
1. How do you want to address this standard? Examining facts, opinions, and reasoned judgment in primary and secondary resources involving a topic in: (a) Science, health, or medicine (b) Mathematics (c) Society (d) Media (e) Art (f) Other: Please Specify
2. What specific area in your topic do you want to focus on? (a) COVID-19 is not spread by children (fact, opinion, reasoned judgment). (b) The 2020 COVID-19 pandemic positivity rates increase at twice the rate of the 2020 influenza outbreak (fact, opinion, reasoned judgment). (c) COVID-19 contributed to the racial tensions in 2020 (fact, opinion, reasoned judgment). (d) Media used reliable sources during reporting on the COVID-19 pandemic (fact, opinion, reasoned judgment). (e) During 2020, many cities were decorated with Graffiti depicting Black Lives Matter. Graffiti is art (fact, opinion, reasoned judgment). (f) The media spread panic about the 2020 pandemic and could not be trusted (fact, opinion, reasoned judgment). (g) Other: Please explain
3. What are your SMART goals (Elias, 2014) for your plan of study? (example below) (a) Specific: I will collect reliable evidence on how COVID-19 is spread by children. (b) Measurable: I will find at least 5 primary sources of information. (c) Attainable: I will determine if the sentence is a fact, opinion, or reasoned judgment based on the evidence that I collect. (d) Relevant: I will prepare a presentation with my evidence. (e) Time-Bound: I will complete this study in five days.

Table 11.2 *Continued*

Standard: CCSS.ELA-Literacy.RH.6–8.8: Distinguish among fact, opinion, and reasoned judgment in a text.	

4. What materials will you need to complete your study and presentation?
  (a) Appropriate websites to search
  (b) Access to mentors or guest speakers using Skype
  (c) Virtual Field trip
  (d) iPad or Chromebook
  (e) Please specify anything else you need	

5. How will you complete your presentation?
  (a) Infographic
  (b) E-book
  (c) Poster Board
  (d) Slideshow
  (e) Nearpod
  (f) Augmented reality experience
  (g) Other—Please Specify	

Learner encourages students to take an active role in choosing how they will demonstrate their competency and self-assess their learning progress.

To achieve these student outcomes, evidence-based practices include providing access to gifted programming services in respect to the school population, using universal screening and multiple indicators of potential to identify students for gifted programming services, selecting assessment tools and identification procedures to eliminate possible biases, designing appropriate services to meet the individual needs of gifted students, and utilizing differentiated formative assessment and ongoing alternative assessments to monitor the progress of students. Similar to the evidence-based practices but with a focus on technology, ISTE for Educators-Analyst encourages educators to provide alternative ways for students to demonstrate competency using technology, offer a variety of formative and summative assessments to guide instruction, and use assessment data to communicate and encourage student self-direction. The NAGC Assessment Standard aligns with the ISTE for Educators-Analyst standard by addressing alternative assessments, including assessments that reduce bias and using assessments to modify and inform instruction for student progress in learning and talent development. Both NAGC and ISTE standards encourage using data-driven evidence to guide instruction and student learning. These standards encourage educators to use data to create and/or use fair and equitable assessments that drive instruction and personalized learning (see Figure 11.2).

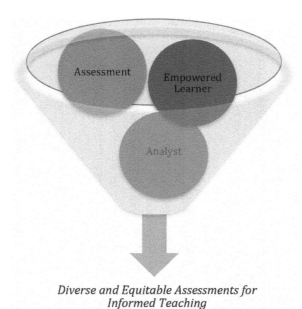

Diverse and Equitable Assessments for Informed Teaching

Figure 11.2 Diverse and Equitable Assessments for Informed Teaching.

Standard 2: Assessment—Practical Application

Revisiting our learning plan in Table 11.2, we can add student choice in types of assessment to the plan. Students can choose how they want to demonstrate their learning through a type of performance-based assessment that would evaluate their application of knowledge using higher-order thinking skills to complete the process. VanTassel-Baska and Baska (2019) suggested that performance-based assessments are helpful when determining student level of performance in authentic type tasks and provide multiple opportunities for differentiation. The assessment could be tied closely to their relationship with mentors or practicing professionals by encouraging students to present their products or solutions to problems to authentic audiences. With virtual meeting platforms easily accessible, audiences are no longer limited by geographical boundaries.

To minimize bias, inform expectations, and be transparent in the grading process, teachers can use a rubric to monitor students' progress. Table 11.3 provides an example of a rubric that would measure the progress on the learning plan from Table 11.2. Additionally, students can use a checklist to monitor their progress and self-assess their learning (see Table 11.4).

Table 11.3 Rubric for Learning Plan.

Criteria	Excellent	Proficient	Needs Improvement
Content	Selected an approved topic. Included specific details, examples, and in-depth analysis to describe the topic.	Selected an approved topic. Included details, examples, and analysis to describe the topic.	Selected an approved topic. Includes few details and examples to describe the topic.
Evidence	Used a minimum of five primary sources as evidence to support claim and base analysis and conclusions Evidence is clear, accurate, and complete and supports the claim.	Used three to four primary sources to support claim and base analysis and conclusions. Evidence is provided to support the claim.	Used fewer than three primary sources to support claim and base analysis and conclusions. Evidence is not provided to support the claim. Or Evidence is incorrectly used to support the claim.

(Continued)

Table 11.3 *Continued*

Criteria	Excellent	Proficient	Needs Improvement
Critical Thinking	Thoroughly analyzes and evaluates alternative points of view. Explains assumptions associated with alternative points of view.	Explains opposing or alternative points of view.	Does not consider alternative points of view.
Self-Reflection	What are some of the most interesting discoveries you made while completing this project? What were some challenges or obstacles you faced in completing this assignment? How would you explain to someone the difference between fact and opinion?		

Table 11.4 Checklist for Learning Plan.

Tasks	Due Date	Completed
Select approved topic		
Select specific area of focus		
Created SMART goals		
Requested needed materials		
Chose presentation mode of delivery		
Completed project		

Standard 3: Curriculum Planning and Instruction

The Curriculum Planning and Instruction student outcomes include growth in academic, social, emotional, and psychosocial skills; development of knowledge and skills for living and contributing in a diverse and global society; achievement in areas of talent and/or interest; and opportunities to become independent investigators with access to quality resources. Just as the NAGC Curriculum Planning and Instruction Standard encourages the development of students as independent investigators, the ISTE Student-Knowledge Constructor Standard also focuses on developing students as investigators by encouraging the use of digital tools to create meaningful learning experiences that will build their knowledge as they explore real-world issues and solve real-world problems. Additionally, the ISTE Student Innovative Designer Standard employs cyclical design processes for developing innovative and creative solutions to real-world problems.

To achieve these outcomes, evidence-based practices should include a comprehensive and cohesive curriculum aligned to appropriate local, state, and national standards that emphasize advanced, challenging, and complex content implemented using evidence-based instructional strategies. Additionally, the curriculum should be responsive to diversity and the needs of the individual learner, provide opportunities for self-directed learning and talent development, employ and respond to multiple voices and perspectives, and integrate technology that allows collaboration locally and globally. Technology should be integrated as a means for students to construct knowledge, solve problems, and communicate. ISTE Educator-Design and Facilitator standards and the NAGC standards share many commonalities concerning curriculum planning and instruction. The ISTE Educator-Designer Standard encourages authentic learning experiences using technology that enables active and deep learning that is responsive to a variety of learners. In turn, the Facilitator Standard recommends using technology to support student learning and creative expression by incorporating student-centered activities involving digital platforms, virtual environments, and hands-on makerspaces. Providing students with opportunities and experiences aligned with these standards will enable students to become independent and collaborative investigators and problem solvers (see Figure 11.3).

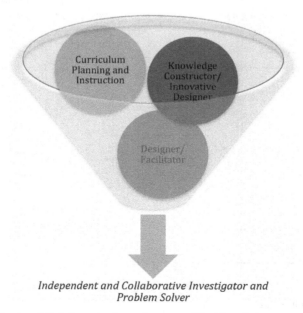

Independent and Collaborative Investigator and Problem Solver

Figure 11.3 Independent and Collaborative Investigator and Problem Solver.

Standard 3: Curriculum Planning and Instruction—Practical Application

Using evidence-based curriculum models such as the Integrated Curriculum Model (VanTassel-Baska & Wood, 2010), teachers should organize learning across dimensions of Issues/Themes, Advanced Content, and Process-Product Dimension. To increase the relevancy and authenticity of learning, it is important to tap into students' interests. One way of doing this is through current events. Using a current event such as the coronavirus, teachers can brainstorm how they can connect their content standards to real-world situations. Additionally, students can create a concept map over the topic to brainstorm paths of study, and monitor and demonstrate their learning. Figure 11.4 illustrates a simple brainstorming map that begins with the topic of COVID-19. There are multiple avenues of study using the theme of COVID-19. Ideally, teachers would develop an integrated unit of study across multiple content areas or students could self-select their learning path from the brainstorming map (see Figure 11.4).

Technology can enhance student learning for discovery and investigation. Utilizing tools such as virtual reality (VR) and augmented reality (AR) allow students to gather information, data, and evidence from a seemingly authentic environment. For example, examining viruses is possible using Google Expeditions: Inside Viruses, Viruses, and What Are Viruses and How Do They Infect. Google Expeditions and other VR/AR applications provide students

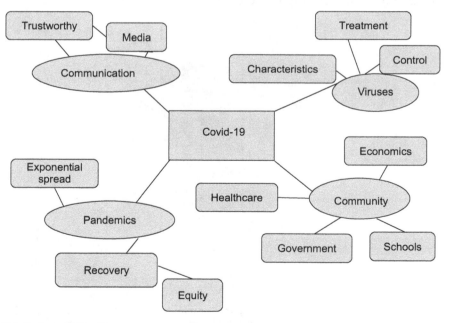

Figure 11.4 Brainstorming Map.

the field trip experience without ever leaving the classroom. Students can visit a place of interest through VR and bring abstract concepts to life with AR—all in Google Expeditions. Through these experiences, students can visit castles and museums, explore the ocean, space, and other geographical areas, and tour landmarks and battlefields. There are multiple other virtual and augmented reality applications, such as Quiver Vision, that allow students to manipulate and bring to life various objects such as cells, volcanos, and the moon. Human Anatomy Atlas enables one to explore and dissect parts of the human body in the virtual world. Through the advances in technology, our students have immersive types of experiences at their fingertips that are not limited by space or time.

Standard 4: Learning Environments

The Learning Environments Standard encourages educators to create environments to develop student's personal, social, cultural, and communication competencies and personal and social responsibility. The focus of ISTE for Students-Digital Citizen is also on ethics and responsibility but in the digital world. To prepare competent and responsible citizens, the evidence-based practices include creating a supportive environment that maintains high expectations and values mistakes as opportunities to learn, providing opportunities for self-exploration and independent studies as well as collaboration and trust-building among diverse groups of students and mentors, giving students voice and choice in shaping their learning environment and using technology to creatively communicate and express themselves.

There are three ISTE for Educator standards that align with the NAGC Learning Environments Standard. ISTE for Educators-Citizen Standard promotes a learning environment that prepares students to make positive, socially responsible contributions to the community and society as a whole, the Leader standard promotes educator advocacy for equitable access to technologies and digital connections for all learners, and the Global Collaborator standard prioritizes working with others using digital tools to solve complex local and global problems. The conceptual thread tying these standards together is the development of students into competent and socially responsible leaders. By creating a low-risk but high expectation environment, students can engage in authentic learning and problem solving, use technology to solve problems and communicate and collaborate with diverse groups of individuals on a local and global scale (see Figure 11.5).

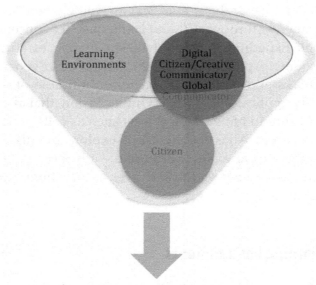

Competent and Socially Responsible Leaders

Figure 11.5 Competent and Socially Responsible Leaders.

Standard 4: Learning Environments—Practical Application

To simulate authentic working environments and to prepare students to work in a global society, students need opportunities to learn in collaboration with others, and from experts outside the classroom. Technology can increase the possibility of matching gifted learners with other students and experts with similar interests and passions. By working in partnership with other classrooms globally, teachers can connect students in a purposeful manner. Video conferencing and video chat software provide students the ability to make connections across the globe through synchronous meetings. A particularly effective and easy tool to use for synchronous collaboration class sessions is Skype Education. Educators use Skype's Collaborative Projects to collaborate with classrooms around the world on creative and community-curated projects. Skype for Education also has numerous guest speaker options that allow students to engage in conversations with practicing professionals.

Asynchronous digital collaboration is also another way to connect students with peers from around the world. If a classroom in the U.S. is wanting to collaborate with a classroom in Europe, it can be difficult to schedule times when synchronous meetings are viable. Using tools like Flipgrid or Seesaw can allow students to communicate with both peers and experts from across the globe. These tools are created to support student safety while increasing asynchronous communication. Students can also use digital collaboration tools like G-Suite applications (Google Docs, Sheets, Slides, and Draw) and Microsoft 360 to create presentations and products that are edited by peers from around the globe.

Technology affords gifted students opportunities to move beyond the physical classroom environment in ways that were previously inconceivable. Real-time collaboration and asynchronous communications allow students to conceive of solutions to real-world problems through collaborative innovation.

Standard 5: Programming

The Programming Standard describes a comprehensive, cohesive, and coordinated variety of services that align with the interests, strengths, and needs of students in all settings. Students who participate in these services demonstrate growth and yearly progress in cognitive, psychosocial, and social-emotional areas, select post-secondary and career goals, and participate in high-quality gifted programming to develop their talent and meet those goals. The ISTE Student-Empowered Learner aligns with the gifted student outcomes on guiding students to set learning and career goals and leveraging technology to help meet these goals and advance their learning opportunities.

The evidence-based practices encourage educators to use multiple approaches to accelerate student learning, including enrichment options in and out of school. Additionally, technology should be used to provide advanced learning opportunities, such as online courses and outside enrichment opportunities, to meet the individual needs of students. Programming and services should be continuously evaluated by educators, students, and parents to assess the quantity and quality of the program. The ISTE Educator Collaborator Standard encourages educators to provide students opportunities to virtually engage with experts, mentors, and other professionals and students in authentic learning experiences. Additionally, the Designer Standard recommends using technology to personalize learning experiences and accommodate independent learning. The commonalities between these standards are the opportunities for individualized and accelerated or in-depth learning using technology and other resources to facilitate student learning, talent development, and post-secondary and career goals. These standards promote opportunities for students to engage in authentic, meaningful, and goal-oriented experiences (see Figure 11.6).

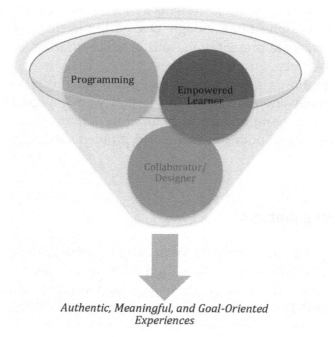

Authentic, Meaningful, and Goal-Oriented Experiences

Figure 11.6 Authentic, Meaningful, and Goal-Oriented Experiences.

Standard 5: Programming—Practical Application

There are several distance learning opportunities for students, especially with the sudden shift away from the face-to-face classroom as a result of COVD-19. However, webquests and other virtual learning strategies have been advancing collaborative learning opportunities in recent years (Warda & Hamid, 2018). When deciding on services that align with the interests, strengths, and needs of students, it is important to remember that the instruction also should meet students' social and emotional needs. Personalized and adaptable learning environments, virtual or not, should incorporate learning material that suits the learning needs of a learner. While budget constraints can create challenges with implementing an online program, there are several free resources for schools and educators to help students virtually engage with professionals and students in authentic learning experiences. Resources such as STEMscopes, the Online Learning Consortium, can provide curriculum adaptable for individualized online learning opportunities. Additionally, talent development centers can be a resource for online learning. For example, Northwestern Center for Talent Development program provides a variety of gifted online courses and programs for students in K–Grade 12. These programs include options for enrichment, acceleration, and family programming, including advanced placement online courses. For additional online resources, see PreK–12 Education and Enrichment at NAGC: www.nagc.org/prek-12-enrichment-educational-resources.

Standard 6: Professional Learning

The Professional Learning Standard's student outcomes include opportunities for students to develop their gifts and talents, experience growth and development in psychosocial and social-emotional skills, and receive high-quality gifted programming services as a result of interacting with educators that who are highly qualified in content and pedagogy, committed to removing access barriers, lifelong learners, and guided by ethical practices. The student outcomes in professional learning align with all of the ISTE for Student standards in that they are representative of strong pedagogical practices used to develop the gifts and talents of students but with an emphasis on using technology to enhance these practices. In particular, the Knowledge Constructor Standard encourages active and student-directed learning, the Innovative Designer Standard promotes student perseverance and open-ended problem solving, and the Global Collaborator Standard focuses on enriching learning through collaboration with others.

The Professional Learning Standard recommends all educators build their knowledge and skills using the NAGC-CEC Teacher Preparation Standards in Gifted and Talented Education (NAGC-CEC, 2013), NAGC-CEC Advanced Standards in Gifted Education Teacher Preparation (NAGC-CEC, 2015), and the Learning Forward–Standards for Professional Learning (Corwith et al., 2019). Professional learning for educators should address the foundations of gifted education, as well as the characteristics, identification, and assessment of gifted learners. Professional learning should also enable educators to create learning environments that promote talent development, facilitate psychosocial and social-emotional development, and address systemic barriers faced by students from underrepresented populations. For reflection and growth of the educator and gifted programming services, the Professional Learning Standard stresses using systematic needs assessments to guide ongoing, high quality, and goal-oriented professional learning. The ISTE Educator-Learner Standard emphasizes the importance of educators continuing their learning especially in relation to effective pedagogical practices using technology. The ISTE Standard encourages educators to create and participate in local and global learning networks and to keep abreast of current research to improve student learning outcomes. The Leader Standard stresses that educators advocate for equitable access to technology and digital content for diverse

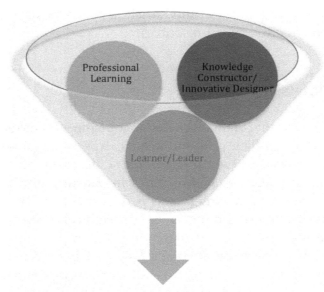

Impactful, Informed, and Effective Educator

Figure 11.7 Impactful, Informed, and Effective Educator.

learners and to seek opportunities to support student empowerment and success. The NAGC and ISTE standards of Professional Learning, Learner, and Leader emphasize the importance of education for the educator. To ensure equitable access and rigorous opportunities for students, educators should be skilled in evidence-based strategies that are acquired through professional learning opportunities. Following the recommendations from these standards can result in impactful, informed, and effective educators (see Figure 11.7).

Standard 6: Professional Learning—Practical Application

Educators choose professional learning opportunities based on a desire to advance their knowledge and skills. Studies showed that continual growth in educators' content knowledge and pedagogical knowledge and skills positively affects student learning and success (Darling-Hammond, 2000; Goldhaber & Brewer, 2000; Hawk et al., 1985). Focusing on improving student learning and success is the foundation toward teacher leader awareness (Wenner & Campbell, 2016). A desire to improve student learning will lead to pursuing actions to create change in the classroom and eventually throughout the school district (Leithwood & Levin, 2010). Professional learning focused on gifted learners can be limited in some areas. Educators may seek to attend state and/or national gifted education conferences to connect with other educators and learn new ideas that can be implemented in their classrooms; however, they often leave the conference ready and willing to change but with limited resources for implementation (Darling-Hammond et al., 2017). For a meaningful change in practices, educators need job-embedded and sustained professional learning (Darling-Hammond et al., 2017) that is often found in federal funded demonstration projects (e.g., Project EXCEL, Project Bright IDEA, Project USTARS Plus, STEM Starters, STEM Starters +).

Recently, there have been more opportunities for educators to engage in remote professional learning through both synchronous and asynchronous formats. Some of these opportunities lead to micro-credentialing. NAGC offers a micro-credentialing program, Gifted Knows No Boundaries, to help educators improve their practices to support gifted learners. ISTE has a myriad of professional development programs that increase pedagogical innovation with technology integration. Additionally, the ISTE Certified Educator program offers teachers the opportunity to earn a microcredential.

There are several avenues toward free professional learning through groups such as Simple K12, Sanford Inspire, and Association for Supervision and Curriculum Development (ASCD), to name a few. Simple K12 offers free online services through community-based learning opportunities. Sanford Inspire offers courses for learning about student social and emotional development. Along with the books, articles, and the journal Educational Leadership, ASCD also provides webinars, conferences, and other professional development in multiple educational areas. As both the NAGC Gifted Programming Standards and the ISTE Standards for Educators emphasize professional learning, this is especially important for general education teachers. General education teachers are the gatekeepers to gifted programming services and they need to be able to recognize characteristics of gifted learners from diverse populations and adequately meet their academic needs (Szymanski & Shaff, 2013).

Conclusion

There are many commonalities between the NAGC Pre-K–Grade 12 Gifted Programming Standards and the ISTE for Educators and ISTE for Students standards. ISTE standards are considered the "technology" standards, but the primary focus of the practices and student outcomes is not necessarily on technology. Both the ISTE and gifted standards support evidence-based practices concerning student-centered and student-directed learning, fair and equitable assessment plans, data-informed instruction, authentic learning and problem solving, communication and collaboration with diverse groups of individuals, and integration of technology to support and enrich student learning. Furthermore, both sets of standards encourage educators to continuously reflect and improve their teaching and programming and participate in high-quality professional learning. In conclusion, ISTE is a great resource and supplement for educators of gifted and talented students. Their online site provides multiple avenues for professional learning to help educators engage their students in evidence-based practices implemented and enhanced with technology.

Resources

- ◆ Association for Supervision and Curriculum Development (ASCD): www.ascd.org/Default.aspx
- ◆ Google Expeditions: https://play.google.com/store/apps/details?id=com.google.vr.expeditions&hl=en_US
- ◆ Human Anatomy ATLAS. www.visiblebody.com/anatomy-and-physiology-apps/human-anatomy-atlas
- ◆ International Society for Technology in Education (ISTE): www.iste.org/
- ◆ NAGC PreK–12 Enrichment & Educational Resources: www.nagc.org/prek-12-enrichment-educational-resources
- ◆ NAGC Giftedness Knows No Boundaries Micro-credentials Program: www.nagc.org/professional-learning/nagc-micro-credentials
- ◆ Nearpod: https://nearpod.com/t/market/init
- ◆ Northwestern Center for Talent Development program: www.ctd.northwestern.edu/program_type/online-programs
- ◆ Pre-K–Grade 12 Gifted Programming Standards: www.nagc.org/resources-publications/resources/national-standards-gifted-and-talented-education/pre-k-grade-12
- ◆ Sanford Programs: https://online.sanfordprograms.org/choose-your-sanford-program/
- ◆ Simple K12: www.simplek12.com/
- ◆ Skype in the Classroom: https://education.skype.com/
- ◆ STEMscopes: www.stemscopes.com/
- ◆ QuiverVision: https://quivervision.com/

References

Darling-Hammond, L. (2000). Teacher quality and student achievement. *Education Policy Analysis Archives, 8*(1), 1–44. https://doi.org/10.14507/epaa.v8n1.2000

Darling-Hammond, L., Hyler, M. E., & Gardner, M. (2017). *Effective teacher professional development.* Learning Policy Institute. https://learning policyinstitute.org/sites/default/files/product-files/Effective_Teacher_Professional_Development_REPORT.pdf

Elias, M. J. (2014, August 27). *Smart goal setting with your students.* Edutopia. www.edutopia.org/blog/smart-goal-setting-with-students-maurice-elias

Goldhaber, D. D., & Brewer, D. J. (2000). Does teacher certification matter? High school teacher certification status and student achievement. *Educational Evaluation and Policy Analysis, 22*(2), 129–145. https://doi.org/10.3102/01623737022002129

Hawk, P. P., Coble, C. R., & Swanson, M. (1985). Certification: It does matter. *Journal of Teacher Education, 36*(3), 13–15. https://doi.org/10.1177/002248718503600303

Hébert, T. P., Sorensen, M. F., & Renzulli, J. S. (1997). *Secondary interest-a-lyzer.* Creative Learning Press.

International Society for Technology in Education (ISTE) (2016). *Standards for Educators-Facilitator and ISTE Standards for Students-Empowered Learner.* www.iste.org/standards/for-educators; www.iste.org/standards/for-students

Leithwood, K., & Levin, B. (2010). Understanding how leadership influences student learning. In *International Encyclopedia of Education,* (pp. 45–50). Elsevier. https://doi.org/10.1016/b978-0-08-044894-9.00439-5.

Maltese, A. V., & Tai, R. H. (2010). Eyeballs in the fridge: Sources of early interest in science. *International Journal of Science Education, 32*(5), 669–685. https://doi.org/10.1080/09500690902792385

National Association for Gifted Children (NAGC). (2019). *NAGC pre-K–Grade 12 Gifted Programming Standards.* National Association for Gifted Children. www.nagc.org/resources-publications/resources/national-standards-gifted-and-talented-education/pre-k-grade-12

National Association for Gifted Children and Council for Exceptional Children (NAGC-CEC). (2013). *NAGC-CEC teacher preparation standards in gifted education teacher preparation.* https://exceptionalchildren.org/standards/intial-gifted-education-professional-preparation-standards

National Association for Gifted Children and Council for Exceptional Children (NAGC-CEC). (2015). *NAGC-CEC advanced standards in gifted education teacher preparation.* https://exceptionalchildren.org/standards/advanced-gifted-education-professional-preparation-standards

National Research Center on the Gifted and Talented (NRCGT, n.d.). *Assessing students' interests.* https://nrcgt.uconn.edu/underachievement_study/curriculum-compacting/cc_section11/#

Reis, S., & Siegle, D. (2002). *If I ran the school. An interest inventory.* https://nrcgt.uconn.edu/wp-content/uploads/sites/953/2015/07/cc_ran-school.pdf

Szymanski, T., & Shaff, T. (2013). Teacher perspectives regarding gifted diverse students. *Gifted Children, 6*(1),1. http://docs.lib.purdue.edu/gifted children/vol6/iss1/1

Subotnik, R. F., Olszewski-Kubilius, P., & Worrell, F. C. (2011). Rethinking giftedness and gifted education: A proposed direction forward based on psychological science. *Psychological Science in the Public Interest,12*(1), 3–54. https://doi.org/10.1177/1529100611418056

VanTassel-Baska, J., & Baska, A. (2019). *Curriculum planning and instructional design for gifted learners* (3rd ed.). Prufrock Press.

VanTassel-Baska, J., & Wood, S. (2010). The integrated curriculum model (ICM). *Learning and Individual Differences, 20*(4), 345–357. https://doi.org/10.1016/j.lindif.2009.12.006

Warda, A., & Hamid, M. (2018). The impact of collaborative learning on web quest strategy used in learning educational psychology. *International Journal of Web-Based Learning and Teaching Technologies, 13*(4), 77–90. https://doi.org/10.4018/IJWLTT.2018100105

Wenner, J. A., & Campbell, T. (2016). The theoretical and empirical basis of teacher leadership: A review of the literature. *Review of Education Research, 87*(1), 134–171. https://doi.org/10.3102/0034654316653478

12

Advocating for Implementation

Susan Corwith and Chin-Wen Lee

Over the past 30 years, an array of standards has been introduced in the field of education. Content standards, such as the Common Core State Standards (CCSS) (National Governors Association (NGA) & Council for Chief State School Officers (CCSSO), 2010); professional standards, including the Interstate Teacher and Support Consortium (InTASC) Model Core Teaching Standards (CCSSO, 2011); and programming standards, like the National Association for Gifted Children (NAGC) Pre-K–Grade 12 Gifted Programming Standards, are entrenched and not likely to disappear any time soon. Still, standards are of no consequence unless they are integrated into classroom, school, district, and state- and national-level policies and practices. The road to adopting and implementing standards is not an easy one, involving knowledge of the standards' content, advocacy at various levels, and the buy-in of decision-makers.

In this chapter, we focus on advocacy for the implementation of the NAGC Pre-K–Grade 12 Gifted Programming Standards (Gifted Programming Standards) at the local and state level. Learning how to advocate for the implementation of the standards at "local" levels—within schools and districts—is critical because educators work directly with students and impact programming on a day-to-day basis. The standards define educators as including all professionals involved with the education of students with gifts and talents

DOI: 10.4324/9781003236863-12

(including but not limited to, central office administrators, principals, general educators, special educators, educators of the gifted, instructional and curriculum specialists, counselors, psychologists, and other support personnel). Regional and state leaders affect policy at that level, but it is educators who can assure the use of evidence-based policies and practices in classrooms.

Importance of Gifted Programming Standards and Advocating for their Use

Though there may be discussion and debate about the content of standards in education, they are and have been for many years the benchmark for defining and evaluating best practices and expectations for learning. The National Association for Gifted Children states,

> [S]tandards provide a basis for policies, rules, and procedures that are essential for providing systematic programs and services to any special population of students. While standards may be addressed and implemented in a variety of ways, they provide important direction and focus to designing and developing options for gifted learners at the local level.
>
> (NAGC, n.d.)

The Professional Standards Committee outlined several uses for the standards, including the following:

1. Assess, evaluate, and improve local policies, rules, and procedures;
2. Plan curriculum;
3. Provide professional learning;
4. Advocate;
5. Develop, improve, and evaluate state standards;
6. Approve gifted plans and programs and monitor for compliance with state regulations.

(NAGC, 2019)

The NAGC Gifted Programming Standards have an important role to play in guiding policy and practice inside and outside of the field. As an example, 25 out of 48 responding states reported having no state program standards or guidelines for gifted education (NAGC & CSDPG, 2020). Yet, there is no national mandate for gifted education and many states are also without a mandate for gifted education. As of the last State of the States report, 31 states require gifted identification and 24 states require programming options/services by law or rule (NAGC & CSDPG, 2020). Adoption and consistent use of the gifted programming standards require significant advocacy, which includes a broad base of stakeholders.

In other words, advocacy must extend beyond gifted education specialists. With the variety of standards that exist, both in type (e.g., programming, professional) and content area (e.g., language arts, math, etc.), a challenge for advocates is how practitioners, administrators, and state and federal leaders integrate and make the best use of the different standards to support student learning and create successful learning environments. For the adoption and implementation of gifted programming standards to continue to expand, and be sustained in use over time, they need to be aligned to the standards and best practices of related areas of education, including special education and general education and to reflect national priorities for equity, inclusion, and diversity.

To that end, the 2019 Gifted Programming Standards contain elements from several other standards-related tools, including both the NAGC and Council for Exceptional Children (CEC) teacher preparation standards and advanced standards (NAGC & CEC, 2013a, 2013b), the Standards for Professional Learning (Learning Forward, 2011), Collaborative for Academic, Social, and Emotional Learning (CASEL) framework for social-emotional learning (CASEL, 2020), the Bill of Rights for Gifted Students of Color (Ford et al., 2018), the APA's Top 20 Principles from Psychology for PreK–12 Creative, Talented, and Gifted Students' Teaching and Learning (2017), and the International Society for Technology in Education (ISTE) Standards for Students (ISTE, 2019).

The point of connecting the gifted programming standards to other standards was to make them more easily incorporated into school- and district-wide plans for improvement and policy development. Gifted education programs should not be separate from the overarching mission, guiding principles, or priorities of a school or district. Aligning gifted education best practices with education best practices as a whole, and the operations of a school or district is intentional and designed to aid advocacy and adoption.

Insights from Common Core State Standards Adoption and Rationale to Adopt the Standards at the State Level

Lord and Clarenbach (2012) wrote that "districts and schools are overwhelmed by federal, state, and local expectations when defining what students should know and be able to do" (p. 256). Districts and schools are also dealing with accountability measures, funding gaps, and the politicization of teaching and learning. So, "how do standards move off the page and into practice," particularly in today's educational environment (Lord & Clarenbach, 2012, p. 256)?

Lord and Clarenbach's work laid important groundwork for advocacy at the state level and the level of schools and districts. Following the adoption of the 2019 Gifted Programming Standards, it seems an appropriate time to re-examine approaches to advocacy, helping educators effectively use principles of organizational change to guide their efforts.

Lessons learned from various states' adoption and implementation of the Common Core State Standards can help inform potential strategies for promoting the adoption of Gifted Programming Standards, particularly at the state level. There are several factors that influenced states making decisions to adopt the CCSS: Rigor of the standards, organizational climate, and incentives (Table 1; Association for Supervision and Curriculum Development (ASCD), 2012; Center on Education Policy, 2011; 2013). When thinking about the Gifted Programming Standards, advocates should consider how the following factors and similar ones provide purpose and opportunity for advocacy.

First, stakeholders need to have confidence in the rigor of the Gifted Programming Standards. "Because the PK–12 Standards are grounded in theory, research, and practice paradigms, they provide an important base for all educational efforts on behalf of gifted learners at all stages of development" (Cotabish et al., 2020, p. 135). In the example of CCSS advocacy, the standards are research-supported college- and career-readiness benchmarks. Adopting the CCSS is "intended to provide consistency among the states in expectations for student outcomes" (Billingsley et al., 2013, p. 173). While the Gifted Programming Standards are not designed for education agencies to achieve *the same level of student outcomes*, they indicate *the desired state of student outcomes* that are very likely to be accomplished by educators performing evidence-based practices.

Second, since the passage of the federal No Child Left Behind (NCLB) law and subsequent Every Student Succeeds Act (ESSA), states, districts, and schools have requirements for accountability that significantly affect decision-making. The ESSA, in particular, includes elements specific to students with gifts and talents:

◆ Student achievement at the advanced level, disaggregated by subgroups, must be available on state and local report cards.
◆ Title I funds may be used to identify and serve low-income gifted and talented students.

- State plans Title II professional development fund usage must address how the state will enable teachers to identify gifted and talented students and provide instruction based on their needs.
- For districts receiving Title II funds, training must be provided to address the learning of gifted and talented students.

(www.ctd.northwestern.edu/blog/
bridging-opportunity-and-excellence-gaps)

Therefore, the climate is right for broader adoption of the Gifted Programming Standards and application in districts. State education agencies, districts, and schools have legitimate reasons to facilitate the application of the Gifted Programming Standards because they uniquely address learning outcomes for advanced students while focusing on equity and inclusion. Beyond the grade-level expectations in academic standards, such as the CCSS, the Gifted Programming Standards provide pathways to acceleration, differentiation, and interdisciplinary learning opportunities for students with gifts and talents (NAGC, n.d.).

Guided by the Gifted Programming Standards, educators are encouraged to exercise their professional judgment carrying out evidence-based practices that best serve their students in their context. Additionally, the Gifted Programming Standards "help define the comprehensiveness necessary in designing and developing options for gifted learners at the local level" (Cotabish et al., 2020, p. 135). Whether or not a school or district has a formal gifted education program, the Gifted Programming Standards are the go-to guide for any development and improvement endeavors and this point can be leveraged by advocates in the current educational climate.

The federal Race to the Top program is credited with the rapid adoption of the CCSS, which had helped grant applicants demonstrate they adopted "internationally benchmarked standards and assessments that prepare students for success in college and the workplace," which was a core requirement of receiving funds (U.S. Department of Education, 2009, para. 1). Because the Gifted Programming Standards are grounded in theory, research, and practice paradigms and are the only known standards that focus on advanced learners' outcomes, the Standards are ready to serve as criteria for selecting data to determine the quality and effectiveness of gifted programs and services. This is helpful for districts needing to fulfill the requirements for student growth under state ESSA plans and should serve as a strong incentive for adoption. Other incentives include the resources available through Title I and Title II for student programming and professional learning. Title I in particular offers an incentive to expand programming to students who have been grossly under-identified and underserved in schools.

Table 12.1 The Rationale for Adopting Gifted Programming Standards.

Major Aspects of	Adopting the CCSS Considered at State Level	Rationale for Adopting Gifted Programming Standards
The rigor of the standards	How recently the state had adopted its current standards; the level of rigor of the CCSS in comparison to the state's current standards which served as a foundation for statewide education improvement; other college- and career-readiness initiatives within the state; whether the standards provided more focus and clarity to teachers, parents and students	Grounded in theory, research, and practice paradigms; gifted education practices fully aligned to the Gifted Programming Standards for curriculum, instruction, and assessment
Organizational climate	The comfort level with having standards that were the same as those for other states; the current landscape of education policies and practices in terms of adopting standards; teacher effectiveness requirements; expectations for measuring growth	The only national standards focusing on advanced learners' outcomes; pathways to acceleration, differentiation, and interdisciplinary learning opportunities for students with gifts and talents; educator autonomy to select evidence-based practices that best serve their students; comprehensiveness necessary in designing and developing options for gifted learners at the local level
Incentives	Federal encouragement (funding, reporting requirements) to adopt internationally benchmarked standards and assessments	Ready to be used in standards-based initiatives and to serve as criteria for selecting data to determine the quality and effectiveness of gifted programs and services; focus on outcomes for student growth required by ESSA; a blueprint for equity and inclusion in programming

Effective Advocacy and Organizational Change at the School or District Level

Adoption of the standards at the state level is one important goal. Local adoption and application of evidence-based practices is also an important goal, which requires a different approach to advocacy. This chapter is not an in-depth exploration of advocacy frameworks or organizational change theory, but when educators intend to create or reform their local policies and practices, it is instructive to review the relevant literature for principles and strategies that result in effective advocacy and sustained change. According to Evans et al. (2012), "[M]any leaders fail to link planned organizational changes with an appropriate theory of change, thus forfeiting opportunities to facilitate more effective and sustained improvement" (p. 155). Considering elements of change theory and examining successful efforts can provide educators with the skills and strategies necessary to orchestrate meaningful change in their settings.

Insights from Gifted Education Advocacy Literature

Generally speaking, advocacy is the act of supporting a cause or working for change. Within the field of gifted education, this means efforts to implement strategies, design services, and craft policies and laws that support students with gifts and talents and reflect the Gifted Programming Standards. The gifted education advocacy literature is largely directed at state and national efforts to influence policy, but this body of literature offers a look at historical models and strategies that are applicable to advocates at the school and district level.

Roberts and Siegle (2012) elaborate on what Burney and Sheldon identified as the "three Ps of advocacy" which are purpose, preparation, and persistence (Burney & Sheldon, 2010; Roberts & Siegle, 2012). Purpose means that advocates have a clear understanding of what they are advocating for and what objectives they seek to accomplish. In the case of standards, this may be adopting the entire set of standards in a district that already has a certain level of programming in place and a community supportive of gifted education. Or, in a school currently without a clear identification process, it may be using the *Assessment* standard to guide the development of a policy and corresponding procedures.

Preparation requires well-informed advocates who collect information and understand school or district needs, priorities, and levers of influence. Developing and nurturing relationships is also an important aspect of preparation according to Roberts and Siegle (2012), because "it is through these relationships that support and, ultimately, change occur … advocates need to be sure that decision makers know their names" (p. 60). An effective advocate for standards implementation will tie student outcomes and evidence-based practices to school and district priorities and share this information with influencers (school administrators, board members, etc.) on a regular basis during meetings, planning sessions, and other places where policy and practice decisions are being made.

Finally, persistence is key because relationship building is a long-term endeavor. Advocacy takes commitment and planning over time. Adopting policies or changing practices is typically a multi-step process requiring a number of knowledgeable stakeholder groups who buy-in to the goals and the approval of individuals at the top levels of leadership.

Robinson and Moon (2003) also identify persistence, collaboration, and knowledge as factors that support positive outcomes. However, they found one additional factor to be important to success, particularly with regard to persistence: having a champion. Champions "were able to get their colleagues or their fellow advocates to support them through persuasion" (Robinson & Moon, 2003, p. 23). In their study of advocacy in state and location contexts, these champions stood out to stakeholders and were given credit for going above and beyond to achieve the goal. These champions are often powerful personalities, with strong motivation, and effective leadership skills.

Insights from Organizational Change Literature

We have identified what it takes to be an effective gifted education advocate and develop an advocacy plan around the standards, but what drives fundamental, lasting changes in educational organizations like schools or districts? There are many proven models of organizational leadership and change, so educational leaders should make the choice that best fits their system and needs (Evans et al., 2012). Rather than focusing on a particular model, we highlight several common themes or factors that align with the advocacy principles described in the previous section. What is important to remember is that "for organizational learning to occur, an organization must employ strategies to systematically integrate individual and collective learning into skills and knowledge that will deeply affect the organization" (Evans et al., 2012, p. 159).

Transformational Leadership

Transformational leadership is a central element of many organizational change theories and frameworks, and this type of leadership comes from individuals with vision, commitment, and the ability to inspire trust and build relationships (Bolman & Deal, 1997). School leaders certainly include superintendents, principals, and program coordinators, but leadership exists well beyond these formal roles. Multiple people are involved in leading schools, taking responsibility for and having an influence on various aspects of teaching, learning, and management (Spillane, 2009). Not all transformational leaders have significant control over decisions about change, but they are able to make use of other forms of power or influence. Consider a department chair or program coordinator who is positioned between policy and practice and who is able to influence change on a practical level through strategic planning, curriculum development, and instruction (Gaubatz & Ensminger, 2015). When it comes to adopting and implementing standards, leadership can come from classroom teachers, department chairs, coaches, and others, depending on the scope of implementation needed and outcomes desired.

Collaboration and Engagement

Relationships are central to advocacy success, and when it comes to organizational change, building networks or coalitions, breaking down barriers between departments, maintaining positive relationships, and leveraging the power of influencers, are core themes (Cooperrider & Whitney, 2007; Demming, 2018; Evans et al., 2012). Collaboration within and across schools can be challenging, but successful organizational change and continuous improvement require strategic and coordinated efforts to "break down silos" and regularly bring together individuals from across the system (Park et al., 2013) for authentic work on improvement efforts. Gifted educators working collaboratively across teams and grade-levels encourage the identification of shared practices, building on strengths, understanding root causes of problems or discrepancies, developing a collective vision for improvement, and executing comprehensive plans and coordinated steps (Cooperrider & Whitney, 2007; Park et al., 2013). Most importantly, collaboration and engagement foster shared accountability among stakeholders, which is critical to including gifted education in school improvement conversations.

Use of Data and Resources

In many models of change, once a priority or issue begins to emerge, the improvement process begins with collecting data and assessing programs, thinking about how to define and understand areas of strength and areas of concern; data collection and analysis continues throughout the process as a means of measuring progress and evaluating performance (Evans et al., 2012;

Gaubatz & Ensminger, 2015). Using data to track progress toward goals is a critical piece of continuous improvement. In the context of gifted education and ESSA, the Gifted Programming Standards articulate the types of data that should be collected and how that data should be used to be able to assess performance and demonstrate progress toward goals for advanced learners (Standard 2.4).

Culture and Community Assets

As Lord and Clarenbach (2012) wrote, "the culture within a school will either facilitate the implementation of gifted program standards or present a resilient barrier to any change" (p. 258), attending to culture is a tenant of many change theories and appropriate use of time and resources. Leaders must consider community values and attitudes and recognize what values are most strongly held and will influence the rate and amount of change that will be embraced, tolerated, or rejected. Understanding the culture also provides an avenue for identifying strengths and assets that can be used in the change process. Cooperrider's Appreciative Inquiry model is particularly illuminating in understanding how assets can be used in change (Evans et al., 2012). In this model, changemakers focus on identifying strengths and positive attributes of an organization on which to build or incorporate new approaches. Starting with what works, provide a place from which to build to create positive change, and identify what is already working well forms the basis from which further exploration can take place, because "building a shared vision for the future is critical in making deep organizational changes" (Evans et al., 2012, p. 167).

Starting the Conversation and Understanding Stakeholder Roles

At the core of working toward the implementation of the Gifted Programming Standards is knowledge of the six standard areas, the related student outcomes, and the evidence-based practices. The National Association for Gifted Children has developed multiple resources to both raise awareness and build the knowledge of educators, facilitating the application of the standards. For example, a self-assessment tool, *Self-Assess Your P-12 Practice or Program Using the NAGC Gifted Programming Standards* (NAGC, 2020), can be utilized to examine local instructional practices, programs, and services. Conducting an honest examination of policies and practices can help identify the priority areas for change. A school that already has programming in place may need only to adopt changes in one standard area. Districts with little to no programming may need to adopt changes in all standard areas, though advocates may choose to focus on one standard area at a time to build capacity and buy-in. Building on the work of Lord and Clarenbach (2012), use the following actions to advocate for Gifted Programming Standards at any level (classroom, building, district).

◆ Know your purpose (what are the assets you are building on and the problems and priorities you are seeking to address).
◆ Present the standards as part of the solution.
◆ Keep the focus on the students (outcomes of the standards and how they connect to priorities, values, and accountability in the system).
◆ Keep the audience focus as wide as possible (broad stakeholder involvement and coalition building).
◆ Build on frameworks, models, policies, and practices already in place (Response to Intervention, acceleration, etc.) into which the standards can be integrated.

Simply possessing knowledge of best practices does not promise a smooth voyage to implementation. Even under ideal conditions (e.g., a mandate to serve advanced learners or designated personnel and funding), legislation alone is not sufficient to promote effective practices for students with gifts and talents in each school and classroom. As an example, Matthews and Shaunessy's (2010) observed a time lag before the best practices made their way into the hands of practitioners, which they believed might have hindered the school district's meeting 80% of the criteria on the standards evaluation checklist. Everyone has a role to play to bring the standards from state adoption to classroom implementation.

Drawing from advocacy and organizational change research and examples of advocacy in a variety of school districts (Matthews & Shaunessy, 2010; VanTassel-Baska & Hubbard, 2019) and at varying levels (ASCD, 2012; Center on Education Policy, 2011, 2013; Lord & Clarenbach, 2012; Roberts & Inman, 2020; Whitby et al., 2013), Table 2 summarizes core responsibilities and activities to affect change categorized by spheres of influence or role. Table 2 is not intended to be an exhaustive list or set of examples. Instead, the actions are either found in practical settings or proposed by professionals with advocacy experiences. Individuals with different spheres of influence, of course, should not feel limited in expanding their course of action.

Table 12.2 Facilitating the Implementation of the Gifted Programming Standards.

	State education agency	Local education agency	School educators	Family and community	Higher education institutions	Professional organizations
Transformational Leadership	Allocating resources and developing policies; mandating implementation with proper supports; evaluating impact through curriculum and assessment guidance and educator preparation, professional learning activities, and effectiveness evaluations	Guiding school leaders; liaising with stakeholders; facilitating implementation; evaluating impact through curriculum and assessment guidance and educator professional learning activities, and effectiveness evaluations	Providing leadership of vision, strategic planning, resource allocation; determining classroom implementation; impacting through the curriculum, assessment, and educator professional learning activities, and effectiveness evaluations	Acting as levers for change; generating local support; identifying resources	Researching and using best practices; leveraging higher education resources; gaining accreditation of teacher education programs; impacting through curriculum and assessment studies and educator preparation, professional learning activities, and effectiveness studies	Liaising and advocating with state, local, and district contacts; connecting influencers with information; creating advocacy teams and agendas; impacting through professional recommendations for curriculum, assessment, and educator preparation, professional learning activities, and effectiveness evaluations

	State education agency	Local education agency	School educators	Family and community	Higher education institutions	Professional organizations
Collaboration and Engagement	Creating state-level workgroups with key stakeholders; providing implementation resources and guidance; developing initiatives to support implementation in targeted districts	Providing professional learning and resources (materials, funds, etc.) for educators; creating regional workgroups with key stakeholders in all areas of education (e.g., special education, ELL, technology)	Presenting standards as part of the solution to school reforms (finding commonalities); keeping the audience focus as wide as possible; offering expertise (share your story)	Building coalitions among parent and community organizations; mapping community asset; sharing goals and messages; offering expertise (share your story)	Building coalitions with professional organizations and district/school leaders	Advocating with parents and educators

(Continued)

Table 12.2 Contiued

	State education agency	Local education agency	School educators	Family and community	Higher education institutions	Professional organizations
Use of Data and Resources	Providing detailed information for students achieving at the advanced level that is disaggregated by student subgroup; developing, adopting, or implementing new assessments that are explicitly aligned with the standards	Providing detailed information for students achieving at the advanced level that is disaggregated by student subgroup; analyzing gifted program demographic data and trends	Analyzing and disseminating local community and gifted program demographics and trends; collecting data to determine progress	Requesting information on students achieving at the advanced level that is disaggregated by student subgroup; analyzing local community and gifted program demographics	Aligning with educator licensures and certification requirements; analyzing accreditation data; studying state and national performance data	Analyzing state report card and state performance data; Analyzing gifted program demographics

Note: Based on ASCD, 2012; Center on Education Policy, 2011; 2013; Lord & Clarenbach, 2012; Roberts & Inman, 2020; Whitby et al., 2013.

Creating a Plan and Getting Started

Understanding the factors that contribute to successful advocacy is important, but so is developing a comprehensive plan of action, using a set of guiding questions (see Table 12.3). Roberts (2012) wrote that a high-quality plan for advocacy includes the following components: clarity, support information, specificity, and inclusiveness. When it comes to advocating for the implementation of standards at any level, articulating your purpose, defining goals, and maintaining transparency with stakeholders are some of the first tasks to address. Given that there is a lot of misinformation about giftedness and gifted education, preparing support information, including performance data, current policies, research, and examples of anticipated outcomes will also go a long way to building coalitions and engaging stakeholders. Specificity helps advocates stay focused and follow through with critical tasks. Specific plans identify who is responsible for what tasks, who makes decisions and on what timeline, and where resources will come from. Finally, inclusiveness is making sure that all stakeholders have a voice in the process, that individuals and groups with similar goals and interests come together, and that gifted programs are seen as an integral part of the school system's response to students' learning needs.

Table 12.3 Guiding Questions for Building an Advocacy Plan.

Theme	Questions
Goals and Outcomes	a. What are the goals and related outcomes? b. What are the priorities and values of the school/district? c. How can the Gifted Programming Standards address the priorities and support the values? d. Which student outcomes are connected to the priorities?
Collaboration and Engagement	a. What is your role and sphere of influence? b. Who makes the decisions? c. What are the coalitions you need to build? d. Who can serve as transformational leaders? e. Who has responsibility for the practice areas addressed by the standards? f. What are the potential assets to build on (active working groups, models, resources, policies, etc.)? g. How can the student outcomes be positioned as helping all students achieve at higher levels? h. What are the barriers?

(Continued)

Table 12.3 *Continued*

Theme	Questions
Communication and Messaging	a. What is the message you need to convey regarding the standards? b. What are the misconceptions or missing pieces of information? c. What data do you have or need? d. What are the opportunities to present the message?
Plan of Action	a. What are the action steps? b. Who will carry out each step? c. Who will coordinate and monitor progress?
Evaluation of Success	a. How will success be measured? b. What are the plans for evaluation? c. How will continuous improvement be maintained?

Note: Adapted from Roberts (2012).

Conclusion

The NAGC Pre-K–Grade 12 Gifted Programming Standards are uniquely developed to focus on student outcomes and evidence-based practices that will benefit students who need instruction beyond a basic curriculum and contribute to the development of rigorous, talent development opportunities for all students. Still, integrating Gifted Programming Standards into the broader educational ecosystem at the local, regional, and state levels takes advocacy and organizational change involving a variety of stakeholders. With the background, examples, and recommendations provided in this chapter, we believe advocates can understand why the Gifted Programming Standards matter, see the need for the Standards to guide the actions to improve current practices to support students with gifts and talents, and will have the tools necessary to work effectively for implementation.

References

American Psychological Association, Center for Psychology in Schools and Education (2017). *Top 20 principles from psychology for pre-K–12 creative, talented, and gifted students' teaching and learning.* www.apa.org/ed/schools/teaching-learning/top-principles-gifted.pdf

Association for Supervision and Curriculum Development (2012). *Fulfilling the promise of the Common Core State Standards: Moving from adoption to implementation to sustainability.* Author. https://eric.ed.gov/?id=ED538575

Bolman, L. G., & Deal, T. E. (1997). *Reframing organizations* (2nd ed.). Jossey-Bass.

Billingsley, B. S., Brownell, M. T., Israel, M., & Kamman, M. L. (2013). *A survival guide for new special educators.* Wiley.

Burney, G., & Sheldon, A. (2010, March). Warrior advocates. *Parenting for High Potential*, 19–24.

Center on Education Policy (2011). *States' progress and challenges in implementing Common Core State Standards.* Author. https://eric.ed.gov/?id=ED514598

Center on Education Policy (2013). *Year 3 of implementing the Common Core State Standards: An overview of states' progress and challenges.* Author. https://eric.ed.gov/?id=ED555415

Clarenbach, J. (2016, Spring). *What the Every Student Succeeds Act (ESSA) means for gifted education.* Center for Talent Development. www.ctd.northwestern.edu/spring-2016-talent-newsletter#main-article

Collaborative for Academic, Social, and Emotional Learning (2020). *CASEL's SEL framework: What are the core competence areas and where are they promoted?* https://casel.org/wp-content/uploads/2020/12/CASEL-SEL-Framework-11.2020.pdf

Cooperrider, D. L., & Whitney, D. (2007). Appreciative inquiry: A positive revolution in change. In P. Holman, T. Devane, & S. Cady (Eds.), *The change handbook: The definitive resource on today's best methods for engaging whole systems* (2nd ed., pp. 73–88). Berrett-Koehler.

Cotabish, A., Dailey, D., Corwith, S., Johnsen, S., Lee, C.-W., & Guilbault, K. (2020). Ushering in the 2019 Pre-K to Grade 12 Gifted Programming Standards. *Gifted Child Today, 43*(2), 135–140. https://doi.org/10.1177/1076217519898226

Council of Chief State School Officers (2011). *InTASC model core teaching standards: A resource for state dialogue.* https://ccsso.org/sites/default/files/2017-11/InTASC_Model_Core_Teaching_Standards_2011.pdf

Demming, W. E. (2018). *Out of the crisis.* Cambridge: The MIT Press.

Evans, L. M., Thornton, B., & Usinger, J. (2012). Theoretical frameworks to guide school improvement. *National Association of Secondary School Principals Bulletin, 96*(2), 154–171. https://doi.org/10.1177/0192636512444714

Ford, D. Y., Dickson, K. T., Lawson Davis, J., Trotman Scott, M., Grantham, T. C., & Taradash, G. D. (2018). A culturally responsive equity-based Bill of Rights for gifted students of color. *Gifted Child Today, 41*(3), 125–129. https://doi.org/10.1177/1076217518769698

Gaubatz, J. A., & Ensminger, D. C. (2015). Secondary school department chairs leading successful change. *International Journal of Education Policy & Leadership*, *10*(6), 1–21. http://journals.sfu.ca/ijepl/index.php/ijepl/article/view/151

International Society for Technology Education (2019). *ISTE standards for students*. www.iste.org/standards

Johnsen, S. K. (2011). A comparison of the Texas State Plan for the Education of Gifted/Talented Students and the 2010 NAGC Pre-K–Grade 12 Gifted Programming Standards. *Tempo*, *31*(1), 10–20. www.txgifted.org/files/Tempo/2011/2011–1.pdf

Learning Forward (2011). *Standards for professional learning*. https://learning-forward.org/standards-for-professional-learning

Lord, E. W., & Clarenbach, J. (2012). Off the page and into practice: Advocating for implementation of the gifted programming standards. In S. K. Johnsen (Ed.), *NAGC Pre-K–Grade 12 Gifted Education Programming Standards: A guide to planning and implementing high-quality services* (pp. 255–268). Prufrock Press.

Matthews, M. S., & Shaunessy, E. (2010). Putting standards into practice: Evaluating the utility of the NAGC Pre-K–Grade 12 Gifted Program Standards. *Gifted Child Quarterly*, *54*(3), 159–167. https://doi.org/10.1177/0016986209356708

National Association for Gifted Children (n.d.). *Frequently asked questions about the Common Core and gifted education*. www.nagc.org/resources-publications/resources/timely-topics/common-core-state-standards-national-science-0

National Association for Gifted Children (2019). *NAGC Pre-K–Grade 12 Gifted Programming Standards*. www.nagc.org/resources-publications/resources/national-standards-gifted-and-talented-education/pre-k-grade-12

National Association for Gifted Children (2020). *Self-assess your P–12 practice or program using the NAGC Gifted Programming Standards* (2nd ed.). Author.

National Association for Gifted Children & Council for Exceptional Children—The Association for the Gifted (2013a). *Advanced standards in gifted education teacher preparation*. www.nagc.org/sites/default/files/standards/Advanced%20Standards%20in%20GT%20(2013).pdf

National Association for Gifted Children & Council for Exceptional Children—The Association for the Gifted (2013b). *Teacher preparation standards in gifted and talented education*. www.nagc.org/sites/default/files/standards/NAGC-%20CEC%20CAEP%20standards%20(2013%20final).pdf

National Association for Gifted Children & The Council of State Directors of Programs for the Gifted (2020). *2018–2019 State of the states in gifted education*. www.nagc.org/2018–2019-state-states-gifted-education

National Governors Association and Council for Chief State School Officers (2010). *Common core state standards.* www.corestandards.org/read-the-standards/

Park, S., Hironaka, S., Carver, P., & Nordstrum, L. (2013). *Continuous improvement in education* [White paper]. Carnegie Foundation for the Advancement of Teaching. www.carnegiefoundation.org/wp-content/uploads/2014/09/carnegie-foundation_continuous-improvement_2013.05.pdf

Roberts, J. (2012). Planning for advocacy. In R. D. Eckert & J. H. Robins (Eds.), *Designing services and programs for high-ability learners: A guidebook for gifted education* (pp. 200–211). National Association for Gifted Children & Corwin Press.

Roberts, J. L., & Inman, T. F. (2020). The basics of advocacy for parents: Getting started. *Parenting for High Potential, 9*(1), 11–14.

Roberts, J. L., & Siegle, D. (2012). Teachers as advocates: If not you—who? *Gifted Child Today, 35*(1), 58–61. https://doi.org/10.1177/1076217511427432

Robinson, A., & Moon, S. M. (2003). A national study of local and state advocacy in gifted education. *Gifted Child Quarterly, 47*(1), 8–25. https://doi.org/10.1177/001698620304700103

Spillane, J. P. (2009, November). Managing to lead: Reframing school leadership and management. *Phi Delta Kappan, 91*(3), 70–73. https://doi.org/10.1177/003172170909100315

U.S. Department of Education. (2009). *Programs: Race to the Top.* www2.ed.gov/programs/racetothetop/factsheet.html

VanTassel-Baska, J., & Hubbard, G. F. (2019). A review of the national gifted standards implementation in eight districts: An uneven picture of practice. *Gifted Child Today, 42*(4), 215–228. https://doi.org/10.1177/1076217519862336

Whitby, P., Marx, T., McIntire, J., & Wienke, W. (2013). Advocating for students with disabilities at the school level: Tips for special educators. *Teaching Exceptional Children, 45*(5), 32–39. https://doi.org/10.1177/004005991304500504

Appendix A
2019 *Pre-K-Grade 12 Gifted Programming Standards*

Programming Standard 1: Learning and Development

Introduction

Educators must understand the learning and developmental differences of students with gifts and talents in order to provide curriculum, instruction, assessment, and programming that will develop students' talents and abilities fully and help them become aware, self-directed learners. Learning and developmental differences provide the rationale for differentiated and specialized programming and services. While educators need to understand the cognitive development of students with gifts and talents, they also need to know about psychological and social and emotional needs that need to be addressed that support talent development in the contexts of school, home, and the larger community.

Standard 1: Learning and Development	
Description: Educators understand the variations in learning and development in cognitive, affective, and psychosocial areas between and among individuals with gifts and talents, creating learning environments that encourage awareness and understanding of interest, strengths, and needs; cognitive growth, social and emotional, and psychosocial skill development in school, home, and community settings.	
Student Outcomes	**Evidence-Based Practices**
1.1. Self-Understanding. Students with gifts and talents recognize their interests, strengths, and needs in cognitive, creative, social, emotional and psychological areas.	1.1.1. Educators engage students with gifts and talents in identifying interests, strengths, and needs.
	1.1.2. Educators engage students with gifts and talents in identifying their intellectual, academic, creative, leadership, and/or artistic abilities.
	1.1.3. Educators engage students in developmentally appropriate activities that help them discover their talents and develop noncognitive skills that support their talent areas.

Student Outcomes	Evidence-Based Practices
1.2. Self-Understanding. Students with gifts and talents demonstrate understanding of how they learn and recognize the influences of their identities, cultures, beliefs, traditions, and values on their learning and behavior.	1.2.1. Educators develop activities that match each student's developmental level and culture-based learning needs.
	1.2.2. Educators assist students with gifts and talents in developing identities consistent with their potential and areas of talent.
	1.2.3 Teachers create a learning environment that promotes high expectations for all children, support for perceived failures, positive feedback, respect for different cultures and values, and addresses stereotypes and biases.
1.3. Self-Understanding. Students with gifts and talents demonstrate understanding of and respect for similarities and differences between themselves and their cognitive and chronological peer groups and others in the general population.	1.3.1. Educators use evidence-based instructional and grouping practices to allow students with similar gifts, talents, abilities, and strengths to learn together, and also create opportunities for students to interact with individuals of various gifts, talents, abilities, strengths, and goals.
	1.3.2. Educators model respect for individuals with diverse abilities, interests, strengths, learning needs, and goals.
	1.3.3. Educators discuss and explain developmental differences and use materials and instructional activities matched to students' varied abilities, interests, and learning needs.
1.4. Awareness of Needs. Students identify and access supplemental, outside-of-school resources that support the development of their gifts and talents (e.g., families, mentors, experts, or programs).	1.4.1. Educators provide role models for students with gifts and talents that match their interests, strengths, and needs.
	1.4.2. Educators identify outside-of-school learning opportunities and community resources that match students' interests, strengths, and needs.
	1.4.3 Educators gather information and inform students and families about resources available to develop their/ their child's talents.

(Continued)

Student Outcomes	Evidence-Based Practices
1.5. Cognitive, Psychosocial, and Affective Growth. Students with gifts and talents demonstrate cognitive growth and psychosocial skills that support their talent development as a result of meaningful and challenging learning activities that address their unique characteristics and needs.	1.5.1. Educators use evidence-based approaches to grouping and instruction that promote cognitive growth and psychosocial and social-emotional skill development for students with gifts and talents.
	1.5.2. Educators design interventions for students that are based on research of effective practices and provide accommodations for learning differences to develop cognitive and noncognitive abilities that support growth and achievement.
	1.5.3. Educators develop specialized, research-supported intervention services for students with gifts and talents who are underachieving (whose learning is not commensurate with their abilities) to develop their talents.
1.6. Cognitive Growth and Career Development. Students with gifts and talents identify future career goals that match their interests and strengths. Students determine resources needed to meet those goals (e.g., supplemental educational opportunities, mentors, financial support).	1.6.1. Educators help students identify college and career goals that are consistent with their interests and strengths.
	1.6.2. Educators implement learning progressions that incorporate person/social awareness and adjustment, academic planning, psychosocial skill development and college and career awareness.
	1.6.3 Educators provide students with college and career guidance and connect students to college and career resources.

Programming Standard 2: Assessment

Introduction

Knowledge about different uses of assessment is essential for educators of students with gifts and talents. It is important to understand assessments when assessing abilities and achievement, designing services and identifying students in need of services, and assessing each student's learning progress. In order for assessment to yield useful information, the definition or operationalization of giftedness must align with the identification procedures, tools, and programming to be provided.

Educators need to create a classroom environment that encourages students to express their gifts and talents and collect multiple types of assessment information so that all students have equal access to the identification process. Educators' understanding of technically adequate and equitable approaches that minimize bias will enable them to select and use the assessment tools needed to identify students who represent diverse backgrounds. They also need to differentiate their curriculum and instruction by using data from pre- and post-, performance-based, product-based, and other assessments that measure student growth. As a result of each educator's use of ongoing assessments, students with gifts and talents are aware of their learning progress and demonstrate growth commensurate with their abilities.

Standard 2: Assessment	
Description: Assessments provide information about identification and learning progress for students with gifts and talents.	
Student Outcomes	**Evidence-Based Practices**
2.1. Identification. All students in Pre-K through grade 12 with gifts and talents have equal access to the identification process and proportionally represent each campus.	2.1.1 Educators develop environments and instructional activities that prepare and encourage students from diverse backgrounds to express characteristics and behaviors that are associated with giftedness.
	2.1.2. Educators provide parents/ guardians with information in their preferred language for communication regarding behaviors and characteristics that are associated with giftedness and with information that explains the nature and purpose of gifted programming options.

(Continued)

Student Outcomes	Evidence-Based Practices
	2.1.3 Educators use universal screening and multiple indicators of potential and achievement at various grade levels from Pre-K through grade 12 to provide multiple entry points to services designed to meet demonstrated needs.
2.2. Identification. Students with gifts and talents are identified for services that match their interests, strengths, and needs.	2.2.1. Educators establish comprehensive, cohesive, and ongoing policies and procedures for identifying and serving students with gifts and talents. These policies include referral, informed consent, the assessment process, review of all assessment information, student retention, student reassessment, student exiting, and appeals procedures for both entry and exit from gifted programming and services.
	2.2.2. Educators select and use assessments that relate to services provided and identify abilities, interests, strengths, and needs based on current research.
	2.2.3. Educators use assessments that provide qualitative and quantitative information from a variety of sources.
	2.2.4 Educators use assessments that provide information related to above-grade-level performance.
	2.2.5. Educators select assessments that minimize bias by including information in the technical manual that describes content in terms of potential bias, includes norms that match national census information or local populations, shows how items discriminate equally well for each group, and provides separate reliability and validity information for each group.

Student Outcomes	Evidence-Based Practices
	2.2.6. Educators have knowledge of student exceptionalities and collect assessment data while adjusting curriculum and instruction to learn about each student's developmental level and aptitude for learning (i.e., dynamic assessment).
	2.2.7. Educators interpret multiple assessments in different domains, and understand the uses and limitations of the assessments in identifying the interests, strengths and needs of students with gifts and talents.
	2.2.8 Educators inform all parents/guardians about the identification process. Educators obtain parental/guardian permission for assessments, use culturally sensitive checklists, and elicit evidence regarding the child's interests and potential outside of the classroom setting.
2.3. Identification. Students with identified gifts and talents represent diverse backgrounds.	2.3.1. Educators select and use equitable approaches and assessments that minimize bias for referring and identifying students with gifts and talents, attending to segments of the population that are frequently hidden or underidentified. Approaches and tools may include front-loading talent development activities, universal screening, using locally developed norms, assuring assessment tools are in the child's preferred language for communication, or nonverbal formats.
	2.3.2. Educators understand and implement district, state, and/or national policies designed to foster equity in gifted programming and services.

(Continued)

Student Outcomes	Evidence-Based Practices
2.4. Learning Progress. As a result of using multiple and ongoing assessments, students with gifts and talents demonstrate growth commensurate with abilities in cognitive, social-emotional, and psychosocial areas.	2.4.1. Educators use differentiated formative assessments to develop learning experiences that challenge students with gifts and talents.
	2.4.2. Educators use differentiated ongoing product-based and performance-based assessments to measure the academic and social-emotional progress of students with gifts and talents.
	2.4.3. Educators use standardized (e.g., adaptive, above-grade-level) and classroom assessments that can measure the academic progress of students with gifts and talents.
	2.4.4. Educators use and interpret qualitative and quantitative assessment information to develop a profile of the interest, strengths and needs of each student with gifts and talents to plan appropriate interventions.
	2.4.5. Educators interpret and communicate assessment information to students with gifts and talents and their parents/guardians, and assure information is provided in their preferred language for communication.
2.5. Learning Progress. Students self-assess their learning progress.	2.5.1. Educators provide opportunities for students to set personal goals, keep records, and monitor their own learning progress.

Programming Standard 3: Curriculum Planning and Instruction

Introduction

Educators need to develop and use a comprehensive and cohesive curriculum that is aligned with local, state, and national standards, then differentiate, accelerate, and/or expand it. Curriculum must emphasize advanced, conceptually challenging, in-depth, and complex content. Educators need to possess a repertoire of evidence-based instructional strategies in delivering the curriculum (a) to develop students' talents, enhance learning, and provide students with the knowledge and skills to become independent, self-aware learners, and (b) to give students the tools to contribute to a diverse and global society. The curriculum, instructional strategies, and materials and resources must engage a variety of gifted learners using practices responsive to diversity.

Standard 3: Curriculum Planning and Instruction	
Description: Educators apply evidence-based models of curriculum and instruction related to students with gifts and talents and respond to their needs by planning, selecting, adapting, and creating curriculum responsive to diversity and by using a repertoire of instructional strategies to ensure specific student outcomes and measurable growth.	
Student Outcomes	**Evidence-Based Practices**
3.1. Curriculum Planning. Students with gifts and talents demonstrate academic growth commensurate with their abilities each school year.	3.1.1. Educators use local, state, and national content and technology standards to align, expand, enrich, and/or accelerate curriculum and instructional plans.
	3.1.2. Educators design a comprehensive and cohesive curriculum and use learning progressions to develop differentiated plans for Pre-K through grade 12 students with gifts and talents.
	3.1.3. Educators adapt, modify, or replace the core or standard curriculum to meet the interest, strengths, and needs of students with gifts and talents and those with special needs such as twice exceptional, highly gifted, and English language learners.

(Continued)

Student Outcomes	Evidence-Based Practices
	3.1.4. Educators design differentiated curriculum that incorporates advanced, conceptually challenging, in-depth, and complex content for students with gifts and talents.
	3.1.5. Educators regularly use pre-assessments, formative assessments, and summative assessments to identify students' strengths and needs, develop differentiated content, and adjust instructional plans based on progress monitoring.
	3.1.6. Educators pace instruction based on the learning rates of students with gifts and talents and compact, deepen, and accelerate curriculum as appropriate.
	3.1.7. Educators integrate a variety of technologies for students to construct knowledge, solve problems, communicate and express themselves creatively, and collaborate with others in teams locally and globally.
	3.1.8. Educators consider accommodations and/or assistive technologies to provide equal access to learning opportunities with twice-exceptional learners and other students with developmental differences.
3.2.Talent Development. Students with gifts and talents demonstrate growth in social and emotional and psychosocial skills necessary for achievement in their domain(s) of talent and/or areas of interest.	3.2.1. As they plan curriculum, educators include components that address goal setting, resiliency, self-management, self-advocacy, social awareness, and responsible decision making.
	3.2.2 Educators design learning experiences for each stage of talent development to cultivate social and emotional and psychosocial skills that support high achievement and talent development.

Student Outcomes	Evidence-Based Practices
3.3. Cultural Responsiveness. Students with gifts and talents develop knowledge and skills for living in and contributing to a diverse and global society.	3.3.1. Educators develop and use curriculum responsive and relevant to diversity (race, ethnicity, culture, language, age, (dis)abilities, family status/composition, gender identity and expression, sexual orientation, socioeconomic status, religious and spiritual values, geographic location, and country of origin) that connects to students' real-life experiences and communities and includes multiple voices and perspectives.
	3.3.2. Educators encourage students to connect to others' experiences, examine their own perspectives and biases, and develop a critical consciousness.
	3.3.3. Educators use high-quality, appropriately challenging materials that include multiple perspectives.
3.4. Instructional Strategies. Students with gifts and talents demonstrate their potential or level of achievement in their domain(s) of talent and/or areas of interest.	3.4.1. Educators select, adapt, and use a repertoire of instructional strategies to differentiate instruction for students with gifts and talents.
	3.4.2. Educators provide opportunities for students with gifts and talents to explore, develop, or research in existing domain(s) of talent and/or in new areas of interest.
	3.4.3. Educators use models of inquiry to engage students in critical thinking, creative thinking, and problem-solving strategies, particularly in their domain(s) of talent, both to reveal and address the needs of students with gifts and talents.

(Continued)

Student Outcomes	Evidence-Based Practices
3.5. Instructional Strategies. Students with gifts and talents become independent investigators.	3.5.1. Educators model and teach metacognitive models to meet the needs of students with gifts and talents such as self-assessment, goal setting, and monitoring of learning.
	3.5.2. Educators model and teach cognitive learning strategies such as rehearsal, organization, and elaboration.
	3.5.3. Educators scaffold independent research skills within students' domain(s) of talent.
3.6. Resources. Students with gifts and talents are able to demonstrate growth commensurate with their abilities as a result of access to high-quality curricular resources.	3.6.1. Educators use current, evidence-based curricular resources that are effective with students with gifts and talents.
	3.6.2. Educators use school and community resources to support differentiation and advanced instruction appropriate to students' interests, strengths, and academic learning needs.

Programming Standard 4: Learning Environments

Introduction

Effective educators of students with gifts and talents create safe learning environments that foster academic achievement, emotional well-being, positive social interaction, creativity, leadership development, and cultural understanding for success in a diverse society.

Knowledge of the impact of giftedness and diversity on cognitive, psychosocial, and social-emotional development enables educators of students with gifts and talents to design environments that encourage academic growth, personal and social competence, responsibility, and the development of leadership skills. They understand the role of language and communication in talent development and the ways in which culture and identity affect communication and behavior. They use relevant strategies and technologies to enhance oral, written, and artistic communication of students whose needs vary based on area(s) and level(s) of ability, language proficiency, and cultural and linguistic differences. They recognize the value of multilingualism in today's global community.

Standard 4: Learning Environments	
Description: Learning environments foster a love for learning, academic, personal and social responsibilities competence with diverse people and interpersonal and technical communication skills to ensure specific student outcomes.	
Student Outcomes	**Evidence-Based Practices**
4.1. Personal Competence. Students with gifts and talents demonstrate growth in personal competence and dispositions for exceptional academic and creative productivity. These include self-awareness, self-advocacy, self-efficacy, confidence, motivation, resilience, independence, curiosity, and risk taking.	4.1.1. Educators maintain high expectations for all students with gifts and talents as evidenced in meaningful and challenging activities.
	4.1.2. Educators provide opportunities for self-exploration, development and pursuit of interests, and development of identities supportive of achievement (e.g., through mentors and role models) and a love of learning.
	4.1.3. Educators create environments that establish trust, support, and collaborative action among diverse students.

(Continued)

Student Outcomes	Evidence-Based Practices
	4.1.4. Educators provide feedback that promotes perseverance and resilience and focuses on effort, on evidence of potential to meet high standards, and on mistakes as learning opportunities.
	4.1.5. Educators provide examples of positive coping skills and opportunities to apply them.
4.2. Social Competence. Students with gifts and talents develop social competence manifested in positive peer relationships and social interactions.	4.2.1. Educators provide learning environments for both solitude and social interaction.
	4.2.2. Educators provide opportunities for interaction and learning with intellectual and artistic/creative peers as well as with chronological-age peers.
	4.2.3. Educators assess and provide instruction on psychosocial and social and emotional skills needed for success in school, their community, and society.
4.3. Responsibility and Leadership. Students with gifts and talents demonstrate personal and social responsibility.	4.3.1. Educators establish a safe and welcoming climate for addressing personal and social issues and give students a voice in shaping their learning environment.
	4.3.2. Educators provide environments for developing many forms of leadership and leadership skills.
	4.3.3. Educators provide opportunities to promote lifelong personal and social responsibility through advocacy and real world problem-solving, both within and outside of the school setting.

Student Outcomes	Evidence-Based Practices
4.4. Cultural Competence. Students with gifts and talents value their own and others' language, heritage, and circumstance. They possess skills in communicating, teaming, and collaborating with diverse individuals and across diverse groups. They use positive strategies to address social issues, including discrimination and stereotyping.	4.4.1. Educators model appreciation for and sensitivity to students' diverse backgrounds and languages.
	4.4.2. Educators model appropriate language and strategies to effectively address issues such as stereotyping, bias, and discriminatory language and behaviors.
	4.4.3. Educators provide structured opportunities to collaborate with diverse peers on a common goal.
4.5. Communication Competence. Students with gifts and talents develop competence in interpersonal and technical communication skills. They demonstrate advanced oral and written skills and creative expression. They display fluency with technologies that support effective communication and are competent consumers of media and technology.	4.5.1. Educators provide opportunities for advanced development and maintenance of first and second language(s).
	4.5.2. Educators provide resources that reflect the diversity of their student population to enhance oral, written, and artistic forms of communication.
	4.5.3. Educators ensure access to advanced communication tools, including assistive technologies, and use of these tools for expressing higher-level thinking and creative productivity.
	4.5.4. Educators provide an environment where students use technology to communicate responsibly and express themselves creatively using the platforms, tools, styles, formats, and digital media appropriate to their goals.

(Continued)

Programming Standard 5: Programming

Introduction

The term programming refers to a continuum of services that address the interests, strengths, and needs of students with gifts and talents in all settings. Educators develop policies and procedures to guide and sustain all components of comprehensive and aligned programming and services for Pre-K through grade 12 students with gifts and talents. Educators use a variety of programming options such as acceleration and enrichment (depth and complexity) in varied grouping arrangements (cluster grouping, resource rooms, special classes, special schools) and within individualized learning options (independent study, original research, mentorships, online courses, internships) to enhance students' performance in cognitive, psychosocial, and social-emotional areas and to assist them in identifying future post-secondary and career goals and talent development pathways. They augment and integrate current technologies within these learning opportunities to increase access to high level programming such as online courses and to increase connections to resources outside of the school walls. In implementing services, educators in gifted, general, special education programs, and related professional services collaborate with one another and with students, parents/guardians, advocates, and community members to ensure that students' diverse interests, strengths, and needs are met. Administrators demonstrate their support by allocating sufficient resources for programming options and evaluation activities so that all students with gifts and talents receive appropriate educational services.

Standard 5: Programming	
Description: Educators use evidence-based practices to promote (a) the cognitive, social-emotional, and psychosocial skill development of students with gifts and talents and (b) programming that meets their interests, strengths and needs. Educators make use of expertise systematically and collaboratively to develop, implement, manage, and evaluate services for students with a variety of gifts and talents to ensure specific student outcomes.	
Student Outcomes	**Evidence-Based Practices**
5.1. Comprehensiveness. Students with gifts and talents demonstrate growth commensurate with their abilities in cognitive, social-emotional, and psychosocial areas as a result of comprehensive programming and services.	5.1.1. Educators use multiple approaches to accelerate learning within and outside of the school setting.
	5.1.2. Educators use enrichment options to extend and deepen learning opportunities within and outside of the school setting.

Student Outcomes	Evidence-Based Practices
	5.1.3. Educators use multiple forms of evidence-based grouping, including clusters, resource rooms, special classes, or special schools.
	5.1.4. Educators use individualized learning options such as mentorships, internships, online courses, and independent study.
	5.1.5. Educators leverage technology to increase access to high-level programming by providing digital learning options and assistive technologies.
5.2. Cohesive and Coordinated Services. Students with gifts and talents demonstrate yearly progress commensurate with ability as a result of a continuum of Pre-K-12 services and coordination between gifted, general, special, and related professional services, including outside of school learning specialists and advocates.	5.2.1. Educators who provide gifted, general, special, and related professional services collaboratively plan, develop, implement, manage, and evaluate programming and services for students with gifts and talents.
	5.2.2. Educators develop a Pre-K through grade 12 continuum of programming and services in relevant student talent areas that is responsive to students' different levels of need for intervention.
	5.2.3. Educators plan coordinated learning activities within and across a specific grade level, content area, course, class, and/or programming option.
5.3. Career Pathways. Students with gifts and talents create future career-oriented goals and identify talent development pathways to reach those goals.	5.3.1. Educators provide professional guidance and counseling for individual students regarding their interests, strengths, challenges, needs, and values.
	5.3.2. Educators facilitate programming options involving mentorships, internships, and career and technology education programming and match these experiences to student interests, strengths, needs, and goals.

(Continued)

Student Outcomes	Evidence-Based Practices
5.4. Collaboration. Students with gifts and talents are able to continuously advance their talent development and achieve their learning goals through regular collaboration among families, community members, advocates, and the school.	5.4.1. Educators regularly engage students, other educators, families, advocates, and community members in collaboration to plan, advocate for, implement, and evaluate systematic, comprehensive, and ongoing services.
5.5. Resources. Students with gifts and talents participate in gifted education programming that is adequately staffed and funded to meet students' interests, strengths, needs.	5.5.1. Administrators demonstrate support for gifted programming and services through equitable allocation of resources and demonstrated willingness to ensure that students with gifts and talents receive consistent educational services aligned to their interests, strengths, and needs.
	5.5.2. Administrators track expenditures at the school level to verify appropriate and sufficient funding for staffing, curriculum and materials, gifted programming, and services.
	5.5.3. Administrators hire a diverse pool of educators with knowledge and professional learning in gifted education and the issues affecting students with gifts and talents.
5.6. Policies and Procedures. Students with gifts and talents participate in general and gifted education programs guided by clear policies and procedures that provide for their advanced learning needs (e.g., early entrance, acceleration, credit in lieu of enrollment).	5.6.1. School policy-makers create and approve evidence-based policies and procedures to guide and sustain all components of the program, including assessment, identification, acceleration, and grouping practices.
	5.6.2. Educators align programming and services with local, state, or national laws, rules, regulations, and standards.

Student Outcomes	Evidence-Based Practices
5.7. Evaluation of Programming and Services. Students with gifts and talents demonstrate yearly learning progress commensurate with abilities as a result of high-quality programming and services matched to their interests, strengths, and needs.	5.7.1. Educators assess the quantity and quality of programming and services provided for students with gifts and talents by disaggregating assessment and yearly progress data and making the results public.
	5.7.2. Educators ensure that the assessments used in program evaluation are reliable and valid for the purposes for which they are being used.
5.8. Evaluation of Programming and Services. Students with gifts and talents have access to programming and services required for the development of their gifts and talents as a result of ongoing evaluation and program improvements.	5.8.1. Administrators provide the necessary time and resources to implement an annual evaluation plan developed by persons with expertise in program evaluation and gifted education.
	5.8.2. Educators create and implement evaluation plans that are purposeful and evaluate how student-level outcomes are influenced by fidelity of implementation in the following components of gifted education programming: (a) identification, (b) curriculum, (c) instructional programming and services, (d) ongoing assessment of student learning, (e) counseling and guidance programs, (f) teacher qualifications and professional learning, (g) parent/guardian and community involvement, (h) programming resources, (i) programming design, management, and delivery, and (j) school equity efforts for underrepresented students.
	5.8.3. Educators disseminate the results of the evaluation, orally and in written form, and explain how they will use the results.

(Continued)

Programming Standard 6: Professional Learning

Introduction
Professional learning is essential for all educators (administrators, teachers, counselors, and other instructional support staff) involved in the development and implementation of gifted programs and services. Professional learning is the intentional, sustained development of professional expertise as outlined by the NAGC-CEC Teacher Preparation Standards and NAGC-CEC Advanced Standards in Gifted Education and is an integral part of gifted educators' professional and ethical practice. Professional learning should be based on systematic needs assessments and professional reflection.

Since students with gifts and talents spend much of their time within general education classrooms, general education teachers should receive instruction and coaching that enables them to recognize the characteristics of giftedness in diverse populations, understand the school or district referral and identification process, and implement an array of high quality, evidence-based practices that challenge all students including those with gifts and talents. Institutions of higher education should use these standards as a guide to address professional learning related to gifted education in their teacher preparation programs.

Standard 6: Professional Learning

Description: All educators (administrators, teachers, counselors, and other instructional support staff) build their knowledge and skills using the NAGC-CEC Teacher Standards for Gifted and Talented Education, NAGC-CEC Advanced Standards in Gifted Education Teacher Preparation, and the Standards for Professional Learning. Institutions of higher education utilize these standards and the NAGC Faculty Standards to ensure quality professional learning experiences in pre-service, initial, and advanced educator preparation programs. Educators frequently assess their professional learning needs related to the standards, develop and monitor their professional learning plans, systematically engage in coaching and learning to meet their identified needs, and align outcomes with educator performance and student curriculum standards. Administrators assure educators have access to sustained, intensive collaborative, job-embedded, and data-driven learning and assure adequate resources to provide for release time, fund continuing education, and offer substitute support. The effectiveness of professional learning is assessed through relevant student outcomes.

Student Outcomes	Evidence-Based Practices
6.1. Talent Development. Students identify and fully develop their talents and gifts as a result of interacting with educators who possess content pedagogical knowledge and meet national teacher preparation standards in gifted education and the Standards for Professional Learning.	6.1.1. State agencies, institutions of higher education, schools and districts provide comprehensive, research-supported professional learning programs for all educators involved in gifted programming and services. This professional learning addresses the foundations of gifted education, characteristics of diverse students with gifts and talents, identification, assessment, curriculum planning and instruction, learning environments, and programming. High-quality professional learning is delivered by those with expertise in gifted education as guided by the NAGC-CEC Teacher Preparation Standards.
	6.1.2. State agencies, institutions of higher education, schools and districts provide sustained professional learning for educators that models how to develop learning environments responsive to diversity and instructional activities that lead to student expression of diverse characteristics and behaviors that are associated with giftedness.

(Continued)

Student Outcomes	Evidence-Based Practices
	6.1.3. State agencies, institutions of higher education, schools and districts provide educators with professional learning opportunities that address social issues, including anti-intellectualism, equity, and access.
	6.1.4. Administrators plan for, budget and provide sufficient human and material resources needed for professional learning in gifted education (e.g., release time, funding for continuing education, substitute support, webinars, and/or mentors). Administrators access Title I and Title II funds as allowed under ESSA to meet this expectation.
	6.1.5. Educators use their awareness of local, state and national organizations and publications relevant to gifted education to promote learning for students with gifts and talents and their families.
6.2. Psychosocial and Social-Emotional Development. Students with gifts and talents develop critical psychosocial skills and show social-emotional growth as a result of educators and counselors who have participated in professional learning aligned with national standards in gifted education and Standards for Professional Learning.	6.2.1. Educators participate in ongoing professional learning to understand and apply research to practice with regard to psychosocial skills necessary for the development of gifts and talents and social-emotional development of individuals with gifts and talents.
6.3. Equity and Inclusion. All students with gifts and talents are able to develop their abilities as a result of educators who are committed to removing barriers to access and creating inclusive gifted education communities.	6.3.1. Educators participate in professional learning focused on curriculum and pedagogy responsive to diversity for individuals with gifts and talents.

Student Outcomes	Evidence-Based Practices
	6.3.2. Educators recognize their biases, develop culturally responsive philosophies, commit themselves to removing barriers, and create inclusive learning environments that meet the educational interests, strengths, and needs of diverse students with gifts and talents.
	6.3.3 Educators understand how knowledge, perspectives, and historical and current issues influence professional practice and the education and treatment of individuals with gifts and talents both in school and society.
6.4. Lifelong Learning. Students develop their gifts and talents as a result of educators who are lifelong learners, participating in ongoing professional learning and continuing education opportunities.	6.4.1. Educators regularly reflect on and assess their instructional practices, develop professional learning plans, and improve their practices by participating in continuing education opportunities.
	6.4.2. Educators participate in professional learning that is sustained over time, incorporates collaboration and reflection, is goal-aligned and data-driven, is coherent, embedded and transferable, includes regular follow-up, and seeks evidence of positive impact on teacher practice and on increased student learning.
6.5. Ethics. All students with gifts and talents, including those who may be twice exceptional, ELL, or who come from underrepresented populations receive equal opportunities to be identified and served in high-quality gifted programming as a result of educators who are guided by ethical practices.	6.5.1. Educators use professional ethical principles and specialized program standards to guide their practice..
	6.5.2. Educators comply with rules, policies, and standards of ethical practice and advocate for rules, policies, and standards that promote equity and access.

(Continued)

Appendix B

Assessments for Measuring Student Outcomes

Tracey N. Sulak and Susan K. Johnsen

The assessments in this appendix were gathered from journals in gifted education, state departments of education, gifted education associations, universities, university-based centers in gifted education, and other centers, regional laboratories, foundations, and institutes that assess outcomes found in the gifted education programming standards. Our process included these steps:

1. We searched the dissertations and theses database for "gifted education," "gifted assessment," "gifted students," and "gifted" and found instruments used in studies with gifted U.S. samples. These instruments were then examined more closely by checking to see if they were published in the Buros *Mental Measurement Yearbook* or used in other studies.

2. We reviewed journals in gifted education (e.g., *Gifted Child Quarterly*, *Gifted Child Today*, *Journal for the Education of the Gifted*, and *Roeper Review*) from 1986 to present. We looked for instruments that appeared in the journal that were accessible and used in research studies with U.S. gifted students.

3. We examined all of the information listed on the websites at state departments of education and state associations in gifted education and listed unpublished or free instruments.

4. We examined university centers in gifted education to identify instruments that might be available for free.

5. Finally, we examined other centers, laboratories, and foundations that might provide additional instruments.

In all of our searches, we attempted to find assessments that might be used informally in assessing student outcomes and were available without charge or with only the author's permission. We therefore did not include any assessments that were available primarily from publishers at a particular cost.

While some of these instruments do have technical information, which we included in Table B.1 and in our descriptions, others do not. Therefore, users are obligated to conduct their own validity and reliability studies if they plan to use the assessments in high-stakes testing such as in identification, program evaluation, or research. In those cases, we recommend that users seek test information from Buros *Mental Measurements Yearbook* and test publishers. When evaluating the technical qualities of tests, Robins and Jolly (2018) provided these questions (pp. 73–74):

1. What is assessment's purpose?
2. Is the assessment valid for this purpose?
3. Is the test reliable?
4. When was the test last normed?
5. Does the sample used to norm the test reflect current national census data and the school district's population?
6. What types of scores does the instrument provide?
7. How is the test administered?
8. Are there qualified personnel available to administer the instrument?
9. What is the cost of the instrument?

Along with these criteria, Robins and Jolly (2018) provide a list of 27 instruments that are frequently used in the identification of gifted students and their technical qualities. It is important that educators review assessments in terms of these questions before using instruments to assess student outcomes in their classrooms.

While many of the referenced assessments do not have technical information, they still may provide helpful guidance in developing informal classroom assessments. As educators administer assessments that lack technical information, data can be collected to determine their technical adequacy over time. In all cases, you need to contact the author to make sure that using the instrument is acceptable.

Assessments with technical information are presented in Table B.1. Following this Table are descriptions of all of the assessments. Assessments are organized alphabetically by category. Within each category, instruments with technical information are indicated by an asterisk next to their name. These instruments are followed by resources that might assist you in finding other assessments. Descriptions include the purpose of the test, its format, age or grade level of students who were administered the test, technical data (if available), and retrieval information. We acknowledge from the outset that this set of assessments is not by any means complete and that more work needs to be done in developing a bank of assessments that all educators might use in assessing student outcomes. We would appreciate your sending any assessments that may have been inadvertently omitted to Dr. Susan K. Johnsen at Susan_Johnsen@baylor.edu. Any assessments that you find helpful in your program will be shared online with others.

Table B.1 Assessments with Technical Information

Name	Purpose	Date	Sample	Internal Consistency	Test-Retest	Inter-rater	Validity	Source of Information
Clark's Drawing Abilities Test (CDAT)	To screen gifted students who are talented in the visual arts.	1991	Elementary to high school			.86–.94	Concurrent; discriminant	Clark, G., & Wilson, T. (1991). Screening and identifying gifted/talented students in the visual arts with Clark's Drawing Abilities Test. *Roeper Review, 13*(2), 92–97. Clark, G., & Zimmerman, E. (1992). *Issues and practices related to identification of gifted and talented students in the visual arts.* (Research Monograph No. 9202). Storrs, CT: The National Research Center on the Gifted and Talented. Clark, G., & Zimmerman, E. (2001). Identifying artistically talented students in four rural communities in the United States. *Gifted Child Quarterly, 45*(2), 104–114.
Classroom Instructional Practices Scale	To assess how teachers organize their classrooms in adapting for learner differences in content, rate, preference, and environment	1992	Teachers			.92	Content	Johnsen, S. K., Haensly, P. A., Ryser, G. R., & Ford, R. F. (2002). Changing general education classroom practices to adapt for gifted students. *Gifted Child Quarterly, 46*(1), 45–63.
Cross-Cultural Counseling Inventory-R	To assess cross-cultural competence.	1991	Adolescents and young adults	.95			Construct validity—factor analysis	LaFromboise, T.D., Coleman, H. L., & Hernandez, A. (1991). Development and factor analysis of the Cross-cultural Counseling Inventory-Revised. *Professional Psychology: Research and Practice, 22*(5), 380–388.

Table B.1 Continued

Name	Purpose	Date	Sample	Internal Consistency	Test-Retest	Inter-rater	Validity	Source of Information
Dance, Music, and Theater Talent Items and Behavioral Descriptors	To assess artistic talents and identify those who are ready for advanced instruction in the arts.	2003	Grades 2–6	.67–.82	.67–.82		Content validity—expert consultant; construct validity—factor analysis; discriminant and convergent validity reported	Oreck, B. A., Owen, S.V., & Baum, S. M. (2003). Validity, reliability, and equity issues in an observational talent assessment process in the performing arts. *Journal for the Education of the Gifted, 27*(1), 62–94.
Diet Cola Test	To assess science process skills; some sources indicate the test may be appropriate for identification of gifted students.	1990	All grade levels		.76	.89–.91	Discriminant validity;	Fowler, M. (1990). The diet cola test. *Science Scope, 13*(4), 32–34
ElemenOE	To measure overexcitability.	2004	Elementary	.88 total scale .66–.90 subscales			Construct validity—factor analysis; discriminant validity	Bouchard, L. L. (2004). An instrument for the measure of Dabrowskian Overexcitabilities to identify gifted elementary students. *Gifted Child Quarterly, 48*(4), 339–350.
Goals and Work Habits Survey	To assess perfectionism	1994	Middle and high school	.87			Content	P. A. Schuler's (1999). *Voices of perfectionism: Perfectionistic gifted adolescents in a rural middle school.* Storrs, CT, National Research Center on the Gifted and Talented, University of Connecticut.

(Continued)

Table B.1 *Continued*

Name	Purpose	Date	Sample	Internal Consistency	Test-Retest	Inter-rater	Validity	Source of Information
Harter's Self-Perception Profile for Adolescents	To measure eight domains of self-concept and a general domain of self-worth.	1988	Middle and high school	.62-.94			Construct validity—factor analysis	Harter, S., Whitesnell, N. R., & Junkin, L. J. (1998). Similarities and differences in domain-specific and global self-evaluation of learning disabled, behaviorally disabled, and normally achieving adolescents. *American Educational Research Journal, 35*(4), 653–680.
Implicit Theories of Intelligence Scale for Children	To measure growth mindset and the extent to which a child believes intelligence can be improved.	1999	Adolescents	.94-.98	.80		Predictive validity	Blackwell, L. S., Trzesniewski, K. H., & Dweck, C. S. (2007). Implicit theories of intelligence predict achievement across an adolescent transition: A longitudinal study and an intervention. *Child Development, 78* (1), 246–263. Dweck, C. S. (1999). *Self-theories.* Taylor & Francis. Napolitano, C. M., & Job, V. (2018). Assessing the implicit theory of willpower for strenuous mental activities scale: Multigroup, across-gender, and cross-cultural measurement invariance and convergent and divergent validity. *Psychological Assessment, 30*(8), 1049–1064.

Table B.1 Continued

Name	Purpose	Date	Sample	Internal Consistency	Test-Retest	Inter-rater	Validity	Source of Information
Learning Behaviors Scale	To measure effective learning behaviors	1999	Secondary students	.61-.86			Criterion validity—convergent and discriminant	Worrell, F. C., & Schaefer, B. A. (2004). Reliability and validity of Learning Behaviors Scale (LBS) scores with academically talented students: A comparative perspective. *Gifted Child Quarterly, 48*(4), 287–308.
Metacognitive Awareness Inventory	To identify metacognition in academic settings.	2001	Grades 6–12	.76-.82			Criterion-related; Construct validity—factor analysis	Kearney, L. J. (2010). *Differences in self-concept, racial identity, self-efficacy, resilience, and achievement among African-American gifted and non-gifted students: Implications for retention and persistence of African Americans in gifted programs.* (Doctoral dissertation). Available from Proquest Dissertations and Theses database. (UMI 3404513). Sperling, R. A., Howard, B. C., Miller, L. A., & Murphy, C. (2002). Measures of children's knowledge and regulation of cognition. Contemporary *Educational Psychology, 27,* 57–79.
Morgan-Jinks Student Efficacy Scale	To assess the level of student efficacy beliefs and how they relate to school success.	1999	Grades K–8	.66-.82			ContentCriterion-related	Jinks, J., & Morgan, V. (1999). Children's perceived academic self-efficacy: An inventory scale. *The Clearing House, 72*(4), 224–230.

(Continued)

Table B.1 *Continued*

Name	Purpose	Date	Sample	Internal Consistency	Test-Retest	Inter-rater	Validity	Source of Information
Multidimensional Inventory of Black Identity (MIBI)	To measures racial identity along three dimensions: centrality, ideology, and regard.	1997	Grades 7–11	Data available for some subscales; .60–.79			Construct validity—factor analysis; criterion validity—predictive	Kearney, L. J. (2010). *Differences in self-concept, racial identity, self-efficacy, resilience, and achievement among African-American gifted and non-gifted students: Implications for retention and persistence of African Americans in gifted programs.* (Doctoral dissertation). Available from Proquest Dissertations and Theses database. (UMI 3404513). Sellers, R. M., Smith, M. A., Shelton, J. N., Rowley, S. J., & Chavous, T. M. (1998). Multidimensional model of racial identity: A reconceptualization of African-American racial identity. *Personality and Social Psychology Review, 2*(1), 18–36. Sellers, R.M., Rowley, S.A., Chavous, T.M., Shelton, J.N., & Smith, M.A. (1997). Multidimensional inventory of Black identity: A preliminary investigation of reliability and construct validity. *Journal of Personality and Social Psychology, 73*(4), 805–815.
The Multigroup Ethnic Identity Measure	To measure ethnic identity.	1992	High School	.81			Construct; factor analysis	Phinney, J. S. (1992). The Multigroup Ethnic Identity Measure: A new scale for use with diverse groups. *Journal of Adolescent Research, 7*(2), 156–176.

Table B.1 Continued

Name	Purpose	Date	Sample	Internal Consistency	Test-Retest	Inter-rater	Validity	Source of Information
								Worrell, F. C. (2007). Ethnic identity, academic achievement, and global self-concept in four groups of academically talented adolescents. *Gifted Child Quarterly, 5*(1), 23–58.
My Way . . . An Expression Style Inventory	To assess students' interests in developing different types of products.	1998	All Grades	.72–.95			Construct validity—factor analysis; content validity—expert consultant	Kettle, K. E., Renzulli, J. S., & Rizza, M. G. (1998). Products of mind: Exploring student preferences for product development using my way. . . an expression style instrument. *Gifted Child Quarterly, 42*(1), 48–57.
Peer Competition Rating scale; Teacher Competition Rating scale; Self-Competition Rating Scale	To measure perceptions of competitive goal orientations.	2005; 2006	Middle and High School	.55–.82			Construct validity—factor analysis; criterion validity—correlation between teacher and student ratings	Schneider, B. H., del Pilar Soteras del Toro, M., Woodburn, S., Fulop, M., Cervino, C., Bernstein, S. et al. (2006). Cross-cultural differences in competition among children and adolescents. In X. Chen, D. C. French, & B. H. Schneider (Eds.), *Peer relationships in cultural context* (pp. 31–338). New York: Cambridge University Press. Schapiro, M., Schneider, B. H., Shore, B. M., Margison, J. A., & Udvari, S. J. (2009). Competitive goal orientations, quality, and stability in gifted and other adolescents' friendships: A test of Sullivan's theory about the harm caused by rivalry. *Gifted Child Quarterly, 53*(2), 71–88.

(Continued)

Table B.1 Continued

Name	Purpose	Date	Sample	Internal Consistency	Test-Retest	Inter-rater	Validity	Source of Information
Possibilities for Learning Survey	To rate students' preference for features of learning experiences.	2011	Grades 3–8	.63–.77			Content and face validity	Kanevsky, L. (1999). *Tool kit for curriculum differentiation.* Burnaby, British Columbia, Canada: Simon Frasier University. Kanevsky, L. (2011). Deferential differentiation: What types of differentiation do students want? *Gifted Child Quarterly, 55*(4), 279–299.
Psychological Well-Being Scale	To measure six domains of psychological well-being.	1989	Adolescents	.86–.93	.81 to .88		Construct validity—factor analysis; criterion validity—discriminant and convergent	Jin, S., & Moon, S. M. (2006). A study of well-being and school satisfaction among academically talented students attending a science high school in Korea. *Gifted Child Quarterly, 50*(2), 169–184. Ryff, C. D. (1989). Beyond Ponce de Leon and life satisfaction: New directions in quest successful aging. *International Journal of Behavioral Development, 12*(1), 35–55.
Rubric for Scoring Persuasive Writing	To assess persuasive writing.	1996	Upper Elementary through High School			92%	Yes	VanTassel-Baska, J., Johnson, D. T., Hughes, C. E., & Boyce, L. N. (1996). A study of language arts curriculum effectiveness with gifted learners. *Journal for the Education of the Gifted, 19*(4), 461–480.

Table B.1 Continued

Name	Purpose	Date	Sample	Internal Consistency	Test-Retest	Inter-rater	Validity	Source of Information
School Attitude Assessment Survey-Revised	To measure attitudes toward school, attitudes toward teachers, goal-valuation, motivation, and general academic self-perceptions.	2003	Grades 9–12	.88–.93			Content' Construct-factor analysis; criterion-related	McCoach, D. B., & Siegle, D. (2003). The school attitude assessment survey-revised: A new instrument to identify academically able students who underachieve. *Educational and Psychological Measurement, 63*(3), 414–429. Matthews, M.S., & McBee, M. T. (2007). School factors and the underachievement of gifted students in a talent search summer program. *Gifted Child Quarterly, 51*(2), 167–181.
Social Support Scale	To measure students' perceived social support.	2015	Grades 6–11	.60–.87			Confirmatory factor analysis	Lee, S-Y., Olszewski-Kubilius, P., Makel, M. C., & Putallaz, M. (2015). Gifted students' perceptions of an accelerated summer program and social support. *Gifted Child Quarterly, 59*(4), 265–282.
Student Product Assessment Form (SPAF)	To assess both individual aspects and overall excellence of products.	1997	All			86% to 100%	No	https://gifted.uconn.edu/wp-content/uploads/sites/961/2015/02/spaf.pdf

(Continued)

Table B.1 *Continued*

Name	Purpose	Date	Sample	Internal Consistency	Test-Retest	Inter-rater	Validity	Source of Information
Student Social Attribution Scale	To assess the causal attributions (e.g., ability, effort, chance, and task difficulty) for success and failure by using social situations.	1995	Grades 4–6	.76–.93	.74 to .84		No	Bain, S. K., & Bell, S. M. (2004). Social self-concept, social attributions, and peer relationships in fourth, fifth, and sixth graders who are gifted compared to high achievers. *Gifted Child Quarterly, 48*(3), 167–178.
Teacher Observation Scales for Assessing Programs	To provide feedback on effective classroom practices in gifted education.	2010	Teachers	.95			Content	Peters, S. J., & Gates, J. C. (2010). The teacher observation form: Revisions and updates. *Gifted Child Quarterly, 54*(3), 179–188.
Teacher Rating of Student Performance	To measure the degree that students meet overall program objectives.	1997	Teachers	.97			Content	Johnsen, S. K., & Ryser, G. R. (1997). *The validity of portfolios in predicting performance in a gifted program. Gifted International, 8*(1), 44–47.

Table B.1 *Continued*

Name	Purpose	Date	Sample	Internal Consistency	Test-Retest	Inter-rater	Validity	Source of Information
Test of Critical Thinking	To assess formulation of a written argument.	2003	Grades 3–6	.83–89			Content validity	Center for Gifted Education, College of William and Mary https://education.wm.edu/centers/cfge/_documents/resources/tctfinalmanual.pdf https://education.wm.edu/centers/cfge/_documents/resources/tctinstru.pdf
William and Mary Observation Scales, Revised	To evaluate gifted education teachers' classroom practices.	2003	Teachers	.91–93		.87–89	Content validity— expert consultant	VanTassel-Baska, J. et al. (2008). A study of differentiated instructional change over 3 years. *Gifted Child Quarterly, 52*(4), 297–312. VanTassel-Baska, J. et al. (2008). A cross-cultural study of teachers' instructional practices in Singapore and the United States. *Journal for the Education of the Gifted, 31*(3), 214–239. VanTassel-Baska, J. (2012). Analyzing differentiation in the classroom: Using the COS-R. *Gifted Child Today, 35*(1), 42–48.

References

Buros Center for Testing (n.d.). *Mental measurements yearbook*. https://buros.org/test-reviews-information

Robins, J. H., & Jolly, J. L. (2018). Technical information regarding assessment. In S. K. Johnsen (Ed.), *Identifying gifted students: A practical guide* (3rd ed., pp. 73–116). Prufrock Press.

Assessments

Creativity

Rubric for Assessing Creativity. This sample rubric includes the dimensions of fluency, flexibility, originality, elaboration, and usefulness for specific creativity strategies (Shively et al., 2018). The rubric may be found in the following reference:

> Shively, K., Stith, K. M., & Rubenstein, L. D. (2018). Measuring what matters: Assessing creativity, critical thinking, and the design process. *Gifted Child Today*, 41(3), 149–158. https://doi.org/10.1177/1076217518768361

Resource: Assessing Creativity (Center for Creative Learning). The Center for Creative Learning provides an index of 72 instruments to assess creative thinking. For some tests, they provide the author, copyright date, age/grade level, cost, source, technical qualities, use, and reviews. The index may be retrieved from www.creativelearning.com/index.php/free-resources/assessing-creativity-index

Resource: Creativity Guide (Wisconsin Association for Talented and Gifted). This guide contains teacher, parent, student, and peer nomination forms for identifying creative potential. The forms are appropriate for all grade levels. The guide may be retrieved from www.mel-min.k12.wi.us/faculty/schwarzs/creativity%20guide.pdf

Resource: Creativity Tests (Indiana University BobWeb). This Indiana University website provides example items from divergent thinking, convergent thinking, artistic, and self-assessments. Test examples include Guilford Alternative Uses Task, Wallach and Kogan, Torrance Tests of Creative Thinking, Insight Problems, Remote Association Task, Barron-Welsh Art Scale, Khatena-Torrance Creative Perception Inventory, How do you think?, Things Done on Your Own, The Creativity Behavior Inventory, Creative Attitude Survey, Statement of Past Activities, Creativity Assessment Packet, Preschool and Kindergarten Interests Descriptors, and others. The assessments may be administered by anyone and are appropriate for a variety of ages. Examples from these assessments may be retrieved from http://curtbonk.com/bobweb/r546/modules/creativity/creativity_tests.html

Critical Thinking

International Critical Thinking Essay Test (The Foundation for Critical Thinking). This test provides a method for assessing students' critical thinking. The test is divided into two parts: an analysis of a writing prompt and an assessment of the writing prompt. Intellectual standards and criteria used in the test and directions for Part I are provided at this website: www.critical thinking.org/pages/international-critical-thinking-test/619

Rubric for Assessing Critical Thinking. This sample rubric includes these dimensions of critical thinking: summarizes topic or argument, considers previous assumptions, communicates point of view, provides evidence of research, analyzes data, considers other perspectives and positions, draws implications, and assesses conclusions (Shively et al., 2018). The rubric may be found in this reference:

Shively, K., Stith, K. M., & Rubenstein, L. D. (2018). Measuring what matters: Assessing creativity, critical thinking, and the design process. *Gifted Child Today*, *41*(3), 149–158. https://doi.org/10.1177/1076217518768361

Rubric for Assessing Design Thinking. This sample rubric assesses the students' processes as they design the solution for specific problems. Based on the Design Thinking Model, it includes these processes: empathy, define, ideate, prototype and test, and reflection (Shively et al., 2018). The rubric may be found in this reference:

Shively, K., Stith, K. M., & Rubenstein, L. D. (2018). Measuring what matters: Assessing creativity, critical thinking, and the design process. *Gifted Child Today*, *41*(3), 149–158. https://doi.org/10.1177/1076217518768361

Seven Levels of Interaction in Seminar: Metric and Reflection (Scarborough, n.d.). The instrument provides a measure of student engagement in seminar discussions. It is self-report and used as discussion tool for adolescents and older populations. The metric includes descriptors for the least (e.g., silence) to the most interactive behaviors (e.g., discriminating). The instrument may be found in Appendix I in a *Collection of Materials on Seminar*

Approaches and Evaluation Strategies. www.hcc.edu/Documents/Courses-Programs/Integrative%20Learning/Seminar%20Resource%20Packet.pdf

*The Test of Critical Thinking (Center for Gifted Education, The College of William & Mary, 2003). The instrument uses scenarios and requires the student to select among the provided choices. The selection of choices requires use of critical thinking skills and assesses across seven life domains: social, affect, competence, environmental, physical, family, and academic. The instrument is appropriate for third through sixth grade. A manual for interpretation and administration is available on the website. Reliability ranges from a = .83 to .89 and a validity study indicate scores from the TCT correlate with other ability measures.

The Student instructions may be retrieved from: https://education.wm.edu/centers/cfge/_documents/resources/tctinstru.pdf

The Examiner's manual may be retrieved from: https://education.wm.edu/centers/cfge/_documents/resources/tctfinalmanual.pdf

Resource: Critical Thinking (Kansas State Department of Education). The Kansas State Department of Education provides a website with rubrics for assessing critical understandings for elementary, middle, and high school students. These assessments may be retrieved from www.ksde.org/Agency/Division-of-Learning-Services/Career-Standards-and-Assessment-Services/Content-Area-F-L/History-Government-and-Social-Studies/HGSS-Assessment

Curriculum Assessments

Arts Talent identification (Haroutounian, 2017). In this framework, criteria are provided for potential talent in these arts: music, visual arts, dance/movement and theater/drama. The criteria are divided into these areas: perceptual awareness and discrimination, creative interpretation, behavior and performance/product, and commitment and critique. The instrument and content validity may be found in this reference:

> Haroutounian, J. (2017). Artistic ways of knowing in gifted education: encouraging every student to think like an artist. *Roeper Review, 39*(1), 44–58. https://doi.org/10.1080/02783193.2016.1247397

*Clark's Drawing Abilities Test (CDAT; Clark & Wilson, 1991). This instrument may be used as a screening device for identifying elementary through high school gifted students who are talented in the visual arts. The instrument correlates with the Torrance Tests of Creativity and state achievement tests. The journal article referenced below found the CDAT differentiated between students with and without artistic instruction. Additional information may be found in these references:

Clark, G., & Wilson, T. (1991). Screening and identifying gifted/talented students in the visual arts with Clark's Drawing Abilities Test. *Roeper Review*, *13*(2), 92–97. https://doi.org/10.1080/02783199109553321

Clark, G., & Zimmerman, E. (1992). *Issues and practices related to identification of gifted and talented students in the visual arts.* (Research Monograph No. 9202). Storrs, CT: The National Research Center on the Gifted and Talented. https://nrcgt.uconn.edu/wp-content/uploads/sites/953/2015/04/rbdm9202.pdf

Clark, G., & Zimmerman, E. (2001). Identifying artistically talented students in four rural communities in the United States. *Gifted Child Quarterly*, *45*(2), 104–114. https://doi.org/10.1177/00169820104500204

*Dance, Music, and Theater Talent Items and Behavioral Descriptors (Oreck, Owen, & Baum, 2003). The instrument is designed to assess artistic talents of elementary students, Grades 2 through 6, and identify those who are ready for advanced instruction in the arts area. Two trained arts instructors may administer it to classes over a five-class series. Each student is rated on a written checklist of eight music, ten dance, or four theater items. Scoring is done on a simple notice/not notice scale for each. Each assessor then gives an overall, holistic score for each student at the end of every class. Students are invited to a fifth session based either on predetermined cutoff scores or by the number of students that can be accommodated in the fifth session. Reported interrater reliability coefficients were .67 for music, .82 for dance, and .74 for theater. Stability reliability estimates were calculated over three separate intervals and ranged from .35 to .68. Ratings were able to predict future ratings with 82% of identified students making good to excellent progress on written semiannual evaluations by arts instructors. More technical information and the instrument may be found in this reference:

Oreck, B. A., Owen, S.V., & Baum, S. M. (2003). Validity, reliability, and equity issues in an observational talent assessment process in the performing arts. *Journal for the Education of the Gifted*, *27*(1), 62–94. https://doi.org/10.1177/016235320302700105

*Diet Cola Test (Fowler, 1990). The Diet Cola Test or Fowler Science Process Skills Assessments may be used to assess science process skills at all grade levels. The checklist contains descriptors related to safety, problem statement, hypotheses, steps, materials, repeat testing, definitions, observations, types of measurements, data collection, interpretation of data, conclusions, and control variables. The checklist may be used as a formative and summative assessment. Interrater reliability has been reported in the range of .89–.91; test-retest reliability, .76. The Diet Cola Test may be retrieved from

Fowler, M. (1990). The diet cola test. *Science Scope, 13*(4), 32–34. https://education.wm.edu/centers/cfge/_documents/curriculum/science/dietcolatest.pdf

NAGC Rubric for Rating Outstanding Curricular Material (Beasley et al., 2017). The NAGC Curriculum rubric is a tool to support the development of quality curriculum and select and award exemplary curricula for addressing advanced academic needs of students with gifts and talents. The rubric may be found in this reference:

Beasley, J. G., Briggs, C., & Pennington, L. (2017). Bridging the gap 10 years later: A tool and technique to analyze and evaluate advanced academic curricular units. *Gifted Child Today, 40*(1), 48–58. https://doi.org/10.1177/1076217516675902

Rigor Rubric (North Carolina Department of Public Instruction, 2006). This rubric rates the dimensions of assessments, instruction, and curriculum of a lesson or a unit on a four-point scale. The rubric and content validity information may be found in this reference:

Matusevich, M. N., O'Connor, K. A., & Hargett, M. V. P. (2009). The nonnegotiables of academic rigor. *Gifted Child Today, 32*(4), 44–52. https://doi.org/10.1177/1076217509032004

*Rubric for Scoring Persuasive Writing (VanTassel-Baska, Johnson, Hughes, & Boyce, 1996). This performance-based persuasive writing assessment requires students to develop an argument in written form. It was developed as a pre- and post-measure for use in a curriculum unit and scored using a rubric. Interrater reliability agreement was reported at 92%. The rubric and more technical information may be found in the following reference:

VanTassel-Baska, J., Johnson, D. T., Hughes, C. E., & Boyce, L. N. (1996). A study of language arts curriculum effectiveness with gifted learners. *Journal for the Education of the Gifted, 19*(4), 461–480. https://doi.org/10.1177/016235329601900405

Rubric for Highest Level Achievement Tests (HLAT; Edmonton Public School Board, 2008). This trait-based rubric uses a 4-point scale (limited, satisfactory, proficient, excellent) to evaluate writing samples. The rubric may be found in these references:

Edmonton Public School Board (2008). *Highest Level Achievement Test writing rubric.* Edmonton, Alberta, Canada.

Roessingh, H., & Bence, M. (2017). Intervening in early written literacy development for gifted children in grade 2: Insights from an action research project. *Journal for the Education of the Gifted, 40*(2), 168–196. https://doi.org/10.1177/0162353217701201

Rubric for Assessment of Individual Debate Skills (Field, 2017). This rubric rates debate skills in the two areas of preparation and speech on a four-point scale from novice to highly skilled. The rubric may be found in these references:

Field, K. (2017). Debating our way toward stronger thinking. *Gifted Child Today, 40*(3), 144–153. https://doi.org/10.1177/1076217517707235

Rubric for Inventions Portfolio Project (Powers, 2008). This rubric rates the dimensions of an inventions portfolio project on a three-point scale: expert/problem, notebook, research, invention, PowerPoint presentation, presentation, portfolio. The rubric made be found in this reference:

Powers, E. (2008). The use of independent study as a viable differentiation technique for gifted learners in the regular classroom. *Gifted Child Today, 31*(3), 57–65. https://doi.org/10.4219/gct-2008–786

Rubric from Florida's Frameworks for K-12 Gifted Learners (Weber et al., 2008). This rubric presents a four-tiered scale (Know, Understand, Perform, and Accomplish) for measuring student outcomes within a particular trait for each objective. The scale qualitatively describes student behaviors and attitudes. The rubric may be found in this reference:

Weber, C. L., Boswell, C., & Smith, D. (2008). Different paths to accountability: Defining rigorous outcomes for gifted learners. *Gifted Child Today, 31*(1), 54–65. https://doi.org/10.4219/gct-2008–695

Resource: Assessment Design Toolkit (Reform Support Network, U.S. Department of Education). The Toolkit includes 13 modules divided into four parts: key concepts, five elements of assessment design, writing and selecting assessments, and reflecting on assessment design. www2.ed.gov/teachers/assess/resources/toolkit/index.html

Resource: Curriculum-Based Measurements (CBM). Several websites have curriculum-based generators that may be used to create off-level materials for gifted students. The assessments may be customized to meet the specific needs for progress monitoring and may be modified for use with all grade levels. The following website contains tools for creating curriculum-based measures: www.interventioncentral.org/curriculum-based-measurement-reading-math-assesment-tests

Interest Assessments

If I Ran the School (Reis & Siegle, 2002). The instrument is designed for students in Grades K–3 to identify their interests within the traditional content areas. Scores from the instrument may be useful for curriculum compacting because it provides information on areas of high interest for the student. It is appropriate for both elementary and secondary students. https://nrcgt.uconn.edu/wp-content/uploads/sites/953/2015/07/cc_ranschool.pdf

Interest-A-Lyzer (Renzulli, 1997). The self-report instrument helps students identify interests, which can be used to plan gifted and talented enrichment experiences. It uses situations, both actual and hypothetical, to stimulate reflection. The instrument should be untimed and the results should not be associated with any type of reward. It is designed for use with middle and high school age students. www.prufrock.com/Assets/ClientPages/pdfs/SEM_Web_Resources/Interest-A-Lyzer.pdf

Primary Interest-a-Lyzer (Renzulli & Rizza, 1997). This self-report interest is designed for students in grade K-3. Picture cues are provided for each question. Teachers may use this instrument informally to identify their students' non-academic interests. www.prufrock.com/Assets/ClientPages/pdfs/SEM_Web_Resources/Primary%20Interest-A-Lyzer.pdf

Secondary Interest-A-Lyzer (Hébert, Sorensen, & Renzulli, 1997). This informal interest inventory is to identify secondary student's interests so that educators might plan ways of nurturing their talents and challenging their learning potential. www.prufrock.com/Assets/ClientPages/pdfs/SEM_Web_Resources/Secondary%20Interest-A-Lyzer.pdf

Learning and Motivation Assessments

Activities and Accomplishments Inventory (AAI; Milgram & Hong, 2001). The self-report instrument for high school students assesses activities and accomplishments in areas like science, computers, mathematics, literature, social activities, drama, music, art, dance, and sports. The instrument has reported validity demonstrated by longitudinal studies showing predictive validity of the AAI with vocation in adulthood. The instrument is located in this reference:

Hong, E., & Aqui, Y. (2004). Cognitive and motivational characteristics of adolescents gifted in mathematics: Comparisons among students with different types of giftedness. *Gifted Child Quarterly, 48*(3), 191–201. https://doi.org/10.1177.001698620404800304

*ElemenOE (Bouchard, 2004). The instrument measures overexcitability in elementary students with a 61-item Likert scale. The authors suggest it may be used as a possible identification measure for students less than 13 years of age. Research shows the internal consistency of the total scale as a = .88, with subscale internal consistency ranging from a = .66 to .90. Validity studies show a five-factor structure supporting Dabrowski's theory of positive disintegration. The instrument is located in this reference:

Bouchard, L. L. (2004). An instrument for the measure of Dabrowskian Overexcitabilities to identify gifted elementary students. *Gifted Child Quarterly, 48*(4), 339–350. https://doi.org/10.1177/ 001698620404800407

*Implicit Theories of Intelligence Scale for Children (ITISC; Dweck, 1999). The instrument measures growth mindset and the extent to which a child believes intelligence can be improved. The ITISC items have a reported internal reliability that ranged from .94 to .98 and a test-retest reliability score of .80 with a two-week interval (Dweck et al., 1995). The test is a significant predictor of mathematics achievement with students who believed intelligence could be improved having a greater increase in mathematics than those who considered intelligence fixed. More information about the instrument may be found in these articles:

Blackwell, L. S., Trzesniewski, K. H., & Dweck, C. S. (2007). Implicit theories of intelligence predict achievement across an adolescent transition: A longitudinal study and an intervention. *Child Development, 78*(1), 246–263. https://10.1111/j.1467–8624.2007.00995.x

Dweck, C. S. (1999). *Self-theories.* Taylor & Francis.

Napolitano, C. M., & Job, V. (2018). Assessing the implicit theory of willpower for strenuous mental activities scale: Multigroup, across-gender, and cross-cultural measurement invariance and convergent and divergent validity. *Psychological Assessment, 30*(8), 1049–1064. http://dx.doi.org/10.1037/pas0000557

*Learning Behaviors Scale (McDermott, Green, Francis, & Stott, 1999). The instrument uses 29 teacher-rated items related to effective learning of secondary students. Internal consistency for the instrument ranges from a =.61 to .86 and validity studies have indicated a four-factor structure explaining 48% of variance in scale scores. The instrument is located in this reference:

Worrell, F. C., & Schaefer, B. A. (2004). Reliability and validity of Learning Behaviors Scale (LBS) scores with academically talented students: A comparative perspective. *Gifted Child Quarterly*, *48*(4), 287–308. https://doi.org/10.1177/001698620404800404

Learning Motivation Questionnaire for Primary School Students (Hu et al., 2016). This 16-item, four-point scale (strongly disagree to strongly agree) addresses surface motivation, deep motivation, and achieving motivation. Cronbach's alpha internal consistency for the subscales ranged from .41–.76. Factor analysis and correlations between each subtest and the whole questionnaire provided some evidence for construct validity. The instrument and its technical qualities may be found in this reference:

Hu, W., Jia, X., Plucker, J. A., & Shan, X. (2016). Effects of a critical thinking skills program on the learning motivation of primary school students. *Roeper Review*, *38*(2), 70–83. https://doi.org/10.1080/02783 193.2016.1150374

*Metacognitive Awareness Inventory (Kearney, 2010). The instrument uses an 18-item survey using a Likert format to identify metacognition in academic settings. Most research using the scale has been in the discipline of math, but the stems for each item could be used in any discipline. The instrument is located in this dissertation:

Kearney, L. J. (2010). *Differences in self-concept, racial identity, self- efficacy, resilience, and achievement among African-American gifted and non-gifted students: Implications for retention and persistence of African Americans in gifted programs.* (Doctoral dissertation). Available from Proquest Dissertations and Theses database. (UMI 3404513).

The instrument is also used in this reference:

Sperling, R. A., Howard, B. C., Miller, L. A., & Murphy, C. (2002). Measures of children's knowledge and regulation of cognition. *Contemporary Educational Psychology*, *27*, 57–79. https://pdfs.semanticscholar.org/1186/bbb43b19c6d26f0bee3589e9d0898c6aeb27.pdf

*Morgan-Jinks Student Efficacy Scale (MJSES; Jinks & Morgan, 1999).
This self-report measure assesses the level of student efficacy beliefs and how
they relate to school success. The thirty-item scale has an overall reliability
coefficient of .82 with subscale alphas of .78 for talent, .70 for context, and .66
for effort. The scale may be retrieved from this article:

Jinks, J., & Morgan, V. (1999). Children's perceived academic self-
efficacy: An inventory scale. *The Clearing House*, 72(4), 224–230.
https://doi.org/10.1080/00098659909599398

*Possibilities for Learning Survey (Kanevsky, 1999). This 110-item instru-
ment asks students to rate their preference for features of learning experiences
on a 5-point Likert-type scale from strongly agree to strongly disagree. The
items relate to content, process, product, and the learning environment. Cronbach alphas vary for different categories: pace (a = .63), collaborative learning
(a = .71), choice (a = .68), curriculum content (a = .71), evaluation (a = .64),
open-ended activities (a = .72), expert knowledge (a = .77), and teacher-
student relationships (a = .69). The instrument may be found in these references:

Kanevsky, L. (1999). *Tool kit for curriculum differentiation*. Burnaby,
British Columbia, Canada: Simon Frasier University.
Kanevsky, L. (2011). Deferential differentiation: what types of
differentiation do students want? *Gifted Child Quarterly*, 55(4), 279–299.
https://doi.org/10.1177/0016986211422098

Preferred Method of Instruction (Krogh, 2010). Part 1 of this Javits Student Survey assesses students preferred method of instruction in Grades
2 through 5 and asks the students to provide reasons for the choice. Part 2
assesses inductive versus deductive learning preferences by presenting information and asking the students to choose the order of learning. Part 1 and
Part 2 assess preferences across all disciplines. The instrument is located in
Appendix A of this reference:

Krogh, J. (2010). *The effects of the models of teaching on student learning*.
(Doctoral dissertation). Available from Proquest Dissertations and
Theses database (UMI No. 3418088).

*School Attitude Assessment Survey-Revised (SAAS-R; McCoach &
Siegle, 2003). This 35-item rating scale is designed to measure five aspects
of adolescents' motivation and attitudes toward school (academic self-
perception, attitudes toward teachers and classes, attitudes toward school, goal
valuation, and motivation/self-regulation). Internal consistency reliability

for the subscales range from .88–.93. The instrument and content, construct, and criterion-related validity may be found in these references:

Matthews, M.S., & McBee, M. T. (2007). School factors and the underachievement of gifted students in a talent search summer program. *Gifted Child Quarterly, 51*(2), 167–181. https://doi.org/10.1177/0016986207299473

McCoach, D. B., & Siegle, D. (2003). The school attitude assessment survey-revised: A new instrument to identify academically able students who underachieve. *Educational and Psychological Measurement, 63*(3), 414–429. https://doi.org/10.1177/0013164402251057

Work Preferences Survey (French et al., 2011). This survey is based on Renzulli and Smith's *How I Like to Learn*, the Piers-Harris's *Children's Self-Concept Scale*, and Hildreth's *Personality and Interest Inventory*. The survey asks gifted students for their opinions of different class activities. Reported Cronbach alphas for projects, peer teaching, and independent study ranged from .70–.80. Along with the instrument, face and content validity is located in this reference:

French, L. R., Walker, C. L., & Shore, B. M. (2011). Do gifted students really prefer to work alone? *Roeper Review, 33*(3), 145–159. https://doi.org/10.1080/02783193.2011.580497

Multicultural Assessments

*Cross-Cultural Counseling Inventory-R (LaFromboise, Coleman, & Hernandez, 1991). The instrument assesses cross-cultural competence with young adults using three subscales: beliefs/attitudes, knowledge, and skills. It contains 20 items with an internal consistency reliability a reported at .95. Validity studies confirm a three-factor structure with all items loading on the hypothesized factor. The instrument is located in this reference:

LaFromboise, T.D., Coleman, H. L., & Hernandez, A. (1991). Development and factor analysis of the Cross-cultural Counseling Inventory-Revised. *Professional Psychology: Research and Practice, 22*(5), 380–388. https://doi.org/10.1037/0735-7028.22.5.380

*Multidimensional Inventory of Black Identity (MIBI) (Kearney, 2010). The MIBI is a research instrument used to measure racial identity along three dimensions: centrality, ideology, and regard. The instrument does not render a composite score. It has been used for research in gifted and talented and may be found in this dissertation:

Kearney, L. J. (2010). *Differences in self-concept, racial identity, self- efficacy, resilience, and achievement among African-American gifted and non-gifted students: Implications for retention and persistence of African Americans in gifted programs.* (Doctoral dissertation). Available from Proquest Dissertations and Theses database. (UMI 3404513).

It is also used in the following references:

Sellers, R. M., Smith, M. A., Shelton, J. N., Rowley, S. J., & Chavous, T. M. (1998). Multidimensional model of racial identity: A reconceptualization of African-American racial identity. *Personality and Social Psychology Review*, 2(1), 18–36. https://doi.org/10.1207/s15327957pspr0201_2

Sellers, R.M., Rowley, S.A., Chavous, T.M., Shelton, J.N., & Smith, M.A. (1997). Multidimensional inventory of Black identity: A preliminary investigation of reliability and construct validity. *Journal of Personality and Social Psychology*, 73(4), 805–815. https://doi.org/10.1037/0022-3514.73.4.805

*The Multigroup Ethnic Identity Measure (Phinney, 1992). The self-report instrument provides a measure of ethnic identity. Four general aspects of ethnic identity are assessed: positive ethnic attitudes and sense of belonging; ethnic identity of achievement; ethnic behaviors or practices; and other group orientation. It is appropriate for use with all ethnic groups and may be used with adolescents. Internal consistency reliability for a high school sample was a = .81. Additional information may be found in these references:

Phinney, J. S. (1992). The Multigroup Ethnic Identity Measure: A new scale for use with diverse groups. *Journal of Adolescent Research*, 7(2), 156–176. https://doi.org/10.1177/074355489272003

Worrell, F. C. (2007). Ethnic identity, academic achievement, and global self-concept in four groups of academically talented adolescents. *Gifted Child Quarterly*, 51(1), 23–58. https://doi.org/10.1177/0016986206296655

Products and Performance Assessments

*My Way … An Expression Style Inventory (Kettle, Renzulli, & Rizza, 1998). This 50-item Likert-scale inventory was designed to assess how interested students are in developing different types of products. Factor analysis produced ten factors or components. Reliability for the scales ranged from .95 to .72. The instrument may be found in this reference:

> Kettle, K. E., Renzulli, J. S., & Rizza, M. G. (1998). Products of mind: Exploring student preferences for product development using my way … an expression style instrument. *Gifted Child Quarterly*, 42(1), 48–61. www. researchgate.net/profile/Joseph-Renzulli/publication/249826200_ Products_of_Mind_Exploring_Student_Preferences_for_Product_ Development_Using_My_Way_An_Expression_Style_Instrument/ links/5bfc184f458515b41d0f71e6/Products-of-Mind-Exploring- Student-Preferences-for-Product-Development-Using-My-Way- An-Expression-Style-Instrument.pdf

Six-Trait Assessment for Beginning Writers (Northwest Educational Regional Laboratory). The assessment identifies strengths in primary students' writing and allows a qualitative indicator to be assigned to the work according to the traits illustrated. It could be used with a student as a self-assessment or as a progress-monitoring tool. The assessment is written specifically for beginning composition writers. The assessment may be retrieved from https://educationnorthwest.org/sites/default/files/scoring-practice-rubrics.pdf

Social Studies Performance Assessment (Moon, 2002). This assessment differentiates instruction for student with varying academic differences in social studies. The performance assessment allows students to choose Individual Components (historical research, integration of the elements of war, format, style), Group Components (group work skills, overall product) and Context (world news, regional news, local news). The performance assessment may be found in this reference:

> Moon, T. (2002). Using performance assessment in the social studies classroom. *Gifted Child Today*, 25(3), 53–39. https://doi.org/10.4219/ gct-2002–75

*Student Product Assessment Form (SPAF; Renzulli & Reis, 1997). The rating scale is composed of 15 items designed to assess both individual aspects and overall excellence of products. Each item is rated using three related parts: the key concept, item description, and examples. Instructions for rating products are included on the form. The form may be used in a variety of disciplines and with all grade levels. Levels of agreement among raters on individual items of the scale ranged from 86.4% to 100%. The authors report a reliability coefficient between raters who assessed the same set of products on two occasions with a period of time between ratings. A copy of the instrument may be retrieved from https://gifted.uconn.edu/wp-content/uploads/sites/961/2015/02/spaf.pdf

Resource: Texas Performance Standards Project. The website includes performance-based assessment tools for students grades in grades four through high school. Tasks are also included and are scaffolded according to the developmental level of the student. The assessments may be used in the disciplines of language arts, mathematics, social studies, and science. The tools may be used as summative and formative assessment of learning. Information on the tasks and assessment tools may be retrieved from website www.texaspsp.org

Social, Emotional, and Psychosocial Assessments

Communication Skills and Competencies Rubric. The rubric may be used to rate written and verbal communication skills in high school students. It is a self-report assessment and focuses on strengths and weaknesses, which makes it appropriate for progress monitoring communication skills. The rubric can be retrieved from www.uwgb.edu/clampitp/Communication%20skills.htm

Empowering Gifted Behavior Scale (Jenkins-Friedman, Bransky & Murphy, 1986). This rating scale is used to identify patterns of enabling and disabling perfectionistic behaviors in gifted students at all grade levels. The teacher rates 11 items that identify the degree to which students might demonstrate perfectionism. The assessment may be found in Appendix B of this reference:

> P. A. Schuler's (1999). *Voices of perfectionism: Perfectionistic gifted adolescents in a rural middle school.* Storrs, CT, National Research Center on the Gifted and Talented, University of Connecticut. https://nrcgt.uconn.edu/wp-content/uploads/sites/953/2015/04/rm99140.pdf

Ethical Decision-Making (Pugh, 1999). This rubric assesses student skills in group discussion and decision-making. Areas addressed include knowledge of subject, use and quality of resource materials, organizing and listening skills, communication skills, analytical and evaluation skills to develop ideas, skills in disagreeing, and flexibility and tolerance. The rubric may be found in this reference:

> Pugh, S. (1999). Developing ethical decision-making through the discussion process. *Gifted Child Today*, 22(1), 26–31, 51–53. https://doi.org/10.1177/107621759902200108

*Goals and Work Habits Survey (Schuler, 1994). The 35-item scale assesses perfectionism by using a Likert-type scale. The assessment uses six subscales: concern over mistakes, personal standards, parental expectations, parental criticism, doubts of actions, and organization. The internal consistency reliability of the total scale during piloting was a = .87. The assessment may be found in Appendix A of this reference:

> P. A. Schuler's (1999). *Voices of perfectionism: Perfectionistic gifted adolescents in a rural middle school*. Storrs, CT, National Research Center on the Gifted and Talented, University of Connecticut. https://nrcgt.uconn.edu/wp-content/uploads/sites/953/2015/04/rm99140.pdf

*Harter's Self-Perception Profile for Adolescents (Harter, 1988). The 45-item questionnaire measures eight domains of self-concept and a general domain of self-worth. The self-concept domains measured are social competence, physical appearance, behavioral conduct, scholastic competence, romantic appeal, close friendship, job competence and athletic competence. A reliability of ranges from a = .62 to .94, and the factor structure appears to support the domains. Further information about the instrument is reported in this reference:

> Harter, S., Whitesnell, N. R., & Junkin, L. J. (1998). Similarities and differences in domain-specific and global self-evaluation of learning disabled, behaviorally disabled, and normally achieving adolescents. *American Educational Research Journal*, 35(4), 653–680. https://doi.org/10.3102/00028312035004653

Leadership Student Self-Assessment and Observation Inventory (Jolly & Kettler, 2004). These instruments were adapted from the Renzulli-Hartman Scales for Rating Behavioral Characteristics of Superior Students and the Gifted and Talented Evaluation Scales. The content of the self-assessment rating scale focuses on social skills. The Leadership Observation Inventory is a teacher observation form that allows the teacher to jot-down student names as they observe their interactions within a group. The self-assessment and observation inventory may be found in this reference:

Jolly, J., & Kettler, T. (2004). Authentic assessment of leadership in problem-solving groups. *Gifted Child Today*, 27(1), 32–39. https://doi.org/10.1177/10762175040200110

*Peer Competition Rating Scale; Teacher Competition Rating Scale; Self-Competition Rating Scale (Schneider et al., 2006; Schneider, Woodburn, del Pilar Soteras del Toro, & Udvari, 2005). All instruments measure perceptions of competitive goal orientations with middle school and high school students. The Peer Competition Rating Scale has 16 items, which address task-oriented and other-referenced competition in the scholastic and athletic domains. The Teacher Competition Rating scale has eight items, which address the students' competition goal orientation in the scholastic domain. The 19-item Self-Rating Competition scale measures the participant's own perception of his or her competition orientation. The self and teacher reports correlate and yield the same factors when examined through factor analysis. Internal consistency ranges from a = .55 to .82 across all scales. More information is reported in these references:

Schneider, B. H., del Pilar Soteras del Toro, M., Woodburn, S., Fulop, M., Cervino, C., & Bernstein, S. et al. (2006). Cross-cultural differences in competition among children and adolescents. In X. Chen, D. C. French, & B. H. Schneider (Eds.), *Peer relationships in cultural context* (pp. 31–338). Cambridge University Press.

Schapiro, M., Schneider, B. H., Shore, B. M., Margison, J. A., & Udvari, S. J. (2009). Competitive goal orientations, quality, and stability in gifted and other adolescents' friendships: A test of Sullivan's theory about the harm caused by rivalry. *Gifted Child Quarterly*, 53(2), 71–88. https://doi.org/10.1177/0016986208330566

*Psychological Well-Being Scale (Ryff, 1989). The 84-item instrument measures six domains of psychological well-being in adolescents. The subscales include autonomy, environmental mastery, personal growth, positive relations with others, purpose in life, and self-acceptance. Internal consistency ranges from a = .86 to .93 with correlations on test-retest of r = .81 to .88 on an unspecified time interval. A confirmatory factor analysis supported the six-factor structure. More information may be found in these references:

Jin, S-U., & Moon, S. M. (2006). A study of well-being and school satisfaction among academically talented students attending a science high school in Korea. *Gifted Child Quarterly, 50*(2), 169–184. https://doi.org/10.1177/001698620605000207

Ryff, C. D. (1989). Beyond Ponce de Leon and life satisfaction: New directions in quest successful aging. *International Journal of Behavioral Development, 12*(1), 35–55. https://doi.org/10.1177/016502548901200102

*Social Support Scale (Lee et al., 2015). This scale consists of 25 items that measure students' perceived social support in these areas: peer support, family support, self-support, general support, and support from nearby students. Cronbach alphas ranged from .60 to .87. More information about this instrument may be found in this reference:

Lee, S-Y, Olszewski-Kubilius, P., Makel, M. C., & Putallaz, M. (2015). Gifted students' perceptions of an accelerated summer program and social support. *Gifted Child Quarterly, 59*(4), 265–282. https://doi.org/10.1177/0016986215599205

*Student Social Attribution Scale (Bell & McCallum, 1995). The instrument assesses the causal attributions (e.g., ability, effort, chance, and task difficulty) for success and failure by using social situations of fourth through sixth grade students. The student rates each situation on a Likert scale to determine causal attributions. The correlations for test-retest on a two-week interval was $r = .74$ to .84 and internal consistency on initial studies was $a = .76$ to .93. More information may be found in this reference:

Bain, S. K., & Bell, S. M. (2004). Social self-concept, social attributions, and peer relationships in fourth, fifth, and sixth graders who are gifted compared to high achievers. *Gifted Child Quarterly, 48*(3), 167–178. https://doi.org/10.1177/001698620404800302

Teacher Social Rating (Coie & Dodge, 1988). The teacher-rating instrument assesses social function in relation to peers. Interrater reliability on initial studies was 100% across four different raters. More information may be found in this reference:

Bain, S. K., & Bell, S. M. (2004). Social self-concept, social attributions, and peer relationships in fourth, fifth, and sixth graders who are gifted compared to high achievers. *Gifted Child Quarterly, 48*(3), 167–178. https://doi.org/10.1177/001698620404800302

Resource: Leadership Instruments. More information about leadership instruments is reported in these references:

Shaunessy, E., & Karnes, F. A. (2004). Instruments for measuring leadership in children and youth. *Gifted Child Today*, 27(1), 42–47. https://doi.org/10.1177/107621750402700112

  Oakland, T., Falkenberg, B. A., & Oakland, C. (1996). Assessment of leadership in children, youth and adults. *Gifted Child Quarterly*, 40(3), 138–146. https://doi.org/10.1177/001698629604000304

Resource: Social and emotional learning skills instruments. This Regional Educational Laboratory Northeast and Islands resource reviews instruments that measure three social and emotional learning skills among secondary school students: collaboration, perseverance, and self-regulated learning.

Cox, J., Foster, B., & Bamat, D. (2019). *A review of instruments for measuring social and emotional learning skills among secondary school students* (REL 2020–010). Washington, DC: U.S. Department of Education, Institute of Education Sciences, National Center for Education Evaluation and Regional Assistance, Regional Education Laboratory Northeast & Islands. https://ies.ed.gov/ncee/edlabs/projects/project.asp?projectID=4583

Program Planning and Evaluation

*Classroom Instructional Practices Scale (Johnsen, 1992). This checklist is designed to measure how teachers organize their classrooms in adapting for learner differences in content, rate, preference, and environment. The description of each area is hierarchical beginning with the least adaptive classroom practice for individual differences and progressing to the most adaptive classroom practice. Interrater reliability was reported at .92. The instrument may be found in this reference:

Johnsen, S. K., Haensly, P. A., Ryser, G. R., & Ford, R. F. (2002). Changing general education classroom practices to adapt for gifted students. *Gifted Child Quarterly*, 46(1), 45–63. https://doi.org/10.1177/001698620204600105

Differentiated Classroom Observation Scale (DCOS; Cassady et al., 2004). The purpose of the DCOS is to examine strategies employed to meet the needs of gifted children receiving instruction in cluster-grouped classrooms.

The DCOS has three components: the pre-observation interview, the observation period, and the post-observation debrief and reflection. The instrument may be found in this reference:

Cassady, J. C., Speirs Neumeister, K. L., Adams, C. M., Cross, T. L., Dixon, F. A., & Pierce, R. L. (2004). The differentiated classroom observation scale. *Roeper Review*, 26(3), 139–146. https://doi. org/10.1080/02783190409554259

Educator and Student Evaluation Surveys (VanTassel-Baska, 2006). The surveys examine student and educator perceptions of the gifted education program. Educator areas include identification, program/curriculum, communication, staff development, and administration. The surveys are found in the following reference:

VanTassel-Baska, J. (2006). A content analysis of evaluation findings across 20 gifted programs: A clarion call for enhanced gifted program development. *Gifted Child Quarterly*, 50(3), 199–215. https://doi. org/10.1177/001698620605000302

Enrichment Cluster Evaluation Forms (Gentry et al., 1999). The Enrichment Triad Model describes the implementation of enrichment clusters, nongraded groups of students who share common interests. Student, parent, and facilitator evaluation forms for enrichment clusters may be found in this reference:

Gentry, M., Moran, C., & Reis, S. M. (1999). Expanding enrichment program opportunities to all students. *Gifted Child Today*, 22(4), 36–48. https://doi.org/10.1177/107621759902200410

Fast-Paced Class Evaluation Survey (Lee & Olszewski-Kubilius, 2006). This one-page survey uses a 5-point Likert scale. Examples of the questions included whether teachers pretest to see what students know before teaching a unit, group students into clusters for instruction based on previous knowledge of subject, allows students to proceed at their own individual pace and so on. The survey may be found in the following reference:

Seon-Young, L., & Olszewski-Kubilius, P. (2006). A study of instructional methods used in fast-paced classes. *Gifted Child Quarterly*, 50(3), 216–237. https://doi.org/10.1177/001698620605000303

Grade-Based Acceleration Scale (Dare et al., 2019). The purpose of this scale is to identify factors that students who accelerate believe to be most important. perceptions related to grade-based acceleration. Using group concept mapping methodology, Dare et al. (2019) identified six belief clusters about grade-based acceleration: best learning environment, child's preferences, abilities across different subjects, peer group, context and school support, and social considerations.

Dare, L., Nowicki, E. A., & Smith, S. (2019). On deciding to accelerate: High-ability students identify key considerations. *Gifted Child Quarterly*, *63*(3), 159–171. https://doi.org/10.1177/0016986219828073

Parent Questionnaire Regarding Child's Gifted Class Performance (PQCP; NRC/GT at UGA, 1993). The PQCP is comprised of 22 items on a 5-point Likert-scale and was developed to determine parents' perceptions of their child's performance in the gifted program. Areas include the parents' relationship with the school, the parents' perception of their child's adjustment to the gifted program, and the parents' perception of the benefits of the gifted program. The PQCP may be useful in program evaluation. The PQCP may be found in Appendix E of this reference:

S. L. Hunsaker, M. M. Frasier, E. Frank, V. Finley, & P. Klekotka (1995). *Performance of economically disadvantaged students placed in gifted programs through the Research-Based Assessment Plan.* Storrs, CT, National Research Center on the Gifted and Talented, University of Connecticut. https://nrcgt.uconn.edu/wp-content/uploads/sites/953/2015/04/rm95208.pdf

Scale for Rating Student Participation in the Local Gifted Education Program (SRSP; Renzulli & Westberg, 1991). The SRSP is used to obtain a gifted education teacher's rating of a student's performance in the gifted program. The SRSP is a 10-item rating instrument with a five-point Likert-scale. The instrument is internally consistent with an alpha reliability coefficient reported to be .95. The SRSP may be useful in program evaluation and studies that might examine the relationship between identification with classroom performance. The SRSP may be found in Appendix D of this reference:

S. L. Hunsaker, M. M. Frasier, E. Frank, V. Finley, & P. Klekotka (1995). *Performance of economically disadvantaged students placed in gifted programs through the Research-Based Assessment Plan.* Storrs, CT: National

Research Center on the Gifted and Talented, University of Connecticut. https://nrcgt.uconn.edu/wp-content/uploads/sites/953/2015/04/rm95208.pdf

Talents Unlimited Lesson Plan and Teacher Self-Rating Scale (Newman, Gregg, & Dantzler, 2009). These assessments are used to evaluate the implementation of the Talents Unlimited model. Educators rate themselves on each of the talents. A copy of this scale may be found in the following reference:

Newman, J. L., Gregg, M., & Dantzler, J. (2009). Summer enrichment workshop (SEW): A quality component of The University of Alabama's gifted education preservice training program. *Roeper Review, 31*(3), 170–184. https://doi.org/10.1080/02783190902993995

*Teacher Observation Scales for Assessing Programs (Peters & Gates, 2010). The purpose of the Purdue University Gifted Education Teacher Observation Form (TOF) is to provide useful "feedback to teachers as to the prevalence of gifted education pedagogical effective practices in their classrooms" (p. 179). The Teacher Observation Form contains 12 items that address these areas: content coverage, clarity of instruction, motivational techniques, pedagogy/instructional techniques, opportunity for self-determination of activities by student, student involvement in a variety of experience, interaction between teacher and student, student, and peers, opportunity for student follow-up on activities and topics on their own, emphasis on higher-level thinking skills, emphasis on creativity, lesson plans designed to meet program, course, and daily objectives, and appropriate use of classroom technology. Observers use the TOF during 30-minute blocks in which they sit quietly in the classroom, mark their observations on the form, and make notes concerning what they observe. The overall alpha reliability estimate was .95. The instrument may be found in the following reference:

Peters, S. J., & Gates, J. C. (2010). The teacher observation form: Revisions and updates. *Gifted Child Quarterly, 54*(3), 179–188. https://doi.org/10.1177/0016986210369258

*Teacher Rating of Student Performance (Johnsen & Ryser, 1997). This assessment measures the degree to which students meet overall program objectives. The instrument consists of 26 items to be rated by the teacher using a 4-point Likert-type scale. Internal consistency reliability for the instrument is a = .97. The instrument may be found in the following reference:

Johnsen, S., Ryser, G., & Dougherty (1993). The validity of product portfolios in the identification of gifted students. *Gifted International*, *8*(1), 44–47. https://doi.org/10.1080/15332276.1993.1167277

*William and Mary Classroom Observation Scales-Revised (VanTassel-Baska et al., 2003). The instrument is designed to evaluate general teaching behaviors and differentiated teaching behaviors (e.g., accommodations for individual differences, problem solving, critical thinking strategies, creative thinking strategies, and research strategies. The instrument, Student Observation Form and Manual may be retrieved from https://education.wm.edu/centers/cfge/resources/instruments/index.php

More information about the instrument is reported in these references:

VanTassel-Baska, J., Feng, A. X., Brown, E., Bracken, B., Stambaugh, T., French, H., McGowan, S., Worley, B., Quek, C., & Bai, W. (2008). A study of differentiated instructional change over 3 years. *Gifted Child Quarterly*, *52*(4), 297–312. https://doi.org/10.1177/0016986208321809

VanTassel-Baska, J., Feng. A., MacFarlane, B., Heng, M. A., Teo, C. T., Wong, M. L., Quek, C. G., & Khong, B. C. (2008). A cross-cultural study of teachers' instructional practices in Singapore and the United States. *Journal for the Education of the Gifted*, *31*(3), 338–363. https://doi.org/10.4219/jeg-2008–770

VanTassel-Baska, J. (2012). Analyzing differentiation in the classroom: Using the COS-R. *Gifted Child Today*, *35*(1), 42–48. https://doi.org/10.1177/1076217511427431

Resource: Gifted Education Unit Reference Series: Creativity, Leadership, Visual and Performing Arts (Colorado Department of Education). This Colorado Department of Education website contains characteristics, observation forms, referral forms, and performance assessment rubrics for identifying students in dance, performing arts, music, and visual arts. www.cde.state.co.us/talentidtools

Resource: Acceleration Institute at the Belin-Blank Center. The website contains books, reports, and other resources for acceleration and grade skipping. *A Nation Deceived, A Nation Empowered, Developing Academic Acceleration Policies, and the Iowa Acceleration Scale are* available for download. The materials are appropriate for all grade levels. Information may be retrieved from www.accelerationinstitute.org/

Resource: Frasier Talent Assessment Profile (F-TAP) (Frasier, 1992). The F-TAP is used to organize multiple assessments used during the identification process. Quantitative data are recorded on a graph producing a profile of each student's strengths and weaknesses. The F-TAP may be found in Appendix C of this reference:

S. L. Hunsaker, M. M. Frasier, E. Frank, V. Finley, & P. Klekotka (1995). *Performance of economically disadvantaged students placed in gifted programs through the Research-Based Assessment Plan.* Storrs, CT: National Research Center on the Gifted and Talented, University of Connecticut. https://nrcgt.uconn.edu/wp-content/uploads/sites/953/2015/04/rm95208.pdf

Resource: State Advisory Council for Gifted and Talented Education and the Kentucky Department of Education Handbook. The Kentucky GT Coordinator Handbook contains forms used by various Kentucky school districts. Appendix A includes teacher and parent checklists, observation forms, student interest forms, and progress reports. http://kagegifted.org/wp-content/uploads/2011/11/sectiona.pdf

*Note: Assessments having technical information